Youth and work transitions in changing social landscapes

the Tufnell Press,
London,
United Kingdom
www.tufnellpress.co.uk
email contact@tufnellpress.co.uk

British Library Cataloguing-in-Publication Data
A catalogue record for this book is
available from the British Library

paperback	*ISBN*	*1872767583*
	ISBN-13	*978-1-872767-58-1*

Copyright © 2013 Helena Helve and Karen Evans

Cover design © 2013 the Tufnell Press
Photographs used of Greek youth demonstration © 2013 Helena Helve

Printed in England and U.S.A. by Lightning Source

Youth and work transitions in changing social landscapes

editors
Helena Helve and Karen Evans

iv

Contents

Acknowledgements

First we wish to thank those who attended the research seminars on the topic of Youth, Work Transitions and Well-being held in Helsinki 2009 and in London 2010 and 2012. We are grateful to the Finnish Institute in London for generously hosting the 2010 and 2012 seminars. These three seminars enabled both experts and newer researchers to share findings and methods from their latest research, generating ideas and insights that have shaped the development of the book. The overarching theme of the book had its origins in the Academy of Finland Research Programme WORK 2008–2011. The book and the seminars would not have been possible without the financial support of the Academy of Finland. The international perspective in the book would not have been possible without the authors from the RC34 (Sociology of Youth) section of the International Sociological Association. We are indebted to them and to all those authors and contributors who have co-operated so positively in bringing the book to fruition. Particular thanks are due to Arseniy Svynarenko for his untiring dedication and thoughtfulness in putting the book into its final form. Finally, we wish to express our appreciation to Tufnell Press for their professionalism and for their advice and support during the publication process.

Helena Helve and Karen Evans
January 2013.

Authors

John Bynner, Emeritus Professor of Social Sciences in Education, Institute of Education, University of London and until retirement in 2004 was Director of the Centre for Longitudinal Studies, the Wider Benefits of Learning Research Centre and founder Director of the National Research and Development Centre for Adult Literacy and Numeracy. He is Executive Editor of the international journal Longitudinal and Life Course Studies. His main research interest is the life course. Recent publications include with Michael Wadsworth, *A companion to life course studies* and papers on *Youth transitions and changing labour markets: Germany and England in the late 1980s* and *Youth transitions and apprenticeship: a broader view of skill*.

Vinod Chandra, Associate Professor of Sociology and Vice-principal of J N Post Graduate College at Lucknow University, India. He is recipient of Commonwealth Academic Staff Scholarship and obtained his Ph. D. degree on *Children's domestic work* from University of Warwick, UK. He has been actively involved in youth and childhood research in the last fifteen years. He was Vice-president of Research Committee of Sociology of Youth at International Sociology Association (ISA) from 2002-2010. Currently, he is Secretary of Research Committee of Sociology of Childhood (RC53), in ISA. He is Executive Secretary of the Circle for Child and Youth Research Cooperation in India (CCYRCI). His recent books are *Growing up in a globalized world* (Macmillan India: 2009), *Revisiting Mahatma's Hind Swaraj* (Manak Publications: New Delhi 2012). His current research interests are Indian Youth and Higher Education, Educational Reforms in India, Youth and Life skill Education, Children's Work, Child abuse.

Helen Cheng completed her Ph. D. in Psychology at University College London, and subsequently worked at the Institute of Psychiatry, King's College London. She participated in the National Evaluation of Sure Start Programme at Birkbeck College London, and also worked for the Learning and Life Chances in the Knowledge Economies and Societies project and the Well-being of Children project at the Institute of Education, University of London conducting structural equation modelling on three British cohorts. Her main research interests are children's cognitive development and behavioural adjustment, and adults' mental health and well-being. Her recent publications include *Determinants of political trust: A lifetime learning model*. Developmental psychology (with Schoon, I. *Developmental Psychology*, 47(3), 2011).

James Côté, Full Professor of Sociology at Western University (Canada). He currently serves as President (2010-14) of the International Sociological Association's Research Committee (34) on the Sociology of Youth, is founding editor of *Identity: An International Journal of Theory and Research*, and served as President (2003-2005) of the Society for Research on Identity Formation (SRIF). He is also an Associate Editor of the *Journal of Adolescence*. His most recent book in the Youth Studies field is *Critical youth studies: A Canadian focus* (2006). He is currently writing the book *Youth studies: Fundamental issues* (for Palgrave).

Rosalind Edwards, Professor of Sociology at the University of Southampton. Her main research interest is family lives. She has published widely in this field, most recently: *Teenage parenting: What's the problem?* (ed. with Duncan and Alexander, 2010, the Tufnell Press), *Key concepts in family studies* (with McCarthy, 2012, Sage), *International perspectives on racial and ethnic mixedness and mixing* (ed. with Ali, Caballero and Song, 2012, Routledge). She is a co-editor of *International Journal of Social Research Methodology*.

Karen Evans, Professor of Education at the Institute of Education, University of London. Her main fields of research are learning in life and work transitions, and learning in and through the workplace. She is an Academician of the Academy of Social Sciences and a leading researcher in the Economic and Social Research Council LLAKES Centre for Learning and Life Chances in Knowledge Economies and Societies. She has directed major studies of learning and the world of work in Britain and internationally and is joint editor of the *Second international handbook of lifelong learning* (2012) and *The sage handbook of workplace learning*, (2011). Books include *Improving literacy at work* (2011); *Learning, Work and Social Responsibility* (2009); *Improving workplace learning* (2006); *Reconnection: Countering social exclusion through situated learning* (2004); *Working to learn* (2002); *Learning and work in the risk society* (2000).

David Everatt, Professor and the Executive Director of the Gauteng City-Region Observatory, a partnership of the University of Johannesburg, University of the Witwatersrand, Johannesburg, and the Gauteng Provincial Government. His most recent book is *The origins of non-racialism: White opposition to apartheid in the 1950s* (Wits University Press, Johannesburg, 2011).

Helena Helve, Emerita Professor of Youth Research in School of Social Sciences and Humanities at Tampere University. She has been a professor for the M.A. European Youth Studies Curriculum Development Project (2009-2011). She was a chair of the Executive Board of the Finnish University Consortium YUNET on Youth Research studies coordinated by Helsinki University, where she is an Adjunct Professor of Sociology and Comparative Religion. She has been the Nordic Youth Research Coordinator (1998-2003), President of the ISA RC 34 (2002-2006) and President of the Finnish Youth Research Society (1992-2005). She has directed several international and national research projects, most recently the Work-Preca project by Academy of Finland. Among her publications are *Youth and social capital* (ed. with J. Bynner, Tufnell Press, 2007), *Contemporary youth research: Local Expressions and global connections* (ed. with G. Holm, Ashgate, 2005) and *Youth, citizenship and empowerment* (ed. with C. Wallace, Ashgate, 2001).

Janet Holland, Professor of Social Research, Weeks Centre, London South Bank University, and was Co-Director of the ESRC funded Timescapes Qualitative Longitudinal Study www.timescapes.leeds.ac.uk. Her research interests and publications are in youth, education, gender, sexualities, family life and methodological development. Recent publications: (2009) 'Young people and social capital: Uses and abuses', *Young: Nordic Journal of Youth Research*, 17 (4): 331-350; with Rachel Thomson, (2009) 'Gaining perspective on choice and fate: Revisiting critical moments', *European Societies*, 11 (3): 451-469; with Sheila Henderson, Sheena McGrellis, Sue Sharpe and Rachel Thomson, *Inventing adulthoods: A biographical approach to youth transitions*. Sage, London; www.lsbu.ac.uk.inventingadulthoods.

Hely Innanen, M. Soc. Sc., and M.E. Her research is in the field of personality, work and organisational psychology. She is working with her doctoral dissertation in the department of psychology in the University of Jyväskylä. Her research focuses primarily on the role of individual achievement (achievement optimism and avoidance) and social strategies (social optimism and social pessimism) and areas of work life (workload, control, reward, sense of community, fairness and values) in burnout and engagement. During her doctoral studies she has assisted the Secretary General in ISSBD from February 2011.

Jaana Lähteenmmaa, D. Soc. Sci., Adjunct Professor (docent) of Youth Research in the University of Tampere. She obtained her doctor degree from the

University of Helsinki in 2000. Her dissertation topic was late-modern youth culture. Her research interests cover the ethics of the young generation, rural young people, youth unemployment and 'moral panics' over youth related issues. Lähteenmaa carried out research on youth unemployment years 2009-2011 on the research project Work-Preca. She is currently researching on the 'YUALP-A' project (2012-2016); both financed by the Academy of Finland.

Tomokazu Makino, part-time lecturer at Waseda University. He is the author of *Jiko keihatsu no jidai : Jiko' no bunkashakaigaku teki tankyū (The age of self- development: A cultural and sociological inquiry into 'self')* (2012), and co-author of *Dokoka mondaikasareru wakamonotachi (Youth at issue)* (2008). His research interests are self and juvenile delinquency.

Sheena McGrellis, visiting Senior Research Fellow, Weeks Centre for Social and Policy Research, London South Bank University located at the University of Ulster. Her research interests are in youth transitions and identities, and health and wellbeing, with a particular concern for those in Northern Ireland. Recent publications: *Growing up in Northern Ireland*, York: Joseph Rowntree Foundation (copies available from www.jrf.org.uk); (2005) 'Pure and bitter spaces: gender, identity and territory in Northern Irish youth transition', *Gender and Education*, 17(5): 515–29; (2005) 'Pushing the Boundaries in Northern Ireland: Young People, Violence and Sectarianism' *Contemporary Politics*, 11 (1) 53-71; (2010) 'In Transitions: young people in Northern Ireland growing up in and out of divided communities', *Ethnic and Racial Studies*, 33 (5) 761-778.

Mette Ranta, Ph. D. student at the Department of Psychology, University of Jyväskylä and the Helsinki Collegium for Advanced Studies, University of Helsinki. Her research interests lie in young adults' well-being, financial situation, transitions and agency in times of economic uncertainty. Her doctoral dissertation is part of the Finnish Educational Transitions (FinEdu) Studies project. Publications include: Ranta, M., Punamäki, R-L., Tolvanen, A. & Salmela-Aro, K. (2012), The role of Financial resources and agency in success and satisfaction regarding developmental tasks in early adulthood, in Sampson Lee Blair (Ed.), Vol 6. Emerald Group Publishing; Ranta, Chow, and Salmela-Aro (forthcoming), *Trajectories of life satisfaction and the financial situation in the transition to adulthood* and Ranta, Punamäki, Tolvanen, and Salmela-Aro (submitted), *The role of financial resources and agency in the success of developmental tasks in early adulthood.*

Tracey Reynolds, Reader in the Families and Social Capital ESRC Research Group, which is situated within the Weeks Centre for Social and Policy Research at London South Bank University. Tracey's research interests focus on transnational families and kinship networks; constructions of motherhood, parenting and childrearing. She has conducted extensive empirical research in the UK across a range of social issues including black and minority families living in disadvantaged communities. Her current research examines Caribbean youths and transnational identities. She is the author of *Caribbean mothers: Identity and experience in the UK* (published by Tufnell Press, 2005); *Transnational families: Ethnicities, identities and social capital*, with Harry Goulbourne, John Solomos and Elisabetta Zontini, (published by Routledge, 2010) and editor of the Special Issue 'Young people, ethnicity and social capital', in the *Journal of Ethnic and Racial Studies* (May 2010).

Katariina Salmela-Aro, Professor in Psychology at Jyväskylä Universit and Research Director in the Helsinki Collegium for Advanced Studies in the University of Helsinki and Visiting professor in the Institute of Education, University of London and director of several ongoing longitudinal studies. Secretary General in the International Society for the Study of Behavioral Development, EC member of the European Society for Developmental Psychology and founding member of the International Collaborative Pathways team. Consulting editor of *Developmental Psychology*, an associate editor *European Psychologist*, and on the editorial board of the *European Journal of Developmental Psychology*. Main interest motivation, well-being, life transitions and related interventions.

Ingrid Schoon, Professor of Human Development and Social Policy in the Department of Quantitative Social Science, Institute of Education, University of London, and Research Director, the Centre for Youth Transitions (CAYT). She is coordinating the post-doctoral Jacobs Foundation Fellowship 'PATHWAYS to Adulthood', and is a member of the International Collaborative for the Analysis of Pathways from Childhood to Adulthood (CAPCA) organised by Michigan University. Her research interests focused on issues of human development across the life course, in particular the transition from dependent childhood to independent adulthood. Her recent publications include: *Transitions from school to work: Globalisation, individualisation, and patterns of diversity* (with Silbereisen, R.K., 2009), Planning for the future: Changing education expectations in three

British cohorts, (*Historical Social Research*, 35(2), 2010) and Teenage career aspirations and adult career attainment: The role of gender, social background and general cognitive ability (with Polek, E., *International Journal of Behavioral Development*, 35(3), 2011).

John Schulenberg, Professor of Developmental Psychology and Research Professor at the Institute for Social Research, Michigan University. He is President of the Society for Research on Adolescence, and helps direct the US national Monitoring the Future study concerning psycho-social development of adolescence. His research concerns the etiology and epidemiology of substance use and psychopathology. His recent publications include: How trajectories of reasons for alcohol use relate to trajectories of binge drinking (with Patrick, M. E, *Developmental Psychology*, 47(2), 2011), Substance use changes and social role transitions: Proximal developmental effects on ongoing trajectories from late adolescence through early adulthood (with Staff, J., Maslowsky, J., Bachman, J. G., O'Malley, P. M., Maggs, J. L., and Johnston, L. D., *Development and Psychopathology*, 22, 2010) and Historical variation in rates of change in substance use across the transition to adulthood: The trend towards lower intercepts and steeper slopes (with Jager, J., O'Malley, P. M., and Bachman, J. G., *Development and Psychopathology*, 2012).

Arseniy Svynarenko, Ph. D. student at the University of Tampere. He has been researcher in the Work-Preca project and he is lecturer in Ukrainian Studies programme at the University of Helsinki. Svynarenko's main research interests are in youth identities, values and generations in Finland, Russia and Ukraine. His most recent research is on identities and work values of young Finns.

Edmund Waite, researcher at LLAKES (Centre for Learning and Life Chances in Knowledge Economies and Societies), Institute of Education, University of London. His research interests and publications relate to adult literacy, workplace learning, comparative education as well as the anthropological study of education in Muslim societies.

Susie Weller, Senior Research Fellow in the Families and Social Capital Research Group at London South Bank University. Her background is in Geography and her research over the past thirteen years has focussed on listening to, and promoting the voices of children and young people. She is the author of *Teenagers' citizenship: Experiences and education* (2007, Routledge) and co-editor of *Critical approaches to care: Understanding caring relations, identities and cultures* (with Rogers, 2012, Routledge), as well as numerous book chapters and articles on young people's participation and social capital, sibling relationships and friendship, and the development of youth-centred research methods. She has worked on a number of major projects including 'Sibling and Friends' part of the 'Timescapes: Changing Relationships and Identities through the Life Course' study (2007-2011).

Johanna Wyn, Professor and Director of the Youth Research Centre, University of Melbourne, Australia. She leads the Life Patterns longitudinal study of two cohorts of Australians. Her work focuses on the interface between young people's learning and wellbeing in formal and informal educational settings, on young people's transitions and on the question of what kinds of knowledge and skills professionals who work with young people in these settings need in the twenty-first century. Her recent publications include: *Youth and society: Exploring the social dynamics of youth* (3rd edition), with Rob White; *Youth health and welfare (2009); Touching the future: Building skills for life and work; The making of a generation: The children of the 1970s in adulthood* with Lesley Andres; and *Young people making it work: Continuity and change in rural places,* with Hernan Cuervo.

Julia Zubok, Professor and the head of the Department of Sociology of Youth at the Institute of Social-Political Studies, Russian Academy of Sciences. She is engaged in studying of the fundamental problems of the sociology of youth, including the mechanisms of social integration and social exclusion and the features of these processes in the conditions of social instability, uncertainty and risk as the factors in the social development of young people, functioning of the social regulation mechanism in its institutional and individual forms and self-regulation of behaviour in social interactions of youth. Her recent publications include *Social regulation in conditions of uncertainty: Theoretical and practical problems in the study of young people* (with Chuprov, V.I., M.:, ACADEMIA, 2008), *Youth extremism: Its nature, manifestations, trends* (with Chuprov V. I., M. ACADEMIA, 2009 and *Sociology of youth: The textbook* (with Chuprov V. I., M., Norma, 2011).

Part 1

Chapter 1

Introduction

Youth and work transitions in changing social landscapes

Karen Evans and Helena Helve

How do the young people of today in different countries and regions of the world find their way to adulthood? What are the opportunities and risks in their work transitions? What does the economic recession and rising youth unemployment mean for young people's trajectories into adulthood. The particular focus of this book is about the importance of successful transitions to adult life as manifested in psychological and physical wellbeing. Based on a series of case studies from Europe and perspectives from the USA, Canada, South Africa, the Caribbean, India, Japan, Russia, Australia and New Zealand it is examining the structural forces that affect the choices young people are able to make. The case studies analyse how social, psychological, economic and cultural factors influence young people's attempts to control their lives, their ability to respond to opportunities and to manage the consequences of their choices. This book is about the changing constellations of risk and opportunity in the transitions from school to work transitions.

Analysis of the effects of precarious work histories—temporary and part-time present employment and unstable work history—on work related psychological well-being among young people is adding to the understanding of the roles that work transitions play in youth and across the life-course. The traditional model of work transitions is under pressure from a number of changes. Not only has the nature of work changed, but so have the organisation of work and the ways in which young people enter the labour market. Jobs have been relocated to other parts of the world and the labour market as a whole has become less stable. In many countries young people are those who are suffering most from changing labour markets. As the recent recession across the world has affected young people more than older cohorts, many have no frame of reference for what is happening; they have grown up with strong economic growth and optimistic assumptions that they would be better off than their parents. Now many have difficulties in navigating work transitions. However, the rapid ageing of the population for example in Europe and Japan has put the onus on young people and their work transitions and inflexibilities in the existing social security systems in terms of their ability to guarantee a subsistence income to all citizens. This timely topic reflects now global social and economic changes in labour markets. Work transitions of young people and their relationships with well-being form a field of action for youth policies, needing research that explores the flows of influence across these areas of young people's lives.

This book approaches the situation of young people in the current labour markets around the world, from a variety of disciplinary and transdisciplinary perspectives. It is based on the strong foundation of international researchers' cooperation in the field of youth research. The ideas for the *Youth, Work Transitions and Wellbeing* book were brought to fruition in a series of papers presented in two seminars of Finnish and English researchers held at the Tieteiden Talo (House of Sciences and Letters) at Helsinki 2009 October 8-9, and at the Finnish Institute in London on October 25-26, 2010. The contributors were affiliated to research programmes in their respective countries concerned with youth work transitions in various ways: in Finland based in the Academy of Finland Research Programme on *The Future of Work and Well-being* at University of Tampere, Helsinki and in Jyväskylä; and in England, based in South Bank University, and in the Economic and Social Council LLAKES Centre (Centre for Learning and Life Chances in Knowledge Economies and Societies), Institute of Education, University of London. This volume based on Finnish and British research groups is linked to *ISA RC 34* Youth Sociology and youth research colleagues researching wellbeing and the work transition of young people in different parts of the world. These research programmes, together with the international contributors, have generated high quality research papers that make a significant contribution to understanding young people's work transitions and wellbeing internationally. A selection of these papers has been brought together in this edited collection.

The recent economic dow nturn ha s presented ne w challenges for organisations and individuals globally. The scope of the book is to present recent research in youth work transitions, wellbeing, employment, career interventions, and research-practice gaps internationally. Wellbeing, leisure and personal relationships are often relegated to side issues to the main game of education and employment; their influence on education and employment patterns and decisions is all too often ignored. This volume adds new knowledge that explores the flows of influence across these areas of young people's lives.

This book is intended as a resource book in a non-traditional sense for students and faculty in youth studies. It is being published at a time of growing concern about the youth unemployment that can lead to marginalisation and social exclusion of the younger generation. The book also gives youth workers, researchers, and policy makers important and timely information about young people's life perspectives in transition to adulthood and work life. Looking at issues from the perspective of different countries deepens our understanding of the realities, shared and culturally differentiated, of youth work transition internationally as well as giving us new ideas how to approach young people and their issues and interests.

Contrasting contexts and the dynamics of change

Youth unemployment and recession are not new phenomena, but there are stark differences in the dynamics of change in the present time England, Finland and the wider world. This book explores these dynamics from contrasting perspectives, asking 'what do we need to understand better in order to find effective ways of supporting youth in a changing world?'

The life chances of young people are profoundly affected by macroeconomic conditions, institutional structures, social background, gender, and ethnicity, as well as by acquired attributes and individual resources such as ability, motivation, and aspirations. As social origin, gender, and ethnicity influence the range of options available to the individual, so too do historical events beyond individual control, such as changes in the labour market, economic downturn, or the outbreak of war (e.g. Elder, 2002; Evans 2009). Young people and adults alike co-regulate their motivation and behaviour in response to the social context (Jones, 2009; Helve, 2007; Schoon and Silbereisen, 2009). Recent changes in education, the labour market and housing opportunities place increasing pressures on young people's initiative and ability to navigate options and demands. On various measures, young people in Europe appear to be at risk of being 'shut out' of opportunities, a situation that is seen as creating conditions for social disorder as well as having a potential long term impact on well-being.

A new generation of research studies is focusing on the ways in which young people respond to and cope with sudden downturns in employment opportunities and the changing pressures involved in decision-making about vocational and higher education. Economic downturn is not new and there is rich previous research on which to build. Research from the 1930s recessions have demonstrated long-term scarring effects that endure from generation to generation. Panel studies internationally are revealing the longer term impacts of experiences rooted in the economic recessions of the 1980s (see for example, chapters by Bynner and Schoon, respectively). There are marked differences in the wider social context in which life and work navigations are being experienced in the aftermath of the financial crises of the early 2000s.

New research has to focus on the reflexive relationships between individual responses of youth to structural shifts in opportunities, inter-generational influences and the ways in which organisational and social practices are changing. As well as understanding the role of life planning and motivation in steering young people on their paths to adulthood, we need to know more about the ways in which social practices are changing (e.g. in civic participation and in career-seeking activity) and how organisational, social, cultural and sub-cultural practices are affected by economic downturn, changing social expectations and the changing socio-political environment. Equally important is how the incentives and disincentives to engagement in education, training and civic participation are changing. By focusing on the intergenerational inter- linkages, parental and wider socioeconomic and cultural influences on attitudes and behaviours of current generations of young people come into view.

LLAKES research (Green and Janmaat, 2011) predicted that civil unrest would be likely to rise during the coming years and young people would be at the centre of social concerns. This has been underlined by recent events, where, according to early estimates young people are amongst the hardest hit by the economic crisis (see Brewer et al., 2009). For example, youth unemployment in the United Kingdom, already rising before the recession (Gregg and Wadsworth, 2011; Goujard et al., 2011), has increased more rapidly since the economic downturn, with already nearly one million 16-24 year-olds, representing over twenty per cent of the age group, without jobs in 2011.[1] In some areas, youth unemployment had reached 35 per cent. As the public expenditure cuts begin to bite, joblessness amongst young people is likely to rise even higher, and disproportionately with the other groups in the labour force. When young people are on temporary, part- time or probationary contracts, they occupy increasingly precarious positions in the labour market. These trends are present, with either greater or less severity in many other European countries affected by the banking crisis. Our initial Finnish-British comparisons, for example,

1   E.g. London Borough of Lewisham

showed the changing ways in which work entry and employment trajectories are profoundly connected to personal, housing and family transitions. Rising rents in major cities make accommodation unaffordable to many young people, which affect both employment options, scope for personal independence and family formation. While there are many similarities in the ways young people navigate changing configurations of work and life, there are also some significant international differences. For example one route to social mobility—through the accumulation of wealth from rising housing assets—that was available to previous generations in the UK through early home ownership (known as 'getting a foot on the housing ladder') is probably now closed, adding further barriers to mobility for a generation whose jobs and earnings prospects are poor and who will be paying increasing contributions to sustain the pensions of their parents (Willetts, 2010). Extending education and training is the obvious response to reduced job opportunities for many young people, but there are widespread concerns that cuts to public finding financial grants and trends towards increases in tuition fees in higher education may deter many less affluent students from further study (Callander and Jackson, 2005). In Finland and the Nordic countries educational entitlements and the principle of free entry to higher education is at present unchanged. Despite these differences, on various measures, opportunities for young people in Europe, relative to those of their parents' generation, appear worse than they have been for many decades (Green and Janmaat, 2011).

Through longitudinal and panel studies of various kinds we can now examine changes in housing, family status and a wide range of personal and wellbeing factors which are crucial to ways in which young people experience and navigate changes that can impact fundamentally on their life chances. We should also be probing young adults' views on the social unrest that has erupted in many parts of Europe, with the wider international contributions bringing these phenomena into global perspective, showing, for example, the harsh realities of youth experiences in countries such as South Africa show how growth in inter- and intra-race inequality leaves the poor, even in wealthy provinces, locked out of the economy (see the chapter of David Everatt in this volume).

Different landscapes of the book

The book is organised into four major parts: *Perspectives on employment transitions and wellbeing changes during economic recession, Biographical negotiations from youth to adulthood, New career aspirations, life chances and risks,* and *Wider international perspectives on youth, working life and wellbeing.* The chapters in these four parts provide more in-depth analysis of issues such as school to work transitions and wellbeing in changing labour markets in England, Finland, Ireland, Russia, Japan, Australia and New Zealand, India and South Africa. A North American perspective on these changes is offered through the commentary by James Côté. The chapters of the book explain in more detail how young people are inventing adulthoods, what kind of regional identities, work values and future expectations they have, what gender, class and ethnicity/race means for work transitions, how youth in education experience working life and how work transitions create different youth pathways to belonging. Furthermore, contributions explore gender differences in achievement and social strategies, the meaning of school motivation and parental aspirations in young people's career development.

The four chapters of the section *Perspectives on employment transitions and wellbeing changes during economic recession* focus on the viewpoints from UK, the US and Finland. *John Bynner* in his chapter *School to work transitions and wellbeing in a changing labour market* compares the current economic recession and young people seeking entry to the labour market with the 1970s recession in the British labour market giving a broad historical perspective to the situation of young people in unstable labour markets by analysing British longitudinal research data. The phenomenon of NEET 'Not in Education, Employment or Training' is discussed. This is coming to known more frequently now in common with other countries, bringing the prospect of reduced life chances and challenges to wellbeing of young people in later life. This section starts by reviewing the historical back ground to these effects and what we can learn from them about the likely consequences for wellbeing of the most recent recession, drawing on evidence collected since the second-world war. The 'scarring' effects damage the expected pattern of school to further, or higher education, and work broken through scarcity of jobs for prospective entrants. A lack of crucial work experience, not only for acquisition of specific work-related skills but the more personally driven attributes of employability ranging from punctuality to taking initiative and team work will give important signals to employers.

Ingrid Schoon and John Schulenberg in their chapter *The assumption of adult roles in the UK, the US, and Finland: Antecedents and associated levels of wellbeing and health* review evidence from two age cohorts in the UK, the US and in Finland making the transition to independent adulthood. Four national and community-based studies from Britain (the 1958 National Child Development Study [NCDS] and the 1970 British Birth Cohort Study [BCS70]), the United

States (Monitoring the Future [MTF]), and in Finland the 1959 Jyväskylä Study of Personality and Social Development [JVLS] and the 1966 Northern Finland Birth Cohort [NFBC]) examined patterns of social role combinations of young people in their mid-twenties, childhood antecedents and associated adult health outcomes. They are comparing using a life course perspective evidence across different cultures and settings to enable a better understanding regarding similarities and differences of how young people negotiate the transition to independent adulthood, the role of early predictors and associated adult health outcomes. Two comparable age cohorts in each country, born in the late 1950s and the late 1960s/early 1970s, respectively, allows across country comparisons. In each country the focus is on the 'big 5' transition events (Shanahan, 2000; Stettersten, 2007) comprising the completion of education, entry into paid employment, partnership and family formation (i.e. parenthood), as well as independent living arrangements. Schoon and Schulenberg take in their chapter a critical view to Arnett (2000) who has postulated a new developmental stage of *emerging adulthood*, characterised by the extended exploration of identity, life styles, and career possibilities. They point out that *emerging adulthood* may be useful synonyms for the prolonged transition to independent adulthood, but it does not take into account the social and economic conditions that have produced extended transitions. Transition outcomes are dependent on structural opportunities and constraints as well as individual resources and capabilities (Elder and Shanahan, 2006; Evans, Rudd, Behrens, Kaluza, and Woolley, 2003).

Mette Ranta in her chapter *Finnish young adults' financial wellbeing in times of uncertainty* presents results based on a Finnish Educational Transitions (FinEdu) longitudinal study, in which 614 adolescents from six upper secondary schools participated. They answered questions on economic conditions (self-reported objective income and subjective appraisal of personal current and near future income adequacy) in measurements after the transition. Statistical analyses revealed four distinct well-being trajectories differing in level and change: two major classes having stable high trajectories and two smaller classes having significant increasing and decreasing changes in wellbeing. Moreover, the stable high classes indicated higher self-reported subjective income levels at the fourth measurement than the changing trajectory classes. *Jaana Lähteenmaa* in the chapter '*Agency vs. structure*' *a view of youth unemployment during the current recession in Finland* analyses the structures of youth unemployment using qualitative material produced in the internet-survey analyses. The theoretical framework for the chapter is build from the 'agency' of unemployed young people.

The Section *Biographical negotiations from youth to adulthood* is divided into four topic areas focusing on issues related to youth work transitions from several different perspectives. This second topic area looks at the more general topics of youth trajectories and pathways to adulthood. *Rosalind Edwards and Susie Weller* in the *Trajectories from youth to adulthood: Choice and structure for young people before and during recession* chapter present a concern about the economic recession and rising youth unemployment in the UK affecting young people's trajectories into adulthood and work transition. The article is based on a qualitative longitudinal study that has been tracking young people's lateral relationships over the past four years or more. A series of case studies of young people's biographical negotiations are used, drawing on a four-fold transitions typology which highlights the structural forces underpinning the choices young people are able to make. Edwards and Weller argue that young people enter a period of economic recession with prior resources and particular trajectories already in play in their lives. Thus, for the young people in this study, rather than recession bringing about a changed or fractured pathway into adulthood, it is providing a certain set of conditions for embedding particular, pre-existing trajectories. The chapter *Inventing adulthoods: Young people growing up in Northern Ireland* by *Sheena McGrellis and Janet Holland* presents a unique qualitative longitudinal study of young people in five socio-economically contrasting sites in the UK through their transitions to adulthood since 1997, when they were aged between twelve and eighteen. In this article the authors discuss about data from the group of young people in Northern Ireland where the study has shadowed the vicissitudes of the peace process and a recent round of interviews were undertaken in 2009/10. This section provides an overview of the young people's experiences of balancing work, education and family in all of the sites over the years, focusing on the Northern Ireland group in more detail. The recent interviews provide insight into the challenges young adults face around work and employment and the effects these have on their health and wellbeing.

The next two chapters present the research on the Finnish Work-Preca research project on young people's work transitions, values and future horizons. *Arseniy Svynarenko* in his chapter *Regional identities, future expectations and work values* analyses young people's changing work values and identities in a time of increased uncertainty and risk of unemployment and how these constitute a challenging and disequilibrating life event in which previously-made identity commitments are no longer workable and an individual may temporarily regress to earlier identity modes. It is a time when new identities and new models may appear. The themes of family, future plans and education are located on the intersections of work identity, local and global identities. The study about work-related values and regional identities of young Finns gives evidence that the employment situation of young people has an impact on their perceptions of future. Those who have successfully found a full-time job see their future in a relatively more optimistic light. In the perceptions of young people's future, one can see reflections of their attitudes and experiences of participation in the existing welfare and political system, negative experiences weaken the sense of national identity. *Helena Helve's* chapter *From higher education to working life: Work values of young Finns in changing labour markets* is based on in-depth narrative interviews and ethnographic observations which were gathered among young people working temporarily in tourism in Lapland. The survey data was gathered on-line on the recruitment websites of the universities and polytechnics from those in higher education seeking jobs. The attitude scales measured attitudes towards education, working life and society, and the future orientation and meaning of life. The paper places its focus on the research questions: How the students of higher education start their working life? Are they combining employment and studies? What kind of jobs do they have and how many employers have they had? What kind of attitudes do they have towards education and work and how are these influenced by their parents and friends? Do they have a short or broad future horizon, is it local or global, positive or negative? How is short-term precarious employment affecting attitudes, lifestyles and worldviews of young adults? The transition into working life no longer takes place as soon as education is finished, but rather it can begin while one is still in education or much later. This study shows that almost every third of the youngest respondents in higher education already combine already studies with work. Nor does moving away from one's parents lead to starting a family of one's own in many cases. The study shows that young people working with short-term employment contracts, or who are temporary unemployed are not doing much long-term planning. The short-term and temporary employment is changing identities, future expectations, work attitudes and values of young people. Drawing on theories of post materialism, values, identity and world views the paper discusses the strategies young people use in their work transitions to manage their life under conditions of precarity and uncertainty.

The section *New career aspirations, life changes and risks* includes five chapters. *Tracey Reynolds* chapter *Youth transitions and wellbeing: The impact of austerity on black youths living in urban 'black neighbourhoods'* draws from the research findings of projects from 'Caribbean families, social capital and young people's diasporic identities'. It included a number of projects within Families and Social Capital ESRC Research Group at London South Bank University (see www.lsbu.ac.uk/families). During 2002-2006 in-depth interviews were conducted with thirty second and third generation Caribbean young people (aged between 16 to 30 years-old) living in Birmingham, London, Manchester and Nottingham. Further interviews took place with fifty of their kinship/family members in Britain and the Caribbean (Barbados, Guyana and Jamaica) across all age groups. The research project explored how family and kinship bonds operate in the lives of Caribbean young people and their construction of ethnic identity and belonging. This paper examines the views and experiences of black youths living in three socially deprived areas of London in order to examine the way in which they recognise the term 'black neighbourhood' as a resource in these austere times. The analysis shows that these neighbourhoods represent urban spaces through which a range of social capital resources are generated including ties of reciprocal ties of trust, solidarity and civic participation. They also provide black youths with a sense of belonging and as such these neighbourhoods are intrinsically valued by them. Research highlights that central to an individuals' overall sense of well-being is the extent to which they perceive a sense of belonging and bonds of trust within their communities (Ryan and Deci, 2001). While the literature suggests that economic hardship adversely affects adults' wellbeing and their community relationships, still little is known about the impact of economic hardship on youths' wellbeing and their perceptions of community and neighbourhood. This issue is particularly pertinent because under the current economic downturn in Britain youths are one of the main groups to be adversely affected as result of high youth unemployment rates and rising numbers of young people not in any form of education or training. With regards to black youths recent figures indicate that nearly fifty per cent are unemployed and this figure is even higher among black youths living in urban neighbourhoods, sometimes colloquially referred to as 'black neighbourhoods'.

Katariina Salmela-Aro's Academic burnout and engagement from adolescence to young adulthood chapter presents recent findings related to academic burnout defined as exhaustion, cynicism and inadequacy at school. How are the three components of burnout related to each other and how do they develop? How are academic burnout and depression related to each other? What is the role of learning difficulties in this context? This article introduces the concept of academic engagement described as energy, dedication towards and absorption in schoolwork. In this context demands-resources model is presented as an approach to study both academic burnout and engagement. The findings as to how academic engagement and burnout change from adolescence to young adulthood, from transition to high school to tertiary education and work life are discussed in this chapter. *Hely Innanen* and *Katariina Salmela-Aro* in their chapter *Gender differences in achievement and social strategies, areas of work life and burnout at the early career stage* have focused on experiences at the early career stage which may include several risk factors for employees' well-being. This study examines gender differences in burnout, in achievement and social strategies and in areas of work life. Research participants were from four organisations: IT, health care, a university, and logistics (N=378, women 56%, age range 18-30 years). The results revealed no gender differences in burnout. Men scored higher in achievement optimism, whereas women scored higher on achievement pessimism and social optimism. Men scored control and fairness to be higher in the organisation than the women. The results showed gender differences in relations between individual strategies, areas of work life, and burnout. These results suggest that employers should pay attention to both the strategies employees use and the areas of work life in the early career, and to do so from the perspective of gender differences.

Helen Cheng and *Ingrid Schoon* in the chapter *The role of school engagement in young people's career development and mental health and wellbeing: Findings from two British Cohorts* examine the role of school motivation as a potential mediating variable, linking family social background and childhood cognitive ability to later educational and occupational attainment and adult mental health and well-being. The study is based on two large representative samples of the British population born in 1958 and 1970, comprising more than 12,000 participants with information on social background, school experiences and subsequent adult outcomes. Structural Equation Modelling (SEM) is used to assess the pathways linking early influences to adult outcomes. Results show that in both cohorts, school motivation is influenced by both family social background and general cognitive ability. School motivation in turn, influences later occupational attainment through its association with educational achievement, and also affects adult mental health and well-being. Thus school motivation shows an independent effect on adult occupational attainment and mental health, even after controlling for family social background and general cognitive ability. The findings suggest experiences and adjustment in the school system can play a significant role in shaping later attainment and levels of health and wellbeing.

Karen Evans and Edmund Waite end this section by introducing a retrospective view in '*Activating events' in adult learners' lives: Understanding learning and life chances through a retrospective lens*. The concept of career trajectories is typically used in work on transitions of young adults into the labour market, providing ideal type segmented routes that can be used to understand a variety of personal histories In adult life, routes diverge, experiences diversify still further and multiple new contingencies come into play. This chapter shows how, in adults' life and work experiences, initial career trajectories take on historical significance. Research into adult learning experiences of workers at the lower end of the earnings distribution highlights the diversity of 'pathways' and social processes by which people come, through youth and adult experiences of various kinds, to the 'destinations' of lower graded jobs. It is argued that these 'destinations' are merely staging posts in highly differentiated occupational and personal learning careers, with considerable implications for lifelong learning.

Part Five *Wider international perspectives on youth, working life and wellbeing* brings together five chapters from different parts of the globe. The contributions from Australia and New Zealand, India, Japan, Russia and South Africa, provide the basis for development of an extended dialogue between ideas and evidence, as they highlight often dramatic differences between normative conceptions of youth transitions and their realities among different sub-groups and in contrasting social and political contexts.

Johanna Wyn in *Young adulthood in Australia and New Zealand: Pathways to belonging* draws on Australian and New Zealand research on young people's lives. Longitudinal and ethnographically based research approaches provide complementary perspectives on the ways in which young people establish a sense of belonging in times of economic recession, and under conditions of employment insecurity. From the late 1980s on, neoliberal policies in Australia and New Zealand have influenced how youth is experienced. Transition approaches tend to be based on set sequences of mobility. It is argued that this approach does not give sufficient purchase on the strategies that young people use to be well, to engage in meaningful activity and to build successful lives in their own terms in different locations. Drawing on concepts from cultural geography and youth cultures this chapter argues that the idea of 'belonging to' enables youth researchers to integrate economic change with other dimensions of life, including wellbeing and relationships to people and place.

David Everatt in '*Ring of fire or a puff of (commentators') smoke?': Youth, unemployment and transitions in Gauteng* is presenting the situation of youth work transitions in South Africa, where youth unemployment remains at staggering levels, well over fifty per cent for the youngest working age cohort, with race, sex and spatial location all impacting. As such, traditional 'transitional' literature and concepts battle to find purchase, most obviously school-to-work and all the child-to-adult signifiers that go with these transitions. Moreover, constructions of youth have gone from anti-apartheid foot soldier and 'lost generation' through 'marginalised youth' and 'potential partners in building democracy'—to again being a threat, a 'ring of fire' surrounding the wealthy cities of Gauteng (Johannesburg, Tshwane (formerly Pretoria) and Ekurhuleni (formerly Germiston). A just-recently completed survey, however, suggests that young people are more optimistic and more engaged than their elders. The author argues that policy-makers should rather look to the inequality that marks South African to identify where the 'threat' they fear can be found, rather than blithely pointing fingers of blame at young people.

Tomokazu Makino's chapter *School to work transition and youth views on labour in Japan* analyses Japanese school to work transition system and labour system looking at Japan's school to work transition system over the last 20 years, as well as youth views and values regarding labour in Japan. In particular, by surveying various studies and statistics, he discusses what social science studies have managed to elucidate since the 'Lost Decade,' as well as the messages (and responses to them) that have been disseminated to society. This paper brings together several perspectives that are usually studied separately, such as changes in the school to work transition system, and youth values, combining them in an integrated story.

Julia Zubok in her chapter *Russian youth in the labour market* analyses the changes in education, employment, and in wealth trends based on the results of sociological research of the Youth Sociology Institute of Social and Political Studies, from 1990 to 2011. The analysed data includes results of studies conducted by a comparable methodology, aimed at tracking the social changes among youth from fifteen to twenty-nine years in connection with the on- going transformation process in twelve regions of the Russian Federation (RF). This monitoring includes the last generation of Soviet youth focusing on the changes of Gorbachev's perestroika, the collapse of the Soviet Union and the country's transition to market economy crisis caused by privatisation and the liberal reforms (so called shock therapies), destabilisation of the economy, the bankruptcy of enterprises, and growth of inflation, which all have been as significant factors in the transitions of Russian young generations. The paper discusses these changes of the post-Soviet period in Russia and what they mean in the lives of Russian young people.

In the *School to work transition in India* chapter, *Vinod Chandra* analyses the ways in which India strives for knowledge society and attempts to improve its labour force. The attempt has been made to increase the gross enrolment rate of secondary, higher secondary and higher education by introducing various subsidies in the study fees and providing grants and scholarships to disadvantaged section of the society. Several central and state government programmes are intended to encourage school and college enrolment and retention. On the basis of a study on 600 school leavers in the districts of Lucknow and Allahabad during 2008-09, the present chapter examines whether school leaving youth in India are equipped to make a successful transition to work roles. It also explores the extent to which they are indeed making that transition. The main probing questions focus on the extent to which this section of the young population succeeds in finding productive employment. What are the career aspirations of young school leavers and how are they linked with employability in various employment sectors? What are the factors which led them to undertake a job without completing their college education?

The commentary chapter of *James Côté* concludes the volume, showing how the papers making up the content of the book offer an exceptionally rich array of evidence to illuminate its major themes. Taken as a whole, the collection highlights the challenges to conventional thinking and methodological issues that future research and theory in the field of youth transitions need to address. The concluding chapter provides a commentary on the contribution of this volume and places the individual chapters within the context of the structure-agency debate and the emerging perspective concerning the importance of agentic resources in overcoming structural obstacles in the transition from education to work in late-modern societies. From his North-American perspective, Côté takes Canadian examples of education-to-work transitions and contrasts them with examples from the UK, where social class appears to structure these transitions to a greater extent than in Canada. A typology of agentic and structural resources is then provided that helps to elucidate the interplay between structure and agency in various societal contexts, and the risks and benefits associated with the transition to work for various subgroups of differentially resourced youth. In turn, these considerations are put in context in terms of current debates concerning what young people are transitioning 'through' and 'to.' This is accomplished by providing an historical analysis of the rise of life course concepts as English-speaking societies underwent the transition from traditional to late-modern societies, with late-modern societies requiring the individualisation of the life course and having different needs for the productive contributions of its younger members. This chapter ends with a call for researchers to understand better the resources needed by young people of all economic backgrounds to strategically manage their life courses under late-modern conditions.

As editors, we have been privileged to work with authors in a process that has extended from Finnish-British dialogue to global debate, through the discussion of new and original research findings. In reaching beyond our national settings, we come not only to appreciate societal and cultural differences but also to understand the situations of young people engaging with the realities of work in our own societies more deeply.

Part 2: Perspectives on employment transitions and wellbeing changes during economic recession

Chapter 2

School to work transitions and wellbeing in a changing labour market

John Bynner

Introduction

Current economic events remind us that young people seeking entry to the labour market suffer particularly from the effects of economic recession. The periodic downturns in the economy that have occurred since the 1970s are currently topped by a recession of exceptional severity. Such economic changes can have damaging outcomes especially for school leavers in the British labour market where experience of employment may be just as important as qualifications to getting and retaining a job.

Economists describe these effects on young people as 'scarring' (e.g. Ellwood, 1982; Arulampalam, Gregg and Gregory, 2001). That is to say individual prospects are damaged when the expected pattern of school to further or higher education and work is broken through scarcity of jobs for prospective entrants. This signals to employers a lack of crucial work experience and the work-related skills involved in doing specific jobs and the more generic attributes of employability ranging from punctuality to taking initiative and team work. Such attributes are likely to be at a premium when the economy recovers and employers are seeking to recruit. The whole employment career of discontinuous employment, interspersed with periods of unemployment and occasional casual jobs is 'scarred' to the extent that the prospects of continuing and fulfilling employment become increasingly weakened. The phenomenon of NEET, as defined originally in the UK as six months over the period 16-18 'Not in Education, Employment or Training' (UK Social Exclusion Unit, 1999), is the consequence. Although the same principle of six months or more disengagement usually defines NEET, the age period over which this occurs is more typically taken now, including in Britain, to be sixteen to twenty-four. This change reflects the extension, in all industrialised countries, of the transition from school to work (Quintini and Martin, 2006). Apart from the damage to employment prospects, NEET also brings the likelihood of reduced life chances and threats more generally to wellbeing in later life.

This chapter starts by reviewing the historical background to these effects since the 1970s and what we can learn from them about the likely consequences of recession for wellbeing. We then move on to longitudinal cohort study evidence focusing particularly on the origins and consequences of NEET and their implications for youth policy.

Recession and unemployment

The magnitude of the effect of the 2008 recession on unemployment among young people (age 16-24) relative to older age-groups (25-49 and 50+) is shown by UK unemployment levels from early 2008 to early 2010.[2] The notable feature was the steady rise in unemployment continuing across the period as job opportunities dried up, especially for the younger age group. From January 2008 to January 2012 the youth unemployment rate rose from 12% to 18% compared with 4% to 6% and 2% to 4% respectively among the two older age groups. As further economic pressures build from the Eurozone to the USA there seems every prospect of the rise continuing and a damaged generation not seen since the collapse of the Soviet Union (Roberts et al., 2005).

The differential damage unemployment is likely to do to young people's job prospects later in life is shown further from historical data collected over a longer period 1977 to 1999. Figures 1 and 2 compare unemployment rates of young people aged 16-19 with those of older age groups (20-24) and (25+) over the period 1977 to 1999 (Bynner and Parsons, 2002). The younger group's unemployment levels were consistently higher, but particularly in the peak period of recession in the early 1990s reaching 17%. By way of contrast, in the recessions of the early 1980s and 1990s, both of the youngest groups (16-19 and 20-24) shared the experience of unemployment to much the same extent, with peaks above 16% for both of them. Another interesting feature of these graphs is the gender difference, which shows consistently higher unemployment levels for young men than for young women. This time the highest unemployment rate was restricted to the early 1980s for 16-19 year-old women, staying for six years at around 12%. In the 1990s rising unemployment barely featured at all for women, whatever their age group. This reflects the more economically vulnerable manual jobs that young men compared with young women were still

2   UK Office of National Statistics 2008-2010.

seeking to enter in the 1990s. It also reflects the transformation of the labour market towards service industry and the decline in manufacturing with the shift towards more flexible working hours facilitating the balancing of job and family commitments that tended to suit women's lives better (Ashton and Bynner, 2011).

Figure 1: Unemployed young people as percentage of the age group, 16-19 year olds and 20-24 year olds, 1977 to 2000–young men.

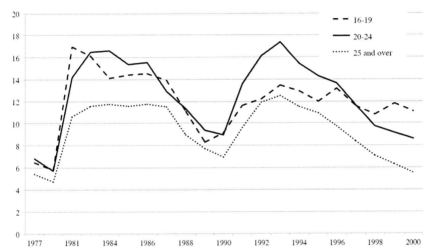

Figure 2: Unemployed young people as percentage of the age group, 16-19 year olds and 20-24 year olds, 1977 to 2000–young women

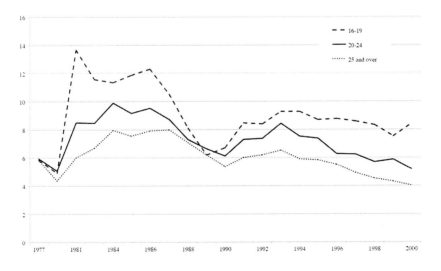

Labour market transformation

Periodic economic recession is one feature of most industrialised societies from the 1970s to the present day. But its causes are not simply restricted exclusively to the actions of bankers as typically perceived now. The current recession is better viewed as merely adding to the long-term trends that have transformed the nature of employment and the labour market. The information and communications technology (ICT) revolution, which began in the late 1970s, coupled with the collapse of heavy industry, the decline of unskilled work and an increasingly globalised economy, broke traditional patterns of entry to employment via the established routes. In place of transition pathways from education to the workplace rooted in the family and community, there was growing prominence for personal choice and the marshalling of individual and family resources in reducing risks and uncertainty in transition decisions. The new 'choice biographies', originating in the ideas of 'Individualisation' and the 'Risk Society' (Beck, 1986), and driven more by the exercise of personal agency than structural demands, became increasingly characterised by the need for various kinds of 'vocational insurance', i.e. accumulating the resources that would ensure later access to work (Bynner, 1999).

Other analysts were less convinced that the structural pressures of gender, and especially social class, on the transition from school to work had diminished to any great extent (e.g. Roberts, Clark and Wallace, 1997; Evans and Furlong, 1997; Furlong and Cartmel, 1997). Nevertheless, personal resources were becoming critically important in shaping the transition the most significant form of which was staying on in education and gaining qualifications. These could be the best protection not only in accessing jobs but retaining them at a time when the labour market for young people was continually contracting.

The consequence was an ever-extending transition in which the full time employment and independence that went with it was increasingly postponed—described as 'quasi citizenship' (Jones and Wallace, 1992). Such a status underpins the somewhat contested claim, emanating more recently from the USA, that a new psycho-socially driven stage of the life course can be identified, *emerging adulthood* (Arnett, 2004), in which a kind of moratorium in the twenties is placed on establishing a career. (For an extended debate on the subject, advancing alternative interpretations of the changes in young people's life courses that had taken place, see Bynner, 2005, Côté and Bynner, 2008, Arnett et al., 2011.)

However, prolonging the transition from education depends critically on the availability of family maintenance and support, including that needed for breaks to broaden experience, e.g.'gap years' before or after going to university, over a much longer period than in the past. In the 1980s, persisting to the present day, young people without such buttressing more typically attempted to pursue the traditional routes of leaving school at the minimum age, often without qualifications. They faced the risk of poor prospects in the labour market, including low quality training schemes instead of jobs and the possibility of long term occupational and social exclusion (Banks et al., 1992; UK Social Exclusion Unit, 1999). Such polarising effects with the marginalisation of those at the bottom end of education and employment'trajectories' has been the main feature of youth transitions ever since (Ashton and Bynner, 2011).

Though the status of NEET, is a grossly over-simplified categorisation suppressing the heterogeneity of the trajectories that such young people are on, including 'gap years', internships, and career shifts (Coles et al., 2010), it does include within it a sizable group, without qualifications or the requisite work experience, whose prospects in the labour market are bleak. For them long term wellbeing is jeopardised in numerous ways. Persistent unemployment may lead to much reduced self-esteem followed by compensation for it by drugs and alcohol and turning to crime, (Banks and Ullah, 1988; Farrington et al., 1986). Partnership and parenthood may either be accelerated for young women, teenage parenthood, (Hakim, 1996), or for young men, indefinitely postponed, 'perpetual adolescence' (Wallace, 1987). Mental health may also come under strain as feelings of hopelessness hold sway (Banks and Ullah, 1988). Such problems may be particularly a problem in countries with a highly institutionalised system of vocational education and training, such as Germany, where failure to get certification through an apprenticeship or other routes will close the doors to recognised occupations and all but the fringes of the adult labour market (Bynner and Evans, 1994).

Youth transitions

Central to the outcomes of the transition to work is the shaping of the identity that the young person will carry with them into adult life. We need to consider first what constitutes a good transition to adulthood and secondly the key personal and social resources that are needed to underpin it. Successful transitions comprise what the French call vividly *'insertion'*-or in UK terms *'integration'*—into the labour market. This makes the point that in France it is seen as the job of the State to ensure that young people gain access to adult jobs as well as that of the individual to take advantage of opportunities when available. Such a transition will be characterised by the achievement of some kind of occupational identity, though this itself-even in the highly institutionalised German system—has become increasingly difficult to identify in many occupational sectors for some time (Bynner, 2010).

Occupational identity is identified with the knowledge, skills and experience to secure continuing employment and progression in a particular sector of the labour market (Brockmann, Clarke and Winch, 2011). In the broader sense of 'general' as opposed to 'occupational' identity there is also the acquisition of the values of commitment, cooperation and tolerance and strong social relationships in the community, the family, the workplace and the peer group' (Côté and Levine, 2002). The other critical component is good physical and psychological health and a healthy lifestyle (Banks and Ullah, 1988).

In contrast, unsuccessful transitions are characterised by what the French call *précarité*, i.e. spells of casual work and unemployment, often coupled with drug and alcohol abuse, and in the case of young women, the risks associated with early parenthood in advance of secure employment. Trouble with the police and mental health problems may be another significant feature (Farrington, et al., 1986).

Resources needed to achieve the successful as opposed to the unsuccessful transition to adulthood are best described, following the conceptualisation of the development economist Amartya Sen (1992), as *capabilities*. Sen defines capability as the means of *gaining access* to and *achieving* desired outcomes—'freedom to achieve wellbeing'—comprising the life goals and competences needed to achieve them. For young people during the transition to adulthood the key goal is autonomy as reflected in financial and social independence. But as we have seen, in the contemporary world this independence is increasingly difficult to achieve.

Capabilities include the core facets of the developing identity through which individual agency is exercised including, apart from cognitive skills as certified through educational attainment, those stressed by developmental psychologists such as 'planfulness', 'self-efficacy', 'self-regulation', 'motivation', 'resilience', 'social competence'. Developing such attributes is critically dependent on learning opportunities and absence of obstacles to those that exist. Managing the transition in ways that will foster these attributes thus lies at the core of life course construction during the youth phase of the life course on which adult wellbeing is founded, 'life management' (Helve and Bynner, 1996).

Capabilities may be usefully grouped into three goal-directed areas of competence also described as *capitals* (Côté, 1996; Côté and Levine, 2002). As applied to young people, *human capital* comprises the qualifications and work experience that reflect the skills that employers will seek in offering opportunities for first and subsequent employment. *Social capital* comprises the trust-based relationships that young people have access to ('strong and weak ties') in carrying through transition decisions, including the crucial one to future wellbeing of whether to stay on in education or leave. The family's position in the social structure facilitates or constrains access to a range of opportunities in education and the labour market, as well as imparting norms of behaviour and lifestyle *habitus* that have a high premium in gaining and retaining employment (Bourdieu, and Passeron, 1977). Hence the most important function of social capital in this respect is as a family resource to be drawn upon; while at the same time young people are striving to achieve autonomy by replacing their parents' social capital with social capital of their own (Helve and Bynner, 2007).

The third form of capital is described as *identity capital*, that is to say those attributes that make up not only the sense of personal wellbeing but at as we saw earlier the key capabilities of self-efficacy, motivation, team work, creativity, flexibility, initiative and drive—mainly gained in the family but developed further through interactions with others in the peer group at school and outside. But education has to be seen as almost conditional for all the others, as without the key competences and certification that education brings prospects in the labour market are likely to be severely curtailed (Bynner, 1998).

Effects of economic change

Some of the effects of economic change on youth transitions are illuminated by comparative analysis of data for thirty year-olds collected in Britain's 1946, 1958 and 1970 birth cohort studies—longitudinal surveys that, since they began, have followed large samples of 5,000 up to 17,000 individuals at regular intervals from birth through to adult life (Ferri, Bynner and Wadsworth, 2003). The 1946 study has over three and a half thousand cohort members still actively participating and the second (1958) and third (1970) up to twelve thousand each.

The particular value of the British cohort studies is in enabling us to chart changes in youth transitions and their outcomes over a period of unparalleled industrial and economic transformation (Wadsworth and Bynner, 2011). The comparison between the 1958 and 1970 studies is particularly informative because it coincides with the shift in the UK from two thirds of the work force entering jobs at sixteen, down to first one half and subsequently one third, a large proportion of whom during the 1980 and 1990 recessions failed to find employment. At the same time as Figure 3, shows polarisation of the youth population was increasing with a widening social class gap between those from professional families continuing in education leading to university and those from unskilled working class homes. A much higher percentage of the 1970 cohort, compared with the 1946 cohort, had gained a university degree. But at the same time there was a substantial social class gradient in this achievement that steepened from the earlier to the more recent cohort. In other words, the polarisation between social classes with respect to access to this key feature of human capital acquisition was increasing.

Figure 3: University or college degree (by family social class) %.

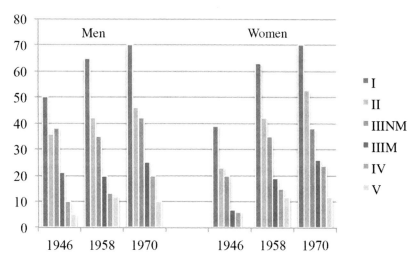

Key: UK Registrar General's classification of occupations: I professional; II Intermediate; IIINM skilled non-manual; IIIM skilled manual; IV semi-skilled; V unskilled.

In contrast, average earnings, analysed by gender showed a quite different picture, a narrowing across cohorts of the gender gap (Dearden, 2003). Notably, in the three successive cohorts, the patterns of women's earnings shifted from a relatively narrow earnings band in the 1946 cohort, with a substantially lower average than that for the much wider earnings band for men. By age thirty in the 1970 cohort, the gap had reduced between men and women and the distribution of earnings was increasingly matching that of men's. In other words from a relatively narrow range of female occupational opportunities, with family responsibilities taking the major role when the 1946 cohort had reached age thirty in 1976, the range of occupational outcomes in terms of associated earnings had expanded considerably for the same age group in the 1970 cohort The less positive side of this latter shift was that it pointed to increasingly class-based polarisation among women, matching that which had traditionally been the experience of men.

Changes of this kind relating to wellbeing were also evident in other areas of the thirty year-olds' lives. Partnership and parenthood was increasingly postponed from the earliest to the most recent cohort with seventy per cent of women and eighty per cent of men still childless at age thirty in the 1970 cohort compared with half this proportion in the 1946 cohort. Suspension from school and trouble with the police, including being arrested, were also reported by a substantially higher proportion of the most recent cohort, as were feelings of 'not getting what you want out of life' and lack of political interest.

Steepening social class gradients were also apparent in these attributes as illustrated for feelings of depression among women (Figure 4). From lack of

Figure 4: Percentage reporting depression in relation to own social class: women

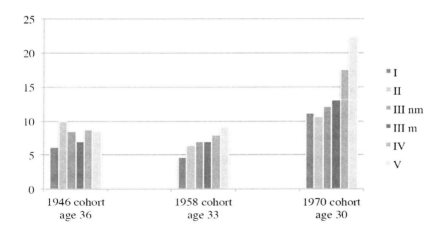

Key: UK Registrar General's classification of occupations: I professional; II Intermediate; IIInm skilled non-manual; IIIm skilled manual; IV semi-skilled; V unskilled.

any gradient in the 1946 cohort, and a modest one in the 1958 cohort, there was a massive rise in feeling of depression concentrated among the semi-skilled and unskilled in the 1970 cohort. Although the average depression level among women was lower for men than for women, much the same picture was maintained of increasing depression concentrated in the unskilled and semi-skilled occupational groups.

Who is NEET?

This descriptive evidence of rising transition difficulties for young people growing up during the recessions of the 1980s and 1990s takes us directly to the possible consequences for today's young people. This was achieved by examining in the 1970 cohort the origins and consequences of not being in education, employment or training for at least six months over the period 16-18 (NEET) (Bynner and Parsons, 2002).

Where does NEET come from and what follows it? Logistic regression analysis of a 10% sample of the 1970 cohort study data for those young people who had spent six months not in education, employment or training over the period 16-18 identified the key predictors of NEET status and its outcomes (Figures 5 and 6). Thus Figure 5 shows that absence of any qualifications 'living on an inner city estate,' not being read to as a child' and 'low birth weight' were the

Figure 5: Predicting NEET including highest qualification achieved by age 30 (odds ratios).

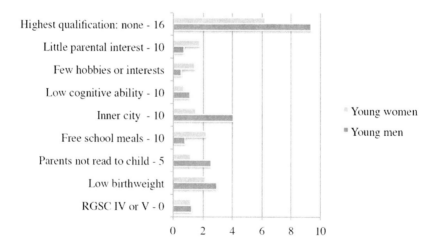

key predictors of NEET for young men—lack of qualifications dominating the rest—more so for young men than for young women. In contrast, 'little parental interest', 'few hobbies and interests' and poverty, as reflected in receiving 'free school meals', were the key predictors for young women. Notably, when highest qualification was removed from the analysis the strength of the relationships with all the other variables increased substantially. This suggests that lack of qualifications mediates part of the effect of other variables while substantial residual effects remain. Or looking at it another way, lack of qualifications in company with other factors such as growing up in an inner city estate is likely to add substantially to a young person's propensity towards NEET

The analysis was extended to investigate the wellbeing outcomes of NEET when the sample had reached age twenty-one (Figure 6). For young men the most significant outcome, separating them from young women, was continuing in the status of NEET, typically reflected in unemployment or further NEET status at age twenty-one. For young women, the key outcomes were feeling that they had 'problems with life', 'lack of control over life' and 'dissatisfaction with life', plus being in a married or co-habiting relationship typically with children. Although these latter outcomes were less strongly identified for young men, they were still featuring in their lives though overshadowed by their poor labour market outcomes

Figure 6: Predicting the outcomes of NEET at age 21 (odds ratios).

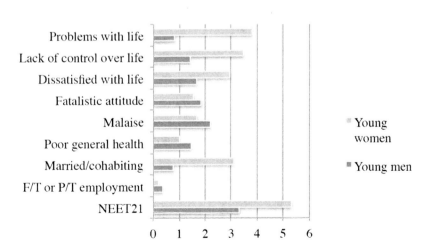

Conclusions

This chapter has set out to demonstrate the likely significance of recession for young people's transitions to the labour market and wellbeing in adult life. Although the great majority of young people, through resilience built on family support and personal attributes, will resist economic recession's worst effects, others without these assets are more likely to be 'scarred' by the experience. This applies not only in the labour market but in the family and community and in their personal lives. The antidote in the modern world is increasingly one of building resources, i.e. especially capabilities of different kinds, accumulated in capitals that can be deployed—human, psychological, and social.

The phenomenon of NEET—virtually unknown from the end of the second world up to the end of the 1970s—is the potential status of those who fail to build such resources. A disadvantaged childhood, typically based in the inner city for boys and accompanied by lack of parental interest in education for girls, supplies the context in which such difficulties may arise. The consequence for boys is continuing on the same track of little continuous and fulfilling employment. For young women, many of whom become young mothers, the consequences tend to be more psychological—e.g. feelings of depression and lack of self worth coupled with lack of the work experience that might lay the foundations for re-engagement with the labour market later through a rewarding job. The experience raises the question of how such vulnerable young people can best be helped to withstand the economic pressures and their lack of confidence in themselves. Clearly in policy terms, the windows of opportunity that the period of full-time education provides and what follows it, are critical to heading off the worst outcomes for young people. Without this help their already poor prospects are likely to get worse. The solution must lie in ensuring that the learning opportunities leading to productive outcomes are kept open for as long as possible and that financial and counselling support is available to maximise the chances of such young people taking them up (Wolf, 2011).

A notable feature of the NEET analysis was that although the importance of educational achievement as reflected in certification had been increasing, social class and the accompanying features of disadvantage continued to exercise an independent and powerful effect even when highest qualification achieved was also taken into account. This suggests that the components of identity capital derived from family circumstances and experience add to, rather than operate through, educational achievement in driving some young people towards NEET.

Thus neighbourhood, family circumstances, and parental lack of support for education predict entry into NEET status, which itself predicts continuing labour market problems (men and women) and psychological distress (women). The role of inner city housing estate residence for boys gives particularly striking endorsement to the problematic nature of this experience for boys' life chances (e.g. Power and Tunstall, 1997). For girls the significance of educational interest in the home (or rather lack of it) appears to push them along a path that for many in the NEET category is identified with early motherhood (Wallace, 1987; Bynner and Parsons, 2002). Capability thus extends beyond performance in classrooms and is needed as the means of achieving a successful transition to adulthood and wellbeing in all the domains of adult life.

However, the differences in the life goals of men and women that begin to crystallise in the teens through transition processes question the application, of the NEET category to girls in the same way as it is applied to boys. The centrality of child bearing in the construction of female careers (Wallace, 1987; Hakim, 1996; Evans and Heinz, 1994), suggests that young women's 'dropping out' through pregnancy has a certain functional equivalence to young men's disengagement from education employment and training but in their case it can also be viewed as an occupational choice in its own right. The dominance of poor labour market experience as the main outcome associated with NEET for young men does query whether NEET status does damage young women's identity capital development in Côté's broad sense of the term (2002) in quite the same way, rather than just its human capital component.

The experience of NEET simply compounds a history of educational failure, reducing prospects of employment or for acquiring human capital through education or training even further—a 'staging post' on the downward path to the margins of the labour market and social exclusion. For young women the NEET experience appears to impact more clearly on other facets of identity as well. The association of NEET with negative psychological states including (self-reported) lack of a sense of control over life, problems and dissatisfaction with life, points perhaps to more fundamental damage occurring. And this is at a time when, in terms of educational achievement and progress in the middle to higher echelons of the labour market, women's prospects have never been better (Hakim, 1996; Arnot, David and Weiner, 1999). Perhaps it is their powerlessness to take advantages of these opportunities that underpins these NEET young women's negative feelings about themselves. On the other hand, we need to qualify such a conclusion on methodological grounds. Women tend to be more willing to express such feelings openly than men, so young NEET men's lack of acknowledgement of psychological difficulties does not rule out their existence.

More complex ways and means of developing capabilities are evident in more recent cohorts and a stronger role for capabilities in later labour market outcomes. Early leaving typically predicts a disadvantaged employment career, including unemployment spells, poor jobs, lack of ICT experience and lack of opportunity (Bynner, et al. 2008). Thus recession compounded with the globalising pressures towards polarisation increases the precariousness of the pathways to adulthood. This is especially the case for those young people lacking the individual and family resources vested in the capabilities needed for successful transition. The *trajectory of disadvantage* leading to social exclusion begins early; but given the right resources to bolster and develop learning opportunities through education, the family, the work place and the community its damaging effects can be mitigated if not reversed. Trajectories reflect statistical tendencies not inevitability: there are opportunities for intervention to raise education levels at every age and stage of the youth phase of the life course.

Chapter 3

The assumption of adult roles in the U.K., the U.S.A., and Finland: Antecedents and associated levels of well-being and health

Ingrid Schoon and John Schulenberg

Introduction

In this chapter we review evidence from two age cohorts in the UK, the US and Finland making the transition to independent adulthood. Drawing from four recent analyses based on four well established national and community-based studies from Britain (the 1958 National Child Development Study [NCDS] and the 1970 British Birth Cohort Study [BCS70]) (Schoon, Kneale, Jager, and Chen, 2012), the United States (Monitoring the Future [MTF]) (Maggs, Jager, Patrick, and Schulenberg, 2012), and Finland [the 1959 Jyväskylä Study of Personality and Social Development [JVLS] (Räikkönen, Kokko, and Pulkkinen, 2012) and the 1966 Northern Finland Birth Cohort [NFBC] Salmela-Aro, Ek, and Chen, 2012)), we summarise evidence regarding patterns of social role combinations of young people in their mid twenties, childhood antecedents and associated adult health outcomes. These studies are part of a special issue of *Longitudinal and Life Course Studies* concerning comparative studies of the transition to adulthood (Schulenberg and Schoon, 2012). Adopting a life course perspective, we compare evidence across different cultures and settings to enable a better understanding regarding similarities and differences of how young people negotiate the transition to independent adulthood, the role of early predictors and associated adult health outcomes. Importantly, included are two comparable age cohorts in each country, born in the late 1950s and the late 1960s/early 1970s, respectively, allowing for within and across country comparisons. Cross-study comparisons in general, and international comparisons in particular, are essential for theory advancement. Such studies assist in matters of generalisability as well as in disentangling how country-level culture and expectations play out in opportunities and limitations during the transition to adulthood.

In each country, the focus was on the 'big 5' transition events (Shanahan, 2000; Stettersten, 2007) comprising the completion of education, entry into paid employment, partnership and family formation (i.e. parenthood), as well as independent living arrangements. Becoming an adult is conceived as a status passage involving several role and status changes guided by age-related informal and legal norms (Buchmann and Kriesi, 2011; Elder and Shanahan, 2007; Macmillan, 2005). Such normative patterns are however subject to change, either through influences from the wider socio-historical context, through individual agency or through collective action (Elder, Johnson, and Crosnoe, 2004; Schoon and Silbereisen, 2009). The transition process has traditionally been regarded as complete when an individual has experienced all five transition events (Shanahan, 2000). In recent years this requirement has been contested, for example by Arnett (2000) who has postulated a new developmental stage of 'emerging adulthood', characterised by the extended exploration of identity, life styles, and career possibilities. Although the term 'emerging adulthood' may be a useful synonym for the prolonged transition to independent adulthood, it does not take into account the social and economic conditions that have produced extended transitions, instead offering a strictly psychological model of free choice focusing on the postponement of commitments (Bynner, 2005; Côtè and Bynner, 2008). Transition outcomes are however dependent on social structural opportunities and constraints as well as individual resources and capabilities (Elder and Shanahan, 2007; Evans, Rudd, Behrens, Kaluza, and Wooley, 2003). Moreover, the assumption of a new, universal life stage leads to an ever increasing marginalisation of those who continue to pursue the traditional routes to adult life through early entry to the labour market, or who due to lack of personal and family resources cannot take advantage of the moratorium opportunities available, especially regarding participation in further and higher education (Heinz, 2009; Macmillan, 2005; Schoon and Silbereisen, 2009). Structural forces, as mediated by the family and local opportunity structures, continue to shape the timing and sequencing of transitions to independent adulthood, and young people from less privileged backgrounds leave education and enter paid employment earlier than their more privileged peers (Blossfeld, 2005; Schoon, Ross, and Martin, 2009).

In the following we will describe variations in the five transition markers achieved by cohort members in their mid twenties, patterns of role combination, examine similarities and differences in predictive influences and associated health outcomes. It has been argued that country differences in completing the five transition markers are largest around age 25 and relatively small before age 20 and after age 35 (Cook and Furstenberg, 2002). Examining transition outcomes and role combinations of cohort members in their mid twenties thus provides a unique snapshot and important insights into similarities and differences in transition experiences of young people growing up in different cultural contexts and in different historical periods. The three countries considered here differ largely in their institutional arrangements, cultural heterogeneity, and economies. How these societal differences are related to diversity in pathways to adulthood is at the core of current scientific debates, questioning whether there has indeed been a destandardisation of transition pathways (Brückner and Mayer, 2005; Macmillan, 2005; Schoon and Silbereisen, 2009). Although the changing nature of the life course in modern society has been, and still is, the focus of speculation and discussion, there is a lack of systematic empirical research, in particular of comparative studies of the transition to adulthood.

Why is it important to study variations in the transition to adulthood?

The transition to adulthood is characterised as a demographically dense life period, involving the assumption of new social roles and responsibilities, and the negotiation of several, often competing transition events (Buchmann and Kriesi, 2011; Elder, 1985; Shanahan, 2000). Often, these events are themselves either the end or starting point of trajectories. Within life course theory (Elder, 1985) transitions denote changes in status or social roles, such as leaving school and entering full-time employment. Transitions are usually short in duration and indicate a change in a single state, moving from one social role or status to another. Transitions are embedded within trajectories that give them a distinctive form and meaning. Trajectories take place over an extended period of time and capture sequences of roles and experiences. The life course is, however, not defined by transitions and trajectories as such, but is characterised by the interplay of multiple role transitions and trajectories. The combination of multiple social roles at a given time has been conceptualised by the notion of role or status configurations to describe age-specific matrices of discrete social roles that individuals occupy at given points in the life course (Macmillan and Eliason, 2003). Negotiating the multiple, often competing role transitions in a relatively short time requires careful conciliation and compromise, which in turn can have implications for health and wellbeing (Schulenberg, Bryant, and O'Malley, 2004). Educational and employment decisions, for example, have implications for family formation and vice-versa. There is evidence to suggest that multiple simultaneous transitions completed in a relative short time result in reduced health and wellbeing (Coleman, 1989; Schulenberg and Maggs, 2002), although failure to achieve key transition markers is also be associated with psychological distress (Sacker and Cable, 2010; Schulenberg, et al., 2004). In this chapter we therefore report the health outcomes associated with variations in role combinations attained by age 26 to gain a better understanding of heterogeneity in transition experiences across different contexts, and how associations have changed over time. We furthermore take into account socio-demographic and adolescent predictors (i.e. educational aspirations) of different transition patterns, to control for variations in structural and individual resources.

The cohort studies
UK

The 1958 National Child Development Study (NCDS) and the 1970 British Cohort Study (BCS70) are two of Britain's richest research resources for the study of human development (Ferri, Bynner, and Wadsworth, 2003). NCDS took as its subjects all persons living in Great Britain who were born in March 1958. In six follow up studies, data were collected on the physical, psycho-social and educational development of the cohort at age 7, 11, 16, 23, 33, 42, 46 and 50 years. The BCS70 has followed children born in April 1970. Data collection sweeps have taken place when the cohort members were aged 5, 10, 16, 26, 30, and 34 years. In these analyses, data cover childhood through to age 26 comprising 9,171 cohort members in NCDS and 9.897 in BCS70 (Schoon et al., 2012). In both cohorts the sample population is predominantly white (about 3 to 4 per cent are from Indian, Pakistani, Bangladeshi, African, Caribbean, Chinese or mixed origin), reflecting the ethnic diversity of the UK population at the time (Ferri et al., 2003; see also www.cls.ioe.ac.uk).

US

The ongoing Monitoring the Future project has recruited nationally representative samples of about 16,000 students in the 12th grade (modal age, 18 years) annually since 1975 (Johnston et al., 2010). Approximately 2400 of these participants are selected each year for biennial follow-ups using mailed surveys. These longitudinal follow-ups begin one year after the baseline for a random half of the participants, and two years after the baseline for the other half; these two halves are combined in these analyses. Thus, longitudinal data on approximately 3000 respondents collected at age 18 and at ages 25/26 are used in analyses reported here for 1958-59 and for 1970-71 birth cohorts (Maggs et al., 2012). More detailed information about the MTF design and methods is available in Johnston et al. (2010b) and at www.monitoringthefuture.org.

Finland

The ongoing Jyväskylä Longitudinal Study of Personality and Social Development (JYLS) follows the lives of 369 individuals from 12 randomly selected second-grade classes in the town of Jyväskylä, Finland (Pulkkinen 2006, Pulkkinen, Kokko 2010). The study began in 1968, when most cohort members were aged 8 years (thus, 1959 birth cohort) with data collections at ages 14, 27, 36, 42, and 50. In the present study, adult transitions were studied up to age 27 (Räikkönen et al., 2012). At age 27 (in 1986) data was collected with a mailed Life Situation Questionnaire (LSQ) and a semi-structured interview. The LSQ was completed by 155 women (90%) and 166 men (85%), and interviews conducted with 142 women (82%) and 150 men (77%).

The Northern Finland Birth Cohort provides data from 12,055 pregnant women and their 12,058 live-born children born in 1966 in the provinces of Lapland and Oulu in Finland. Data on the biological, socio-economic, and health conditions, living habits, and family characteristics of cohort members were collected during pregnancy with follow-up studies via postal questionnaires at age 14, 16, and age of 31. In addition register data have been collected online. The present study is based on those cohort members for whom relevant register data could be obtained at the age of 25-26 (N=11,825) (Salmela-Aro et al., 2012).

Prevalence of transition markers of cohort members in their mid twenties

Before looking at the data, some limitations of our comparative approach should be noted. The data collection in each country was not designed for comparative analysis, and is strongly influenced by national conventions. Furthermore, the sampling frames for data collection were not similar in the different countries, involving large scale prospective cohort and panel data, as well as, in the Finnish case, a small scale community sample. The purpose for which the data were gathered, the criteria used and the method of collection varied considerably from one country to another, and the criteria adopted for coding data has changed over time. For example, regarding the coding of educational attainment, differences in the structure of the three countries' education system make a direct comparison difficult—but not impossible. Furthermore, in the 1966 Northern Finland Study no information on part-time employment has been collected, and no differentiation between single, cohabiting, divorced, or widowed family status has been coded. Identifying comparative indicators was thus not always as straightforward as we hoped for, and in some cases the available information is limited. As a solution, we reduced the classifications of the transition markers to a common base, jointly agreeing with the studies' authors about the parameters and units of comparison.

Table 1 shows the observed characteristics of the cohort members in their mid twenties, differentiated by country and age cohort. The later born cohorts are generally better educated, are less likely married and less likely to have children then the earlier born cohorts. Compared to the other countries, educational attainment was highest (i.e. percentage of cohort members with a completed bachelor or higher degree) among US cohort members at both time points— and lowest (i.e. high school or less), especially during the mid 1980s. Young people in Finland were least likely to have degree qualifications by age 26/27 at both time points, but the younger 1966 Northern Finnish cohort was more likely than their peers in the other countries to be still in education. Regarding highest academic qualifications achieved by age 26 young people in the UK were somewhere in the middle between the US and Finland.

There are no great differences in employment status, as most young people were employed full-time by age 26—in both age cohorts. In the mid 1980s part-time work is more prevalent (around 5-6 per cent) in the UK and Finnish sample (compared to the US sample). To be a full-time home maker at age 26 appears to be more prevalent in the UK sample (about one in ten) than in Finland or the US. Compared to the UK, more young people in the US and Finnish sample were still in education at age 26/27, particularly in the mid 1990s.

For both cohorts, the majority of young people live away from home by age 26, especially so in Finland, where we find the lowest proportion of young people living with their parents at that age. However, the proportion of young people in Finland living with their parents has more than doubled at the later assessment point.

Regarding relationship status we observe a major shift in living arrangements, especially in the UK and in Finland, where the proportion of young people being married by age 26 has considerably reduced for the younger cohorts. Likewise we see an increase in the proportion of young people who are childless at age 26. In the US samples the proportion of young people being married or having children has reduced for the younger cohort, but not to the same extent as for the UK and the Finnish samples.

Despite many similarities across the UK, Finland, and the US, there are some clear differences in educational opportunities and independent living. In particular, the three countries differ regarding academic and vocational tracking in secondary school (explicit split at age sixteen in the UK and Finland; opaque and less formal tracking in the US) and public funding of post-secondary college (fully funded in the UK until 1998, fully funded in Finland, and largely self funded in the US). Nonetheless, we find for the US cohorts a considerable increase in degree level qualifications, suggesting substantial private investments in young people's education. On the other hand, the Finnish welfare state supports the move to independent living among young people, and post-secondary students are entitled to social security support; this is not the case in the UK and the US. A consequence is that by age 25-27 most Finns—in both age cohorts—live independently from their parents, while in the UK and US we find in both age cohorts a distinct group of young people who at age 25-27 are living with their parents (having either never left or returning to the parental home after difficulties in launching). The greatest changes in transition experiences across cohorts however, have occurred regarding marriage and family formation, with fewer young people in the later born cohorts making the step into marriage and family formation, especially in the UK.

Combination of social roles by age twenty-six: their antecedents and associated levels of wellbeing

How do these different roles combine within individuals? The interdependence of education, work and family related transitions suggest the need for empirical methods that account for the multidimensional associations between variables, enabling the simultaneous consideration of multiple dimensions, which interact in important ways. All studies reviewed here used Latent Class Analysis (LCA) to identify patterns in social role combinations. LCA is a statistical method that enables us to examine latent structures among a set of categorical scored variables and to identify underlying types, groups, or classes (Goodman, 1974; Lazarsfeld and Henry, 1968). The usefulness of the latent class approach to map out diversity and heterogeneity in role configurations has been demonstrated in a number of previous studies (Macmillan and Copher, 2005; Osgood, Ruth, Eccles, Jacobs, and Barber, 2005; Ross, Schoon, Martin, and Sacker, 2009; Sandefur, Eggerling-Boeck, and Park, 2005).

After identifying distinct groups, the associations between group membership and a number of predictor variables (parental social status and education,

education aspirations, own school grades) were estimated by multinominal logistic regression. The association between group membership and indicators of wellbeing were assessed using ordinary regression as the measurement level for both variables was continuous.

In the UK samples five distinct groups could be identified (Schoon, et al., 2012), in the US and Finnish samples four distinct groups were found (Maggs, Jager, Patrick, and Schulenberg, 2012; Räikkönen, Kokko, and Pulkkinen, 2012; Salmela-Aro, Ek, and Chen, 2012). The profiles of the different groups can be summarised as those who are highly educated, as work orientation without children, traditional families, fragile transitions, and slow starters.

The highly educated

Each of the studies could identify a group of young people with relative high academic attainment, no children, full-time employment, often single or cohabiting, living independently from their parents. This group of young people comprises about 20 per cent in both British samples, about 10 per cent in the US and Finnish samples (8 and 9 per cent in the two US cohorts and 13.6 and 12.4 per cent in the two Finnish samples). In the US samples the group of the highly educated were still in full-time education at age 25/26, in the UK samples they were working full time and were mostly single, in the 1959 Finnish sample most were working full-time and were either single or cohabiting. In the 1966 Finnish cohort however, the 12.4 per cent with the highest academic qualifications had also made the step into marriage and family formation (Salmela-Aro, et al., 2012), unlike their counter parts in the other studies. This finding maybe reflect the available state support for the younger North Finnish cohort, encouraging young people to be independent adults and to fully assume all adult roles.

In all cohorts the highly educated group of young people is the most advantaged, regarding socio-demographic family background (i.e. parental education and social status), they also had high education aspirations and the highest exam scores. In adulthood this group showed relative low levels of psychological distress and medium to high levels of life satisfaction.

Work orientation without children

Another group that could be identified in each of the studies comprises young people with medium level qualifications, mostly working full-time, with no children. In the British samples this group is mostly married or in a relationship, comprising about a third of all young people (30.1 per cent in NCDS and 33.9

per cent in BCS70); in the US this group includes married, cohabiting and single young people, comprising 45 per cent in the older sample and 46 per cent in the younger sample; in the Finnish samples this group is mostly single or cohabiting, comprising 42.1 in the older 1959 cohort and 32.3 per cent in the 1966 Northern Finnish cohort.

In all samples this group generally comes from a moderate to higher level family background, had moderate education aspirations and medium exam scores. They show the lowest levels of psychological distress and high levels of life satisfaction.

Traditional Family Track

Young people with medium to low level qualifications, who have made the step into family formation, parenthood, independent living and full-time employment were categorised as traditional families. This group comprises about one in four in the UK samples (20.2 per cent in NCDS and 17 per cent in BCS), about one third in the US samples (31 per cent in the older versus 27 per cent in the younger cohort), nearly 40 per cent in the 1959 Finnish cohort and about 22 per cent in the 1966 North Finland study. While in the UK and Finland this group had medium level qualifications, in the US this was the group with the lowest level of qualifications.

Across all countries and assessment points this group includes more females, and is associated with moderate family social background (skilled occupation, low to medium parental education), moderate education aspirations and low exam scores. This group shows relative high levels of life satisfaction—but also signs of psychological distress.

Slow starters

This group could be identified within the UK (18 per cent in the 1958 cohort and 15 per cent in the 1970 cohort) and the US samples (16 per cent in the older and 18 per cent in the younger cohort), the 1966 Finnish sample (about 33 per cent), but not in the older 1959 Finnish sample. Slow starters typically have medium to low levels of educational attainment, are single with no children, are employed, and—with the exception of Finland—are living with their parents.

More males than females are identified in this group, which comes from moderate family background (skilled occupation, medium level parental education), had moderate education aspirations, and showed relative low school performance. They show some signs of distress and moderate to low levels of life satisfaction.

Fragile transitions

A distinct group of fragile or precarious transitions could be identified within both UK samples (about 12 per cent in each cohort), and the 1959 Finnish sample (5 per cent). In the UK samples this group is characterised by low educational attainment, parenthood status, and living in rented accommodation. In the 1959 Finnish sample this group has the lowest qualifications, is generally married and has 2 or more children, and often comprises a full-time home marker.

In the UK and in Finland this group is predominantly female, is the most disadvantaged regarding family background (i.e. low social status and low levels of parental education), and has the lowest exam scores of all groups. They also show the highest levels of psychological distress and the lowest levels of life satisfaction in both age cohorts.

Conclusions and Implications

The studies reviewed in this chapter show the relevance of structural, developmental, national, and historical factors in shaping youth transitions; variation and diversity in the transition to adulthood; and the importance of objective transition markers and their combination as predictors of well-being. Generally the findings point towards the need for a broader definition of what comprises a 'successful' transition to adulthood. Across the three countries and two birth cohorts there is more than just one pattern of role configurations corresponding to high life satisfaction and well-being. In particular, the active engagement in and commitment to meaningful social roles predict higher levels of life satisfaction and well-being, highlighting the importance of reaching objective developmental tasks during the transition to adulthood (Sacker and Cable, 2010); Schulenberg, et al., 2004). The timetable when to achieve certain tasks, however, appears to be variable and depends on the resources available to the individual.

Although the later-born cohorts in each country are better educated and more likely to be single and without children at age 26 compared to the earlier-born cohorts, the distinct patterns of role combinations largely remains unchanged within each country, not supporting the assumption of an increasing destandardisation of transition patterns. What we do see, however, is a polarisation of fast versus slow transition prevalences, with those from less privileged backgrounds making the transition to employment and parenthood earlier than others, potentially due to insufficient resources to take advantage of educational opportunities and to support an extended period of education (Heinz, 2009; Macmillan, 2005; Schoon and Silbereisen, 2009). Fast track transitions to adulthood are however not necessarily associated with lower levels of life satisfaction and wellbeing, as the active engagement with meaningful social roles can present turning points in the lives of young people, opening up opportunities to experience competence and accomplishment.

For good reason, developmental scientists rarely talk anymore about universality of stages and sequences of development. The understanding and demonstration that the occurrence and meaning of developmental milestones depend on the multi-level context in which the individual is embedded yield little justification for conceptualizing universalities in development (e.g., Conger, Conger, and Martin, 2010). Yet, when we find, as we do across different studies conducted in different cultural contexts, involving different age cohorts, that there are many points of commonality in the transition into independent adulthood, we gain an appreciation for some coherence and consistency of individual experiences, especially within social demographic groups. This coherence of experiences across cultures and history highlights the clear advantage of cross-country and cross-cohort comparisons, for they allow more convincing conclusions about commonalities and uniqueness of experiences across the transition to adulthood.

Replication of research findings across independent longitudinal studies is essential for advancing developmental science. Of course, cross-country comparisons depend on similarities in methods; for us, although constructs are remarkably similar across countries, sampling frames are not, especially in the two Finnish studies. When interpreting the data one therefore has to ensure that discrepancies are not forgotten or ignored and to be wary of using what may be a sampling bias as an explanatory factor. In interpreting the results, findings have to be examined in relation to their wider societal context and with regard to the limitations of the original research parameters. Other more intensive analytic approaches involving integrative or pooled data analysis will be possible when common measures across studies are available (Curran and Hussong, 2009). However, the complexity of longitudinal designs and cross-study differences in sample composition and measurements often impede or lessen the utility of such approaches. Nonetheless, a collaborative, coordinated analytic approach can provide needed leverage and a broad foundation for cumulating scientific knowledge by facilitating efficient analysis of multiple studies in ways that maximise comparability of results and permit evaluation of study differences (Hofer and Piccinin, 2009). Future steps, building on what we have here, include extending this framework across other countries, time periods, and constructs to get a fuller multi-level understanding of this pivotal time of life.

Acknowledgments:

Work on this manuscript was supported in part by grants from the National Institute on Drug Abuse Grant (R01 DA01411, R01 DA016575), the National Institute of Alcohol Abuse and Alcoholism (R01 AA019606, R21 AA020045), the UK Economic and Social Research Council (ESRC: RES-594-28-0001), and the National Science Foundation (BCS 0818478) to the Integrative Research Activities for Developmental Science (IRADS) Collaborative on Contexts Affecting Pathways from Childhood to Adulthood. The findings and conclusions in this report are those of the authors and do not necessarily represent the views of the NIH, ESRC, or NSF.

Table 1: Observed[3] % of the 'big 5' transition outcomes by country and cohort study.

	age 26 in mid 1980s			age 26 in mid 1990s		
	UK:NCDS	US: MTF	FI: JYLS	UK:BCS70	US: MTF	FI:NFBC[4]
Education						
High-school or less	12.1	37.4	31.8	15.1	19.4	19.1
Some college	49.0	22.4	42.0	44.2	23.8	33.1
Associates/ technical degree	17.3	12.3	15.3	13.3	11.7	37.7
Bachelor's or advanced degree	21.7	27.9	10.8	27.4	45.1	10.1

3   The N's and % values on table 1 for UK and Finland are from observed values while for US-MTF are weighted values.
4   For Finland-NFBC, education was measured at age 25, employment status at age 24, and marital status and parental status at age 26 from registered data while living arrangement was measured at age 31 from survey.

	age 26 in mid 1980s			age 26 in mid 1990s		
	UK:NCDS	US: MTF	FI: JYLS	UK:BCS70	US: MTF	FI:NFBC[4]
(available n)	(9171)	(2607)	(352)	(9897)	(2427)	(11584)
Employment status						
Unemployed/ Out of LF	4.4	7.63	5.8	4.1	5.15	10.7
Full-time home maker	12.2	7.15	3.2	9.4	3.89	--
Full-time education	1.1	8.93	6.6	3.2	14.4	18.3
Works part-time	5.7	1.14	5.2	7.6	1.15	--
Works full-time	76.6	75.15	79.2	75.7	75.01	71.1[5]
(available n)	(9171)	(2376)	(346)	(9897)	(2234)	(10126)
Living arrangements						
Lives with parents	18.7	18.9	4.1	19.8	20.8	11.2[6]
Lives away from home	81.3	81.1	95.9	80.2	79.2	88.8
(available n)	(9171)	(2555)	(345)	(9897)	(2386)	(8627)
Relationship status						
Married	54.9	49.3	47.1	27.7	40.0	30.3
Cohabit/ divorce/ widow/single	45.0	50.8	52.9	72.3	60.0	69.7
(available n)	(9171)	(2602)	(344)	(9897)	(2426)	(11817)
Parental status						
Childless	63.3	66.2	53.5	70.1	71.3	63.9
Had child	36.7	33.8	46.5	29.9	28.7	36.1
(available n)	(9171)	(2603)	(346)	(9897)	(2429)	(11825)
Total N	9171	2614	354	9897	2434	11825

Note: Some of % not summing up to 100 are due to rounding errors. Findings are summarised from Schoon et al., 2012, Maggs et al., 2012, Räikkönen et al., 2012, and Salmela-Aro et al., 2012.

5   For Finland-NFBC, no distinction on full-time versus part-time employment is made.
6   For Finland-NFBC, living with parents including living arrangement other than rent or own apartment.
7   For Finland-NFBC, no distinction on full-time versus part-time employment is made.
8   For Finland-NFBC, living with parents including living arrangement other than rent or own apartment.

Chapter 4

Finnish young adults' financial well-being in times of uncertainty

Mette Ranta

Introduction

From a sociological point of view, the youth of Finland today form an interesting group: they have been socialised into a western, materialistic and consumption-based society, in which the processes of identity and lifestyle formulation are based largely on consumption habits, and increasingly so. On the other hand, consumption options are restricted by many factors, such as life situation (mainly being in the life stage between education and employment), irregular and uncertain income, increasing individualisation and the transition to independent living (Wilska, 2004). In addition to these changes taking place in this life course phase, the restructuring and imbalance of labour markets characterised by irregular and part-time employment possibilities and the current economic recession, as well as economic pressure since the 1990s have led to a downfall in young adults' personal finances. Their finances have not improved in comparison with those of older age groups, partly because of the high unemployment rate and the cutbacks in social welfare support aimed at young adults (Allianssi, 2006; Wilska, 2001). The problems of young people form a strong indicator of well-being at societal level (Furlong and Cartmel, 2007; Wilska, 2001).

Concern over financial problems relating to the entrance to adulthood has attained increasing public awareness (see e.g. The Finnish Medical Society Duodecim, 2010; Furstenberg, 2001; *Helsingin Sanomat* 2010a, 2010b; *The Youth Indicator*, 1994- 2009) and academic research attention (see e.g. Autio, 2006; Orr, Gwosc and Netz, 2011; Wilska, 2001), both in a national and international context. Economic difficulties challenge life management and eventually influence overall well-being. When young adults fail to obtain a stable career, yet alone build a financially secure household for themselves, their life may appear unstable as a whole. Studying young adults' financial well-being can address numerous fundamental questions. These might include the growing rate of youth unemployment, the length of studying time, how studying is financed through part-and full-time jobs, governmental financial aid and parental support, the housing situation, the relationship between young adults and their parents and many more topical, socially acknowledged, and politically loaded topics.

Social exclusion and polarisation as threats to individuals can be present in young adulthood. This is why it is important period for the multidisciplinary research of socio-political significance for both the economic and social structures of society, as well as of individual factors affecting the life management of youth (Helve, 2002). Young adults must constantly manage changing circumstances and tolerate insecurity (Myllyniemi, 2004). They are often seen as a vulnerable group while facing a society characterised by high unemployment rates and demands for flexibility, where they are expected to find a job which fits their personal interests and capabilities. In youth research, young adulthood and adolescence have not been frequently linked with opportunities for positive development (Takanishi, 1993), although the majority of young adults do pass through youth with no severe problems (Graber and Brooks-Gunn, 1996; Powers, Hauser, and Kilner, 1989). This article utilises a more constructive and comprehensive perception on the transition to adulthood and aims by means of a theoretical overview to give a multidisciplinary view on how young adults' economic conditions construct the future and the multi-faceted transition to adulthood.[9] The transition is depicted by two discrete processes: the social and demographic passages from compulsory comprehensive education to the labour market and further studies and from the parental to the individual household, thus entering into roles considered typical for adults, which researchers view from a life course perspective (see e.g. Billari, 2001). Many of these changes have to do with economic status, which in this context includes economic independence meaning being responsible for one's own personal finances. The fact that individuals are active agents is emphasised; through employment and thus improving one's income and financial situation as a resource, one is protected from financial distress.

New dimensions of the transition to adulthood

It is important to acknowledge young adults' lives as a life phase of building and reflecting one's own life situation, identity, expectations, hopes and the future. Alan France (2007) has introduced the notion of young adults' lives *blending*, which means that it is common among young adults to combine different tasks and activities instead of concentrating merely on one thing, this being especially

9   An article by the author on this topic has been published in Finnish in a leading national journal of psychology (Ranta, M., (2010) Taloudellinen tilanne ja elämäntyytyväisyys siirtymässä aikuisuuteen [The financial situation and life satisfaction in the transition to adulthood], Psykologia, 45(05/06): 433-447).

true in working and educational contexts. Due to the fact that several things occur during a relatively short time period but also for each individual to a different extent and content, transition studies require a dynamic approach which allows examining individual variety in adopting the adult role in terms of employment, living situation and economic resources.

At least in postmodern societies, transitions in life are not specifically institutionalised nor do they contain formal rites but they are indeed important life stages (Giddens, 1991). In the transition to adulthood, an individual's status or role usually alters gradually (as opposed to comprising an *event*) although it can also include very concrete changes, such as moving out of the childhood home. Some transitions, such as this one, can include multiple changes and decisions, which affect the progression of the transition to adulthood (Elder and Johnson, 2003; Hagestad, 2003; Settersten, 2003).

Demands for life management

In the transition to adulthood, the individual must adopt a new, young adult phase in life which might be perceived as challenging as it involves the adjustment to a new role in society. As options multiply and individualisation increases, the transition phase is increasingly seen as a stressful life phase while the phase of exploration and preparing for adult roles is often prolonged (Schwartz, Côté, and Arnett, 2005). Additionally, decisions often need to be made in a relatively short period, which also have long term effects into the future (du Bois-Reymond and Stauber, 2005).

Discussion of biography helps to understand how individuals experience uncertainty and maintain life management, and as a concept has an important place in youth studies. Biographical approaches have been used to study how individuals make sense of their lives in a state of transition or change, and how they plan their future (Furlong and Cartmel, 2007). The life course is not as structured as before, and contains more freedom to make individual choices. Du Bois-Reymond (1995) has introduced the notion of the transition from the *normal biography* to the *choice biography*, a phenomenon occurring throughout Europe. With it comes an increase in options and the need to adapt to circumstances over which there is little or no control. With adulthood one faces independence, choices and freedom, which are opposed by insecurity, anxiety and stress. Choice and goal-making are the basis for subjective life management, or in this case more specifically, financial situation. On the other hand, faced with endless possibilities and choices, one might also end up being submerged by numerous demands and expectations from society and the social environment. Thus life management from young adults is required and individual responsibility and decision making is anticipated, also in financial matters. This individualisation in turn leads to the postponement of decision making and transitions to a later life phase, another result of the social and financial concerns of society affecting both adults and the young.

Prolonged transitions and financial independence

Young adulthood is understood to begin in the early twenties and is characterised by 'establishing personal and economic independence, career development, and selecting social contexts' (Grob, 2001). Adolescence itself, or young adulthood for that matter, should not be seen merely as a kind of contrast to adulthood but as a process, a transition between the two phases in life which builds a broader perspective to this topic. This issue becomes especially prominent as multiple life domains intertwine, as young adults gradually shift between education and work and thus engage in multiple tasks and responsibilities. The development occurring in late adolescence is not separate from other life phases, as it happens in the context of the past, present and anticipated future (Settersten, 2003). Jeffrey Arnett (2000) has brought forth the concept of *emerging adulthood*, the phase between ages eighteen and twenty-five as a prolonged life phase of adolescence where the transition to adulthood is put forward into the near future. This phase has moulded itself into a new phase of searching for independence, departing from the strings of the childhood home and not yet adopting adulthood responsibilities. This can be identified in practice for example in the transition to employment, which takes longer as one extends studying time (Salmela-Aro and Helve, 2007). According to Arnett (2011), a new developmental stage between adolescence and young adulthood in terms of relationships and vocational life is formed: transitions are postponed as individuals engage in 'self-focused exploration as they try out different possibilities in love and work'.

This new life phase may be permitted to only the selected few, however, and certain aspects of culture, gender and class need to be considered. The critiques of Hendry and Kloep (2007a, 2007b) as well as Bynner (2005, 2006) on the concept of *emerging adulthood* emphasise the fact that it is impossible to group young adults into a homogeneous group, with a normative developmental pathway into adulthood irrespective of individual differences, varying resources and encountered challenges. Arnett's theory is strongly based on Western industrialised societies and lifestyles, through research conducted mainly in the United States (Arnett, 2007; Bynner, 2005). It is generally agreed by both groups that in Britain and the United States social class has a strong impact on educational opportunities, where middle-class emerging adults have greater educational opportunities, but for Hendry and Kloep (2007a, 2007b), this life phase of *emerging adulthood* with its possibilities, independence and choices is available for only young adults in an economically stable situation, either through own income or financially supportive parents. This, as well as social class, makes a difference in how this life phase is subjectively perceived; either positively, as a possibility and as a result of personal choice, or negatively, as a constraint (Bynner, 2005; Hendry and Kloep, 2007a). However, financial independence as a criterion for adulthood seems to remain across social classes (Arnett, 2006).

Furthermore, Arnett's theory does not take into account the overlapping and irregular processes and mechanisms of change, which would evidently be important in inspecting the trajectories of change as individuals shift from one transition to the other, for example relating to education, work, romantic relationships and independent living. Both Arnett's (2006) *descriptive* analysis as a framework, as opposed to the *explanatory* and systemic models proposed by Hendry and Kloep (2007a, 2007b) are relevant in the discussion of transitions to adulthood and as the authors suggest, a synthesis may offer a solution to the debate.

It is nevertheless evident that adolescence as a phase in life has extended well into the twenties, and a period of *semiautonomy*, common a century ago, or *social semi-dependency*, has re-emerged with prolonged dependence on families or the State for economical and social support (Elder and Shanahan, 2006; Furlong and Cartmel, 2007). According to the 2005 *Youth Indicator*, an annual study on Finnish young adults, the age limit of young adults financially dependent on their parents is about twenty years-old (Myllyniemi, 2005). Finnish young adults move out of their childhood home relatively early compared to others in the European Union member states, although according to Eurostat statistics (2010), more than half of young men aged eighteen to twenty-four still live with their parents in their childhood home, and of women approximately thirty-two per cent. In Finland it is fairly easy to rent an apartment and the housing supplement of the student financial aid package promotes leaving the childhood home (Eurostat statistics, 1997).

According to the *market-income hypothesis*, a stable income is the most significant predictor of the transition to independent living. Because of difficulties in the transition to employment, the process of financial independence may also be prolonged (Guerrero, 2001; Kuure, 2001; Wilska, 2001). Additionally, even if independence is prominent in the stage of transition and the young adult does make the physical transition to independent living, emotional and economic attachment to family and parents may remain. Nevertheless, even though settling down as such may not be as evident, we can still suppose that individuals do take a certain amount of responsibility in terms of their own finances even if the future is seen to be uncertain and filled with risks, a supposition proposed by Furlong and Cartmel (2007).

One of the nine developmental tasks of adolescence, as proposed by Havighurst (1948), was achieving assurance of economic independence, which is also an adulthood criterion in Arnett's (2000) studies. Adulthood is often seen as being accomplished by means of the financial ability to earn and maintain one's livelihood through life management. In the transition to adulthood, employment becomes an important part of everyday life, enabling a sufficient income but also being a strong indicator of well-being, self confidence and capability (Cunnien, MartinRogers, and Mortimer, 2009; Karvonen, 2006).

Financial well-being development and challenging labour markets

Emerging adults must negotiate a pathway into adulthood for themselves, and the length and direction of that pathway may differ greatly from one individual to another (Elder and Shanahan, 2006; Furlong and Cartmel, 2007; Luyckx, De Witte, and Goossens, 2011; Salmela-Aro, Kiuru, Nurmi, and Eerola, 2011; Schwartz et al., 2005). The inherent, unstable nature of the transition phase can lead to uncertainty, ill health and maladaptive functioning in life satisfaction or in different life domains, such as working life (Luyckx et al., 2011; Reifman, Colwell, and Arnett, 2007; Wilska, 2004). Finding a job, the reliability of the job, its duration and personal livelihood are significant factors that may lead to uncertainty, especially among young women (Myllyniemi, 2004). In addition to the drastic changes taking place during the transition in personal lives, young adults face profound change in the surrounding society. Because of uncertain labour markets, young adults' lives become unstable and complicated and career lives disjointed.

The significance of well-being has been pondered by Veenhoven (2004): the subjective view of individuals concerning the state of their own lives can be seen as important in socio-political decision making. It is after all the fundamental goal of country officials to see that people perceive their life as fulfilling. However, focusing on youth in particular can be problematic. This is because even if young adults' low income is a reflection of a degree of poverty, they themselves might perceive this life phase (during their studies, for example) as temporary, and as a kind of investment for the future which will eventually turn into better employment possibilities and higher income (Ylitalo, 2009). The situation is thus to some extent accepted and is regarded as a personal choice. Secondly, even though fixed-term and part-time employment possibilities are most common for young adults, even irregular and short-term working possibilities and the additional income attained may help to relieve the financial constraints that young adults might have to cope with. Some flexibility in balancing employment with education is possible in this situation, and even temporary fixed-term contracts are accepted (Myllyniemi, 2005; Saarela, 2002).

The income of young adults in Finland is to a great extent composed of salary through employment, being approximately a third of overall individual income in adolescence and gradually increasing to about seventy per cent. According to recent Statistics Finland (2011a) data, more than half (fifty-five per cent) of Finnish students are employed while studying. However, Finnish young adults also greatly rely on governmental financial support, according to international comparisons (Orr, D., Gwosc, C., Netz, N., 2011). In Finland, students in upper secondary schools, vocational institutes or higher education institutes receive governmental financial aid, which consists of a study grant, a housing supplement and a government guarantee for a student loan. Study grants and housing supplements are cash benefits and do not need to be paid back. Before the national economic recession in the early 1990s, the student financial aid system was mainly based on subsidised student loans. The system was reformed in 1992 with the abolishment of government loans as subsidies for students, but the study grant amount was more than doubled. This resulted in the unpopularity of student loans and shifted students' interest from loan-based to employment- based income (Häkkinen, 2004; Häkkinen and Uusitalo, 2003).

Agency

Another topic that should be discussed in the context of transitions is young adults' development of agency: forming actions reflecting life management through employment and improvement of income as supportive mechanisms, thus being protected from economical problems and promoting a smooth financial transition. Individuals are not passively exposed to circumstances which they do not understand nor do they encounter the future as a series of forthcoming events, but rather they organise the future themselves (Giddens, 1991; Settersten, 2003). Agency has attained a new position in research as it has been seen that individuals as social actors are important producers of subjective identity in numerous social processes and experiences (France, 2007).

All of the factors relating to the transition to adulthood also demand *life planning*, a complex network of numerous goals and strategies aimed at obtaining these goals. Strategic life planning fits well into the thematics of youth and change since reflexive preparation for the future decreases uncertainty and personal concerns and helps control stress, vulnerability and forthcoming subjective risks (Furlong and Cartmel, 2007; Giddens, 1991; Smith, 1999). An individual does not merely react to outer stimuli or the objective environment and its resources. However, decision-making takes place in a context of structural and institutional possibilities and constraints of life events, as well as social and normative pressures of what is appropriate for a certain age group. If an individual does not fulfil these expectations or live up to the norms and, for example, fails in financial decision making and life management from an individualistic perspective, the fault is attributed to the individual. According to Giddens (1984), rather than material scarcity being the greatest obstacle to well-being, the prosperity of societies and the liberation of behavioural norms have caused new problems relating to decision-making in life.

Age-related developmental tasks format the life course according to personal preferences, competences and actions. These tasks are also related to specific challenges and restrictions faced by certain age groups. By focusing one's own motivation it is possible to face a challenging life situation and its related decision-making processes. The life course perspective can help in perceiving the situation and in creating different models of ways in which the situation is handled. For example, in the transition to adulthood, the challenges faced by youth in the shift to employment can be better understood by studying their own personal subjective views or by looking at what other challenges and changes are related to this transition in other life domains (Salmela-Aro and Nurmi, 2005). Researchers adopting the life course theory as an overall framework for research are often concerned with the concept of transition or change from one state to another, such as entry into employment, adulthood or parenthood. During a transition period individuals are able to negotiate their lives according to imposed constraints and opportunities on individual agency (Salmela-Aro, 2009).

Current human developmental theories emphasise how the social and cultural environments and individuals' relationships towards them change the identity and life course but how simultaneously the personal activity and decisions made as an agent have a significant effect as well—this being called *agency within structure* (Elder and Johnson, 2003; Settersten, 2003). The social environment on the one hand creates opportunities, and on the other hand, assigns restrictions on human action. Nevertheless, individuals do exercise freedom in formulating their identities rather than adopting them directly from previous generations or homogenous societies, for example (Giddens, 2001). Agency is not about the intention of carrying out a certain action but the capability, or power, to do these things. There is a possibility to act differently and with these personal interventions, the action can be influenced (Giddens, 1984).

On the basis of what has been presented, it can be stated that during this transition phase, the young adult must be active and find an individual path in life which to follow. The quest for finding one's own place in the world has begun and young adults may aim to manage their financial resources by being agents of their lives, for example, through employment. However, financial independence is restricted by the available financial resources which regulate financial behaviour and agentic strivings. Social, economic and cultural factors influence young adults' attempts to control their lives and structural factors such as macro-social circumstances and the labour market may influence development, educational transitions and the chosen pathways, but nevertheless, individual decision-making and actions reflecting agency need to be highlighted too. Agency needs to be conceptualised as limited, with *an internalised frame of reference* formed by the environment but still supported by individual choice-making and actions (Evans, Schoon, and Weale, 2010). This aspect of *bounded agency* (Evans, 2002; 2007) is helpful in understanding the current choices of young adults between the transitions from school to work and aiming for a financially secure lifestyle through employment. This type of agency takes past habits, the present moment and future possibilities into consideration, where all of them equally guide and shape actions within the social structure offered by the society. In times of economic uncertainty, both in society and within an individual life, transitions into adulthood may be adjusted according to personal judgement and subjective perceptions of the structures individuals need to negotiate with (as in Evans, 2007).

Conclusions

Even though previous and future life course phases do contain unique characteristics, the aim of this article was to show how young adulthood can be a fascinating research topic itself, being an exceptionally important phase with many simultaneous transitions and changes taking place at once. Young adults must face this life phase filled with exploration and decision-making processes including those related to education, employment, and living situation (see e.g. Côté, 2002; Schwartz et al., 2005). As proposed by Arnett (2006), young adults frequently opt for trying different educational and occupational paths while formulating their identities. In Finland, for example, the education system provided free by the State and the financial support granted for all, make these pathways and the prolonged transitions possible.

Life transitions are also always part of social trajectories that give them distinct meaning and form. Secondly, individuals have multiple trajectories, of which the developmental implications are the basic elements of the life course (Elder, 1998). This development is shaped by a set of principles including individual agency, timing of events, linked lives and how development is embedded in its sociohistorical context. Research on transitional events and the transition to adulthood need to be tied to the cultural and macro-economic contexts in which the young adults are bounded to (Hendry and Kloep, 2007a).

This article, with its theoretical introduction on the theme of agency, aimed to emphasise the factors and resources which promote successful transitions to adulthood in order to promote financial well-being and coping with uncertainty. Additionally, although this important life phase has certain age-related normative characteristics, financial situations are very diverse as life situations differ greatly especially in factors determining financial independence: employment, mode of income and living situation. The transitions relating to education, employment and living situation are frequently interlinked: in young adulthood one usually becomes detached from the childhood home, begins further studies, familiarises oneself with working life, and becomes engaged in social life and relationships.

Chapter 5

'Agency *vs.* structure': A view of youth unemployment during the current recession in Finland

Jaana Lähteenmaa

Introduction

Youth unemployment is a highly topical and relevant question in Finland and in several other European and Asian countries, not only as the object of sociological inquiry, but also as a social problem. In Finland, unemployment among youth has increased rapidly during the current recession, more than doubling in two years to twenty-three per cent in January 2010. It was still more than double the overall level of unemployment, which was about eight to nine per cent in autumn 2010, as the Finnish economy showed a slight upturn. Youth unemployment is expected to remain high for a long time despite the overall economic recovery of the economy. The present situation is similar to the recession in Finland in the early 1990s.

In the relevant Finnish literature on unemployment, one of the main research questions is how and to what extent people can maintain their health and ability to work. Specifically, what are the structural preconditions needed for this (e.g., Kortteinen and Tuomikoski 1998). However, youth unemployment has been overlooked in these studies, regardless of its somewhat different characteristics. Whilst economic factors (the level of poverty) and networking (social trust) are decisive as to whether or not adults can maintain their employability, no clear structural patterns have so far been discerned as regards youth unemployment.

One perplexing aspect is the fact that among the young unemployed there is a minority, both in Finland and in many other countries, who do not find periods of unemployment a problem. They are looking for an alternative lifestyle, with a desire to 'be freely creative' (Sell, 2005; see also Schnapper 1981). Either they have chosen to belong to the precariat (*la precarité*) or they have adapted to their precarious situation in the labour market so that they do not think they would lose their agency during their short but persisting temporary unemployment periods (Sell 2005).

However, feelings of loss of capacities and opportunities have been more typical among the unemployed during times of very high youth unemployment, with more young people who would genuinely like to work for a salary but who do not have the possibility to do so. This was revealed in studies done in Finland during the previous recession in the 1990s (Paakkunainen 1997; Suutari 2002). Even so, even young people who are unemployed against their will can find meaningful activities and social networks (Suutari 2002). For young people, who have never gained a foothold in the labour market and who can also build their agency on things other than paid work, the question of maintaining or losing their capacity to act, in other words their agency, seems to be more complex than in the case of adults, who become unemployed from a position of permanent salaried work. However, this question has never been studied systematically.

During the 1990s and more recently, youth unemployment has been studied quite actively in Europe and in other countries including Japan, but there has been no focus on maintaining agency. Certain research results about youth unemployment and labour market policies directed at the young in Europe have been collected in *Youth unemployment and social exclusion in Europe; a comparative study* (Hammer, 2003). In their article, Carole and Pastore (2003) compare the situation and the effectiveness of activating labour market policy in Germany, Spain and Sweden and conclude that the measures have had a weak positive effect, and only in Sweden. They assume that effectiveness of the activation measures implemented depends on the overall functioning of the market and on education, training and employment scenes. This is a very interesting finding in the context of the role and function of activating labour market policies in countries hit hard by the current global recession—not least Finland with its high unemployment and exceptionally high youth unemployment rates. We can only guess that the public response to activating labour market measures is far from unproblematic when the whole labour market is depressed.

So-called activating labour market policies were introduced in the Western countries in the 1990s, Britain was among the pioneers, gradually followed by the Scandinavian countries (Kildal 2001). In Finland, such measures were adopted during and after our former heavy recession in the early 1990s, and they were—and still are—directed especially at the young generation (ibid.) The rationale of the measures is to encourage and activate young unemployed people during their periods of unemployment periods in order to keep them employable. These measures include both 'sticks' and 'carrots', although the 'sticks' tend to play a larger role (ibid.). With the labour market experiencing serious problems and with high unemployment rates, a serious problem can emerge if these measures begin to function repressively and depressingly, rather that activating and maintaining the young people's ability to act, or their agency. On this latter question no studies have yet been done.

In Finland, only a few studies on the effect of the measures have been done in circumstances of recession (Aaltojärvi and Paakkunainen, 1995; Päällysaho, 1997). According to the results obtained, certain measures seemed to work during the recession of the 1990s, at least for some people, while other measures did not have an effect. However, the measures are today somewhat different and more numerous. Among them is the law from 1997, which insists, with a threat of sanctions, that youth below the age of twenty-five study for a 'profession', if they do not already have one. This law has many dysfunctions. One of them is the well known but not systematically studied fact that some young people who are not motivated to study attempt to enter polytechnics whose entrance criteria are extremely tough. These people do not succeed in gaining entry, but avoid also sanctions because they can show that they have made an *attempt* to enter (Kojo 2010).

I argue that in this new situation, in which there are plenty of unemployed youth who have a fairly high level of education (at university or polytechnic level), activating measures can be even more dysfunctional. Some can be experienced as humiliating and discouraging. Some of the young also begin to 'play' with these 'sticks' and 'carrots', and manage base their whole lives accordingly (Kojo, 2010). These young people may view the approach as life management but from the perspective of society it leads in totally unplanned directions, at least if we assume that the State really means to activate and support these young unemployed citizens.

Theoretical background

In a recent study on young unemployed people and on measures of activating labour market policies (Carole and Pastore 2003), the theoretical point of view of 'agency' has been used in an interesting way. In both of these studies, the agency has been theorised through Bourdieu's theory on *habitus*. The main finding of both of these studies (one was made in the UK and the other in the UK and Germany) is that the activating labour market policy works best in helping and supporting those whose *habitus* is fitting, or is good enough, for the labour market niche at hand. This is a relevant and interesting finding but does not reveal how these activating measures work when there is no functioning labour market 'at hand'—as is the current Finnish situation for most unemployed youth. I will discuss these speculations about *habitus* and labour market 'field' or niche but in the context of recession the mechanism is not the one suggested by these researchers.

On a more theoretical and general level, the notion of the agency of unemployed youth touches one of the central issues in sociology: the debate concerning the primacy of structure and agency in human behaviour (see, e.g., Abercrombie and Turner, 2006, 9). In the context of this debate, 'agency' refers to the capacity of an individual to act independently and to make his own free choices (Bakker et al., 2005). 'Structure' refers to the recurrent patterned arrangements which seem to influence or limit the choices and opportunities that individuals possess.

The tension between agency versus structure, which in sociological theory is typically handled as a highly abstract relationship, is extremely real and concrete in the lives of the unemployed young. This is particularly the case in contemporary so-called welfare states. The unemployed live in a society where 'autonomy'—the core of agency in modern (and late-modern) Western cultures— is highly appreciated, even over-valued (see Lawler 2008, 66-67; Sulkunen 2009). At the same time, they are not just hindered from working for pay ('hindered' because most of them really would like to find work) but most of them also suffer from shortage of money which sets limits on their consumption and even on their day-to-day life in many ways—in other words, on their autonomy and agency as consumers.

A further strain on unemployed people is that they have to report about their lives to get the unemployment benefits, as well as their studies (as already mentioned, there are special regulations and rules concerning especially the unemployed under twenty-five year-olds) and all small jobs, in order to satisfy labour officials. They also have to obey the myriad rules that are applied to the unemployed, and especially the young Finnish unemployed. The 'forcing structures' are something very concrete in their lives. The question of internalised structures, which can be conceptualised as *habitus*, work in much more complex ways in such a situation.

Typically, and especially in Anglo-Saxon (British and American) sociological youth studies, speculations on *habitus* and 'reflexivity' are connected with the problems of those whose *habitus* is not sufficiently middle-class and who have had limited opportunities to reflect on their lives (Woodman 2009). It is my aim also to shed light on the opposite social strata and the problems that youth unemployment causes there. When one has been socialised to be well-educated and 'upper-class', becoming unemployed may make the *habitus*, one's 'internalised structure, especially painful. To see whether this is indeed the case is one of the aims of my ongoing research.

I see agency as a matter of struggle and conflict, in the same way as French sociologists usually do (Martuccelli and de Singly 2009, 50-53). As Pierre Bourdieu (1980) said, agency is not only a matter of representation but also of reputation. Much of a young unemployed person's struggle for agency is connected also with handling the shame or stigma of being unemployed.

Research objectives

This chapter is based on my ongoing research.[10] The research questions to which I seek preliminary answers in this chapter are:

- how do the young unemployed describe their desires, capacities and skills, their struggle to maintain them, or their loss when unemployed)? How can their 'agency' be approached through these descriptions?
- how do today's young unemployed people describe both societal structures and practices and the internal 'forces' that prevent them from achieving their aims and that suppress their aspirations and capacities?

Research Material

The empirical material on which I lean in this chapter consists of 448 non-structured answers to the open-ended question concerning the everyday life and feelings and thoughts as unemployed. These answers are part of the data gathered in a survey by myself in April and May 2009 (N=770). The sample is non-representative; the survey was directed at young people and young adults (ages from sixteen to twenty-nine year-olds), using the web-based services of MOL (the Ministry of Labour). The respondents were currently unemployed or had experienced unemployment-periods (or both). Those, who visit these web-pages are mainly unemployed people who would like to find work, but there are also some, for example, who are seeking information about subsidies. It is obvious that those who are really marginalised do not visit these web-pages. They comprise a group which is very difficult to reach, for research purposes at least.

There was a technically unlimited space to answer which could extent to more than a single page. Some of these essay answers are short and laconic but the majority are long and 'rich' descriptions not only of every-day life, but also the feelings, experiences of meetings with the labour authorities and reports

---

10 The research started as a part of 'Work-Preca' project (2008-2011) and is continuing in 'YUALP-A' project (2012-2016); both financed by the Academy of Finland.

on the rules and duties imposed on an unemployed person, or narratives of the (collapsed) plans for the future of these people. Some are optimistic, some laconic, some angry, some full of disappointment and despair.

Analysis

How is it possible to analyse the agency from texts in which people write about themselves? How can one deconstruct and reconstruct analytically the structures described in these texts that may be more or less ambivalent?

Wanting something, and doing something—being able or capable of acting in a certain way—is the core of being a social actor, 'an agent'. An ideal 'agent citizen' in late-modern society should possess his/her own autonomy, intimacy and biography that are not ruled by others (see Sulkunen 2009). Facing obstacles and overcoming them, or at least trying to overcome them instead of adapting to everything, all kinds of 'structures' and necessities, constitute characteristics of an agent (*sujet d'action*, as they say in French). If a person is not at all an agent, she/he is just an object of actions. Psychologists and psychoanalytical theory since the times of Freud's texts have tried to define 'actor' from the psychological point of view (see Wallvorck 1991). However, from a sociological point of view, it is essential to also consider the obstacles and structures which one has to handle and cope with, when we try to understand and interpret 'agency' from a sociological perspective.

The socio-semiotic model, originally developed by the French philosopher and semiotic A.G. Greimas, further developed in Finland by Sulkunen and Törrönen (1997) and in France by Greimas' college Eric Landowski (1991), seems to be a promising tool for analysis, at least as suggested by my preliminary 'testing'. (The limitations of the model can be taken as a challenge. As far as I face limitations of this 'Greimas model' when trying to use it this way, I admit them and maybe even try to develop the model further.)

The main elements of this model are so-called modalities (*les modalités*). There are four of them: I present them here in the original language, then English, then Finnish:

- *vouloir* (wanting/*haluta*);
- *pouvoir* (being able to …/*voida*);
- *devoir* (having (a duty) to do …/*olla velvoitettu/pakotettu tekemään*);
- *savoir faire* (be competent to do …/*osata; omata taito tehdä*)

Greimas has not stated that other modalities are not possible, but he has stated that these four are the driving forces in the acts of a *sujet d'action* (agent)

(Sulkunen and Törrönen 1997). They can overlap each other and there can be several 'modalities' in a single act. However, these are the most important modalities. In any event, when analysing texts or 'texts' (films, etc.) with this model it is relevant to look at the modalities connected with the actor (in the text, or 'text'). As far as I know this model has not been used before to interpret the agency of speakers/writers describing themselves and their acts. I will try to do so.

Struggling to maintain one's agency

Words that are directly 'wanting' (*haluta*), 'being able to' (*voida*) and the other two modalities are not as often used in the accounts of the young unemployed in the data as is the verb *yrittää*, which means 'to try' or 'attempt.' Yet this 'trying' can also be analysed using the modalities, when the context of the verb is taken into account. Let us take some of those accounts from the research material, namely answers to the open-ended question: Describe your everyday life as an unemployed person. You can also tell, how your time passes by (or, passed by) and what you feel and think.[11]

> I try to keep certain routines going on, like waking up early in the morning. Life is quite boring and the days similar to each other. I don't have too many success feelings.

> My aim is to wake up and do something, which would develop my activity and possible learning processes. Always I just don't have enough energy … but I try, even the very small moments! Motivations—they come and go …

There are almost a hundred accounts in which 'trying' is mentioned in one way or another.' Trying' is not a modality in itself. However, it can be seen to consist of *wanting* (something) and being unsure whether one will *manage* in pursuing this aim. The latter can be further read as 'not being sure in one's ability to do the thing X' (*savoir faire*), which can be due to a *lack of competences* and/or *lack of possibilities* (*pouvoir*). Unemployed young people with these kinds of worry struggle with themselves (fear of becoming passive and maybe also depressive) and the circumstances in which they have to live as unemployed people.

---

11 The imperfect form is used in deference to those who have experienced unemployment but are not unemployed right now.

The external circumstances which are described as crushing include: living with the shame or stigma of unemployment; shortage of money all the time; social isolation and having to account for one's life and plans to labour and other officials. The 'internal forces' against which one has to struggle are in the descriptions: depression; shame; feelings of being totally worthless; terrible disappointment (especially among highly educated ones) and self-accusations. The young people who are writing about this internal struggle try to manage their inner life, their 'souls', which is increasingly typical for late-modern people who are aware of psychological theories (see Rose 1999).

There are many texts in which the mood is very depressive. That 'correlates' with minimum expressions of any agency. There are no expressions of wanting, being able to, having competence to or even having duties to do something (that is, other than reporting about one's life to labour offices), nor any duties which rise from a moral duty felt by the person her/himself). Even the verb-forms used are mainly passive (as in 'it is done' or 'one does'), and do not express that the speaker is talking about him/herself. Here is an example of this kind of text:

> The rhythm of days and nights is upside down, there is no reason to wake up in the mornings. The day passes by slowly, with eating breakfast there is no hurry, one can eat it at lunchtime. Because there is nothing to do, the energy is not consumed, so one eats less. All these aspects make the feeling tired, and there is no motivation in order to activate oneself. The time is spent reading, watching television and surfing the internet. I decided to start to study again and I am reading now for the entrance exams, but I really suspect that I don't have enough motivation to study again for another five to six years. I feel worthless ... and don't understand how anybody could stand this kind of situation for a long time.

The writer begins to talk directly about herself, using the 'I do' form once when she tells about her decision to start to study again. 'Own decision' implies (one's) will: here she talks shortly about herself as an agent. But instantly after that she begins to suspect her motivation, her own will, to do the thing she has decided to do. The writer's agency seems to be very weak and fragile; she does not define herself as 'depressive', like some of the writers do—but when looking for the expressions of agency it becomes quite clear that she is really 'down', and her agency is in danger.

In some cases the disappointment comes out as bitter anger; the writer does not (want to) hate her/himself, but instead the whole Finnish society.

> I can thank the economical recession and the Finnish state for my unemployment. This has just strengthened my decision to move away from here! I will quit as soon as I have finished my education in this country. I don't owe anything to this country!

In this account the agency of the subject is strong. 'My decision' has to do with a strong will. Speaking about 'I don't owe anything to X' has to do with (moral) duty: the writer wants to underline that he or she does not perceive any duties to the State. (Who has ever said she/he would have any? Nobody.) The speaker wants to underline how disappointed with 'this country' he or she is, and wants to underline that all his/her possible duties to the Finnish society have now faded away, because the State has 'betrayed' her. This is a sentence with modality 'having duty to', but with negation (I don't have any duty to …). The strong agency of the writer is built in underlining, that the writer can 'cancel' the contract with the 'Finnish state' (a contract, which the writer first constructs in the text).

In several other accounts written in an angry state of mind, the word *vituttaa* is used, one of the strongest swear words in the Finnish language which means in this context something similar to 'all fucked up'. Derivatives of the same word, as an adjective, as a noun and in all other senses, are used in many of the texts. For example:

> Bloody moneyless shit … and the bloody bitches from the labour management centre should go themselves, without getting a penny for all these 'training programmes' and other 'chartings' which are from hell! They really should think a bit about their 'practices'!

Although in this kind of very aggressive texts the modalities of 'wanting', 'being able to', 'having the competence to' or 'having the duty to' cannot be found, the marks of agency of the writer are still evident. *Vituttaa*, declined to convey 'I am fucked off' is in the Finnish language a way to express very deep disappointment and anger—and the sense that cannot be disappointed if one has never hoped for anything. So the modality of 'wanting' is present as it is a part of 'hoping'— hoping for something which has not been fulfilled and has in fact been denied.

There are also those accounts in which the mood is almost positive. Interestingly, typically elements of the modality of 'being able to (do something, just because one is unemployed)' are then present. For example:

> Being unemployed has always made me feel rather insecure, and caused more or less worries about the future (especially if it has lasted quite a long time …). Although sometimes it has also offered the opportunity to rest for a bit longer, which has been also needed. Now my time unemployed passes with a renovation project of my own, in everyday practices, with the family, and in small-scale hobbies.

This text gives an impression of peacefulness, almost happiness, although the writer also tells explicitly also about anxiety. The writer also seems to be a subject, although without using the verb form 'I do' at all. Yet the modality of 'being able to' is present in the text. The writer tells that sometimes, thanks to being unemployed, he or she has been able to rest enough. The agency is implied in the text—although paradoxically, through the mention of being able to rest.

There are also accounts in the same 'mood', in which people tell how being unemployed has made it possible to practice one's hobbies more frequently: sports, arts, reading, walking one's dog, and so on. The possibility to spend more time with one's small children was also mentioned. In some of them being unemployed is described to be both positive (in this sense) and negative (from another point of view: shortage of money, worries about the future, etc.). In some texts unemployment is described only in positive terms, as it makes it possible to organise one's days and pursuing one's hobbies as much as one wants. One person says that being unemployed in summer is 'OK', because of the more frequent access to sun and sand, for instance, but that in winter it is not. Even so, these descriptions are a small minority of all the accounts.

The 'Having the ability to do' (*savoir faire*) modality can be found from the texts mainly connected with 'possibility to' in negative form, or not having the possibility to use one's skills (*ne pouvoir pas*). Especially for those young unemployed people who have just finished university-level education, this is a bitter situation which causes much frustration.

> My competencies to do the work I was trained for, as well as my self-consciousness, diminish from day to day … It is really easy to start feeling uneasy and depressed. There might be some cleaning work available

which one could get. Soon you really have to take it. On the one hand it is good if there is at least something to do. On the other hand it really irritates me; you can get cleaning work without having to get such a high education! It won't feel so nice to have to answer when someone asks, so what's the brand new Master of Sciences doing as a job?

The writer has competencies received in extensive university training in the university which he or she cannot use. Part of the writer's potential agency is in this way taken away. There are many young people with good education in this situation, and there are many texts like this in my data. 'Reflection' praised by Giddens (1991) among others, as an important late-modern competence is of no real assistance to these people: the more they consider and reflect on their situation, the more they suffer. At least my research material would suggest that this is the case.

Agency and the employment authority measures

There are many comments in the questionnaire responses on labour authorities, employment offices and courses, and practicum systems organised by them. The practicums can be organised in 'real working places' where participants are paid an extremely small 'salary' (which is in fact paid by the State, so is a component of activating labour market policy). There are also different kinds of workshops for the young unemployed. Many but not all of those training courses and practicums can be obligatory: if the unemployed person does not attend, he or she loses the benefits that are otherwise due, firstly for a certain period, but if refusal to attend continues systematically, then totally. (Subsequently, an application can be made for benefit but the process is considered to be somewhat humiliating by most citizens, not least those who are poor).

It is extremely rare for anyone in Finland to be allowed to die of hunger or the effects of cold weather, but in social offices it is necessary to lay bare the smallest details of one's life. As a client of *sossu* (social office in Finnish slang), one loses intimacy and autonomy. In Finland unemployed people would rather deal with labour market offices, although in most cases neither is this a pleasant experience.

Most comments on labour market measures in this data are negative. For instance:

... I also experience the visits to the employment office as extremely painful. I feel that I don't get any help there. I would prefer to get information and encouragement, instead of being tended and forced to participate in all these training sessions and courses from which I don't get anything useful. You just have to sit there! I am in fact afraid of going there, and to speak with the counsellor ...

The modality 'having (a duty) to' is present in almost all the comments on labour market measures. As a modality it—*devoir*—is somewhat difficult to grasp. When it is an internalised duty it is an 'inner' driving force in a sense, experienced as neither positive nor negative. But if it is a duty forced from outside, a 'must' (*pakko* in Finnish, the word explicitly used by the young person woman quoted above), that may even be backed up possible sanctions, then it may crush the agency of the person in question, especially individual will is contradicted.

Even so, in some less frequent instances, positive things are said about these same measures. For example:

The courses organised by labour market offices are really JEES' ('yes' according to Finnish pronunciation)

The 'structures'—in other words, the measures and sanctions of the labour market offices—which force young unemployed people to take part in these courses and practicums are experienced as genuinely humiliating and unpleasant by many young unemployed people in the data. But there are also some who find that these same things are positive, especially those who lack higher or any education and who may need some help in finding their way in life in general. Of course, there are those among this group who may find the measures repellent and irritating (Lähteenmaa and Kojo 2010).

Discussion

Many relevant dilemmas of the agency of the young unemployed people can be identified using the methodological apparatus of modalities for the attempt to identify both explicit and hidden expressions of *vouloir*, *pouvoir*, *devoir* and *savoir faire* is especially helpful in the search for the paradoxes in the (young) unemployed person's agency, and its obstacles and restrictions.

Certain paradoxes concerning youth unemployment as a 'social problem' also seem clearer after this kind of analysis. Put briefly, the young unemployed person should not become passive and depressive; yet he or she should not enjoy being unemployed, and should not feel that unemployment opens up opportunities—

not in any large number, at least. This has to do with *pouvoir*/ being able to. The unemployed person should not feel that she/he is able to do pleasant things or enjoy life thanks to unemployment. This discourse is strong in Finland and surely also in most other countries (see for example Ervasti and Venetoklis 2010).

Connected with this is *vouloir*/wanting to do or be something. Nobody should *want* to be unemployed. The moral panic (at least in Finland) around unemployment, especially youth unemployment, has very much to do with this 'threat'. Young unemployed people especially should want to get into the labour market, even desperately, even during times of economic recession when there are insufficient jobs available for everyone.

Young unemployed people should consider it their duty to work—this is the opinion at least of those who have power in society, and also the predominant assumption in media, at least in Finland and other European countries, as well as in Japan (Honda 2009). Just the same, because it is possible, and in some countries even self-evident, that not all unemployed people have internalised this ethos, sanctions to back up labour market measures are needed and they are directed especially towards the young—not least in order to promote this ethos among them. This is connected with *devoir*/having the duty of do something.

Savoir faire/having competence to: as a result of unemployment, a significant dilemma is connected with the lost competences of young people, both at individual and societal level. Young people are schooled, educated and trained in most European countries, as well as in Japan and in many other countries to an increasingly advanced level, then end up in situations where they cannot find work in which they can use their competences. The rise of academic unemployment is a growing problem and not just in Finland. This production of a surplus of well-educated young people for a labour market that cannot employ them selves results in a big loss of competences achieved by young people by means of hard work. This situation causes huge frustration, as my research material makes clear. Certainly, it will have also societal consequences, and in some countries, for example, such as Greece, it already has manifested itself in the form of riots. In Finland individualism is so internalised that collective popular movements—especially connected with a topic that is also considered as to some extent shameful—are very rare. In fact, a much older ethos than modern and or late-modern individualism is prevalent—that of 'every man for himself' (*yksinpärjäämisen eetos*; see Kortteinen 1997, Kirves et al. 2010)

Activating labour market policy with all its measures, systems, norms and sanctions, is really a social structure to which unemployed citizens as agents have either to adapt, or against which they have to struggle. In the life-sphere of an unemployed, and especially young unemployed person, this structure is everywhere, mainly limiting but also constructing and directing one's actions, practices and possibilities. I see this sociological topic, which is often discussed very abstractly and on a macro-level as a 'structure versus agency' dilemma, as very concrete and real in my own research topic. The 'structures' and 'discourses' need not always be enigmatic, hidden or complicated. The 'structure-agency' dilemma and struggle are present, in a very concrete sense, in the lives of the unemployed.

Part 3   Biographical negotiations from youth to adulthood

Chapter 6

Trajectories from youth to adulthood: Choice and structure for young people before and during recession[12]

Rosalind Edwards and Susie Weller

Introduction

This chapter explores change and continuity in young people's trajectories from youth into adulthood as the economic backdrop to their lives undergoes rapid change. Over the past decade youth unemployment in the UK has risen from under twelve per cent in 2000 to over twenty-two per cent in 2011 (ONS, 2009, 2011). Changes in Britain's economic conditions have generated changing political and media commentary on the opportunities available to young people. This commentary has moved on from notions of prosperous growth where, in the face of abundant chances to better themselves, young people only have to exercise application and responsible choice. It has progressed through ideas about the need for young people and the population generally to infuse themselves with self-confidence in order to overcome the negative psychological impact of the credit crunch, to concerns about economic downturn and full recession where the spotlight is focusing more and more on the dangers of a 'lost generation' of young people—especially NEETS who are not in education, employment or training.'

Further, the shadow of a previous cohort of large scale youth unemployment during the 1980s has fallen across the 'lost generation' discussion, and particularly the long-term effects as young people grow up into an adulthood that is 'scarred' by material and psychological depression (Burgess et al., 2003; Gregg and Tominey, 2004, Shaheen, 2009). Direct extrapolation of the consequences of mass unemployment from the 1980s is complicated by major transformations in the youth labour market since that period, however. Fewer young people in their late teens now are in paid work, and many more are in education or training, or mixing part time work and education or training (Barham et al.,

12 Updated version of an article published in *21ˢᵗ Century Society*, 2010, 5(2): 119-124 now called *Contemporary Social Sciences.*

2009). Nonetheless, a preoccupation of the contemporary commentary on youth unemployment has been the effects of economic circumstances on young people's sense of the opportunities available to them, implying that downturn knocks them off-course on their pathway into adulthood, replacing a smooth trajectory of resourceful optimism with a fractured turn into demoralisation.

Other trends affecting the nature of contemporary childhood and youth also form a backdrop to young people's conceptions of self in relation to the economic opportunities and constraints open to or facing them. Three wide-ranging processes have been identified as broadly affecting the lives and trajectory into adulthood of young people in post-industrial countries: a process of familialisation whereby children are positioned as the responsibility of and economically dependent on their parents for longer periods of their life; an accompanying process of institutionalisation that reinforces the deferment of independent adulthood, encompassing upward extension of the period of compulsory schooling and children's exclusion from paid work; and a process of individualisation. The latter represents an increasing general emphasis on children as individual social actors who reflexively construct their own biography and whose subjectivity is shaped by a sense of ability to make choices and carve out their own destiny, in this context an expansion of the idea of individualisation from adults to children and young people. The inherent contradiction between familialisation and institutionalisation processes and individualisation is mitigated somewhat by the harnessing of the extension of family life and schooling to produce this individualisation. (See more detailed discussion of these processes in Edwards, 2002.) These other, social, changes reshaping dependence and independence in contemporary childhood and youth call into question any simple, direct causal relationship between changed youth labour market opportunities and young people's life course shifts into adulthood outside of any consideration of their interaction with shifting circumstances in the sphere of social relations (Irwin, 1995).

The focus of this chapter is on what rising youth unemployment might mean for trajectories into adulthood for the young people of the new millennium. What has been the place of economic recession in contemporary young people's sense of the choices and resources available to them over time? Has the changing economic backdrop to young people's lives meant that they are knocked off course and onto new pathways? Or has economic change reinforced trajectories that young people were already embarked upon, entrenching their sense of the options and the constraints that are shaping their future? In-depth exploration of changes and continuities in young people's perceptions of choice and structure in their lives over time requires qualitative longitudinal data, and so we draw on our study following the unfolding of children's biographies since 2002. This means that our material begins in the period of apparent prosperous growth and self-responsibility, and proceeds through what was initially seen as a credit crunch and then a full-blown economic recession.

Before we consider the material from our study however and draw out some implications, we initially consider ideas about different sorts of trajectories into adulthood for young people, and their relationship to choice and structure, and provide some details of our qualitative longitudinal research.

Trajectories of choice and structure into adulthood

One theme of the evidence put forward on rising youth unemployment is its spatial inequality, steeper in urban areas in the north of the country than it is in the south (Shaheen, 2009), albeit with far less attention paid to rural areas. The ideas noted above about (i) a 'lost generation', focused in the north of Britain, and (ii) the process and production of individualisation, both tend to portray the implications for the length and nature of young people's trajectory into adulthood as similar for all. But even in a single northern city—or indeed one in the south of the country—young residents will not all be positioned similarly in relation to the rising tide or otherwise of youth unemployment. There is evidence from studies of young people in the period of apparent economic prosperity pre-2008 that structural positioning of gender and social class cuts across processes such as individualisation to mould differential trajectories into adulthood. Janet Holland's (2007a, 2009) longitudinal case studies of young people moving into adulthood between 1996 and 2007, for example, show how the social and material environment in which they grew up acted to shape the values and identities that they adopted, and the differential 'choices' they made and resources available to them in attempting particular life pathways. Indeed, choice and agency do not stand alone but are an integral part of changing social structures, and need to be analysed accordingly (Irwin, 1995, 2005).

In Julia Brannen and Ann Nilsen's view (2005), the notion of choice, however differential, seems to be one that is often unquestioned by both researchers and researched. They present a nuanced and evidenced argument that ideas about individuals having a 'choice biography' have eclipsed attention to the contexts and conditions under which the choices are made—in other words, structural forces. They say that this is the case both conceptually, in terms of the theories that sociologists have applied to analyse people's lives, but also within the public discourses that people themselves draw on to understand their own and others' biographies. Structure is 'the silent discourse'. Similarly, with regard to those public discourses, Andy Furlong and Fred Cartmel have suggested that, in late modernity, 'young people are forced to reflexively negotiate a complex set of routes into the labour market and in doing so, develop a sense that they alone are responsible for their labour market outcomes' (1997: 52), albeit this is an epistemological fallacy since they are attempting to take responsibility for something that is beyond their control.

Brannen and Nilsen's empirical evidence concerning individualisation, choice and silent structure draws on their research on young people's views of work and family in the future (Brannen et al., 2002). In contrast to some overarching assertions of a stretching or extension of trajectories into adulthood linked to familialisation and individualisation (Jones, 2005), they identify four main, empirically grounded, types of transition into adulthood for the young people they spoke to, which articulated with aspects of social structure, namely, gender, class and race/ethnicity. These types of transition, which are discussed in more detail later in this piece, represent different timeframes for the relationship between youth and adulthood. The period of youth and embarkation on adulthood may be stretched for some young people, as posited in processes of familialisation and institutionalisation, but for others it may be abbreviated:

1) *long period of youth*, involving financial dependency on family and a mutuality mentality;

2) *young adults*, involving semi financial independence from family and a contingency mentality;

3) *early adulthood*, involving a precarious financial independence and 'getting by' mentality; and

4) *short youth*, involving financial independence and a planning mentality.

Brannen and Nilsen's study, however, was conducted against a backdrop of apparent economic prosperity. In times of an economic recession that has a high public profile, however, issues of structural constraint may become more apparent for young people, in how they think about the options and resources available to them. This may represent a fracture or turn in the long or short nature of the trajectory into adulthood that they were previously set upon. Or coming face to face with an inability to make choices may be a confirmation and further embedding of a particular timeframe trajectory.

Our study and methods

The material we draw on for this article comes from the 'Your Space! Siblings and Friends' project (www.lsbu.ac.uk/ahs/research/yourspace/index.html), part of the wider Timescapes study. 'Your Space!' aims to document and track the meanings, experiences and flows of prescribed (sibling) and chosen (friendship) relationships for children and young people, and how these relate to their sense of self as their individual and family biographies unfold. It follows just over fifty children and young people from a variety of backgrounds and living in a range of family circumstances, distributed nationally across Britain.[13] We first interviewed our participants when they were aged between six and thirteen years-old (wave

From this overall sample, we focus in this chapter on young people at the older end of the age range: 16+ during our most recent wave of data collection in 2009. We have used Brannen and Nilsen's empirically grounded timeframe typology of transition into adulthood, identifying what we consider to be typical male and female cases[14] for each of the four forms of youth into adulthood trajectory in our wave 3 data. In this sense, we are not concerned so much with young people's explicit (or not) discussions of the economic recession, but with identifying their life circumstances within the transition typology. From this position, we then looked back longitudinally, to the previous interviews with those cases (2003-5 and 2007) to see if the trajectories of, respectively, long youth, young adulthood, early adulthood, short youth, were ones that—so far as we could tell—were actually smooth trajectories that our participants were already embarking upon from four to six years earlier, or represented a recent turn away from another sort of trajectory.

Working backwards in this way may appear quite strange when we are used to seeing longitudinal qualitative case studies written up in a progressive chronological narrative, following participants 'forward' in an apparently unknowing fashion to see how things turned out for them. As Andrew Abbott (2001) points out in his detailed consideration of the concept of 'turning point' in relation to trajectories, however, social analysts (whether lay or academic) can only judge whether or not there has been a change from one trajectory to another retrospectively. We thus make this retrospective nature explicit in how we write

13 Participants were drawn from three previous studies: (1) a study of sibling relationships for children in middle childhood, accessed through a nationally representative survey sample of parents distributed across Britain; (2) a study of sibling relationships in childhood and youth, drawing on an informal snowballed sample in the south-east of England; and (3) a study of the transition from primary to secondary school recruiting from schools located across England.

14 Participants chose their own pseudonyms, which are used throughout this chapter.

up our analysis, starting from where our cases are positioned on Brannen and Nilsen's typology, and then proceeding to trace change or continuity in this positioning into the young person's past.

Case study trajectories

1. Long period of youth

Brannen and Nilsen characterise young people in a 'long period of youth' as living at home and financially dependent on their family. They hold a 'family mutuality' understanding, which implicitly shapes their trajectory into adulthood. This trajectory echoes ideas about the familialised and institutionalised nature of contemporary childhood and youth referred to above. Brannen and Nilsen refer to young people from middle class backgrounds, as well perhaps as those from a minority ethnic background, as most likely to be experiencing a long period of youth. Alisha and Michael are examples of a long period of youth trajectory from our study. Both live in the South-East of Britain, but in different sorts of areas: Alisha in an affluent gated community and Michael in a disadvantaged inner city neighbourhood.

Alisha is a middle class[15] British Pakistani young woman who has been privately educated and brought up as an ambitious, liberal Muslim. During 2009, aged eighteen, she was waiting to go to a nearby university, supported in an affluent lifestyle at home by her mother, a self-employed business woman, and expecting to have this support continued through university (as it has been for her older sister). In turn, Alisha occasionally lends a hand in her mother's business, likes to help out around the house, and plans to visit her mother weekly from university to ensure her mother does not feel lonely: 'I'm thinking maybe I'll come home for three nights a week and [my sister] can come home because I don't want my Mum to be alone, it's not fair on her'.

Michael is a socially mobile black British young man whose parents migrated to Britain from Nigeria. Both his parents work for public services, his father works in public transport and his mother as a nurse. Michael attends a selective state school and is being brought up as a practising Christian. During 2009, aged sixteen years-old, he was intending to go into the sixth form and was looking for work experience during the summer vacation. There is a strong sense of family collectivity: Michael looks up to his older brother and looks out for his younger brother, and has a weekly rota of household responsibilities. He thought that he would stay at home to continue involvement in family life when he was at

15 Participants' social class is based on parental occupation.

university, as did his older brother: 'no matter how much I think I'm ready for it [moving away to university], I just don't think me personally I'll be able to handle it at that time'.

Both Alisha's and Michael's long period of youth trajectories are shaped by expectations about their academic achievement and eventual professional careers. These are the sorts of background 'silent structures' to which Brannen and Nilsen refer—cultural expectations, and parental expectations and financial support—that underlie any assertions about 'choice biographies'. In Michael's account, there is also a hint that, in the face of recession, the need to succeed and achieve is reinforced: 'The one thing I don't want to happen is I get to a point where I do something [a job] because I have to rather than because I want to'. But neither Alisha nor Michael is embarking on a different trajectory because of the recession.

Working backwards, it is clear that, while they each have expressed an interest in a short youth trajectory at different points over the past seven years or so, this has not resulted in an actual change of trajectory. In 2003, aged eleven, Alisha envisaged moving to America and working as a lawyer, and in 2009, aged eighteen, she mused on how she had not felt able to pursue her love of drama as a career. In 2007, aged fourteen, Michael considered pursuing the opportunity to become a professional footballer. In each case, though, they knew their choices would have been met with disapproval: 'Having my Asian culture kind of pressing on my back because the person that I want to be isn't often acceptable in my culture and there are sacrifices that I have to make for it' (Alisha); 'My football coach has told me that I could do football when I'm older as well but not many people in my family like that idea' (Michael). Indeed, it is clear from their discussions respectively at age eleven (Alisha, 2003) and twelve (Michael, 2005) that ideas about attending university were already established. Thus each 'chose' to continue on the long youth trajectory that fulfilled cultural and parental expectations.

2. Young adults

'Young adults', in Brannen and colleagues' typology, are semi-independent from their parents, perhaps living on a mix of financial support from their family, state benefits, student loans and/or part-time paid work. They may be living away from home or wanting to live separately from their parents, and have a 'contingency' approach to life where they try to seize opportunities as they arise in what they can see as a constantly changing world. In this sense, young adults are part of the process of individualisation, building their own biographies, cross-cut with familialisation and perhaps institutionalisation. Relatively early attempts to become independent and enter young adulthood are evident in Louise's and Steven's situations of semi-independence, both of whom live in suburban areas in the metropolitan South-East.

Louise is a middle class white British young woman. Her father is in private sector management while her mother is a support worker in the public sector. In 2009, aged nineteen, Louise was living with her parents but often staying over at her boyfriend's house. She was leaving her administrative job of two years standing, which she obtained through a friend of her father's, and also leaving home, to follow the example of a friend of hers and work in a summer camp for young people in the United States. Louise regarded this new venture as a chance to find a pathway in life: 'I don't have anything that I wanna do and that's why I think I should go to America because you learn most about yourself out there'.

Steven is a working class white British young man. His father is a service worker and his mother an administrative assistant, both in the public sector. In 2009, aged nineteen, Steven was playing in a band that had been signed to a record label—an opportunity that 'just came along' when he was asked to join an already formed group. He was not earning enough to pay rent to his parents, although he contributed to the household budget whenever he could, and looked forward to being able to live independently. Steven did have options at the back of his mind, including joining one of the services: 'It's really strange because all I can picture in the future is the band. It's really weird, I shouldn't do it because it might not happen. Yeah, [joining a service] was my plan and if the band fails that would be my plan'.

Both Louise and Steven saw themselves as self-reliant and choosing their own pathways through life, but is clear that in each case this was underpinned by parental backstop support. At this point in time, their independence was 'semi' in that Louise's job and home was provided through her parents, and Steven was financially supported by his parents.

Working backwards, it seems that Louise's and Steven's emphasis on choice and seizing contingent opportunities presented by family and friends as they arise is longstanding in each case. In 2003, aged thirteen, both expressed ideas about choosing what they wanted to do, but had no clear idea of what that choice might be. Louise seemed to herald being a young adult, however, with a paid Saturday job. And while Steven raised the prospect of a long period of youth trajectory in considering continuing his education through to university, a young adult trajectory was also signalled in his expressed hurry to grow up. Later, in 2007, aged seventeen, Louise was pushed out of a long period of youth and into a young adult trajectory when she was asked to leave her school sixth form because she was not studying enough, and then took the opportunity of a job offered by her father's friend. Steven, at that time, was keeping several options in play. He continued to leave a long period of youth trajectory open by studying for A-levels, was playing with friends in a band in the hope that this might prove successful, and also experienced the financial semi-independence of young adulthood through having two part-time jobs.

Clearly the young adult trajectory had become dominant for both Louise and Steven by 2009 but it is also clear that without the intervention of other factors they could each have been on an alternative trajectory. In their world of contingency and responding to opportunities and constraints as they arise, the advent of recession seems to be just another external factor to which they might respond in a number of potential ways.

3. Early adulthood

Young people who have entered adulthood early, or are embarking upon an early adulthood trajectory, experience a precarious financial existence, joining or seeking to join the labour market without further or higher education, and with a focus on 'getting by'. They may assume that they soon will be, or are, living with a partner and, perhaps, have children of their own. In this sense they are placed on the margins of trends towards institutionalisation and individualisation, and familialisation may have a different meaning to them. Brannen and Nilsen note that these are likely to be young people from working class backgrounds. Such marginalisation and early experiences of unemployment are part of Malaky's and Rooney's trajectories into early adulthood, with both of them firmly part of concerns about the 'lost generation'—as NEETS (not in employment, education or training).

Malaky is a white British young woman who lives in a small city in the South-East. She falls between working and middle class, with a father who has a portfolio of manual and administrative skills, and has periods of not working, and a mother who is a specialist administrator in local government. In 2009, aged eighteen, Malaky was living at home with her parents. Rather than feeling supported by her parents, she felt like a burden to them because of her financial dependence. She spoke about financial independence, and expressed feeling pressure from her parents to go out to work. Despite this, Malaky was experiencing a lack of motivation to find employment or undertake the education and training she would need to fulfil her longstanding ambition to become a midwife: 'It's not a fear of not achieving them [necessary qualifications], it's a fear that I just won't be bothered to do it'.

Rooney is a working class white British young man also living in a small city in the South-East. Both his parents are long term unemployed. In 2009, aged sixteen, Rooney was also unemployed, having been sacked on the first day of his first job after leaving school. In the context of recession, he spoke of little choice or availability in jobs. He thought that Connexions (an information and advice service for young people aiming to engage them in education and employment) would get him onto a course at college to study catering and/or music. Rooney was living at home with his parents who were reliant on unemployment benefits themselves, but very much wanted to live independently with his fiancée and start a family. He felt the stumbling block was the lack of availability of social housing for young people. The structural backdrop of material parental support was not available to him. Overall, Rooney felt, 'you can never predict the future can you? Get worse, it could get easier'.

Both Malaky and Rooney experienced the precariousness of an early adulthood through early experience of unemployment, while each wanted to be on a young adult trajectory. Neither, however, felt in control of their lives, and the recession loomed as a silent structure in the background for both of them. Working backwards, it seems that Rooney had never felt any certainty about his employment future but did have a continuous but vague desire for independence. Malaky's goal of becoming a midwife had long roots, being clearly expressed back in 2002 when she was twelve, and she had attempted to realise it through studying at college on leaving school at sixteen, with the intention of moving on to university. After completing the college course, however, Malaky discovered that she had gained the wrong level of qualification for realising her ambition, and found herself derailed from her long period of youth trajectory into early adulthood. In contrast to Rooney's pathway of becoming further embedded on an early adulthood trajectory over the past seven years, Malaky had shifted onto that trajectory from a potential long period of youth pursuing the studies that would enable her to achieve her career aims.

4. Short youth

Brannen and Nilsen identify young people for whom a period of youth has been relatively short, describing them as those who are seeking to achieve or have achieved financial and other independence from their family through getting a 'good job'. Young people who experience a short youth have a 'confident planning' approach to life, often following standard biographical pathways that they assume will resemble their parents' lives. Such young people then exhibit some aspects of individualisation, such as self-responsibility and development, and are moving away from familialisation. Kate and Dan provide good examples of aspects of a short youth, despite challenging educational pathways in each case.

Kate is a working class white British young woman living with her mother, previously a support worker in a public service and now not working due to ill health, in a rural area of the Midlands. In 2009, age sixteen, she had set in motion her plans to attend college to study sport and English, determined to achieve the GCSE grades required, and then be the first in her family to go to university. Kate was looking for part-time work so that she had some financial independence, and it is her desire for financial self-sufficiency and to get a good job that places her on a short youth trajectory even though she is not following the standard family biographical pathway and is planning to go to university: 'Cos like I'm ambitious, I want to go to college, do a part time job, and after college to go university and become a teacher … I know which [university] I want to go to … Cos to be honest with you, I hate asking for money cos I'm independent and I want to get a job, earn my own money.' Indeed, it is evident that Kate has become even more determined to be independent in the face of the recession: 'The recession has started ain't it? Something has to happen! I'm not lucky am I? So now I'm sixteen I'm looking for a job. I don't care *where* it is' (her emphasis).

Dan is a working class white British young man living at home with his parents in a rural area of the South-East. His father works in the voluntary sector, while his mother is a full time home-maker. In 2009, age seventeen, Dan was at college studying agriculture, and undertook part-time work for some financial independence. Dan's vision for his future was a home of his own with his girlfriend and starting a family. In his desired field of employment and wanting his own family life in the near future, Dan was following in the short youth trajectory footsteps of other family members across the generations (grandfather and uncles) and the cultural mores of the area in which he lived; he felt certain that he would achieve his goals and planned his life accordingly.

Working backwards, it is clear that both Kate and Dan have strengthened their short youth trajectory over time. Both have held their ambitions and planned towards achieving them since their early teens. In 2007, age fourteen, for example, Dan remarked: 'My hope is to get into college and do agriculture

… because my granddad, uncle and next-door neighbour and my granddad's best mate and a load of other people and my other uncle works in agriculture'. Nonetheless, both have experienced several difficulties to surmount in their preferred short youth trajectories, which could have derailed them. For Kate, this included eating issues and behavioural problems at school, while Dan had specific learning difficulties and was held back a year at school. Each doggedly worked their way through these challenges and remained on the course they planned for themselves.

Conclusion

In his ground-breaking lifecourse study linking the particulars of individual people's lives to broad currents of historical change, *Children of the Great Depression*, Glenn Elder (1999, originally published 1974) points out that the 'lost' generation of youth during the Depression of the 1930s then turned out to be the 'greatest' generation of the Second World War. Crucially, he argues that people enter a crisis such as economic recession with prior resources of various kinds and uses, and the crisis accentuates whatever it is that they bring to it. On the basis of the findings from our study, it seems that this message may still relevant today in the current period of recession in Britain.

The typology of youth transitions devised by Brannen and colleagues (2002) from their empirical data has been useful in analysing our longitudinal data on young people. Their typology takes account of and enables us to tease out the silence discourse of structure, aspects of social structure including gender, race/ethnicity and class that have an effect on young people's trajectories that can provide the shaping context for any impact of economic disruption.

The young women and men in our case studies were not knocked off-course on their pathway into adulthood by the recession, replacing a smooth trajectory of resourceful optimism with a fractured turn into demoralisation. In particular, the young people following 'long period of youth' or 'short youth' trajectories appeared to be continuing a pathway into adulthood that had become further and further embedded over time and during the recession, despite the transient attractions of other trajectories or facing educational setbacks.

In contrast, the 'young adult' and 'early adulthood' trajectories seemed less stable and more subject to shifts towards and/or away from other trajectories; albeit these other trajectories had not suddenly appeared on their horizon but had been possible alternatives alongside the 'young adult' and 'early adulthood' trajectories for the young people discussed here. In other words, there may have been shifts and changes but these were not in entirely new directions.

A strong sense of individual choice was only apparent for those on the 'young adults' trajectory, responding to contingent constraints and opportunities. Even for these young people, however, 'silent structures' were evident. Indeed, the structural backdrops to young people's lives were important in both continuous and shifting trajectory scenarios, and race/ethnicity and social class shaped these. In the cases discussed above, these included cultural and parental expectations, the material resources available within and to families, wider social networks, the availability of economic and welfare opportunities for full or part-time employment, education and training courses, housing and so on.

Overall then, in the face of assertions that recession has brought about major change to a new trajectory into adulthood, previously not evident, it would seem that either one trajectory continues gaining in strength over time, or a number of prior potential trajectories can be in play in young people's lives with one of these becoming more and more strongly entrenched. The economic recession has provided a certain set of conditions for embedding trajectories rather than fracturing them.

Chapter 7

Inventing adulthoods: Young people growing up in Northern Ireland

Sheena McGrellis and Janet Holland

Introduction

Since 1996 we have been exploring young people's lives in their biographical social/historical and generational context in a prospective qualitative longitudinal study, Inventing Adulthoods (www.lsbu.ac.uk/inventingadulthoods).[15] The one hundred young people in the study are located in five socio-economically contrastive sites across the UK: a leafy suburb, an inner city location, an isolated rural area, a disadvantaged northern estate, and a site in Northern Ireland varying by class and religion. The holistic, biographical and dynamic approach we have employed to understand young lives explores their varied trajectories into adulthood, following the interweaving and potential unravelling of processes over time. In up to six biographical interviews through time, we invited them to create a series of retrospective accounts of the past, and to project themselves into the future from the perspective of a changing present.

A central concern of our analyses has been to examine and reflect how biographies are shaped by structural factors such as locations, social class, gender and family and by concomitant personal, social, physical/material and economic resources available to the individual (Thomson et al. 2002, Thomson et al. 2003, Henderson et al. 2007). In analysing and interpreting our data we employed the concept of the 'reflexive project of self' (Giddens 1991) where the individual is seen as responsible for constructing their own identity in the face of disappearing traditional resources and supports (Beck and Beck Gernsheim 2002), whilst also mounting a critique of late modern theories more generally. We developed concepts from the data, for example that of 'critical moments' to capture events in young people's lives that they or we, or both, considered to be significant and consequential (Thomson et al. 2002, Holland and Thomson 2009). The longitudinal approach allows us to see how young people make and remake their biographies through time, and in this process, both the young person and the researcher can revisit and reconsider critical moments that

15 Research team: Sheila Henderson, Janet Holland, Sheena McGrellis, Sue Sharpe and Rachel Thomson.

perhaps were not initially recognised. We used the concept of social capital, to understand some social and associational aspects of the resources available to the young people, defined as: 'The values people hold and the resources that they can access, which both result in and are the result of collective and socially negotiated ties and relationships.' Methodologically we have been developing aspects of qualitative longitudinal research and practice, including longitudinal case histories, to capture time, duration and change (Henderson et al. 2012).

In this chapter we provide some background from the broader study, but are looking particularly at the young people in Northern Ireland, re-interviewed in 2009/10 funded by the Joseph Rowntree Foundation UK. These most recent interviews provide insight into the challenges young adults face around work and employment and the effects these can have on their health and wellbeing.

The Northern Irish site/study

The young people in the Northern Ireland site were last interviewed in 2004/05, and in 2009/10 we interviewed 18 of them, many for the seventh time since 1996. Of this group, just over half were in full time work, five were unemployed (28%) seven living with their parents, including four who left home for study or work but who have since returned. Ten are single, five are parents, eight stayed in Northern Ireland, while five returned from living outside Northern Ireland during this period.

These figures depict a picture of a small group of young adults moving between college, university, work and unemployment and training, leaving and returning from home and country, with shifting relationship status and caring responsibilities. The stories behind the figures can tell much more.

A period of social and political change in Northern Ireland

The young people from the Northern Irish site, now in their mid-twenties to early thirties, grew into adulthood during a period of significant political, economic and social transition, and our study shadowed these changes. Table 1 indicates their biographical life stages alongside significant political-social-historical events.

Table 1: *Biographical-historical-social-political timeline.*

Biographical	age	year	Historical/social
	12	1994	Paramilitary ceasefires
GCSE, education decisions, expanding social lives	14	1996	IRA bombs London, Manchester
PT jobs/more freedom and independence	15	1997	2nd IRA ceasefire
Leave (continue) school; college/FE	16	1998	Good Friday Agreement 71% support, Omagh bomb
Expanding social and leisure scene in NI/ relationships/educational pressures	17	1999	Devolved government. Assembly set up
Leave home/relationships/social life/work/training /FE/HE, unemployment/ travel	19	2001	IRA decommission arms, power sharing
	20	2002	Assembly suspended
Completed uni/work/ unemployment / emotional health issues /opportunities global level/ social networking/ parenthood	23	2005	
	25	2007	Assembly reinstated
	26	2008	Recession UK
Work/unemployment/parenthood /relationships/emotional health/ restricted opportunities/return community/emigrate	27	2009	Increased Dissident Republicans activity.

While politicians and those in positions of power and influence negotiated, re-negotiated and thrashed out settlements and deals, sectarianism and violence continued in the streets and in the communities where the young people lived. Over time the young people in the study engaged with the political developments and discourse to a greater or lesser extent. In early interviews (1997-1999), discussions on the peace process, community differences, sectarian violence and shared spaces were animated, could be heated, and drew on young people's own lived experience and the historical experience of their families and communities (McGrellis 2005). Subsequent interviews suggested that the young people had largely disengaged from politics, and whatever was happening (or not happening) in the corridors of Stormont (devolved Northern Ireland Government) and Westminster (UK government). But the political changes and developments contributed to their biographical narratives of community, affiliation, identity and perceived opportunity. The ceasefires remained largely intact but the process of moving towards an inclusive and peaceful society has been, and continues to be, delicate, as sectarianism continues to define sporadic violence and the threat of violence from dissident republican groups.

Political changes in Northern Ireland were paralleled by economic change and the young people experienced an opening up of leisure and consumption opportunities during economic growth and boom years. But it was their age group that was most heavily affected by unemployment when plunged into the 2008 recession, and employment prospects for young people currently remain poor. While the population unemployment figures for Northern Ireland are comparable with the UK average, a much higher percentage of those aged between eighteen and twenty-four in Northern Ireland are registered unemployed. With one of the highest youth populations in Europe it is perhaps not surprising, but none the less alarming, that youth unemployment accounts for one fifth of the current jobless total in the province, and 17.4 per cent of this age group are out of work (DETI, 2010). In our revisited sample over a quarter were unemployed.

Broad picture: Education, work, family, class and gender

Education

Years of research tells us that the social class and educational background of parents is the major consistent element affecting the education and work chances of young people, a fact that seems to have re-emerged into public awareness in a situation where there is probably less chance of change than in the past. So it was in our study, although some of the policies of the New Labour government could be seen working positively through the lives of the young people, particularly those targeted at socio-economically disadvantaged groups. The policies we noted included Education Action Zones, Excellence in Cities, mentoring of working-class young people, Connexions, Educational Maintenance Allowances (EMA), and the expansion and massification of higher education. More recent coalition government (Conservative/Liberal Democrat) policies abolishing or strictly means testing EMA and proposing high tuition fees at universities are likely to undermine these gains. Combined with the efforts of the schools in disadvantaged sites to grasp every possibility for their pupils, these earlier policies saw numbers of young people finding their way through various routes, inflected by their class locations, into higher education very often the first in their family to do so. In the early years of the study the young people in the Northern Ireland site were particularly aspirational in the desire for a university education, and as in the sample as a whole, more girls than boys had this aspiration. A significant proportion of the young people had part time work whilst at school, on average 28 per cent through ages eleven to sixteen, but this varied by location, age and gender, all of which also influenced the type of work they undertook. For many this juggling of education and work continued into their further and higher education.

Work

For many in the study securing part time jobs while at school was their first introduction to work, and this provided a valued degree of financial independence from parents, an opportunity to become independent consumers, and the chance to test out career options, or to expand their curriculum vitae with a view to future careers. For those from the more disadvantaged families the income could be essential. As they grew older, helping to meet family bills and ease pressure on their parents' finances was important for them.

Over time there was an increasing focus in the interviews on transition from education to work, and how employment, or the lack of it, defined and influenced so many other aspects of their lives. Social capital in the form of social networks emerged as key in the search for part or full time work. In the fourth interview the young people (aged seventeen to twenty-four) were asked questions about social capital: about communities and belonging, networks of association they were part of and the benefits that might accrue from those contacts, who they could turn to for various types of support (economic/practical, social, emotional), and about feelings of inclusion and exclusion. For some of the young people the idea of networking, building and using contacts was totally familiar, and they were usually well networked. Others had little idea about what it meant, and often minimal networks and contacts. Yet others rejected the idea of networking, preferring to go it alone or deploring the idea of using their friends or family in such an instrumental way.

The major source of support for the young people at that point in their lives was their family, in particular parents who provided emotional, financial and social support and resources. Parents also provided networks of contacts through which their children could secure information and help with educational choices, and work. Young people without this backdrop of support for whatever reason could face difficulties. The examples of the well networked in our sample have tended to be middle class young people, albeit in a range of circumstances. They also tended to be flexible with networks spanning different age groups and communities—local, family, educational, work, leisure—and a range of activities, from bell-ringing to volunteering. They were often well resourced by their family. Putnam has distinguished between bonding and bridging social capital, with bonding being 'inward looking and tend[ing] to reinforce exclusive identities and homogeneous groups' and bridging 'outward looking and encompass[ing] people across diverse social cleavages' (Putnam, 2000: 22-3). Although some of the working class young people in the sample are well networked, keen to be socially mobile upward often through education, and are resourced by their families, many of them have networks that tend to link them into family, community and locality, rather than providing broader opportunities for contacts, education and work Others in the young people's social networks who provided support and resources in various ways included friends, people in their workplaces and communities, college and university teachers, and members of the social services. They could also gain support, networks and social capital through relationships, youth culture, the gay scene, sport and the internet.

In the Northern Ireland sample and our latest interviews, young people from more working class backgrounds, for example, the young men in the construction industry, seemed rather adept at using social networks. As well as being beneficial in terms of securing employment these networks were often the resource point for housing and leisure. But when these structures collapsed or evaporated in relation to work, a chasm of support was left in their wake. Young men who left high earning jobs in a booming building industry, for example, to join the dole queue felt the ignominy of this as a personal failure.

Long term unemployment has been a feature of life for a small number of study participants. Cyclical training schemes, short term work placements and casual work, have defined their twenties, and had a significant impact on their sense of self esteem and identity, all of which make their return to work or education significantly more difficult, and has had an impact on their well-being.

Relationships and family support emerged as a vital resource in relation to work and unemployment. Young parents depended on their own parents and families for childcare in order to return to work. Working did not necessarily pay any more than remaining on benefits, but a desire to be independent and provide for their children motivated young parents in particular in this direction. The 'cost' of returning to work could act as a disincentive. Travel costs and the lack of work-place childcare, the importance of which is little recognised or acknowledged by the state, were both major considerations. The emotional and personal costs were perhaps more poignant as young parents talked about the lack of quality time they could actually spend with their children. Tiredness, time pressure, work demands all ate into this space. In terms of policy interventions none of these young people attract help or intervention, all operate under the radar, but are only doing so with significant and vital family support.

Health and well being

In 2004 the Department of Health acknowledged that mental health problems in children and young people 'are associated with educational failure, family disruption, disability, offending and antisocial behaviour, placing demands on social services, schools and the youth justice system'. In the Inventing Adulthoods data, certain aspects of mental ill-health, particularly depression, came into clearer focus when the young people were aged eighteen to twenty-three years- old. Thirteen young people (nine women and four men) described experiences of depression and stress linked to education, employment, family situations, and relationships. Almost all the young women were from working class backgrounds, mainly in Northern Ireland and the disadvantaged English site, while all but one of the young men were from middle class families living in the affluent commuter site. In addition, five more young women described being affected by the depression of someone they were close to, such as a parent or boyfriend.

Young people living in the disadvantaged estate and some parts of the Northern Irish site were more likely to experience cultures of ill health, poverty, poor housing, unemployment and family breakdown. They found themselves with far fewer material, social and cultural resources on which to draw than others in the study. This harsher landscape with its higher incidence of illness, bereavement and suicide meant there was more potential for 'critical moments' in young people's lives to have a negative impact on their well-being. Bereavement was a key theme that also emerged in this context, sometimes changing the young people's approach to life, and their values, confidence, motivation and hence their life trajectories, leading possibly to either an upward or downward spiral.

The number of young people who reported feelings of stress, depression, or anxiety in the recent Northern Ireland interviews was remarkable in such a small sample. Some talked about the physical effects of these feelings, which included weight loss, weight gain and insomnia. One reported self harming and thinking about and attempting suicide. (Northern Ireland has one of the highest suicide rates in the UK, with rates rising by sixty-four per cent between 1999 and 2008 and fifteen to thirty-four year-olds accounting for most of this rise, particularly young men, Hayes, 2011). Such experiences were linked to education, unemployment, debt, relationships, and sexual and gender identity. Both young men and women suffered, and class background did not seem to discriminate. While earlier interviews suggested that young women from working class backgrounds were more likely to report such stress and anxiety than their middle class counterparts, this later round suggests that the pressures of higher education and demands of work and other commitments contributed to feelings of stress and depression among those from more middle class backgrounds.

The young men in this study seemed particularly vulnerable to life events that resulted in periods of stress, despair and depression. The chance to share their feelings and to be listened to, as in the research interview, was something that a number of them clearly sought—going to the doctor but really just wanting a listening ear, spending hours on social networking sites 'talking' and accessing support from others in similar situations, or writing their feelings down. Few felt able to talk to their family about the nature and depth of their feelings.

Danny, for example, had experienced depression at university, describing himself then as 'severely depressed' for about six months. He couldn't 'get out of bed, eat talk or socialise.' In the latest interview he reported a further experience of depression. Having successfully completed his degree he enjoyed a lucrative job placement in the City of London. High earnings, a 'high life' and high expectations all came to an abrupt end when the company he worked for folded as markets collapsed. This recent experience of depression was linked to the end of a relationship and also coincided with unemployment and loss of status. Danny described himself as 'a wreck' and a 'disaster.' While some found 'talking' helpful, this is not one of Danny's coping responses:

> talking about emotional problems doesn't really help for me, because I talk too much and it just goes on and on and on. I get into loops and cycles and nothing gets resolved. I don't really resolve things by talking them through. I just have to stick it out then it goes away.

In general these young people expressed little knowledge about the nature and availability of support services, or how they might access any services. While the stigma associated with emotional or mental health needs is perhaps less now than in the past, barriers still exist around accessing help and support. Some of these barriers are about a lack of awareness of services; other more fundamental barriers are possibly linked to the lack of education around emotional awareness and resilience.

Case histories

The case history method that we have been developing to capture the longitudinal nature of our study produces extremely long documents, written in the voice of the researcher, but hopefully expressing something of the voice of the young person. (Henderson et al. 2012). We have chosen two examples here to illustrate some of the points raised in the chapter. Both are in fact young parents now, Shelagh working class, and Patrick middle class. Both were aspirational in relation to work and career, but thrown off course, and for each having a child was a critical moment and turning point. They show the challenges associated with low paid work and single parenthood, particularly in the context of the economic downturn and limited opportunities, and the importance of family support in different ways. We can see the impact of financial pressures on relationships and the link between work and identity, and self esteem and well being.

Shelagh
Shelagh's parents separated before she left primary school. Her mother raised Shelagh and her siblings on benefits with little support from their father. Growing up there was no extra money for luxuries, her mother lived from day to day. Their housing executive (social housing) home was basic and from an early age Shelagh was determined that she would gain independence and work towards a life that removed her from the one she saw her mother living.

At sixteen she had babysitting jobs and later worked in a local restaurant. She earned little for the long hours she toiled but did not care—the importance of earning and having her own money was greater than any sense of fair pay. She regarded education as a way out of poverty and a gateway to success and a new and different life. At school she was channelled more than guided into educational choices and options. Her quiet and reserved nature saw her accept the teacher's choices without question and in the end saw her fall behind in her studies. By her own admission she was 'lazy' at school and when not pushed or encouraged she faltered. Ambitions for university and a professional career fell by the wayside before she had turned seventeen. She moved from one Further Education course to another over a five year period, achieving sufficient qualifications to obtain an office job.

A contributory part of Shelagh's disjointed educational journey was early motherhood. At eighteen she 'fell' pregnant when the relationship which led to the pregnancy had already ended. Her strength of character determined that she would live as a single mother, in her own rented house, and prove to all around that she could cope. She wanted her son to see her as a working mother who took care of and responsibility for her situation. This was not necessarily easy, and was wholly dependent on the childcare support provided by her mother. At one point Shelagh discovered that a year long short term contract with the civil service did not financially pay; she was no better off than she was on benefits, was physically exhausted and had little time with her child. When her contract ended Shelagh went back on benefits and worked a few hours in a cafe for low pay, 'just to get out of the house.' At times Shelagh felt the restrictions and responsibilities of motherhood too much, a sense that life was passing her by made her feel down and 'resentful.'

> a year ago I just felt as if everything was passing me by, I was only nineteen and I was living a life of somebody a lot older than me who didn't have to deal with half the complications that I had. –[ ] I felt as if the whole world was against me at one stage. [ ] I was nineteen stuck in with a wee'un and couldn't do nothing about it.   (age 20)

Relationships have always featured strongly in Shelagh's biography. She is now a mother of three, lives with her partner, father of two of her children, and has a mortgage on a new house in a development adjacent to the estate where she was raised. While she has managed to move out of the estate, she remains very close to it (emotionally and physically) and depends on her mother for affordable childcare enabling her to work. Working outside the home continues to be important to Shelagh's identity and sense of self, but the wages she earns are crucial to the household finance. Her partner lost his job in the downturn in the building trade but through family contacts has managed to secure an office job. They are managing.

Patrick

'Single mother' is a well rehearsed public and policy identity label. The 'single father' is perhaps less common, less recognised. Patrick's girlfriend became pregnant when he was in his second year at university. Both took the decision to leave their degree courses and return to Northern Ireland to 'make a go' of being a family. In a competitive economic climate work opportunities were limited, the job Patrick got was low paid, low skilled, and unfulfilling. But determined to be a 'hands on' father, Patrick took the job in order to rent a flat with his girlfriend. To pay bills Patrick worked long hours, putting considerable strain on his relationship and bringing him to a point where he 'just kind of buckled.'

> … to be honest it was grand the first two years but it came down to basically I was working quite a bit and [partner] didn't want to work so it kind of was a bit lopsided … it kind of, it ended up the last year we were together I was working six twelve-hour shifts a week to cover the bills and stuff and after a while I think the pressure just started to get to me [ ] Aw, I'm sure I was a pain in the arse to like—but when you're working that amount of hours a week you're not the happiest person to be with [ ] then I wasn't getting to see the wee'un then as much as I wanted to see her, you know so (.) I just kind of buckled

When the relationship broke down Patrick considered buying a house for himself and his child, but low wages and little job security meant he could not secure a mortgage. Finally he had to move back to his parents, and his girlfriend and child moved into another flat. Experiencing the financial as well as emotional responsibility of parenting, Patrick did not feel able to return to university and instead set about finding a better paid job with some career prospects.

While not in his area of interest, he did secure a relatively good job. His work pattern allows him to have his child for at least fifty per cent of the time and be as involved in the child's care as the mother. Patrick enjoys being a young father, fatherhood has given him a 'better outlook in life … things that mattered before don't really matter any more,' and while he was always highly motivated he feels he now 'has something to work harder for.'

After the end of his relationship with the mother of his child he was reluctant to embark on any other relationships, he became 'basically a hermit,' and noticed that 'when you have a wee'un friends disappear.' When he did start to socialise again he also found that girls 'seemed to kind of run a mile when they found out [he] was a father.' His hesitance to get involved with anyone was both a response to the break up of his relationship and a desire to protect his child. Patrick is now in a steady relationship and hopes to marry when the time is right. He continues to live with his parents.

Towards conclusions

This chapter has examined recent interviews with a group of people growing up in Northern Ireland, whose lives we have followed with multiple biographical interviews since 1996. We placed them in the context of the broader Inventing Adulthood study, which included young people from across the UK, and in the social, political, and historical context of Northern Ireland. Throughout the study, data from the Northern Ireland site gave witness to the particular challenges and opportunities faced by the first generation of young people to grow up in a post ceasefire (1994) and post Good Friday Agreement (1998) society. Falling as they did in some ways between two generations (in terms of experience, culture and history as well as age) this group of young people journeyed into adulthood during a period of significant political, economic and social transition. After the Troubles, they were buoyed up by what appeared to be a new dawn, offering new opportunities and bright hopes, and they sought the realisation of their desires and dreams through opportunities afforded in education, work, leisure and consumption and relationships. But laggard politicians and continued threats and violence from sectarian sources led to disillusionment with the political process and the possibilities for changing Northern Irish society, as historic tensions between communities persisted. Economic conditions of boom and bust exacerbated the effects of these processes, and with the legacy of the Troubles, added to insecurities affecting their (mental) health and well-being. For those who have stayed in or returned to Northern Ireland in our study, family and community support has become possibly even more important than in their past. Practical and emotional resources available through immediate and extended family networks helped young people to cope with unexpected and challenging life changing events, critical moments in their trajectories.

Our two case histories highlight the points made in the chapter in some similar and some different ways. For each of them work was very important for their self image and esteem, and for practical reasons to support their young children. In each case parental support was crucial to enable them to work. For Shelagh independence and providing for her child was a major motivator, and particularly early on, work enabled her as a single parent to have a life other than mother, meet her friends, feel young again and forget for a brief time the major responsibilities she carried. Work also provided her with a safety valve for her own emotional and mental health. Patrick also used work as a way of confirming the positive aspects of parenthood, being responsible and providing for his child and partner, and maintaining, or reclaiming some sense of his own self esteem and self worth. His aspirations were initially quite high, as were Shelagh's, but unlike her he did go to university before his girlfriend became pregnant, so had tasted the first step on the road to fulfilling his early ambition. Both young people displayed significant resilience in coping with early parenthood, and re- aligning their projected pathways. New and fast changing circumstances and responsibilities can contribute to periods of stress, and at times despair, for young people, and had a very direct effect on their real and imagined hopes and aspirations. Qualitative longitudinal study enables us to see lives unfolding, and we wait in the wings to know the next steps in these young lives.

Chapter 8

Regional identities future expectations and work values

Arseniy Svynarenko

Introduction

This chapter as well as the next chapter by Helena Helve is based on Finnish Work-Preca research on young people's work transitions, values and future horizons. During economic recession, increased uncertainty and risk of unemployment constitute a challenging and disequilibrating life event in which previously-made identity commitments are no longer workable and an individual may temporarily regress to earlier identity modes. It is a time when new identities and new models may appear. The themes of family, future plans and education are located on the intersections of work identity, local and global identities. In this article we intentionally did not investigate work identities as such, instead we looked at intersections of work-related values and regional identities of young Finns. The employment situation of young people has an impact on their perceptions of future, as those have successfully found full-time jobs certainly see the future in a relatively more optimistic light. In the perceptions of young people's future, one can see reflections of their attitudes and experiences of participation in existing welfare and political system; negative experiences weaken the sense of national identity. Further findings about youth transitions from education to labour market will be presented by Helena Helve in the next Chapter 9.

Identity

Social identity has often been described as group identity in social psychological literature (e.g., Côté, 1996; Weigert, Teitge and Teitge, 1986). In researching group identities, one approach is to focus on aspects of the self such as native language, country of origin, and ethnic background. Another approach to identity is through the examination of personal identity at the intersection of self and context. Erikson spoke of personal identity as the set of goals, values, and beliefs that one shows to the world. Personal identity includes career goals, sexual preferences, word choices, and other aspects of self that identify a given individual as someone unique and that help to distinguish him or her from other people. In contrast to personal identity, there is also social identity, which is the most contextually-oriented level. This was identified by Erikson as a sense of inner solidarity with a group's ideals, the consolidation of elements that have been integrated into one's sense of self from groups to which one belongs. All individuals, at any given time during their lives, can be placed at some point on Erikson's dimension between identity synthesis and identity confusion. Identity synthesis is needed to facilitate the healthy functioning of an individual; self-knowledge should predominate over confusion. In more concrete terms, identity synthesis represents a sense of 'a present with an anticipated future' (Erikson, 1968, p. 30). An identity-synthesised person's choices and actions are consistent with one another, such that one can predict, with some degree of certainty, what that person is going to decide or do in the context of any particular situation or life choice.

A well-developed identity structure needs to be flexible and open to possible rapid changes in relationships or circumstances. Identity commitments change over time in both content and in how definite they are. Identity is influenced by new contexts encountered during subsequent life phases of an individual. Marcia described these changes in identity in terms of moratorium-achievement cycles in adolescence (Marcia, 2002), or foreclosure-achievement cycles. Longitudinal studies by Päivi Fadjukoff (Fadjukoff, 2007) provide empirical backing to this assumption about the identity process. A general increase in identity foreclosure at the age of thirty-six, instead of generally increasing identity achievement, may reflect normative age-graded influences, with participants relying on traditional values at the time of establishing their families and careers and becoming parents to small children, or history-graded influences on development, with people turning into foreclosure during unstable times (Fadjukoff, 2007). Fadjukoff writes that occupational identity formed along the age-graded developmental sequence from identity diffusion toward achievement from age twenty-seven to forty-two, is more strongly developed in women than in men. During economic recession increased uncertainty and risk of unemployment constitute a challenging and disequilibrating life event in which previously-made identity commitments are no longer workable and an individual may temporarily regress to earlier identity modes (Marcia, 2002). This can be followed by a narrowing of perspective induced by internal personality factors, such as lowered tolerance for ambiguity or openness to experience, or external factors such as circumstances restricting access to a diversity of life experiences. On the other hand, an identity crisis may advance the acquisition of new commitments; in an open society, political opportunities available for the unemployed may facilitate their political participation (Fadjukoff, 2007).

Perceptions of future: optimism/pessimism[16]

Despite the crisis, most of young people have positive expectations about the future, although the today's young are less optimistic if compared to the 1995/6 study by Helena Helve (Helve, 2002). Young people in 1995 and in 2011 were asked to complete the open-ended phrase 'Future is …' (Table 1). Answers were coded into positive, neutral, and negative statements. In 1995/6 future was seen positively by a third (33 per cent) of young people, neutral—54 per cent, negative—13 per cent.[17] Some 15 years later, in 2011 the same tendency prevails among slightly older cohorts; a fourth (25.8 per cent) expressed optimistic opinions about the future (that is less than in 1995/6).[18] There are more than a half who expressed neutral opinions about the future 54 per cent (the same as in 1995/6), and there are slightly more pessimistic young people compared to 1995/6 (19.9 per cent in 2011 and 13 per cent in 1995).

The employment situation of young people has an effect on their evaluation of the future. Working young people are slightly more optimistic, compared to those who do not work: 28 per cent and 24 per cent respectively (Table 2). Furthermore, the gap is greater between those who have full-time employment and those who are employed part-time. Full-time employed young people are more optimistic about the future, when compared to those who have part-time employment contracts: 31 per cent and 22 per cent respectively (Table 2). We should take into consideration the fact that many working young people are also studying at the same time (see the Chapter 9). There is a sharper differentiation

16 Our intention was to collect as many responses to our online questionnaire as it was possible without using a commercial online-panel and to use this quantitative data side by side with our qualitative data to explore the trends and tendencies in value systems of young people. Therefore we were restrained to use sampling without specific predetermined quotas. The only quota was age: all respondents were expected to be between eighteen and thirty years-old. Invitations to join the survey were sent to mailing lists at the recruitment services of universities and vocational schools, other recruitment services and student unions. Thus the online survey involved only conscientious respondents (those who participate because they like surveys or want to help the researchers) and the obtained data cannot be regarded as representative for all young people of Finland aged between eighteen and thirty. We observed that young women were significantly more interested than men in taking part in the survey: in our analysis we are aware that sample is more representative for young female population (N 560 or 81 per cent of all 689 respondents were women), not representative for male population (N 129 or 19 per cent of sample were men) in the same age cohort in Finland.

17 Helve's study in 1995/6 included a greater number of younger-aged people.

18 Mannheim (1972) suggested that fifteen years is a time for change of generations and appearance of a new generation.

in the moods of those who study and those who do not. Most of those young people who do not study full-time are employed. After finding a workplace they became more optimistic about their future. Young people studying are less optimistic and gave more neutral statements about the future: 25 per cent are optimistic and 55 per cent gave neutral answers. In contrast, as many as 36 per cent of those respondents who completed (or interrupted) studies see their own future in positive light (Table 2). Just as in 1995/6 the gender differences in the views of future are small and almost negligible.

Furthermore, peculiarities of the life situations of young people have broader effects, which reach far beyond the feelings of optimism and pessimism about the future. Young people who have pessimistic expectations of the future are more likely to think that skills and hard work have less influence on the employment opportunities of a person (that a 'skilful and hard-working person will always find job'; mean 3.5 for optimists and 2.7 for pessimists, on the scale where '1' is to fully disagree and '5' is to fully agree). Feelings of national identity are relatively more important for optimists ('It is a stroke of luck and privilege to be a Finn': mean 4.1 for optimists and 3.5 for pessimists), while pessimists are more distrustful towards existing political system ('There is no party representing my interests': mean 3.4 for pessimists and 2.9 for optimists; 'Parties are too distant from the problems of ordinary people': mean 3.9 for pessimists and 3.6 for optimists). Overall it appears that optimistically-minded young people tend to share relatively more conservative and materialistic values, while young sceptics tend to be more critical about the state and the existing social order.

Work and regional identity

The peculiarities of regional labour markets, as well as broader cultural factors, may have an impact on the young people's perceptions of the future. Young people living in southern Finland and the capital region, as well as young people who live in northern regions are almost equally optimistic about their personal future: 28 per cent respectively (Table 2). In contrast, young people are more pessimistic in western Finland (a region traditionally considered as more industrialised). But when the question concerns more global issues like the economic crisis, the regional perspectives are different. Young residents in western and northern regions are the least optimistic concerning macro economical situation and more than 35 per cent of young people expect that more hard times are ahead. Only in the southern Finland (including the capital region) young people have a slightly more positive view of macro economic development; 28.6 per cent say that crisis is not over (Table 3).

The majority of young people (86.6 per cent) are confident that they can find job elsewhere outside their home region. There is more confidence in replies given by young people in northern Finland; almost all (93 per cent) agree with a given statement (76.5 per cent fully agree and 16.9 per cent partly agree with this statement). On the contrary, residents of western Finland are least confident (82.2 per cent) about whether they can find a job elsewhere (Table 3).

Across the regions about two thirds of young respondents (59 per cent) are ready to search for a job abroad. Interestingly young people in northern Finland are least willing to search for a job abroad (55 per cent agree and 30 per cent disagree with the statement 'I am ready to search for a job elsewhere in the world') (Table 3). Perhaps there is lack of interest in migrating to neighbouring countries, while they assume that they can find jobs elsewhere in Finland. Compared to young people in other regions, residents of northern Finland are more ready to migrate to another region. Every third young resident of southern Finland feels a stronger attachment to their place of living and even job opportunities elsewhere wouldn't make them to move, although the majority (65.8 per cent) of young people across Finland demonstrate willingness for job-related migration (Table 3). Interviews with young temporary workers of ski centres in northern Finland conducted by Helena Helve demonstrate that despite the readiness of local young people to move and try different kinds of jobs, they also have specific emotional attachment to their home place, and northern nature is one of the most significant elements.

> In regards to the *tunturi* [skiing resort mountain] it became such a heart-touching issue. Somehow I noticed that my mind changed. I do not need the city lights around. But in the coming years it is very likely that I go to Tampere [south-western Finland] for the whole year. I believe I will find a job there too.
>
> (25-year-old man 'Risto', originally from the Tampere region.)

There is interesting intersection of optimism and special attitude towards nature. Optimism is reflected in expectations that a respondent can find work, or can be selective about what kind of work he or she does.

In the times of the growing globalisation of youth cultures, trends, media and communication, questions about the national identities of young people remain on central. Especially young residents of northern Finland feel most proud of being Finnish. Young respondents in southern and western Finland are relatively more cosmopolitan when compared to their peers in the North. In the south and west less than 70 per cent of them said that for them 'it is a stroke of luck and a privilege to be a Finn'. As many as 81 per cent of residents of northern Finland share the same sentiments, and we can say that they have stronger national identity (Table 3). Moreover the young people in the North are more oriented towards traditional values (although we did not define what the concept 'traditional values' means). In the North, some 45 per cent of respondents agreed with the statement that young people do not respect traditional values. At the same time only 34-35 per cent of respondents in southern Finland shared the same opinion (Table 3).

The interviews with young part-time workers of in Finnish Lapland help us better understand the intersections of identities of young people with regards to work values.[19] The theme of part-time employment was the central in the interview and we place it the middle of the Figure 1. When young people spoke about part-time employment, they mentioned both positive and negative experiences, spoke about connecting part-time work and their hobbies, they also spoke about how their part-time employment relates to their profession and career choices.[20] Local and global identities have very important place in the discourses about part-time employment. In the discourse about local identities, a new work-related local identify was created and shared by the young workers in this particular context of employment at the skiing centre. Local identity is actualised in the every-day contacts between young part-time workers from various regions and local residents. Young workers who came from the southern regions as well as those from northern Finland, may equally be identified by the local population as newcomers, or as one of informants described it 'brought by train'.

> Local residents call us 'Those whose were brought by train', not really distinguishing if someone came from the South, we are all similar
> (19-year-old woman 'Anna')

19 We used MaxQDA software to code interview material by Helena Helve. The code co-occurrence model created by the MaxQDA demonstrates the overlapping or co-occurring codes in the interviews and may assist us to understand the linkages between the themes of local and global identity, values, work and future.

20 Interviews were conducted predominantly with workers at the skiing centres in 2009-2010; see more in Chapter 9.

Youth and work transitions in changing social landscapes

The themes of family, future plans and education are located on the intersections of work identity, local and global identities. In almost all interviews we can see that global identities of young people are being formed by their experiences and future plans to travel in the world, to study or work abroad. Most interestingly the family discourses are placed in the middle of this triangle: between local identity, global identity and current part-time employment.

Figure 1: Part-time employment and identities. Code co-occurrence model created in MaxQDA software.

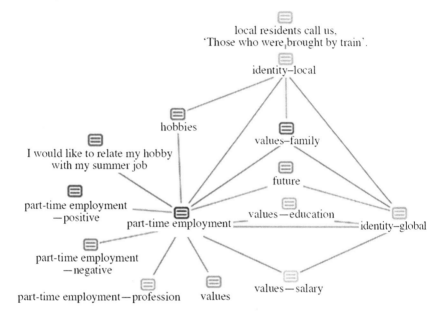

Work values

Work may have various meanings in people's lives. The majority of young people see in it strongly positive meanings, first of all related to personal professional advancement and improvement of skills; secondly, social relations and self-esteem, and also as a means to fund other activities. Only few young people see work in negative light. Furthermore, negative (unfairness, burden, routine) perceptions of work strongly correlate with materialistic treatment of work (as a means to earn money, to fund other activities). Here regional differences are also very visible. A majority of young people across Finland see work as a source for professional growth (76% in the south, 74% in the west and 69% in the north), (Figure 2). There is also a similarity in the view about work as a means to fund other activities (48%, 54%, and 52% respectively), or as obligation of a member of society (31%, 38%, and 34% in the south, west and north).

Figure 2: What work means for you?

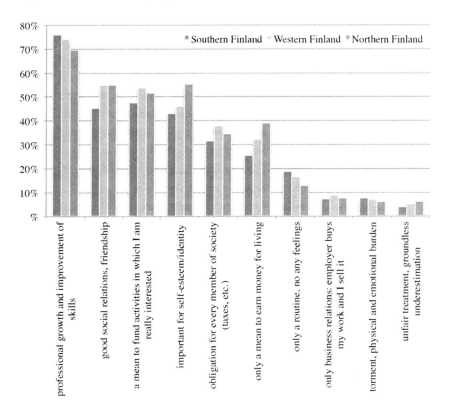

There are also some remarkable differences between young people in these three regions. Residents of capital region tend to give relatively less value to good social relations at the workplace (45 per cent), while it is more important for young people in the western and northern regions (55 per cent in each regions support this statement). It is remarkable that young people in the North more often see work as an important for self-esteem and identity (55 per cent in the North, 46 per cent in the West and 43 per cent in the capital region). Some thirty nine per cent of young people in the North ascribe to work a materialistic meaning as a means to earn money, while only twenty six per cent in the south and thirty two per cent in the west agreed with this statement. Interestingly there is also a strong negative correlation between work as a source of identity and as a source of money. Therefore we may assume that there is greater differentiation among young people in the north: there is a certain group of those who share post-materialistic values and similarly there is a distinct group that shares materialistic views.

Conclusions

The regional differences in regards to identities and work-related values are clearly visible, although the gaps between youths in the regions are not dramatic. There is a space for cultural factors that affect these differences, visible for instance in young people from northern Finland with their attitudes towards nature. But the greater impact may still have the structure of regional economies, employment opportunities and accessibility of international connections in specific regions. For instance young people in the southern and western Finland more often share cosmopolitan identity and post-materialist values.

During economic recession, increased uncertainty and risk of unemployment constitute a challenging and disequilibrating life event in which previously-made identity commitments are no longer workable and an individual may temporarily regress to earlier identity modes. It is a time when new identities and new models may appear. In this article we intentionally did not investigate work identities, instead we looked at intersections of work-related values and regional identities of young Finns. The employment situation of young people has an impact on their perceptions of future, as those have successfully found full-time job certainly see the future in a relatively more optimistic light. In the perceptions of young people's future, one can see reflections of their attitudes and experiences of participation in existing welfare and political system, negative experiences weaken the sense of national identity. Perhaps a grown public support for populist political leaders (for instance, Timo Soini, leader of the True Finns party) is an attempt to express this feeling of national identity and dissatisfaction with traditional political system.

Table 1: Respondents were asked to complete the phrase 'Future is ...'. Their answers were coded according to their positive, neutral or negative meaning. Studies in 1995/6 and in 2011.

'Future is ...' (%)	1995/6	2011
Positive	33	25.8
Neutral	54	54.3
Negative	13	19.9

Table 2 *Respondents were asked to complete the phrase 'Future is ...'. Their answers were coded according to their positive, neutral or negative meaning.*

	'Future is ...'—positive	neutral	'Future is ...' negative
Employment			
Employed	27.7%	53.8%	18.5%
Not employed	24.1%	54.7%	21.2%
Type of employment			
Full-day	30.8%	48.4%	20.9%
Half of a day	50.0%	25.0%	25.0%
Less than half of a day	22.0%	60.4%	17.7%
Other arrangement	32.7%	52.7%	14.5%
Studies			
Study	24.7%	55.5%	19.8%
Do not study	36.8%	42.1%	21.1%
Gender			
Men	21.6%	56.9%	21.6%
Women	26.8%	53.7%	19.6%
Regions			
Southern Finland	28.5%	52.7%	18.8%
Western Finland	20.5%	54.1%	25.4%
Northern Finland	28.2%	58.8%	13.0%
Total	25.8%	54.3%	19.9%

Table 3: Work related statements and regional distribution (N=689 respondents).

	Southern Finland	Western Finland	Northern Finland	Total
'Economic crisis is not over, there are hard times ahead.'				
Yes	28.6%	36.9%	35.5%	32,6 %
Don't know	48.8%	45.8%	47.8%	47,7%
No	22.6%	17.3%	16.7%	19,7 %
'It is likely that I will find job elsewhere outside my home region.'				
Yes	86.4%	82.2%	93.4%	86.6%
Don't know	8.7%	11.2%	5.9%	8.9%
No	4.8%	6.5%	.7%	4.5%
'I am ready to search for a job elsewhere in the world.'				
Yes	59.9%	59.6%	55.1%	58.9%
Don't know	17.2%	16.0%	14.7%	16.2%
No	22.9%	24.4%	30.1%	24.9%
'I feel attached to the place where I live so that I wouldn't move anywhere else even after a job.'				
Yes	29.8%	24.1%	19.7%	25.9%
Don't know	9.6%	8.8%	4.4%	8.3%
No	60.5%	67.1%	75.9%	65.8%
'It is a stroke of luck and privilege to be a Finn.'				
Yes	68 %	67 %	81 %	70 %
Don't know	21 %	23 %	10 %	19 %
No	11 %	10 %	9 %	11 %
'Young people don't respect traditional values'				
Yes	34 %	35 %	45 %	37 %
Don't know	19 %	29 %	20 %	22 %
No	47 %	36 %	34 %	41 %

Chapter 9

From higher education to working life: Work values of young Finns in changing labour markets

Helena Helve

Introduction

I have studied young people over three decades and during these years we have experienced two economic recessions in Finland: in the early 1990s and the most recent one which started in 2008.[21] My perspective on these matters has been coloured by my longitudinal study concerning the world view formation of young people who grew up in the 1970s in a suburb of Helsinki, the capital of Finland. Now they are middle-aged parents with their own children. I have also studied young people's values and attitude shifts from 1989 to 2011. This has involved young people from sixteen to thirty-year-olds from urban and rural areas. During this period Finland experienced intense economic changes, moving in 1989 from a state of economic prosperity where the per capita GDP (gross domestic product) was the third highest in the world (after Japan and Switzerland) to the great recession of the 1990s after the collapse of one of our former largest trading partners, the Soviet Union, to the joining of European Union in 1995, and the explosive growth of the Nokia corporation and other IT businesses in its wake in 1990s.

In the 2000s we have faced a global economic recession, with rather different symptoms from the one in 1990s, when unemployment, especially youth unemployment, came to be a regular feature of capitalist societies, and when a new underclass of the unemployed was growing, especially in Western European countries. These global changes are not affecting all citizens in the same way. Migrants and ethnic minorities and young people living in remote rural areas are most vulnerable in contemporary labour markets (Fangen, Fossan and Mohn, 2010).

The welfare state supports young Finns during their transition from education to work life by providing health insurance, social insurance and free higher

---

21 This chapter uses partly the analysis in the article Helve, H., (2012) Transitions and shift in work attitudes, values and future orientations of young Finns, in Hahn-Bleibtreu, M., and Molgat, M., (eds.) *Youth Policy in a Changing World: From Theory to Practice*, pp. 134-158 Leverkusen: Budrich.

education. Since 1996 unemployed people under twenty years-old, with no vocational education, who enter the labour market for the first time, have no longer been granted labour market support, unless they have actively applied for education or participated in a labour market policy measure such as practical training. The right to support will be restored when the applicant shows that he or she has completed a vocational qualification. At the beginning of 1997, the reform was extended to cover those under twenty-five. A young person's living allowance can also be reduced if he or she has refused education. Youth workshops offer training and work practice to unemployed young people under twenty-five years-old. A new Finnish governmental tool from 2012 for combat youth unemployment and exclusion includes a social guarantee for young people. It guarantees every school-leaver a place in the upper secondary school, in vocational education/training, in apprenticeship training, in a youth workshop, in rehabilitation or by other means. The aim is that every young person gains a post-compulsory qualification; some seventeen per cent of the current under-twenty-five age group has none. The aim for the Government is that by the end of this decade over ninety per cent of the twenty to twenty- four year-olds will have post-compulsory qualifications. (Ministry of Education and Culture, 2012)

The Youth Division in the Ministry of Education and Culture is responsible for the workshops, which should offer a place for young people to learn life skills, grow into adulthood and get hands-on experience of work, encouraging and helping them to seek further training.[22] One of the main policy aims over the decades has been to give everyone the opportunity to study. Almost 90% of the group aged twenty-five to thirty-four had attained at least upper secondary education. In international comparisons the level of education of the young Finns is relatively high. As an example PISA, the OECD's Programme for International Student Assessment 2009, has shown that Finland is among those countries where students reach best reading abilities (OECD, 2009b).[23]

The transition from education to work of young people today is often a time of change, waiting and uncertainty. It has also become a political question in Europe. The EU Strategy 2020s initiatives on youth and employment (i.e. 'Youth on the Move' and 'New Skills for New Jobs') are committed to improve qualifications and skills of young people in order to accelerate their access to the labour market. There are new promotions of a more proactive approach

---

22 In the Finnish Youth Act young people means those under twenty-nine years old.
23 The partner economy Shanghai, China shows the highest average reading performance in PISA 2009, followed by the OECD countries Korea and Finland, the partner economy Hong Kong, China and the partner country Singapore (OECD, 2009b).

by tangible recommendations (e.g., the 'youth guarantee'). (See European Commission, 2010.)

Young people in changing labour markets

There are problems of short-term precarious jobs and segmented labour markets, of a limited entitlement and coverage by social security systems. In Finland recent public discourse and studies of the sociological aspects of work have raised the issues of short-term employment and longer transition periods (e.g. Manninen and Luukannel 2006; Palanko-Laaka 2005). This new short-term employment phenomenon is not comparable to traditional part-time or temporary employment, which was often seasonal or productivity based (Sutela et al. 2001). Short-term employment in the public sector, particularly in nursing, teaching and social services, is a new trend, typified by the 'chaining' (i.e. repeated renewing) of short-term employment contracts, by a high level of education among employees and by low unemployment. The issue is therefore no longer confined to 'typically' uncertain careers as such as art, new media and communications. Many well educated young people seem to value short-time jobs and they are not ready to bind themselves to life-long careers (Sell, 2005).

In 1997 the percentage of the Finnish labour force comprised of those under twenty-five years-old was only 8.1%, the lowest in Europe (see Table 1). Most Finns under twenty-five are still in some form of education at that age. Even so, unemployment rates among Finnish young people were very high by European standards. By August, 2009 Finnish unemployment rates had come down to below average for EU countries, but they are still far too high for a healthy economic system.

The Table 1. shows that during the last fifteen years in fifteen EU countries youth unemployment rates have grown on average in most of the countries. Youth unemployment improved from 2009 to 2011 in Belgium, Sweden, Luxembourg, Germany, Austria, and became worse in Finland, France, Greece, Italy, Spain, Portugal, Great Britain, Netherlands, Denmark and Ireland. The global youth unemployment rate stood at 12.6% in 2010, up from 11.8% in 2007, but down slightly from 12.8% in 2009 (ILO, 2011a). However, the labour force participation among youth was strongly affected by the global economic crisis.

Table 1: *Labour force participation and unemployment percentages among 15–24-year olds in European Union Countries in 1997, 2009 and 2011.*

	Youth as % of the labour force	Youth unemployment rate		
Country:	1997	1997	2009	2011 (month 12)
Finland	8.1	27.4	18.8	19.9
France	8.4	28.9	22.3	23.8
Belgium	8.8	22.9	21.3	20.07
Greece	9.1	31.0	24.2	47.2 (month 10)
Sweden	9.2	21.1	24.2	22.9
Italy	10.4	33.5	24.9	31.0
Luxembourg	10.8	9.1	19.1	15.2
Germany	11.0	9.9	10.5	7.8
Spain	12.4	41.9	33.6	48.7
Portugal	12.8	16.7	19.6	30.8
Austria	14.7	6.0	9.0	8.2
Great Britain	14.9	15.5	17.9	22.3 (month 10)
Netherlands	15.3	11.5	6.0	8.6
Denmark	17.1	10.6	8.9	14.7
Ireland	17.2	18.2	21.5	29,0

(*European Commission, 2009, first quarter; and European Commission, 2012, youth unemployment statistics, 2011; Helsingin Sanomat, 19.3.1999, A 14.*)

During economic downturns, young people are worse off than the older age groups because they have less work experience than older workers. This issue has implications for the school to work transition when young people look for their first job. They often face extended periods of joblessness and many may stop seeking employment opportunities and decide to drop out of the labour market altogether at which point they are no longer defined as officially unemployed. Many choose to study or work in volunteer work. Many young people have to accept part-time jobs in order to get money for living. (UN, 2011; World Youth Report.)

Shifts in work life

Many unskilled young people with lower education are working in precarious non-standard employment which is poorly paid, insecure, unprotected and cannot support a household. In recent decades there has been a dramatic increase in precarious work everywhere due to such factors as globalisation, the shift from the manufacturing sector to the service sector and the spread of information technology. These changes have created a new economy which demands flexibility in the workplace and, as a result, they have caused the decline of the standard employment relationship and a dramatic increase in precarious work.

An important aspect of precarious work is its gendered nature, as women have been over-represented in this type of work. Precarious work is associated with the following types of employment: part-time employment, self-employment, fixed- term work, temporary work, on-call work, home workers, and telecommuting. All of these forms of employment are related in that they depart from the standard employment relationship (full-time, continuous work with one employer). Each form of precarious work may offer its own challenges but they all share the same disadvantages: low wages, few benefits, lack of collective representation, and little to no job security. The process whereby work becomes more precarious is very common among immigrants. From a gendered perspective it is more common in female labour markets than in male labour markets. (Miettinen 2007.)

The inability to find a job carries psychological costs, causes frustration and depression, and undermines motivation. Youth unemployment is also often associated with such social problems as violence, delinquency, alcohol and drug abuse, crime, and suicide (UNICEF, 2000).

Identity formation and future horizon

Many factors mentioned above are affecting young people's transitions to adulthood and these are also related to their values, worldviews and identity formation, which is connected to the concept of future horizon. It characterises the young person's sense of prospects for the future (Côté et al. 2008). The ability to develop a broad future horizon can be undermined by the personal and social vulnerabilities associated with 'identity anxiety', a psychological state that can inhibit personal and moral development (Côté et al. 2008, 77-78; see also Stålsett 2006).

Education can predict that certain family backgrounds produce different levels of academic achievement, which in turn produces different levels of academic engagement (Salmela-Aro 2009; cf. Chapter 11 in this volume). Optimally, family influences are positive, but some are problematic and along with other negative influences can produce alienation and under- achievement, which in turn lead to disengagement/dropout and ultimately to socio-economic exclusion.

This study exploits the future horizon and identity formation model (Côté et al.; 2008, 78). The hypothesis is that prior experiences will broaden or narrow the future horizon that a person perceives for him/herself and that this perceived horizon is anchored in the subjective realm of identity. Those with broader horizons should have more positive assessments of the returns in terms of the relationship between benefits and costs because they can anticipate their future involvement in target environments. In contrast, those with narrower horizons will have less positive assessments because of a blockage in their ability to visualise their involvement in environments that are sensed as 'foreign.'

Those with broader future horizons should thus have more positive perceptions of the potential returns on investments of time, effort, and money devoted to achieving certain goals, and an important source of these perceptions would be parental influences: parents who themselves have broader horizons should promote broader horizons in their children as they grow up.

Conversely, a source of a narrowing effect on horizons may come from parents with low levels of educational and occupational attainment. In addition to having less of a basis from role models for estimating cost and benefits for their own futures, those from these backgrounds may be particularly prone to an 'identity anxiety' (a non-monetary 'personal' cost of change in one's life) because they do not perceive a good fit for themselves in current and future educational or work settings and they lack the level of personal agency necessary to rectify that problem themselves. Moreover, they might have deep-seated apprehensions that they will experience tensions with parents and peers and that they will have to change in ways that are unacceptable to these relatives and acquaintances (Côté et al., 2008; 77-78).

Following Côté et al. (2008, 78) the narrow horizons are more likely to include 'local goals' while broad horizons should include more 'global goals'. Thus, those with narrow horizons will not want to study or work far from where they grew up, while those with broad horizons will have goals that take them away from their local comfort zone into the world at large. The future horizons of young people in higher education will be analysed later in this chapter.

The research questions and data

This chapter places its focus on the following research questions: 1) How the students of higher education start their working life in the age groups of 18-22, 23-25 and 26-30? Are they combining employment and studies? What kind of jobs do they have and how many employers have they had? 2) What kind of attitudes do they have towards education and work and how these are influenced by parents and friends? Do they have a short or broad future horizon, is it local or global, positive or negative? 3) How is short-term employment affecting attitudes, lifestyles and worldviews of young adults?

The in-depth narrative interviews and ethnographic observations made over an eight-week period were gathered in 2009-2010 among twenty (N=20) young people from 17-30 year olds working temporarily in tourism in Lapland. Almost all of them were skilled workers. They were professionals with degrees such as Bachelor of Hospitality, restaurant workers and managers, skiing instructors, wilderness nature guides, and so on. The survey data was gathered on-line between November 15, 2010 and February 15, 2011 on the recruitment websites of the universities and polytechnics (universities of applied sciences) from those in higher education seeking jobs. Together 689 young people from different parts of Finland completed the questionnaire, which included attitude scales from my earlier value studies (1989, 1992-93 and 1995-96; Helve 1993 and 2002), work life scales by EVA (a policy and pro-market think tank financed by the Finnish business community.); the Council of Economic Organisations in Finland (Haavisto, 2010),[24] and future horizon scales by James Côté based on the identity horizon model (Côté et al. 2008, see also Côté and Levine 2002). The attitude scales measured attitudes towards education, working life and society, and the future orientation and meaning of life. Basic socio-demographic data were also gathered.[25]

The on-line survey was targeted at the students of higher education in the process of transition from education to the work life. The hypothesis was that the recruiting websites of the universities/polytechnics are the first places to encounter those searching for a job. Students of higher education are

24 EVA has gathered data on Finnish attitudes and values on a regular basis from 1984. During these years EVA has acquired an extensive and comparable material on the change of values and attitudes in Finnish society. The studies have investigated Finns' attitudes towards politics and politicians, society's structure, the market economy, entrepreneurship, environmental protection, work-life related issues as well as international matters, for example the European Union and Finnish foreigner policy (see www. eva.fi/en/hankkeet/arvo-ja-asennetutkimukset/2425/).

25 Arseniy Svynarenko analyses the same data in the previous chapter 8. 'Regional identities, future expectations and work values.'

experienced Internet users. In this case the students of higher education were very conscientious when filling in the questionnaire with 174 variables. There was very little missing data. The long survey has been divided into several parts in terms of topics. The intention was to collect as many responses to the online questionnaire as was possible without using a commercial online-panel and use this quantitative data side by side with the qualitative data to explore the trends and tendencies in work values of young people. The only quota was age: all respondents were expected to be between 18-30 year olds.

Invitations to join the survey were sent to the mailing lists at recruitment services of universities and polytechnics, and their student unions. The obtained data cannot be regarded as representative for all young people of Finland in higher education aged between 18-30 year olds. Of the respondents, 81% were females (N=560) and 19% were men (N=129). It can mean that the questionnaire interested females more than males and that the females were following the universities' recruiting websites more closely than males. Also in my earlier studies of the world views (Helve 1993) and values of young people (Helve 1996 and 2002) females were over-represented. As a result this sample of young Finns in higher education is more representative for the young females than for the males.

Starting the working life in higher education

This study supports the Finnish student survey 2010 (Saarenmaa et al., 2010; 50-53) about the high proportion of students in higher education who study and work at the same time (46. 1%, N= 627). Mostly they studied and worked part-time (56.2%) but also every fifth (21.5%) worked full-time and studied at the same time. A tenth of those who had finished their studies were unemployed and searching jobs; 85.4% of those who did not study worked already full-time. (See Figure 1.)

Figure 1: Cross tabulation "Do you study?" and "Do you work full time, ½ time, part time, or other arrangement" (total 689 respondents) %.

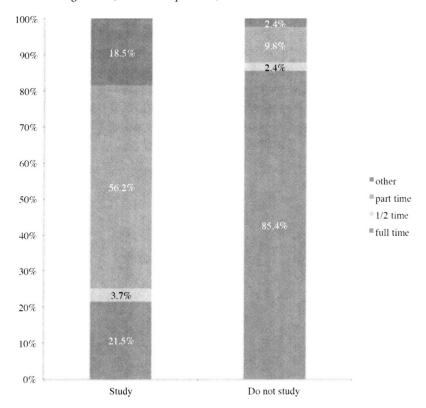

The study shows that almost all of 18-22 and 23-25 year old respondents were enrolled in education (95% and 96% respectively). Even 84.7 % studied still in the age group of 26-30. The great majority (74.5%) of employed students in the youngest cohort (18-22) has part time jobs, every fifth (21%) employed student has other work arrangements, most likely hour-based or occasional employment. Older students (aged 23-25) tend to have more stable jobs, about one in ten (11.6%) has a full time contract, two thirds of students (63%) have part time contracts, and 21% have other work arrangements. The rate of full-time employment increases with the age of studying students, among 26-30 year olds 36.8% have full time contracts and 45.6% have part time contracts, only 14% have other arrangements. The Finnish student survey 2010 shows that of all students 30% work regularly and 30% occasionally during terms (Saarenmaa et al., 2010; 50-53).

Political discussions in Finland in recent years have been about how to get young people earlier into higher education, how to shorten the time young people spend in education and how to get them earlier into the labour markets. This study shows that even almost every third (28.5%) of the youngest respondents already combine studies with work. Among 23-25 year old students the number of employed is even greater: 46% of students in this age cohort combine studies with work. By the end of their professional training students become engaged in the labour market. More than a half (60.4%) of 26-30 year olds still both study and work, and over 31 year olds employment reached 72.2 per cent. (See Figure 2.)

Figure 2: Cross tabulation "Are you employed?" and age groups (total 689 respondents).

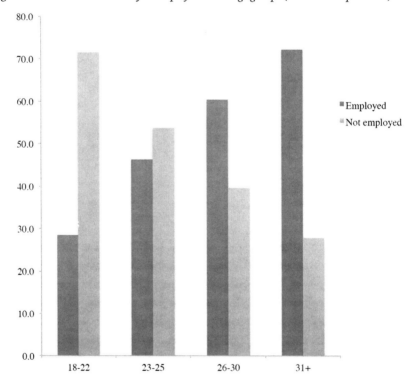

In the younger age cohort 18-22 some 69% of young people already had one to four employers, a quarter (25.6 %) had from five to nine employers. About half of young people in the age of 23-25 and 26-30 have had from five to nine (45.1% and 50.2% respectively) employers. A very significant fact is that 16.5%

of 26-30 year olds have already had more than ten employers (13.3% 10-14 employers, 2%—15-19, 1.2% over 20)., (See Figure 3.)

Figure 3: "How many employers have you had?" and age groups (total 689 respondents).

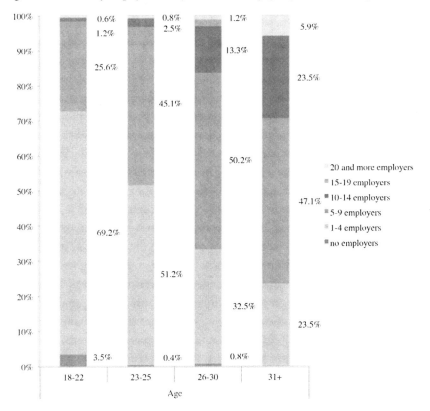

Finnish young people start their higher education later than young people in many other countries. Two in three students (circa 159,000 students) have had a break of at least one year from studies (before or during current studies). The Finnish student survey 2010 shows that 42% of polytechnic students and 38% of university students spent the gap year working in Finland. 26% of students have or have had a study right in some other higher education programme besides their current one.[26] (Saarenmaa et al., 2010; 21-23.).

So we can say that in Finland higher education students having a couple of gap years before the beginning of their studies are typical. That is why the Finnish

---

26 This was most common among medical students, over half of whom had gained a study right in some other field of education.

higher education policy has been concerned about the delay in the beginning of studies as well as the extended duration of studies. In any event, this study of young people in higher education shows that almost half of them studied and worked at the same time. Working became more common in older cohorts. It means that they might progress more slowly in their studies than was targeted. The reasons for slow progress are often employment but there are also many other different life situations and various personal reasons (Saarenmaa et al., 2010; 50-53).

Finnish higher education students enter the labour market already while studying. A third of the eighteen to twenty-two year olds combine already studies with work. Many of them may have had a gap year before they reached the university. They might have continued the job they had during the gap year part-time when starting their studies. The number of those who are combining studies with work is increasing in older cohorts. By the end of their professional training, Finnish students in higher education become engaged in the labour market. More than a half of 26-30 year olds still both study and work.

The time spent at paid work varies according to the age of the student and the stage of studies. Working while studying slows down higher education students' progress. Especially for students of universities of applied sciences (polytechnics) the major reasons could be the reform allowing under twenty-five year-olds not in education or employment to get reduced living allowance if they refuse to attend education or training. This coercion towards education could be the reason for poor study motivation or a sense of having chosen the wrong field of education.

Even though the time spent in education is long in Finland, young people have been able to work and study at the same time getting important work experience. They have a wide range of experience from several employers. At the beginning of their studies young people work mostly part-time. The money they receive gives them an independent life from their parents. Also Finnish young people move out of their family homes quite early on because of government education allowances. These factors have given them independence sooner, as is the case in all the Nordic countries compared to their counterparts in southern Europe and post-communist eastern Europe. In the Anglo-Saxon liberal countries the policy has been to get young people to the labour market early and to economic independence as soon as possible (McNeish and Loncle, 2003; Walther and Pohl, 2005; Walther, 2006; Walther et al., 2006; Pohl and Walther, 2007). In a comparison between transitions from education to the labour market, Finnish young people find it easier after their studies to get the jobs which are funding their studies than, for example, young people in Britain, where young people arrive on to the labour market earlier without work experience (Lindberg 2008).

Future horizon and attitudes of students of higher education

The on-line survey used the attitude statements by James Côté translated into Finnish. Respondents were asked to select how strongly they agree or disagree with the statements on a five point scale. Strongly agree and Agree were categorized in the Figure 4 to Yes, Neither Agree Nor Disagree to the category Difficult to say and Disagree or Strongly Disagree to the category No. For example to the statement *There are probably many job opportunities for me in other parts of the country away from where I was raised* almost all of the respondents (86.6 %) selected Strongly agree or Agree. See the Figure 4.

Figure 4: Future horizon attitude scales.

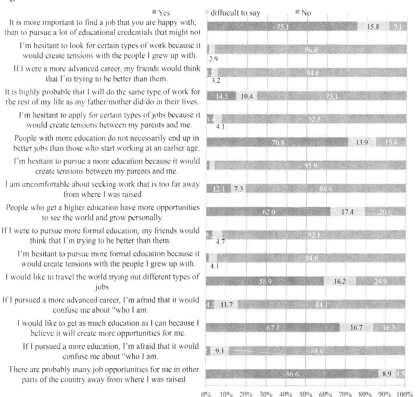

Over half of the respondents (67.1 %, N=683) would like to get as much education as they can because they believe it will create more opportunities for them. Well over half of them thought that people who get a higher education have more opportunities to see the world and grow personally (62%, N= 684). Most of them (70.8%, N= 684) agreed with the claim *People with more education do not necessarily end up in better jobs than those who start working at an earlier age.* This attitude might get support from the employment situation. From the new jobs under half are permanent (Statistics Finland, 2011b). The number of temporary jobs has increased from 2009 to 2010 by 4%.[27] It is no longer sure that young academics who have studied many years could get a better job, at least not a permanent job, than those peers who have started to work at an earlier age.

Almost all (88.6 %, N=683) disagreed with the claim *If I pursued more education, I'm afraid that it would confuse me about 'who I am'.* They (94.6 %, N=684) disagreed also mostly with the claim *I'm hesitant to pursue more formal education because it would create tensions with the people I grew up with* and most (92.1 %, N=682) disagreed with the claim *If I were to pursue more formal education, my friends would think that I'm trying to be better than them.* Almost all (86.6%, N=685) believed that they have many job opportunities in other parts of the country away from where they were raised, and every second (58.9%, N=684) would like to travel the world trying out different types of jobs. They did not experience tensions with parents and peers, and for most (75.1 %, N=683) it is highly probable that he/she will not do the same type of work for the rest of his/her life as father/mother did/do in their lives. A more advanced career compared to friends would not make them (94.6 %, N=683) think that they try to be better than their friends. Almost all of the studied university students (96%, N=684) agreed with the claim *It is more important to find a job that you are happy with, than to pursue a lot of educational credentials that might not lead anywhere.*

We can summarise that Finnish young people in higher education have a positive attitude towards education and work. They have a broad horizon for the future, including 'global goals'. They do not feel uncomfortable searching for a job far away from their home environments. They want to see the world and grow personally. They are ready to travel the world in order to try different types of jobs. These young people seem to have a lot of self-confidence, which may result either from an academic education or home upbringing. They seem not

---

27 Women are working temporarily more often than men. In 2010, women and men in new jobs of limited duration accounted for about 62% and 49% respectively of the totals (Statistics Finland, 2011b).

to be influenced by their parents or their friends' education or work attitudes and values. It should in any case be remembered that these results might skew the gender balance of respondents (81% of the respondents were women).

It was not possible to see a connection between the narrowing effect on horizons by parents and the low levels of educational and occupational attainment. Young people in higher education were ready to change their life and future educational or work settings. Their attitude to the future was positive and had a broad future horizon.

Short-term employment and attitudes, lifestyles and worldviews of young adults

Although Finnish young people are joining the labour force armed with more education than their parents had, and with a broad and optimistic future horizon, the status of many entering the labour market involves greater risk and uncertainty. Many factors point to how this process may not be functioning as quickly and easily as in the past: young people take more time to make the transition to employment, fall back on jobs for which they are often overqualified and receive less pay, and delay forming a family of their own. In a context where the economy is undergoing rapid transformations that favour the expansion of jobs requiring advanced education, those young people are particularly at risk who are without at least a secondary education certificate.

Some young people seem already to be used to the lifestyle of short-term employment. For example many of the interviewed professionally skilled young people who are working temporarily in tourism in Lapland seem to value the lifestyle of short-term jobs, and they are not ready to commit themselves to life-long careers. Below is a quote from Anna, a nineteen-year-old girl who works in a ski shop at a skiing resort. I was asking her about her future expectations:

> *Anna*: I don't know, I am quite satisfied here. I like this kind of seasonal [i.e., temporary] work, even if I can't be sure if I'll get another job after this. I like being up on this mountain [a skiing resort in Lapland]. When others go south for the summer I like to stay here. I haven't done anything else than these mountain jobs. This place has its own magic. I'll be coming back here … I think I'll always find some sort of work here, even if there are a lot of unemployed people … I don't think they've really tried to find work … I know unemployed people who live off of what they get from unemployment … I don't like it that we pay our taxes for these people. I

am annoyed by their attitudes ... I found this job myself from the website at an employment office.

Anyway it is difficult to commit to long-term relationships as twenty five year old Jaana relates:

> ... so here there are many such as nature guides, waitresses or ticket vendors who might have boyfriends but it is very difficult to find anyone for a longer romantic relationship. So we have here what we can find [temporary relationships].
> I was dating last time when I was here but it broke up soon after I left ... here we have our own lifestyle. If you meet someone here you live here together but when you go away you will forget it.

That is why it is hard to find couples in permanent relationships among temporary workers, as the following interviewee confirms:

> Well, at least I do not know anyone here. Most of them are just singles ..., but there's also some coming here as couples to work. They will both work here in the mountains. I have met beautiful couples here, when they both can be wild and free, but still they have their own relationship.

It is difficult also to build up one's own home and plan the future, as twenty-six year old Petri described:

> I cannot build up my own home. I have never had a permanent own home after I left the mother's home [his parents were divorced when he was a child]. However, it is always home, but I'd like my own stuff, and everything else. I don't know even what my next work is after this ...

Young temporary workers tend not to be committed to a relationship. Instead of permanent relationships, social networks with co-workers with the same lifestyle are more important. Even though the young people in higher education had an optimistic future orientation, the biographies of the interviewed temporarily working young people seem to show a loss of the perspective of life-course, and the dimension of continuity associated with it as Lassi (twenty-two year-old) responded:

After all, it is a bit, not ever being able to make bigger plans, I don't know what it is going up [the next job to go] ... people [like me] will always be a bit half-way, especially when on the road ...

The narratives of these young people have fragmented into episodes—each of which has its own past and future. Many still have other professional ambitions for the future. Adult life for many of the interviewed young people does not necessarily mean a family of their own. Friends are more important. Temporary, short-term work gives many of them the possibility to be active in their hobbies with their friends. For example, in skiing resorts in Lapland, young temporary workers get free passes to the ski slopes. For many of them the future is seen as cycle from one winter season to the next. During the summer, when they are unemployed, they travel and live with their parents, who help them if needed. They have formed their own individual concepts of time. This is also part of their identity construction and plurality of identities (Wyn and White, 1997). For older generations working time has coordinated social rhythms with biographies that are constructed around this linear time: eight hours work, eight hours leisure time with family and friends, and eight hours for sleep each day. Now young people are living virtual lives, where time and space have lost meaning in their world views. To them, youth does not necessarily mean preparation for adulthood, work and family life anymore.

Discussion

In the Finnish Youth Barometer of 2009 (Myllyniemi 2009, 107) nine out of ten, fifteen to twenty-five year-olds believed that education is helpful in finding a job. Trust in education among young Finns is still at a high level, and even unemployed young people seem to be optimistic, too, when arguing for education as a means of improving their possibilities of entering the labour market. Yet new flexible types of work for young people, which are temporary, short-term and/or part-time, are changing young people's values. Italian sociologist Carmen Leccardi (2006) says that there is a crisis of time experience which can be seen in young people's understanding of time. Finnish researcher Matti Kamppinen (2000) has written about social transformations which involve changes in people's socially constructed temporal profiles; drawing distinctions between cyclical, linear, absolute and relative conceptions of time. It could be predicted that, in this new information society, with the appropriation of information technology, our conceptions of time will radically be transformed. The Digital

Revolution means a new generation of cell phones: wireless Internet, iPads, handheld computers, and social media which allow us to work anywhere, anytime, 24/7. However, Kamppinen refutes the claim that in the digital information society we are moving into a timeless time where being online and real time are ideals everyone strives for, where modern people work in computer-based jobs and where individual life projects have lost their temporal order. Instead, he concludes that time is transformed in the digital information society but not radically, and that our lives and related processes are temporally ordered even though the processes are speeded up and reshuffled.

Have these changes, brought on by the digital information society and virtual environments, influenced young people's life-styles and values, and their transitions into adulthood? Young people still socialise on the institutional level in their families and in education; and there is still a linear time of transition into adulthood, from school to work.

Young people live under different conditions in different parts of the world. For example, in many European countries such as Finland the transition into working life no longer takes place as soon as education is finished, but rather it can begin while one is still in education or much later. Nor does moving away from one's parents lead to starting a family of one's own in many cases. Young people have greater freedom to live life on their own terms than before, but possibilities of living in a traditional fashion (going straight from school to work and then starting a family) have become weaker.

Impacts of shifts in work are changing the attitudes, values and world views of young people. We have some evidence from interviews with young people working with short-term employment contracts, or who are temporary unemployed, that they are not doing much long-term planning. Leisure activities, such as skiing during winter, are very important to them. These leisure activities and hobbies have become important means of building up their identities and value worlds. Labour markets are structured so that younger generations have to be satisfied with temporary unemployment and short-term low paid employment. Institutionalised society will lose this young generation if they are not brought into labour markets. Yet the young people interviewed gave us the message that they could be happy in the sort of work which we older folk would see as precarious. I think, therefore, we should have flexible jobs for young people and we should accept their viewpoints regarding temporary jobs, an uncertain future and an extended present.

These tentative signals of new attitudes toward working life with new lifestyles, relationships and even ethical principles have a two-part relationship with young people's world views, influencing the way they balance themselves between a collective world view and an individual one. In their world view, past, present and future each have individual/cyclic and collective/institutionalised/linear temporal dimensions (cf. Leccardi 2006). In this process of world view formation, life planning and future planning in the post-modern risk society (Beck, 1992) seem to be in crisis (cf. Leccardi 2006). In the world views of young people I have interviewed, the future is unpredictable and subject to change. Flexible and temporary world views help them to accept temporary jobs and even to value them as part of their lifestyles. They seem to want to keep their future unknown. My interpretation is that many of today's young people in Finland are in no hurry to reach adulthood. Maybe we should listen to young people who, in their transition to work life, emerge from a vague and prolonged youth and stumble on towards a vague and prolonged adulthood, perhaps even an arrested adulthood (see Côté 2000).

Establishing a family and other long-term commitments require a positive trust in the future. Also, life management is based on having a regular income, a steady social situation and a predictable future (see Kuure 2006). In these respects, having a future orientation is particularly important for young people going through developmental and transitional periods where they should be preparing themselves for future challenges.

I will end the chapter with a quotation from the World Youth Report (UN, 2011).

> Young people themselves are crucial stakeholders in the pursuit of decent and productive work for all. They are rights-holders and active participants in society, in addition to representing the future global workforce; often times, they are also pioneers. Yet, too frequently, their voices go unheard and their positive and negative experiences and viewpoints unshared, particularly with decision-makers.

Part 4: New career aspirations, life chances and risks

Chapter 10

Youth transitions and wellbeing: The impact of austerity on black youths living in urban 'black neighbourhoods'

Tracey Reynolds

Introduction

This chapter will examine the views and experiences of black youths living in three socially deprived areas of London in order to examine the way in which they recognise the term 'black neighbourhood' as a resource in these austere times. The analysis shows that these neighbourhoods represent urban spaces through which a range of social capital resources are generated including ties of reciprocal ties of trust, solidarity and civic participation. They also provide black youths with a sense of belonging and as such these neighbourhoods are intrinsically valued by them. Research highlights that central to an individuals' overall sense of well-being is the extent to which they perceive a sense of belonging and bonds of trust within their communities (Ryan and Deci, 2001). While the literature suggests that economic hardship adversely affects adults' wellbeing and their community relationships, still little is still known about the impact of economic hardship on youths' wellbeing and their perceptions of community and neighbourhood. This issue is particularly pertinent because under the current economic downturn in Britain youths are one of the main groups to be adversely affected as result of high youth unemployment rates and rising numbers of young people not in any form of education or training. With regards to black youths recent figures indicate that nearly fifty per cent of them are unemployed and this figure is even higher among black youths living in urban neighbourhoods, sometimes colloquially referred to as 'black neighbourhoods'.

The chapter draws from the research findings of two projects. The first project entitled, 'Caribbean Families, Social Capital and Young People's Diasporic Identities' was one a number of projects within Families and Social Capital ESRC Research Group at London South Bank University (see www.lsbu.ac.uk/families). During 2002-2006 in-depth interviews were conducted with thirty second and third generation Caribbean young people (aged between sisteen to thirty years-old) living in Birmingham, London, Manchester and Nottingham. Further interviews took place with fifty of their kinship/family members in Britain and the Caribbean (Barbados, Guyana and Jamaica) across all age groups. The research project explored how family and kinship bonds operate in the lives of Caribbean young people and their construction of ethnic identity and belonging. The interviews focused on the areas of family and kinship relationships, friendship networks, neighbourhood and community participation, and also investigated how social capital operated as an important social resource within ethnic identity formation. Also highlighted in the analysis was the significance of transnational and cross-cultural kinship networks in shaping ethnic identity (see Reynolds, 2004; 2006a and b).

The second project 'RAW' (2008) involved research and evaluation of five community-based youth programmes spread across the London boroughs of Brent, Haringey and Lambeth. The youth programmes were designed to explore emotional and psychological 'barriers' that prevent black young people of Caribbean/Black British heritage or parentage achieving personal and educational success. Parenting support classes provided a second dimension to the programmes, and these programmes developed support services for parents and children experiencing educational underachievement in schools and also involved in anti-social and criminal behaviour. Expert representatives from personal development, education, youth services and community policing were involved in this study. Whilst the evaluation part of the project focused on assessing programme processes and outcomes of the programmes, the research concentrated on exploring young people's understandings of self and their relationships within their family, local neighbourhoods, and wider ethnic community networks. In total twenty qualitative interviews were undertaken with young people age sisteen to twenty-one years-old (n=18) and their parents (n=12) (Reynolds and Briggs, 2008).

Conceptualising black youths in the 'community'

Broadly speaking much of the research exploring youths in urban city contexts has tended to focus on young people as active agents of social change; and also the social resources and relationships utilised by young people to achieve build independence and their aspirations in urban spaces (Tienda and Wilson, 2002; Briggs, 2010). A second counter-narrative has been to highlight the challenges encountered by young people as a result of urban poverty and deprivation; and also the risk-taking behaviour of inner-city youths (Browning et al., 2004;

Collinson, 1996). An area of research that has received comparatively limited attention is the way that urban spaces can represent social resources for young people in the formation of their ethnic (and racial) identity. In the UK, London is a multi-cultural city that is comprised of urban neighbourhoods and communities that are racially, ethnically, culturally and socio-economically heterogeneous. Some commentators have argued that such 'super-diversity' (Vertovec, 2007) should be celebrated. It is suggested that urban spaces reduce the barriers to social integration, encouraging 'mixing' and the emergence of 'cultural hybridity' among inner-city youths (Alexander, 2007). In addition, second and third generation migrant and minority ethnic youths, living in multi-cultural cities as London, have greater opportunities to social integrate, achieve social inclusion and mobility when compared to the their first generation migrant parents (Platt, 2005; Heath, 2008 Goulbourne et al., 2010).

Yet, some authors take a much for critical stance when considering the extent to which multi-cultural urban spaces represent a mechanism for social integration and inclusion by migrant and minority ethnic youths (Runnymede Trust, 2007). This literature suggests that the traditional problems associated with urban development—such as for example, high rates of unemployment, welfare recipients and 'broken families'—have encouraged a form of voluntarily segregation by individuals from different social class and ethnic communities. There is the concern too that black and minority ethnic youths have become marginalised and isolated from the rest of the city (Commission for Racial Equality, 2005). Black young men in particular find themselves without a place in the public space of the city because whilst within their own neighbourhoods they are accepted and embraced by family, friends and community members, once they leave these community spaces they are immediately stigmatised, avoided, or directly excluded from public engagement. The danger ascribed to black youth is closely linked to their marginal position in the labour market economy. As noted above, statistically speaking black youths living in economically deprived neighbourhoods suffer greater risk of unemployment, lack of education, and job training (Modood, 2004; Cheung and Heath, 2007; Equality Human Rights Commission, 2010). These youths also have very restricted access to places within the city, limiting their rights of citizenship. This marginalisation and alienation of black youths in urban spaces is reflected in public and media debates concerning the dangers of the 'hoodie', gang culture and inter/intra ethnic violence between groups of young men, and increasingly young women (see *The Independent*, 2009). More recently this issue again came to the fore of the public and policy attention following the August, 2011 riots in London and other urban cities.

Despite the relatively high levels of inter-racial mixing across a range of social relationships that goes in large British cities, in policy terms multiculturalism is publicly expressed as diverse ethnic groups living side-by-side in small enclaves or pockets of racial/ethnic defined geographical settlement patterns (Modood, 2007). Debates recognise that tolerance of ethnic diversity rather than a genuine desire to integrate defines much of the social relationships between ethnic groups. Over the past two decades, a number of studies have implicitly and explicitly suggested that different racial-ethnic groups' comparative failure to bridge and work across socio-economic and ethnic divides have contributed to existing social tensions and feelings of social exclusion in Britain today (Zhou, 1997; Parekh, 2000; Ousley, 2001).

There are therefore several dimensions at play when considering young people's relationship to disadvantaged neighbourhoods in urban spaces. Adopting a broader cultural perspective to understand this issue, Hansen's (2008) study of black youths in Zambia, highlighted the different trajectories provided for minorities and marginalised young people in these spaces. Of course Hansen's study operated in a vastly different cultural and social environment to the one in which my study is located. Nonetheless the trajectory framework presented can be applied to minority and marginalised youths in differing social, cultural and economic contexts. Hansen's study took up the position that young people living in crowded households, with a lack of education and limited means of employment and legal income easily fall into 'getting stuck'. The notion of 'getting by' therefore characterised the ability of these young people to navigate their way through a range of educational courses, occasional jobs, statutory funded- community programmes, and also self-employment in order to not 'get stuck' in their existing living and social conditions. In contrast, 'getting on' represented young people's ability to take advantage of networks and contacts to craft options and opportunities for themselves. The young people that typically 'get on' more often live in households where they have the social resources and networks to take advantage of educational and occupational opportunities to move out of these urban spaces. Similar parallels are drawn in Holland (2007b) analysis of youth transitions in disadvantaged communities with the notion of 'getting by' and 'getting on'. Examining social capital in the context of transitions in young people's lives and within the context of family, locality and community relationships, Holland suggests that the young adults living in disadvantaged neighbourhoods and housing estates of northern England and Northern Ireland saw their localised networks as highly constraining, tying them into their community. Whilst such networks allowed them to 'get by' it also stifled individual progression and social mobility. For some of these young people there was a strong desire to 'get out' and 'move out' and they strategically used education and employment opportunities as a means to 'escape from the bubble' of their socially disadvantaged local neighbourhood. My own research of Caribbean youths and transnational families provided a counterpoint to this view. A key research finding was that the notion of 'getting out' to 'get on' did not reflect the everyday social realities of these young people's experiences. Instead attachment to place and the security of belonging in a 'black neighbourhood' was viewed as a platform from which social progress and social mobility can be built (Reynolds, 2006a)

In order to analytically capture the way that diverse groups of young people negotiate routes out of poverty and youth transitions to adulthood debates have drawn on the concept of social capital (Morrow, 2000; Raffo and Reeves, 2000; Kovalainen, 2004; Holland et al.). Social capital theory raises the distinction between bonding ties (involving relationships and networks that reinforce bonds and connections within groups), and bridging ties (involving relationships and networks between different groups). Of course the notion of bridging and bonding social capital, made popular by theorist Robert Putnam (2000), represents one of the many ways in which social capital has been constructed and theorised by various authors, (see Field, 2003). Nonetheless, despite the differing approaches to social capital theory, when taken together a broad understanding of the concept reflects the 'values that people hold and the resources that they can access, which result in, and are the result of, collective and socially negotiated ties and relationships' (Edwards et al., 2004:2). It is regarded as a concept that either deals with the dilemma of collective action and integration, or as one dealing with the dilemma of social injustice and inequality (Holland et al., 2007). An interest in entrenched forms of societal inequality, including the reproduction of social class divisions in society, has been very much influenced by the work of Pierre Bourdieu (1977). His work is significant because its places culture at the heart of social stratification (Bourdieu and Wacquant, 1992). Distinguishing between different forms of capital as Bourdieu does—economic, social, cultural and symbolic capital—highlights variations of social stratification among young people (Schaefer-McDaniel, 2004; Adkins, 2005) and it also highlights the factors that influence young people's social wellbeing, such as for example, belonging, protection and social and economic security. Brann-Barrett (2010) study of youths in disadvantaged working-class communities interpret Bourdieu's notion of *habitus* (ways of being) to identify how youths growing up in disadvantaged communities are linked by a *collective habitus* (2010: 262). This work also suggests that any understanding of community is fundamentally underpinned by ideals of unity, related histories and interconnectedness of its residence despite variations in socio-economic experiences, lived experiences and perceptions. The themes of interconnectedness, shared historical roots, and interrelatedness among social and culture, and also structures and people provides the basis for constructing the term 'black neighbourhood'.

Black neighbourhoods and youth belonging

Historically, as a concept the term black neighbourhood emerged out of African-Caribbean migration patterns and settlement to the UK, particularly in urban neighbourhoods within Greater London, West Midland, Greater Manchester and West Yorkshire (Owen, 2006). In policy terms 'black neighbourhoods' are generally characterised as being poorly resourced neighbourhoods where there are high indices of poverty and deprivation. Factors that correlate with poverty and unemployment—such as, for example, under-achieving schools, large concentrations of social housing, and high rates of mental ill-health—are also portrayed as being significant characteristics of these neighbourhoods. It has been suggested that bonding social capital in 'black neighbourhoods' entrench black youths into these economically deprived urban spaces. This in turn restricts them from accessing resources that are outside of their community, which may facilitate social mobility (Orr, 1999). These same critics argue that in some instances black youths prefer to remain in the 'comfort zone' of such neighbourhoods, with poorly resourced and underachieving schools, instead of moving to the resourced schools that is often found in white middle-class locales geographical areas, and where they would have a greater chance of educational success and social mobility (see also Reynolds, 2006b).

This raises the question of to what extent the ethnic penalty by black youths themselves located in these neighbourhoods because of their willingness to remain in their 'comfort zone'. In many cases the young people were faced with a dilemma. Those that had opted to 'move out' expressed concerns about 'fitting in', acceptance and belonging, whilst those that decided to 'stay put' highlighted concerns that in times of austerity social resources aimed at improving social resources, community cohesion and wellbeing among its residents were further limited. It is important to point out that these youths desire to 'stay put' in their neighbourhoods (even if it is sometimes detrimental to their own personal success) must be understood within the wider context of social exclusion, and the way in which this has in turn encouraged a desire for ethnic and cultural belonging (Reynolds, 2006a). Britain's black community has faced a well-documented history of racial discrimination. Emerging out of, and in response to, these experiences 'black neighbourhoods' from the 1950s onwards acted as critical sites in developing strong bonds and internal institutions to establish a politics of struggle and resistance against racial-ethnic inequality and exclusion. Community bonds in this neighbourhood created public spaces for the development of day-to-day strategies and networks of survival and self-reliance. Through such urban spaces social solidarity was formed (Goulbourne, 1989). With economic austerity and the rise of youth unemployment among black youths in urban areas there is evidence that these young people are again turning 'inwards' towards their neighbourhoods to build up a platform for social progress and motivate them towards success. This involves, for example, their participation in ethnic-specific community networks that respond to the cultural and ethnic specific needs their communities.

On belonging in the urban landscape

There is little doubt that in these austere times unemployment is on the rise generally across all ethnic groups. Nonetheless this problem has been more astute for Black and other minority youths (BME) with a recorded high of them not in any form of employment, education or training (also known as NEETs) (Department of Education, 2011). Statistics show nearly fifty per cent of black people aged between sixteen to twenty-four years-old are unemployed. Additionally, mixed ethnic groups have seen the biggest increase in youth unemployment since the current recession began, rising from twenty-one per cnet to thirty-five per cent. For those black/mixed youths living in neighbourhoods where there exist high indices of poverty and deprivation and with few academic or technical qualifications it is estimated that three-quarters of youths are NEETs. These unemployment figures compares to twenty per cent of white young people nationally in a similar age category (IPPR, 2010). Such is the scale of the problem in these socio-economic disadvantaged neighbourhoods that some commentators now refer to these youths as representing the 'lost generation'; unlikely ever to secure upward social mobility and legitimate success via the conventional routes of employment, education and training.

The youths interviewed confirmed that with the current economic downtown there is more competition for the scarcity of jobs and there are more people looking work in a declining job sector. However, as a consequence of this they felt there was even greater reliance on community networks to secure work experience, in either a paid or voluntary capacity.

> Man-dem [men] look out for their own anyways, that's human nature, but we're now feeling the squeeze [economic pressure] so naturally man-dem is going to take care of their own first and foremost. The way it is, it's a jungle out there and its survival of the fittest, you're more likely get work from 'your people' [emphasis added] and 'Johamundo' [black community organisation] provides legitimate opportunities for lots of peeps [people] that live round here and it's rare that people like us are given in life opportunities to earn papers [money] the legitimate way.
>
> (Cameron, age 19, interview Haringey, London, 2008.)

As the quotation by Cameron intimates it is often during episodes of economic austerity that values associated with the 'survival of fittest and 'looking out for one's own' hold even more prominence as people compete over fewer employment opportunities. It was felt by the youths that ethnic-specific community networks and voluntary organisations provided greater support in looking for work than the more mainstream employment agencies and they preferred to use these networks. Such was the case of Chantelle, a twenty-one year old, youth worker who utilised her neighbourhood connections on the housing estate where she lived to gain work at the local youth centre. Chantelle had previously left school with no qualifications, but her current work allowed her to attend college to study for NVQ qualifications in youth work. She has since gone onto advance her career by studying for further courses in youth studies and by also recently enrolling for a part-time degree in childhood and youth studies at her local university.

Whilst the young people's accounts stress the important function the neighbourhood provides to its residents faced with economic hardship, there were also very aware that austerity created heightened feelings of mistrust, insecurity and lack of safety in the neighbourhood. The following quotation by Chibeze provides some indication of this viewpoint also expressed by many other participants interviewed:

Man's are becoming desperate and they will use any means necessary to find that money. They want fast cash, easy money and so anything can happen on the streets. People getting shot or shanked [stabbed] anytime, it's not surprising. It can happen anytime and to anyone. Me I trust no-one because things are getting worse every day, and we're living in a cycle of fear. You can lose your life over the mundane stuff. We're living in desperate times so it things can get a whole lot worse

(Chibeze, age 17, London Borough of Brent, 2008.)

The perception of a rise in crime and related anti-social behaviour was commonly blamed on the cuts in public funding to local youth services. There was a sense among those interviewed that there existed limited resources and fewer opportunities for young people to participate in organised leisure activities within the neighbourhood. Chantelle, a youth worker, who lives in her local neighbourhood comments:

Organised youth activities like our youth club are the first things in youth services to be cut back on during the [economic] recession. It's very depressing and short-sighted because we have shown time and time again that our work with the young people positively improves their lives. Often we're the only ones there for them and well, you never know, maybe we can provide that one chance in life because on the streets anything can happen. We try really to keep them off the streets and provide [them] a focus and purpose in life, you'd be surprised just how many young people round here don't have that in their lives

(Chantelle, age 21, London Borough of Lambeth, 2008)

There was also evidence that faced with economic hardship communal activities that took place in the neighbourhood—such as music festivals and local carnivals—and that traditionally reinforce bonding networks, were either cancelled or much more scaled down in size reaching a lower demographic of people. This reduction in neighbourhood-wide activities reduced the opportunities of young people to generate social and economic capital with diverse, and cross-ethnic, networks of young people and other people across various ages and stages in the life-course. To some extent some young people may be able to compensate for this loss of community networking by using social networking sites and other technology to build wider social and transnational connections (see Song and Parker, 2009). However, it could be argued that if black youths are socialising less in different forms of social activities and diverse groups of people in their locality then this further limit their opportunities to obtain work, particularly because, as noted above, argued previously, many of those interviewed heavily relied on information provided by friends and family and social connections to bring them out of the NEET trajectory.

Economic hardship also created fewer opportunities to form the kinds of bonds that help people survive during difficult times. It was noted, for example, that the provision of informal loans and gifts of food, money and other forms of help to friends and neighbours became more limited. Yet, during austerity these kinds of informal support increased in importance (Hossian et al., 2009). The decline in, or absence, this kind of informal support has the potential to propel young people into harmful coping strategies that are detrimental to their well-being, such as joining gangs to foster sense of belonging.

In the RAW study the spectre of gang membership as route to belonging among the youths was all too pervasive. The vast majority of those interviewed were NEETs and whilst many did not admit to being current gang-members themselves they discussed the rationale for many youths in their neighbourhoods joining gangs. A common theme in the narrative was that youths in their neighbourhoods had little opportunity of finding work, outside of immediate vicinity of the neighbourhood and community networks, and as such there was the sense that these youths felt they had little stake in wider British society. In essence these young people's accounts highlighted that gang membership served important multiple social and economic functions in this economic climate. It provided youths with a sense of belonging that was denied to them in wider society. Still others joined gangs and undertook illegal activities because it allowed them to contribute money to the household and family income. Also, for others gang-membership was about personal survival and safety. A small number of participants had left the parental home from a young age after experiencing social and economic conflict here and so were living on their own and had to support themselves through legal (e.g. paid work and welfare support) or illegal means (e.g. mugging and burglary).

A primary objective of 'RAW' youth-centred programmes was to develop understanding of the causes of urban youth poverty and marginalisation, as opposed to the much publicly debated consequences of this. By assuming a holistic approach and focusing on a whole range of social, psychological and material conditions that affect black youths living in 'black neighbourhoods,' attention was focused on encouraging programme participants to develop strategies in building self-esteem and autonomy as they try to negotiate the social landscape of their urban neighbourhoods.

As part of the programme the young participants were asked to consider the extent to which their neighbourhoods informed their everyday lived experiences. Similar to other studies (Clay, 2009), the youths identified that 'street culture', 'the streets' or 'being on road', in particular, played a significant role in shaping their daily lives and that their existed immense pressure for them to conform to the code of the 'streets'. In addition many of the participants in the RAW study had difficult relationship with their schools, which confirmed a belief that institutional routes to success were either unavailable to them. They spoke of a culture whereby 'avoiding school', 'dropping out' or being excluded from school represented a way in which they could retain self-respect among their peers in the neighbourhoods. 'Street culture' allowed them to build respect and where, with luck and the right connections, could also enable them to achieve status within their locales.

The programmes created the space and 'safe environment' for the youths to be able to re-evaluate this valourisation of the 'street culture' and to (re)consider their dreams and future aspirations. In the group discussions that took place in the workshop sessions various practices and techniques were used—an example being the 'truth chair'—so that the youths were able to talk freely about future aspirations in a space where they would not be judged against the normative code and values of the 'streets'. For instance, in one of the sessions with the 'truth chair', Ethan aged seventeen and unemployed reflected on his childhood dream to become an airline pilot when he grew up. Ethan had gone as far as visiting the career office at the Town Hall and researching the necessary qualifications and skills needed to achieve this aspiration. However, he never pursued this aspiration further because in order to realise this ambition the next step would be for him to attend the local Further Education College to study for the required qualifications that he failed to obtain at school, and which could set him onto a trajectory of higher education. Ethan believed that returning to school did not conform to the 'street code', and the type of street culture he associated with his neighbourhood. During this session Ethan also expressed concern about being ostracised and victimised by his friends in the neighbourhood if he admitted to wanting to develop a transition pathway into adulthood that might eventually require him to 'move out' of his locality. Ethan's example demonstrates the cultural and social constraints that existed for these youths in seeking to bring about changes in their lives.

Conclusion

To conclude this discussion introduces the notion of the 'black neighbourhood' and brings into sharp focus the way in which such urban neighbourhoods provide black youths with different trajectories of transition into adulthood, which range from being viewed as 'getting stuck', 'getting by', or 'staying put to get on'. To a large extent the meanings and knowledge of their local neighbourhood is informed by the particular types of cultural and social resources they are able to access. For those black young people's who view their networks as strongly embedded within their locality, 'black neighbourhoods' represent a social resource in actively combating racial inequality and exclusion, which they experience as part of their everyday lives. The social resources that exist here generate acceptance, belonging and social progress. Yet, it must also be acknowledged that 'black neighbourhoods' also create a negative outcome for black youths The evidence suggests the cultural and social conditions existing within these urban spaces played an important part in shaping attitudes and expectations. In particular 'street culture', 'the streets' or 'being on road', played a significant role in shaping the young people's aspirations and attitudes towards social mobility and to varying degrees had a direct effect on their motivation to engage in crime and anti-social behaviour.

The current climate of economic recession had significant implications for black youths 'getting on' and getting' in black neighbourhoods. Statistically, black and 'mixed' youths have some of the higher youth unemployment rates in Britain. Intersecting levels of disadvantage create the feeling among black youths living in disadvantaged 'black neighbourhoods' that it is virtually impossible to enter the labour market or training, especially those youths with no formal educational qualifications. Cuts to public sector funding to programmes and social enterprise schemes also penalise black youths because these were traditionally their routes into employment and entrepreneurship industries within the local neighbourhood. Cuts in funding to programmes such as the 'RAW' project also affect participants and there is the very real fear that will end up live in poverty and frustration, all of which is detrimental to their wellbeing.

Chapter 11

Academic burnout and engagement from adolescence to young adulthood

Katariina Salmela-Aro

Introduction

Adolescence is characterised by rapid physical, psychological and social changes, and the extent of these changes is probably higher in adolescence than in any other phase of life (Salmela-Aro, 2011). Academic demands increase and the adolescent is required to learn various roles and cope alone in increasingly complex situations. It has been found that stressful experiences in life and the emotions they generate may predict depression (Ge, Lorenz, Conger, Elder, and Simons, 1994) and burnout (Salmela-Aro, 2009) among adolescents.

While the concept of burnout has largely developed and been applied to occupational fields, the application of the construct to academic domains has been of interest to educational psychology in relation to student well-being and achievement (e.g., Fimian and Cross, 1986). The conclusions of such research have largely matched those in occupational settings where academic burnout has been found to be related to a number of important well-being and achievement factors. In particular, the research suggested that school burnout is associated with depression and anxiety (state and trait), and negatively associated with school engagement and self-esteem (Fimian and Cross, 1986; Salmela-Aro, Kiuru, Leskinen, and Nurmi, 2009). Academic burnout has also been linked with tedium, poor school life quality, external locus of control, self-handicapping and failure-avoidant achievement strategies (Covington, 2000; Fimian and Cross, 1986).

In recent years however, research has moved beyond the consideration of burnout as one of many well-being outcomes of various institutional and intrapsychic processes and has begun to explore the construct validity of school burnout from a multidimensional perspective (Salmela-Aro et al., 2009). This perspective is particularly important as it brings academic burnout into line with the theoretical approach of Maslach and colleagues (see Maslach, Schaufeli, and Leiter, 2001 for a review); a framework which is the central research framework in occupational settings and which has provided a number of important substantive and applied findings (Schaufeli and Enzmann, 1998). According to multidimensional theory, burnout consists of emotional exhaustion, cynicism, and feelings of inadequacy (Schaufeli and Enzmann, 1998). Burnout in the work context is defined as a syndrome of emotional exhaustion, cynicism or depersonalisation, and reduced professional efficacy (Maslach et al., 2001). Exhaustion refers to feelings of strain, particularly chronic fatigue resulting from overtaxing work. Cynicism consists of an indifferent or a distal attitude toward work, in general, and the people with whom one works; losing interest in one's work; and not seeing work as meaningful. Lack of professional efficacy refers to diminished feelings of competence, as well as less successful achievement and accomplishment in one's job.

Although burnout has generally been regarded as a work-related disorder (Maslach et al., 2001) it is useful in the school context. School is a setting in which students work: Students attend classes and do assignments in order to pass exams and acquire a degree (Schaufeli, Martinez, Pinto, Salanova, and Bakker, 2002). Hence, the concept of burnout can reasonably be extended to the school context (Kiuru, Aunola, Nurmi, Leskinen, and Salmela-Aro, 2008) and a valid and reliable instrument to measure it has recently been developed (SBI [School-Burnout Inventory], Salmela-Aro, Kiuru, Leskinen and Nurmi, 2009). The SBI consists of three subscales, exhaustion at school, cynicism at school, and inadequacy at school.

In the present chapter I present recent findings related to academic burnout. How are the three components of burnout related to each other and how do they develop? How are academic burnout and depression related to each other? What is the role of learning difficulties in this context? Second, I will introduce the concept of academic engagement. In this context I present the demands- resources model as an approach to study both academic burnout and engagement. Finally, I present findings as to how academic engagement and burnout change from adolescence to young adulthood from transition to high school to tertiary education and work life.

Developmental models

Golembiewski (1989) suggests that burnout develops in phases, where the three factors can be split into high and low categories, resulting in eight distinct clusters. The progression from phases I to phase VIII is considered to indicate the increase in the feelings of burnout experienced with low emotional exhaustion characterising the initial four stages and high emotional exhaustion characterising the final four phases (Golembiewski, 1989; Schaufeli and Enzmann, 1998). From a developmental perspective, this phasing model suggests that cynicism develops first and is followed by feelings of inadequacy with emotional exhaustion emerging in the final, more virulent stages of burnout (Golembiewski, 1989; Taris, Le Blanc, Schaufeli, and Schreurs, 2005). This framework suggests that cynicism represents a poorly adapted coping strategy that begins as a legitimate attempt to distance oneself from stressors but results in an inability to form helpful attachments and feel a sense of accomplishment. Over time this causes emotional exhaustion (Taris et al., 2005). Support for this model has been found with research suggesting that progressive phases are associated with greater distress and disengagement as well as increased physical symptoms of strain (Golembiewski, 1989).

Leiter's model (1989) has been shown in some empirical research to represent a far better fit to the data than Golembiewski's model. In Leiter's model cross-lag paths showed a reciprocal relationship between emotional exhaustion and cynicism and a consistent relationship between cynicism and feelings of inadequacy. This model indicates that emotional exhaustion is the initial component of burnout which leads to cynicism developing as an ineffective coping strategy, cumulating in feelings of inadequacy (Leiter, 1989). Empirical research in the occupational field has generally supported the link between emotional exhaustion and cynicism but the lack of evidence for the link between cynicism and feelings of inadequacy has resulted in alternative models to account for this discrepancy. These use the Leiter model as a foundation but include differing relationships between cynicism and feelings of inadequacy. Thus for example, Lee and Ashforth (1993) provided longitudinal support for an alternative model in which emotional exhaustion predicted both cynicism and feelings of inadequacy.

The developmental models of burnout were tested by using data on academic burnout among 670 high school students who were followed three times, one year apart (Parker and Salmela-Aro, 2011). Leiter's (1989) and Golembiewski's (1989) developmental frameworks fitted the data equally well. The Lee and Ashforth model was the worst fitting hypothesised model. The results were consistent with the Taris et al. (2005) research as it showed that their integrative model, which combined the Leiter and the Lee and Ashforth theoretical frameworks, was the best fitting model. The results of development revealed that cynicism and emotional exhaustion were consistent predictors of feelings of inadequacy. Inadequacy was thus the final phase of academic burnout.

Academic burnout, depression and learning difficulties

By using the same data we then examined the extent to which burnout predicts depressive symptoms or *vice versa*. Longitudinal cross-lagged paths between school burnout and depressive symptoms revealed that school burnout more strongly predicted subsequent depressive symptoms than *vice versa*. Clear cumulative cycles between school burnout and depressive symptoms were found (Salmela-Aro, Savolainen, and Holopainen, 2009): academic burnout predicted subsequent depressive symptoms rather than *vice versa*. Moreover, cumulative cycles between school burnout and depressive symptoms were also found to some extent in both studies. These results support earlier findings in the working life context. In a two-wave longitudinal setting, burnout and depression have been found to be reciprocal: occupational burnout predicted new cases of depressive symptoms and, in turn, depression predicted new cases of burnout (Ahola and Hakanen, 2007). Burnout and depression might thus develop 'in tandem' (McKnight and Glass, 1995). These are important findings, revealing the detrimental effects of school burnout later on. Stressful experiences in school life and the emotions they generate may thus predict depression among adolescents (Ge et al., 1994). This adds to and supports the findings among adults. Among adults mental health has been shown to deteriorate as burnout advances and the more severe burnout is, the closer it resembles depression in its symptoms. Those who suffer from school burnout might not have sufficient resources to meet the demands of their school work and this situation might predispose them to depressive symptoms. Furthermore, those who are depressed perceive and evaluate their situation at school more negatively than those who are not depressed. Consequently, one way to prevent depression among adolescents is to reduce their school burnout. Thus in the future an effective preventive focus is needed (Salmela-Aro, Mutanen, Koivisto, and Vuori, 2010).

The role of learning difficulties was also examined in the context of burnout (particularly the component of inadequacy) and depressive symptoms (Kiuru et al., 2011). Learning difficulties prospectively predicted depressive symptoms. Furthermore, the impact of learning difficulties was mediated via feelings of inadequacy as a student: Learning difficulties predicted a higher level of inadequacy which then contributed to a greater increase in depressive symptoms. Gender moderated the association between learning difficulties and depressive symptoms: Being both a girl and having a high level of learning difficulties predicted a higher initial level of depressive symptoms. The impact of learning difficulties on depressive symptoms was mediated via feelings of inadequacy as a student. The results support the thesis according to which difficulties in achievement tasks can constitute a stress factor that triggers depressive reactions among adolescents suffering from learning difficulties. The cumulative effects of academic difficulties and failures among adolescents with learning difficulties may lead to exhaustion at school and feelings of being overwhelmed by academic demands. They may also increase failure expectations, negative attitudes towards school and eventually weaken academic self-concept (see also Marsh, Trautwein, Lüdtke, Köller, and Baumert, 2005). As a consequence of this maladaptive cycle, depressive symptoms may increase among adolescents for whom dysphoric mood is a typical reaction to difficulties.

Although results importantly shed light on the processes via which learning difficulties impact on depressive symptoms, it is important to remember that stress and failures in the academic domain are not the only factors contributing to depressive symptoms. According to the competence-related feedback model of depression, depressive reactions are most likely to emerge when deficits in several areas of competence coincide (i.e., social, academic, behavioural).

Academic Engagement

In recent years the concept of engagement has received a lot of attention in both school (Fredricks, Blumenfeld, and Paris, 2004) and work contexts (Schaufeli et al., 2002). Active engagement is vital to a student's educational success and development into competent members of society. Students who are more engaged in school earn higher grades and show better personal adjustment to school. Conversely, students who are disengaged from school are more likely to experience academic failure, school dropout, and a host of other negative psycho-social outcomes (Archambault, Janosz, Fallu, and Pagani, 2009). Researchers, educators and policy makers are increasingly focused on student engagement as a means to addressing problems of student boredom and alienation, low achievement, and high dropout rate because it offers several benefits for research and practice (Fredricks et al., 2004).

Engagement in the work context is defined as a positive, fulfilling work-related state of mind characterised by energy, dedication and being absorbed (Schaufeli et al., 2002). Energy refers to high levels of mental resilience while working, dedication to being strongly involved in one's work and experiencing a sense of significance, and absorption to being fully concentrated on work so that time seems to pass quickly. In line with this theory and definition (Schaufeli et al., 2002), schoolwork engagement could be described as energy, dedication towards and absorption in schoolwork. Energy in this context refers to a positive approach to schoolwork, dedication to a positive cognitive attitude and perceiving schoolwork as meaningful, and absorption to full concentration on studying so that time seems to pass quickly.

Salmela-Aro and Upadyaya (2012) created a short, valid and reliable instrument capturing the key factors of schoolwork engagement EDA-inventory (energy, dedication, absorption) and its potential transformation to work engagement. We included data on students from post-comprehensive schools where they begin to focus on their careers, and where engagement with work might be assumed to originate.

Academic engagement and burnout

Using job demands-resources model as a guiding framework, we documented pathways from study demands and resources to later engagement and burnout as well as later life adjustment in a sample of students during their transition from comprehensive school to academic and vocational track. Results showed that the model fitted well and can thus be used as a theoretical background for demands, resources, burnout, and engagement in the study context. Study demands (D) were positively related to burnout at secondary education one year later, while study resources (R) were positively related to engagement one year later. In addition, personal resources were positively related to engagement and negatively to burnout. Engagement and burnout were both stable during secondary education and negatively associated. The cross-lagged paths between engagement and burnout revealed that burnout predicted negatively engagement one year later. Next, engagement was positively related to life satisfaction two years later, while burnout was positively related to depressive symptoms and negatively to life satisfaction two year later. Results thus suggest that D-R model is a suitable framework in the study context explaining students' pathways to adjustment and maladjustment.

Filling the gap, support for the two processes of the demands-resources model were found (Demerouti, Bakker, Nachreiner, and Schaufeli, 2001). First, an effort-driven, energetic process of overtaxing and wearing-out, in which high study demands exhaust a student's energy and lead to diminished mental health such as depression. Second, the motivational process in which the availability of resources precludes dealing effectively with high study demands leads to engagement and foster life satisfaction. Engagement mediated the relationship between study resources and life satisfaction, while burnout mediated the relationship between study demands and mental health outcomes. Overall, a particularly strong relationship existed between study demands and burnout and between burnout and depressive symptoms. In contrast, the paths from study resources and engagement and from engagement and life satisfaction were weaker. Similarly, the cross-lagged paths from study resources to burnout and from burnout to life satisfaction were much weaker. The cross-lagged paths to engagement from demands and from engagement to depressive symptoms were not even significant. This agrees with the two processes of energetic effort-related process: study demands to burnout to depressive symptoms and motivation process from study resources to engagement to satisfaction with life.

In line with the demands-resources model (Bakker and Demerouti, 2007), the more depressive symptoms and school burnout adolescents suffered and the lower their GPA and self-esteem, the lower was their EDA. In accordance with the hypothesis those on the academic track had lower schoolwork engagement than those on the vocational track. This supports earlier findings showing that students following the academic track experience more exhaustion than those on the vocational track because academic demands are typically higher (Salmela-Aro, Kiuru, and Nurmi, 2008, see also Salmela-Aro and Tynkkynen, 2012). Upper-secondary schools are typically larger and more bureaucratic than comprehensive schools, and provide fewer opportunities for students and teachers to get to know each other. Such environments are likely to undermine further the motivation and involvement of many students, especially those not doing particularly well academically. These signs of disaffection might be signs of impending school failure, school dropout, and risk behaviours. By comparison, the vocational track focuses more on hands-on and practical activities, which might lead to improved schoolwork engagement.

Gap year

Psychological thinking on the 'gap year' phenomenon can be traced back to Erikson (1968) who suggested the transition to adulthood is often characterised by a period of moratorium where young people disengage temporarily from their long-term career/educational paths. Erikson adds that unlike other forms of career/educational disengagement, this period is often a socially approved period of disengagement during the early stages of young adult development. Despite this long history, research on the effects of an educational moratorium period is scarce (Heath, 2007). However, the research that is available generally suggests that the period is potentially beneficial. For example Rose Birch and Miller (2007), found that those who took a moratorium period before entering university had higher levels of achievement than those who did not and that these benefits were particularly apparent for male students of average ability. Likewise, Martin (2010), after controlling for demographic variables, found a number of motivational benefits suggesting that a 'gap year' may be particularly beneficial for individuals with problematic achievement and motivation profiles including low levels of task-orientated motivation and greater avoidance behaviours. In addition, the benefits of an educational break have been identified in relation to skill development, well-being, and making young people more competitive in educational and career markets (Heath, 2007; Jones, 2004; Martin, 2010). The hypothesis that a moratorium period provides a break from achievement pressures during which young people can consider their long-term plans is intuitively appealing, and is in part the basis upon which such a period is promoted to young people (e.g. Heath, 2007). Indeed, empirical research indicates that school students do experience high levels of stress and burnout in both school (Parker and Salmela-Aro, 2011; Pines, Aronson, and Kafry, 1981) and university (Schaufeli et al., 2002). Thus, the advantage of a break between these two high stress environments seems obvious. Likewise, the idea of taking time for oneself to carefully consider future plans and resolve uncertainty appears self evident (Heath, 2007).

It is important to note, however, that for many young people an educational moratorium period is not a complete break from achievement pressures. Rather, many young people enter into the labour market (or other achievement domain) while attempting to enter university. Indeed some researchers consider the entry into temporary employment or another achievement domain to be a defining feature of a 'gap year.' Furthermore, such an achievement context is associated with experience and skills development, which are suggested to be central benefits of a 'gap year' (Heath, 2007).

Thus, young people may not be gaining the break from achievement pressures that they expect to receive from this period (Jones, 2004). We aimed to explore assumptions used to explain why an educational moratorium after school is beneficial for later educational attainment. First, the research explored whether those on an educational break experience less achievement pressure than comparable youth who go directly to university. Second, the research explored whether a moratorium period helped young people resolve uncertainty about long-term educational and career goals. The results suggested that youth who took advantage of a moratorium period did have lower levels of burnout than the matched university group and slightly higher engagement. The evidence did not, however, support the assumption that an educational break helps resolve uncertainties about long-term educational and career goals. Indeed, individuals in the moratorium group had moderately lower levels of commitment to their long-term educational and career goals and reported slightly lower expectations about their ability to successfully obtain their goals. Taken together, these results suggest that a break from education is associated with a break from achievement pressure (though the break associated with engagement was inconsistent across methods) but that this break may not be associated with a resolution of educational (and occupational) career uncertainty. Thus, while being in a period of moratorium was beneficial in terms of well-being, results for goal pursuit suggest that it may not be without costs. In relation to the assumption that a 'gap year' provides a break from achievement pressures, the results suggest that such young people are not only experiencing lower burnout but may be gaining well-being advantages as they reported high levels of engagement during their planned short-term period in the labour force or other achievement contexts.

Importantly, these differences were present despite the moratorium group being selected on the basis of their educational break consisting of full-time presence in the labour force (or other achievement domain). Illustrating the validity of these results, no group differences were observed in the general domains of well-being (depression and satisfaction with life). As indicated in the literature review, individuals on an educational break are only taking time out from achievement pressures, not from all pressures associated with young adulthood. Thus a gap year would be unlikely to affect these more general outcomes. While the current research suggests that such a break is beneficial in relation to obtaining a relief from achievement pressure, it does not appear to help resolve uncertainty about long-term educational and career goals. Results appear to contradict previous research conclusions that the motivational benefits of 'gap year' are due to the advantages gained in the moratorium period. It is also possible that the moderate break from achievement pressures observed in this research is sufficient to overcome the effects of greater goal uncertainty in terms of the benefits of a 'gap year' found in research based on students who have returned to their educational trajectories.

Another hypothesis for this discrepancy relates to what occurs during the 'gap year' period. While the moratorium participants in the current research indicated both at pre and outcome time that they intended to go to university, it is possible that the lower commitment to an educational trajectory and the greater goal uncertainty noted in this research means that many in this group will never re-enter university. Thus it is possible that this period imposes strong selection pressures which means that youth at risk of doing poorly at university never re-enter education. With such individuals excluded, the comparison of non-deferment students with at-risk youth included compared to a educational break group without such individuals may be biased. It was outside the scope of the current research to directly assess such hypotheses. However, the current research does suggest that more research is needed before a 'gap year' is promoted to young people based on the results of research drawn from the experiences of those who succeed in re-entering education.

Conclusion

In the present chapter I presented recent findings related to academic burnout and engagement. I presented findings of how the three components of burnout are related to each other and how they develop. Next I presented findings of how academic burnout and depression are related to each. I also presented findings about the role of learning difficulties in this context and introduce the concept of academic engagement. In this context I presented the demands-resources model as an approach to studying both academic burnout and engagement. Finally, I presented findings on how academic engagement and burnout change from adolescence to young adulthood, from transition to high school to tertiary education and work life, and the role of the gap year in academic burnout and engagement.

School-related maladjustment was conceptualised in terms of academic burnout, which comprises three dimensions: exhaustion due to school demands, a cynical and detached attitude towards school, and feelings of inadequacy as a student (Salmela-Aro et al., 2009). In turn, schoolwork engagement was described as energy, dedication towards and absorption in schoolwork (Salmela-Aro and Upadyaya, in press). The transition from comprehensive school to the next stage of education is a significant context for change in burnout. A higher level of academic engagement, in turn, seems to predict a successful educational trajectory. Increasing engagement and support for those suffering from burnout would also help them in their later educational trajectories and transition to working life.

Chapter 12

Gender differences in achievement and social strategies, areas of work life, and burnout at the early career stage

Hely Innanen and Katariina Salmela-Aro

Introduction

Recent research has shown that stressful experiences in academic life may predict burnout among adolescents (Salmela-Aro, Savolainen and Holopainen, 2009). Further, it has been shown that girls experience more academic burnout than boys (Salmela-Aro, Kiuru and Nurmi, 2009). Previous results have found that the achievement and social strategies that individuals use in academic life can predict burnout in their later work life (Salmela-Aro, Tolvanen and Nurmi, 2009, 2011). Findings of continuity in experiences of burnout, and especially age and gender differences in experiences of burnout (Ahola, Honkonen, Virtanen, Aromaa and Lönnqvist, 2008), suggest that more attention should be given to research on burnout in the early career. Maslach and Leiter (1997) have defined job burnout as a psychological syndrome of exhaustion, cynicism, and professional inefficacy—referred to as *dimensions of burnout*. Exhaustion refers to a lack of emotional energy (Maslach, 1993; Toppinen-Tanner, Kalimo and Mutanen, 2002). The cognitive dimensions of job burnout are cynicism and professional inefficacy (Leiter, 1991). It has been found that experiences of unfavourable work characteristics may play a significant role in burnout (Bakker, Demerouti and Euwema, 2005; Buunk and Schaufeli, 1993; Schaufeli and Enzmann, 1998). One possible psychological process in burnout may relate to employees' individual ways of reacting in demanding work situations (Langelaan, Bakker, van Doornen and Schaufeli, 2006; van den Heuvel, Demerouti, Bakker and Schaufeli, 2010). The preventing role of individual characteristics and appropriate work context against exhaustion and cynicism, and supporting role to professional efficacy needs further attention.

The role of gender in relation to individual characteristics and experiences in work life remains a question of interest. Research has shown highly inconsistent results for gender differences concerning experiences of job burnout. In the present study, in regard to underlying gender experiences, we have focused on young employees' achievement and social strategies, experiences in particular areas of work life, and burnout.

Gender, burnout, and achievement and social strategies

Previous research has shown gender differences in experiences of burnout (Maslach and Jackson, 1985). Moreover, burnout is reported to be higher among young employees (eighteen to twenty-nine years-old) than among employees who are between thirty to forty years-old (Maslach, Schaufeli and Leiter, 2001). Some research on burnout suggest that women generally are more likely to experience emotional exhaustion than men, whereas men experience more cynicism (Maslach, et al., 2001; Purvanova and Muros, 2010; Schaufeli and Bakker, 2004), and higher professional efficacy than women (Leiter and Maslach, 2004). One reason for the gender differences in burnout might be employee achievement and social strategies. Eccles (2011) has recently suggested that motivational and social factors influence individuals' efforts and choices in achievement and other life situations. Thus, these factors may underlie gendered decisions on the basis of beliefs linked to cultural norms, expectations of success, and the values that young employees attach to their choices in working life.

Individual differences can be divided into achievement strategies and social strategies (Eronen, Nurmi and Salmela-Aro, 1997; Onatsu-Arvilommi and Nurmi, 2000). Achievement and social strategies are usually classified as *achievement optimism* and *social optimism* (i.e., *functional*) in contrast to *achievement pessimism* and *social pessimism* (i.e., *dysfunctional*) (Aunola, Stattin and Nurmi, 2000; Eronen, 2000; Eronen, Nurmi and Salmela-Aro, 1997; Onatsu-Arvilommi and Nurmi, 2000). Eccles (2011) has found that social experience and gender-role beliefs may have an influence on working life through their impact on employees' expectations and task values. *Achievement optimism* means task-focused performance (Salmela-Aro et al., 2009), which in academic research has been shown to predict low burnout in the early part of individuals' careers. In work life, active problem-solving strategies (Schaufeli and Enzmann, 1997; Wilk and Moynihan, 2005), optimism (Mäkikangas, 2007; Scheier, Carver and Bridges, 2001), and expectations of positive outcomes (Seligman, 1991; Seligman and Csikszentmihalyi, 2000) have been suggested to be related to high professional efficacy (Lee and Ashforth, 1993; Salmela-Aro et al., 2009). On the other hand, *achievement pessimism* is characterised by high task-avoidance (Eronen et al., 1997), which in turn contribute to exhaustion, cynicism, and professional inefficacy (Salmela-Aro and Nurmi, 2007; Salmela-Aro et al., 2009).

Employee social strategies may also be relevant to burnout, which has been examined in an interpersonal context in terms of individuals' relationships with co-workers (Maslach, 2003). *Social optimism* has been described as positive emotions and a sense of community, whereas *social pessimism* is characterised by social withdrawal (Eronen and Nurmi, 1999; Langston and Cantor, 1989), and pessimistic social interaction strategies (Langston and Cantor, 1989; Nurmi and Salmela-Aro, 1997). Positive expectations (Folkman, 2008) and optimism (Carver, Scheier and Weintraub, 1989; Savicki, 2002) sustain employee well-being (Mäkikangas and Kinnunen, 2003; Otero-López, Mariño and Bolaño, 2008), whereas social pessimism is related to stress. Sondaite and Zukauskiene (2005) have found that, in adolescence, women's social withdrawal, and thus *social pessimism*, is higher than the men's. Masten, Desjardins, McCormick, Kuo and Long (2010) have emphasised the stability of individual early social competence and its role in predicting social success in later working life. Most previous research viewing young individuals' burnout from a perspective of strategy has been conducted in academic contexts and achievement situations (Nurmi, Aunola, Salmela-Aro and Lindroos, 2003; Määttä, 2007). Only few studies have focused also on work life (Salmela-Aro et al., 2009, 2011). The study of the role of individual strategies in work life among young employees needs more attention, especially since employee-organisation match/mismatch has been emphasised as a determining factor for either well-being or burnout in employees (Leiter, Gascón, and Martinez-Jarreta, 2009; Siegall and McDonald, 2004).

Gender, burnout, and areas of work life

Maslach and Leiter (1997) defined six critical areas that contributed to burnout in the context of work (workload, control, reward, community, fairness, and values). Previous results by Leiter and Maslach (2004) have found that young employees in the early career experienced lower exhaustion, and professional efficacy, higher work load, lower control, and sense of reward, higher sense of community and fairness, and lower value congruence with their organisation than their older co-workers. Men generally scored higher in regard to workload, control and fairness than women did, whereas women tend to score higher with respect to values, while no gender differences were found concerning reward or sense of community. Nonetheless, Bildt and Michélsen (2002) suggest that especially among women, low reward and low social support, and thus lack of community, are related to burnout. Price and Spence (1994), as well as Greenglass (1991) suggest that causes for burnout would develop from different primary sources among men and women. In this respect, higher cynicism among men might be partly a result of a masculine gender role, such as a strong role of achievement in the workplace (Eccles, 2011). Work demands such as work overload and role ambiguity would be primary sources of exhaustion among men, whereas among women, exhaustion and cynicism result from both work and home-based stressors (Price and Spence, 1994; Greenglass, 1991). High stress is the price that women have to pay for their decisions concerning the balance of their occupational behaviour with other life roles when social services and rewards for their achievements are inadequate (Abele and Spurk, 2011).

Areas of work life have been widely described in previous research. Work overload, or gradually working overtime without sufficient recovery and psychological detachment, has been proved strongly related to occupational burnout and primarily to exhaustion (Hakanen, Bakker and Schaufeli, 2006; Sonnentag and Fritz, 2007). Lack of control over one's work combined with high job demands is linked to professional inefficacy (Glass and McKnight, 1996). In combination with poor relationships with co-workers (Fernet, Gagné, and Austin, 2010) lack of control is associated with exhaustion (Spence Laschinger, Wong and Greco, 2006; Leiter, Gasgón and Martinez-Jarreta, 2010). Reward can refer to external rewards (e.g., financial benefits) or to intrinsic rewards (e.g., an employee's pride in his or her work) (Maslach et al., 2001). Sense of community, including positive relationships with co-workers, can buffer against exhaustion (Richer, Blanchard and Vallerand, 2002). Experiences of fairness buffer against exhaustion and cynicism (Elovainio, Kivimäki and Vahtera, 2002; Elovainio, van den Bos, Linna, Kivimäki, Ala-Mursula, Pentti and Vahtera, 2005). Results by Moliner, Martinez-Tur, Peiro, Ramos and Cropanzano (2005) have shown a higher negative relation between perceived organisational fairness and exhaustion or cynicism among women than among men, but reported no significant gender differences between perceived organisational fairness and professional efficacy. Value congruence (see Gabel, 2011) between the values of an employee and those of an organisation (Siegall and McDonald, 2004; Winefield and Jarrett, 2001) decrease experiences of exhaustion and cynicism (Leiter et al., 2010). To clarify factors in employee exhaustion, cynicism and professional efficacy in the early career, and previous contradictory results regarding gender differences reported in related research literature, we conducted an extensive analysis of burnout, individual work-related strategies, and areas of work life among young employees.

The aim of the present study and research questions

The main aim of our study was to examine gender differences in exhaustion, cynicism and professional efficacy, and further in achievement and social strategies, and in areas of work life in a sample of 378 young employees in the early career. First of all, we examined to what extent dimensions of burnout, achievement and social strategies, and areas of work life (workload, control, reward, community, fairness, and values) differ from each other between genders. On the basis of earlier studies, we hypothesised (Hypothesis 1) that young men's score in relation to cynicism and professional efficacy would be higher than that of the young women, while women would score higher on emotional exhaustion than men (Maslach, et al., 2001; Purvanova and Muros, 2010; Schaufeli and Bakker, 2004).

Second, we examined gender differences in the usage of achievement and social strategies. To reveal gender differences in relations between achievement and social strategies and burnout, we examined to what extent achievement and social strategies are related to the dimensions of burnout among young men and women. We hypothesised (Hypothesis 2a) that due to a high stability in strategies and gender roles, women's score for achievement optimism (see Eccles, 2011) would be lower and for social pessimism higher than that of the men (Sondaite and Zukauskiene, 2005). We hypothesised (Hypothesis 2b) that achievement and social strategies would be related to dimensions of job burnout in both genders (Salmela-Aro et al., 2009, 2011) but that the significance levels of these relations would differ from each other between young men and women.

Third, we examined differences in the levels of areas of work life between genders. To reveal gender differences in relations between areas of work life and burnout, we examined to what extent areas of work life are related to burnout among men and women. According to previous studies (Leiter and Maslach, 2004), we hypothesised (Hypothesis 3a) that the men participating in our study would score higher on workload, control and fairness than the women, while women would score higher on value congruence than the men. Also in line with previously reported results (Leiter and Maslach, 2004), we hypothesised (Hypothesis 3b) that gender differences in the levels of sense of community and reward would not be statistically significant. Since reward plays a strong role in women's experiences of achievement in working life and regarding stress (Abele and Spurk, 2011), we hypothesised (Hypothesis 3c) that rewards would have a stronger preventing role against burnout among women than among men, that fairness would prevent exhaustion and cynicism more so among women than among men, and that it would not be related to professional efficacy in the early career (Bildt and Michelsen, 2002; Moliner et al., 2005).

Method

Participants
The subjects were employees in the early career from four organisations: logistics (N=176; 46%), health care (N=39; 10%), a university (N=86; 22%), and a IT company (N=85; 22%). The data was collected in group meetings using questionnaires, which were returned by 55% of the employees. The majority (56%) of the study's participants were women. The mean age of both the male and female participants was 26 years (SD = 3.11 men; 3.19 women),

Measures
The Strategy and Attribution Questionnaire (SAQ) was used to examine achievement and social strategies (Nurmi, Salmela-Aro and Haavisto, 1995). The SAQ contains twenty items ranked on a 4-point Likert scale (1 = *completely disagree*, 5 = *completely agree*). Achievement strategies were measured according to optimism (six items, for example, '*When I begin a task, I am normally sure that I will succeed in it*') and pessimism (four items, for example, '*When I have a difficult task to carry out, I often find something else to do instead*'). Social strategies were measured according to social optimism (4 items, for example, '*I usually get on well with other people*') and social pessimism (4 items, for example, '*Because I am afraid of meeting people, I am often alone*'). For men the Cronbach's alpha reliabilities for achievement strategies were .67/.76, and for social strategies .77/.69. For women the Cronbach alpha reliabilities for achievement strategies were .69/.74 and for social strategies .79/.72.

Methods from the *Areas of Worklife Survey (AWLS)* (Leiter and Maslach, 2000) were used to measure employees' experiences relating to workload, control, reward, sense of community, fairness, and values. The AWLS consists of twenty-nine items ranked on a 5-point Likert scale (1 = *completely disagree*, 5 = *completely agree*). The sum variables were: workload (six items, for example, '*I do not have time to do all that I have to do*'), control (three items, for example, '*I am professionally independent in my work*'), reward (four items, for example, '*My work is appreciated*'), sense of community (five items, for example, '*I do not feel close to my co-workers'*), fairness (six items, for example, *Resources are divided fairly at my workplace'*), and compatibility of employees' values with those of the organisation (five items, for example, *My values and the values at my workplace are similar'*). The Cronbach alpha reliabilities for men were for workload (.77), control (.72), rewards (.70), sense of community (.73), fairness (.68) and values (0.69). The Cronbach alpha reliabilities for women were for workload (.72), control (.71), rewards (.61), sense of community (.78), fairness (.78) and values (.75), respectively.

Maslach Burnout Inventory–General Survey (MBI-GS). The MBI–GS was used to measure job burnout (Byrne, 1994; Schaufeli, Leiter, Maslach, and Jackson, 1996). The MBI–GS consists of 16 questions. Respondents are asked to assess their feelings about their work by using the scale 0 (*never*)–6 (*daily*). The sum variables were: exhaustion (five questions), cynicism (five questions), and professional efficacy (six questions). The Cronbach alpha reliabilities for men were for exhaustion (.88), cynicism (.85) and professional efficacy (.77), and for women for exhaustion (.88), cynicism (.82) and professional efficacy (.83), respectively.

Data Analysis

The analyses were conducted separately for men and women. To examine the gender differences in the variable means, *t*-tests were carried out. The extent to which the achievement and social strategies and areas of work life contributed to the dimensions of burnout in the early career was examined by using a hierarchical regression analysis. In this analysis, burnout was first explained by achievement and social strategies and then by the areas of work life.

Results

The correlations between all variables, mean values and standard deviations are presented in Table 1, separately for men and women. The descriptive statistics showed that women had higher level of education than the men had (p<.05). Our first aim was to examine gender differences in employee evaluations of dimensions of burnout. The results showed no gender differences in dimensions of burnout in the early career. Our second aim was to examine gender differences in employee achievement and social strategies and to examine what extent achievement and social strategies would be related to the different dimensions of job burnout among men and women. Men scored higher on achievement optimism (t(374)=2.19, p<.05), and women scored higher on achievement pessimism ($t(373)$ =2.07, p<.05, and social optimism ($t(372)$=4.28, p<.001). The strategic factors were related to exhaustion, cynicism and professional efficacy among both genders, but the significance of the relations differed between genders (Table 2). The *beta* values for the independent variables indicated that the less men used achievement optimism, the more exhausted and cynical they were. The more men showed achievement optimism and the less they used pessimism, the more professional efficacy they experienced. Further, the *beta* values for the independent variables indicated that the less women showed achievement optimism, the more exhausted they were. The more women showed achievement optimism, the higher a sense of professional efficacy they had.

Our third aim was to examine gender differences in the levels of areas of work life and to reveal what extent areas of work life (workload, control, reward, community, fairness, and values) would be related to the dimensions of job burnout among men and women. The results showed that men scored higher on control ($t(368)$=2.01, p<.05) and fairness ($t(375)$=2.22, p<.05) than the women did. Women rated no areas of work life higher than did the men. The results of the regression analysis showed that the areas of work life were significantly related to exhaustion, cynicism and professional efficacy among both genders, but the significance levels of the relations differed between genders. The *beta* values for the independent variables indicated that among men, the higher the workload, the lower the perceived reward, the more they experienced exhaustion. The lower the control and sense of community, the higher the workload and value conflicts, the more cynical they were. The more the reward and congruent values, the higher a sense of professional efficacy they had. Among women, the relations between areas of work life and burnout differed from the results of men. The *beta* values for the independent variables indicated that the greater the workload and the less control held, the more exhaustion the women experienced. The less control, reward, sense of community and value congruence, the more cynicism women experienced and the higher the reward and value congruence, the higher a sense of professional efficacy women experienced.

Discussion

Psychological characteristics, such as achievement strategies (Nurmi et al., 2003; Salmela-Aro et al., 2009) and social strategies (Eronen et al., 1997; Salmela-Aro et al., 2011), as well as the areas of work life (Maslach et al., 2001, Leiter and Maslach, 2004) can contribute to burnout in the early career. The gender differences have been examined separately for achievement and social strategies (Eccles, 2011; Sondaite and Zukauskiene, 2005), areas of work life, and dimensions of burnout (Leiter and Maslach, 2004). To the best of our knowledge, no other research has combined achievement and social strategies with areas of work life in order to simultaneously examine their contributions to burnout while also considering gender differences. The main aim of this study was to reveal gender differences in levels of burnout, types of strategies, and areas of work life. Moreover, our aim was to reveal how both achievement and social strategies and the areas of work life are related to the dimensions of burnout, and whether there are gender differences in these associations in the early career.

Based on previous research, we first hypothesised that also in their early career, men would score higher on cynicism and professional efficacy than would women, and that women would score higher on exhaustion than men would (Leiter and Maslach, 2004; Maslach et al., 2001; Purvanova and Muros, 2010; Schaufeli and Bakker, 2004). However, the results did not support our hypotheses and previous research. Unexpectedly, our results did not show any gender differences in exhaustion, cynicism, or professional efficacy during participants' early career. One reason might be the preventing role of some areas of work life against burnout. Previous results have highlighted the relation between insufficient rewards and burnout, especially in regard to cynicism (Bildt and Michélsen, 2002; Leiter, Price and Spence Lashinger, 2010). Our results are in line with previous results showing the preventing influence of satisfactory rewards on cynicism and the supportive influence of rewards on professional efficacy in women. Noteworthy, satisfactory rewards had a preventing role on exhaustion in men. Previous results have found work overload to be highly related to exhaustion (Maslach et al., 2001). In line with this, our results showed a strong preventing role of appropriate workload against exhaustion among both genders. These might be reasons for no gender differences having been detected as regards exhaustion and cynicism. Furthermore, the reason for there having been no gender differences in the levels of exhaustion, cynicism, and professional efficacy might be at least partially due to cultural factors. In Finland, among women in their early careers, having a good level of education may predict expectations of success rather than emotional exhaustion (see Eccles, 2011), and would lead one to assume there to be a high level of professional efficacy among young Finnish working women. Child care and social services are well-organised, meaning that women have less home-based and other life stressors than may be expected in some other cultures, and they have opportunities equal to those of men concerning achievements at work and thus career progression (see Abele and Spurk, 2011).

We further hypothesised, according to previous research (Salmela-Aro et al., 2009, 2011) emphasising the role of achievement and social strategies in burnout, that achievement and social strategies would be related to dimensions of job burnout among both genders. However, we also expected that the levels and the relations would differ between genders. Our findings partially supported our hypotheses. In our study, the men scored higher on achievement optimism than did the women, and the women scored higher on achievement pessimism and social optimism. These results did not support the results relating to other research fields and other cultures investigated by Sondaite and Zukauskiene (2005), who reported social withdrawal (i.e., social pessimism) to be higher among women than among men. Our results regarding work context support the results of Eccles (2011), according to whose findings individual achievement and social factors influence effort and choices, and may underlie decisions in working life that are linked to cultural norms, expectations and values regarding choices. Furthermore, achievement optimism among men played a preventing role against both exhaustion and cynicism, whereas among women, achievement optimism buffered against emotional exhaustion. Along this line, among men, the frequent use of achievement optimism and social optimism and the lesser use of achievement pessimism supported professional efficacy. In line with this also among women achievement optimism was strongly related to professional efficacy in their early career. A high preventing role of achievement optimism might be one reason for no gender differences in exhaustion, cynicism and professional efficacy in the early career. These results offer further information about the role of individual strategies in work life. The results are also in line with previous results (Savicki, 2002; Wilk and Moynihan, 2005; Salmela-Aro et al., 2009, 2011) showing active problem solving, optimism and expectations of success to have a preventing role against exhaustion and cynicism, and a supporting role to professional efficacy. The usage of achievement and social strategies among men and women in their early career may be partly related to cultural norms and expectations of success in work life (see Eccles, 2011).

In our results pertaining to their early careers, the men scored higher on control and perceived fairness than the women did. These results of gender differences in areas of work life are partially in line with our hypotheses and the results by Leiter and Maslach (2004), in whose research the men rated workload, control, and fairness to be higher than did the women, and women rated the emphasis on values to be higher than did men—but with no gender differences concerning sense of community and rewards. Surprisingly, in their early career, employees' experiences of workload and values did not differ between genders. Further, our results supported the findings by Eccles (2011), who reported that, as a result of men's work-related gender role, men could be expected to gain more control over their work and to perceive there to be greater fairness at work. As mentioned earlier, the reasons for this may also partially be cultural. Our results supported our hypothesis regarding the higher significance of the relation between reward and burnout in women compared to men (Able and Spurk, 2011). In contrast to the results by Leiter and Maslach (2004), the women in our sample did not score higher on value congruence with their organisation than did the men. Our results revealed that value congruence plays a high preventing role against cynicism and a supporting role in professional efficacy—among both genders. This result suggests that values play a strong role in the well-being of both genders in men and women's early professional career. This is also in line with the results by Gabel (2011) and Winefield and Jarrett (2001), according to whom basic individual values play a key role in the person-organisation match and are related to employee professional efficacy and engagement, and, when mismatched, to burnout. The results suggest that supporting value congruence between the organisation and its male and female employees in their early career can play a significant role in the employees' well-being, which, in turn, could be expected to be of benefit to the organisation.

Finally, the results of our study supported our hypothesis related to the findings by Leiter and Maslach (2004), in whose study the men rated control and fairness in their organisation to be higher than did the women. Unexpectedly, our results did not support our hypothesis related to earlier findings by others as follows. Our results did not support the results of Leiter and Maslach (2004), according to whom men rated workload higher than did the women, and the results of Bildt and Michelsen (2002) as well as Moliner et al. (2005), according to whom perception of unfairness is related to exhaustion and cynicism among women in particular. These results, which pertained to employees in their early career, appear to suggest that it is important for an organisation's management to pay attention to the workload of both genders. These results emphasise the role of the fairness perceived by female employees as management try to sustain a balance between their occupational responsibilities and other life roles (Abele and Spurk, 2011; Eccles, 2011).

The results of our gendered approach to achievement and social strategies as well as areas of work life in relation to burnout suggest that occupational burnout can be prevented by improving both individual strategies and certain areas of work life in individuals' early career. The findings also promote encouraging men to develop more positive attitudes in social situations and for women to increase even more their achievement optimism, and expectations of positive outcomes in work life (Seligman, 1991; Seligman and Csikszentmihalyi, 2000). This chapter supports the findings of previous research that employees' achievement and social strategies could provide a basis for success (Aunola, Stattin and Nurmi, 2000) together with evaluations of organisational characteristics (Leiter and Maslach, 2004; Maslach, 2001; Schaufeli and Enzman, 1998), and that this applies to both men and women.

The added value of our study lies in the fact that our sample of participants was heterogeneous enough to represent both male and female employees in the early career sufficiently. The present research yields useful theoretical information about the relationships between employee strategies, areas of work life, and job burnout using gendered approach. The results of our research can be of value in organising and leading positive work initiatives within organisations and in seeking to support well-being in organisations (Ablele and Spurk, 2011; Eccles, 2011; Leiter and Maslach, 2000; Mäkikangas and Kinnunen, 2003). Our findings can be useful in interventions offering special solutions to account for the gender differences in experiences of burnout (Purvanova and Muros, 2010; Schaufeli and Bakker, 2004). Naturally, our research also has some limitations. First, the cross-sectional design does not allow causal inferences to be made, and second, the data is based on self-reports.

Conclusions

In conclusion, there were differences between men and women in regard to levels of achievement and social strategies, experiences of work life and burnout in the early career. Both achievement and social strategies and areas of work life could prevent exhaustion and cynicism and support professional efficacy, but the role of the strategies and the work context differed somewhat between genders. Thus, taking into account gender differences in young employee achievement and social strategies and experiences of areas of work life (workload, control, reward, sense of community, fairness, and values), organisations can create new ways to decrease and prevent employee burnout and strengthen employee professional efficacy and engagement in the early career. It would be useful for further research to examine with a larger research sample of working age people how job burnout occurs in different organisations. A longitudinal design would be required in order to test the causal relations between the employees' strategies, areas of work life and burnout or engagement during the career.

Table 1: *Correlations, Means and Standard Deviations of study variables (male and female).*

Variables	1.	2.	3.	4.	5.	6.	7.
1. Optimism	1.00	-.36 ***	.28 ***	-.60 ***	.24 ***	.31 ***	.23 **
2. Avoidance	-.34 ***	1.00	-.02	.32 ***	-.07	-.02	-.11
3. Social optimism	.44 ***	-.17 *	1.00	-.51 ***	.19 **	.21 **	.13
4. Social pessimism	-.60 ***	-.20 *	-.43 ***	1.00	-.21 **	-.27 ***	-.25 ***
5. Workload	.18 *	-.12	-.19 *	-.08	1.00	.22 **	.18
6. Control	.39 ***	-.19 *	.41 ***	-.32 ***	.18 *	1.00	.36 ***
7. Reward	.24 **	-.06	.33 ***	-.26 **	.42 ***	.18 *	1.00
8. Community	.35 ***	-.03	.38 ***	-.39 ***	.13	.13	.39 ***
9. Fairness	.22 **	-.10	.27 ***	-.20 **	.18 *	.18 *	.47 ***
10. Values	.39 ***	-.28 ***	.40 ***	-.30 ***	.21 **	.21 **	.34 ***
11. Exhaustion	-.31 ***	.23 **	-.26 **	.19 *	-.67 ***	-.67 ***	-.10
12. Cynicism	-.42 ***	.28 ***	-.39 ***	.32 ***	-.31 ***	-.46 ***	-.28 ***
13. Professional efficacy	.36 ***	-.28 ***	.32 ***	-.18 *	.02	.36 ***	-.31 ***
M1	4.04	2.05	3.87	1.81	3.42	3.60	3.17
SD1	.55	.73	.71	.70	.80	.89	.80
M2	3.91	2.21	4.17	1.93	3.28	3.48	3.27
SD2	.58	.80	.65	.75	.81	.92	.90

Variables	8.	9.	10.	11.	12.	13.
1. Optimism	.24 ***	.23 **	.14 *	-.33 ***	-.27 ***	.44 ***
2. Avoidance	-.00 **	-.02	-.13	.16 *	.14 *	-.23 **
3. Social optimism	.25 ***	.16 *	.10	-.17 *	-.29 ***	.15 *
4. Social pessimism	-.27 ***	-.20 **	-.16 *	.33 ***	.35 ***	-.31 ***
5. Workload	.18	.25 ***	.25 ***	-.54 ***	.20 **	.06
6. Control	.26 ***	.45 ***	.37 ***	-.42 ***	-.43 ***	.19 **
7. Reward	.52 ***	.49 ***	.33 ***	-.34 ***	-.53 ***	.32 ***
8. Community	1.00	.50 ***	.32 ***	-.30 ***	-.45 ***	.27 ***
9. Fairness	.54 ***	1.00	.41 ***	-.39 ***	-.40 ***	.21 **
10. Values	.44 ***	.47 ***	1.00	-.36 ***	-.45 ***	.26 ***
11. Exhaustion	-.23 **	-.25 **	-.31 ***	1.00	.53 ***	-.24 **
12. Cynicism	-.40 ***	-.35 ***	-.58 ***	.56 ***	1.00	.24 ***
13. Professional efficacy	.26 **	.25 **	.42 ***	-.08	-.31 ***	1.00
M1	3.84	3.18	3.37	1.91	1.98	4.32
SD1	.69	.71	.71	1.15	1.35	.95
M2	3.79	3.01	3.37	2.04	1.91	4.23
SD2	.83	.78	.70	1.17	1.30	1.04

*Note., Values for male are below the diagonal and for female above the diagonal. M1, SD1 are for male; M2, SD2 are for female. * p < .05. ** p < .01. ***p < .001*

Table 2: The results of hierarchical regression analyses in predicting employee exhaustion, cynicism and professional efficacy in the early career (male/female).

Antecedent	Exhaustion 152/202				Cynicism 150/198			
Step No.	1		2		1		2	
	M	F	M	F	M	F	M	F
Optimism	-.23 *	-.19 *	-.08	-.03	-.25 *	-.08	-.08	.02
Avoidance	.12	.05	10	.06	.14	.06	.11	.06
Social optimism	-.14	-.01	-.04	.05	-.17 *	-.16	.00	-.13 *
Social pessimism	-.08	.20 *	-.04	.12	.05	.23 *	.02	.11
Workload			-.62 ***	-.40 ***			.15 *	-.02
Control			-.10	-.20 **			-.22 *	-.17 **
Reward			.19 **	-.07			.05	-.30 ***
Commu-nity			-.07	-.03			-.17 *	-.14 *
Fairness			-.07	-.09			.06	.02
Values			-.07	-.10			-.33 ***	-.24 ***
ΔR²	.11 **	.14 ***	.31 ***	.31 **	.21 ***	.16 ***	.22 ***	.31 ***
R²	.11	.14	.42	.45	.21	.16	.43	.47
F			15.1 ***	15.9 ***			10.6 ***	16.7 ***

Antecedent	Professional efficacy 152/199			
Step No.	1		2	
	M	F	M	F
Optimism	.29 **	.39 ***	.22 *	.40 ***
Avoidance	-.16 *	-.06	-.14	-.04
Social optimism	.21 *	-.04	.09	-.02
Social pessimism	.10	-.10	.15	-.05
Workload			-.14	-.13
Control			.11	-.08
Reward			.18 *	.22 **
Commu-nity			.04	.07
Fairness			-.00	-.06
Values			.19 *	.18 *
ΔR^2	.19 ***	.22 ***	.11 **	.09 ***
R^2	.19	.22	.30	.31
F	6.2 ***			8.5 ***

*Note. M = male, F = female. The betas are standardised coefficients. *$p < .05$, **$p < .01$, ***$p < .001$*

Chapter 13

The role of school engagement in young people's career development and mental well-being: Findings from two British cohorts

Helen Cheng and Ingrid Schoon

Introduction

Active engagement in school is critical to a student's educational success. Research suggests that students who are more engaged in learning earn higher grades and show better personal adjustment to school (Archambault et al., 2009; Salmela-Aro and Upadyaya, 2012; Wang and Holcombe, 2010). Conversely, students who are disengaged from school are more likely to experience academic failure, school dropout, and a host of other negative psycho-social outcomes during adolescence (Finn and Rock, 1997). The role of school engagement in promoting successful career development has been demonstrated in a number of studies across different cultural contexts (Eccles, 2004; Fredricks, Blumenfeld and Paris, 2004; Wang and Holcombe, 2010). There is, furthermore, evidence to suggest that school engagement is an important resource capacity for younger students planning their careers (Salmela-Aro, Tolvanen and Nurmi, 2009; Schoon, 2008) and promoting their mental health (Wang, Willet and Eccles, 2011). School engagement is of particular interest to researchers because it is both a malleable state that can be shaped by social context and a robust predictor of a wide array of educational and career outcomes (Eccles and Wigfield, 2002; Fredricks et al., 2004). There are however relative few studies examining the association between school engagement and long-term outcomes, in particular regarding psychological wellbeing. Using longitudinal data from two age cohorts we examine the role of school engagement as a predictor of adult mental health in addition and above educational and occupational attainment. We furthermore investigate the role of school engagement as a potential mediating variable, linking family social background and childhood cognitive ability to later educational and occupational attainment and well-being. Testing our model in two age cohorts provides vital evidence regarding the generalisability of findings.

Figure 1 gives a diagrammatic depiction of the model to be tested using Structural Equation Modelling (SEM). The usual SEM conventions are used, with latent variables shown as circles and manifest variables as rectangles. Singe headed arrows represent causal influences. The double-headed arrow represents the correlation between independent variables. Unique and error variance for each manifest variables and disturbance on the latent variables are included in the model (not shown in the diagram). There are independent variables (family social class and childhood cognitive ability), mediating variables (motivation, education, occupational attainment) and an outcome variable (adult mental

Figure 1: Pathways to career development and wellbeing.

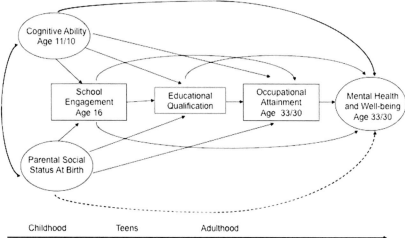

health). Family social status at birth is assumed to be associated with general childhood cognitive ability. The two variables share some genetic as well as environmental influences, and were operationalised as correlated independent variables. This approach is considered as a preferable, theory-neutral, position until more is known about the causal relations and patterns of interaction of these two variables (Deary et al., 2005). The effects of family social status and cognitive ability on adult mental health are hypothesised to be direct and also mediated via school motivation and subsequent educational and occupational attainments. The paths in the model track development over time. As parental social status and childhood cognitive ability were assessed at an earlier age than the other variables in the model, they are assumed to be causally prior. It is hypothesised that a) parental social status and childhood cognitive ability have a direct influence on adult career outcomes, which in turn affects adult mental well-being; b) the influence of parental social status and childhood cognitive ability on adult career outcomes and mental well-being is at least partly mediated via school engagement; c) school engagement has a significant association with adult career attainment and mental well-being in addition and above parental social background, after controlling for childhood cognitive ability.

Method

Participants

The study draws on two nationally representative cohort studies: the 1958 National Child Development Study (NCDS) and the 1970 British Cohort Study (BCS70). The study participants were recruited as part of a perinatal mortality survey. In both cohorts the sample population is predominantly white (about three to four per cent are from Indian, Pakistani, Bangladeshi, African, Caribbean, Chinese or mixed origin), reflecting the ethnic diversity of the UK population at the time (Ferri et al., 2004). NCDS comprises 17,415 individuals born in Great Britain in a week in March 1958 (Power and Elliott, 2006), and BCS70 comprises 16,571 individuals who were born in Great Britain in a week in April 1970 (Elliott and Shepherd, 2006).

The following analysis is based on data collected at birth, age sixteen, and in early adulthood, at ages thirty (BCS70) and thirty-three (NCDS), when most cohort members have completed their education, and established their working careers. The analytic sample comprises 6,221 cohort members in NCDS (50.5 per cent females) and 6,632 in BCS70 (51.2 per cent females), for whom complete data were collected at birth and the follow-ups at age thirty and thirty-three, respectively. Analysis of response bias in the cohort data showed that the achieved adult samples did not differ from their target sample across a number of critical variables (social class, parental education and gender), despite a slight under-representation of the most disadvantaged groups (Plewis, Calderwood, Hawkes and Nathan, 2004). Bias due to attrition of the sample during childhood has been shown to be minimal (Butler, Despotidou and Shepherd, 1997; Davie, Butler and Goldstein, 1972; Fogelman, 1976). Potential bias due to missing variable information is addressed in the section on estimating the model. It was possible to identify variables that enable a comparison of experiences among individuals in the two cohorts and to examine changes and continuities in the patterns of association observed between family social status and cognitive ability, and how the effects of both variables on adult occupational attainment and psychological well-being are mediated through school engagement.

Measures

Family Social Status at Birth

In both cohorts family social status is indicated through parental occupational social status and parental education. Parental occupational status at birth was measured by the Registrar General's measure of social class (RGSC). RGSC is defined according to occupational status and the associated education, prestige (OPCS, 1980) or lifestyle (Marsh, 1986) and is assessed by the current or last held job. Where the father was absent, the social class (RGSC) of the mother was used. RGSC was coded on a four-point scale: I/II professional and managerial class; III skilled non-manual; IIIM skilled manual; IV/V semi-and unskilled occupations (Leete, 1977).[28] Class I/II is associated with the highest level of prestige or skill, and class IV/V the lowest. For ease of interpretation the scores were reversed, so that a high score represents the highest level of prestige. A second indicator of parental social status is parental education which is measured by the age either parent had left full-time education.

Childhood Cognitive Ability

Cognitive ability was measured differently in the two cohorts, yet assessing the same construct of general cognitive ability comprising both verbal and nonverbal skills. In the 1958 cohort cognitive ability was assessed at age eleven in school using a general ability test (Douglas, 1964) consisting of forty verbal and forty non-verbal items. Children were tested individually by teachers, who recorded the answers for the tests. For the verbal items, children were presented with an example set of four words that were linked either logically, semantically, or phonologically. For the non-verbal tasks, shapes or symbols were used. The children were then given another set of three words or shapes or symbols with a blank. Participants were required to select the missing item from a list of five alternatives. Scores from these two set of tests correlate strongly with scores on an IQ-type test used for secondary school selection (r=0.93, Douglas, 1964) suggesting a high degree of validity.

Cognitive ability of the 1970 cohort was also assessed in school, using a modified version of the British Ability Scales (BAS) which can serve as a measure for childhood IQ (Elliott, Murray and Pearson, 1978). The assessment involved the administration of four sub-scales: word definitions and word similarities which were used to measure verbal ability, and recall of digits and matrices which

---

28 The occupational categories used in the US census and other European countries are similarly based on the skills and status of different occupations (Krieger and Williams, 1997)

were used to measure non-verbal ability. For the word definitions subscale, the teacher articulated each of thirty-seven words in turn and asked the child about its meaning. For each of the forty-two items in the word similarities subscale, the teacher enunciated three words and asked the child to name another word consistent with the theme. For the thirty-four items subscale of recall of digits, the teacher read out digits at half-second intervals and asked the child to repeat them. For the twenty-eight items matrices subscale, the teacher asked the child to draw in the missing part of an incomplete pattern.

Teenage School Engagement

At age sixteen members of both cohorts completed a five-item school engagement scale (e.g. 'school is largely a waste of time'; 'I do not like school'). Items were measured on a 5-point Likert scale in NCDS and on a 3-point Likert scale in BCS. Item analysis suggests good internal consistency for both cohorts, with coefficient alpha = .77 for NCDS and .75 for BCS samples. The validity of the school engagement scale has been established in previous studies, showing significant correlations between school engagement and educational aspirations (Schoon et al., 2007) and time spent in education (Schoon, 2008). A high score indicates positive school engagement and a low score school disengagement. Scores in NCDS and BCS were standardised for further analysis.

Educational Qualifications

At age thirty-three in NCDS and at age thirty in BCS, participants were asked about their highest academic or vocational qualifications. Responses are coded to the six-point scale of National Vocational Qualifications levels (NVQ) which ranges from 'none' to 'higher degree level': 0 = no qualifications; 1 = some qualifications [Certificate of Secondary Education Grades 2 to 5]; 2 = O-level [equivalent to qualifications taken at the end of compulsory schooling]; 3 = A-level [equivalent to university entrance level qualifications]; 4 = post secondary degree/diploma and equivalent; and 5 = higher post-graduate degrees and equivalent.

Occupational Attainment

Data on current or last occupation held by NCDS and BCS cohorts members at age thirty-three and thirty respectively are coded according to the Registrar General's Classification of Occupations (RGSC), described above, using a four point classification (professional-managerial, skilled non-manual, skilled manual, and semi-or unskilled) in both cohorts. In this study RGSC for both parents and participants was reverse coded on a four-point scale. Thus 1=semi-and unskilled occupations, and 4 = professional and managerial class.

Mental Health and Well-being

Adult mental health and well-being is defined by a latent variable comprising adult psychological distress and a sense of control over one's life were assessed at age thirty-three (NCDS) and age thirty (BCS70) respectively. Psychological distress was assessed using Rutter Malaise Inventory (Rutter, Tizard, and Whitmore, 1970). It comprised of twenty-four items with Yes/No (a twenty-two item version was used in NCDS and the twenty-four item version was use in BCS70). The 'sense of control over one's life' is a scale comprised of three items ('Never get what I want out of life', 'Usually have control over my life', and 'Can run my life how I want') used in the cohorts. Two choices were given for each item, for example, 'I usually have a free choice and control' or 'Whatever I do has no real effect'. The combined scores were used for the following analyses.

Results

Correlational Analysis

Tables 1 and 2 show the correlations between the observed variables in the study, as well as the means and standard deviations for both cohorts. Please note that the measures of cognitive ability, school engagement and adult wellbeing were assessed with different instruments or different responses and are not directly comparable. In both cohorts gender shows only small but significant (p<.001) associations with childhood intelligence (girls scored higher on verbal test in NCDS as well as on tests of matrices and recall of digits in BCS, whereas boys scored higher on tests of word similarities and word definitions in BCS), school engagement (girls scored higher than boys in both cohorts), mental distress (women scored higher than men in both cohorts), education and occupation (men scored higher on educational qualifications in NCDS and women scored higher on occupational attainment in BCS). Higher parental social status indicators and childhood cognitive ability were significantly (p<.001) associated with higher levels of school engagement, higher academic and occupational attainment in adulthood, as well as adult mental health and well-being. School engagement was significantly (p<.001) associated with career outcomes and adult mental health and well-being in the expected direction, with higher school engagement predicting higher educational qualifications, higher occupational attainment, and a lower score on mental distress and a higher score on a sense of control over one's life.

Structural Equation Modelling

Structural Equation Modelling (SEM) was used to assess the pathways linking family social background, childhood cognitive ability, school engagement, adult career outcomes and mental health and well-being at age thirty-three in NCDS and at age thirty in BCS70. Paths in the models are designed to correspond with the time sequence in which the variables occurred. All SEM pathway models were carried out using the structural equation modelling program AMOS 18 (Arbuckle, 2009). The AMOS program uses maximum likelihood estimation that can be based on incomplete data, known as the full information maximum likelihood (FIML) approach. FIML estimation is a theory based approach based on the direct maximisation of the likelihood of all the observed data, not just from cases with complete data. FIML is preferable to maximum likelihood estimation based on complete data (the listwise deletion (LD) approach) since FIML estimates tend to show less bias and are more reliable than LD estimates even when the data deviate from missing at random and are non-ignorable (Arbuckle, 1996).

The full model has two components: one giving the relationships between the latent variables and their indicators (the measurement model) and the other defining the relationships among the latent and observed variables (the structural model). Table 3 shows the indicators for each of the latent variables identified in the models (the measurement model). The measured variables that represent parental social status, childhood cognitive ability, and adult mental health and well-being load strongly on the latent variables.

Model Fit

In line with current practice, several criteria were used to assess the fit of the data to the model. The χ^2 statistic is overly sensitive to model misspecification when sample sizes are large or the observed variables are non-normally distributed. The root mean square error of approximation (RMSEA) gives a measure of the discrepancy in fit per degrees of freedom ($<.05$ indicates a good fit). The final index of choice is the comparative fit index (CFI) where values above .95 indicate good fit (Bentler, 1990).

The model described above showed a good fit in both cohorts. In NCDS the Chi-square was 168.2 (df = 23, p<.001), the CFI was .992, and the RMSEA was .032. The model explains 33 per cent of variance in adult occupational attainment, 95% CI [.30, .36] and 16 per cent of variance in adult mental health and well-being indicated by mental distress and a sense of control over one's life, 95% CI [.14, .18]). In BCS70 the Chi-square was 372.1 (df = 42, p<.001), the CFI was .980, and the RMSEA was .034. The model explains 27 per cent of variance in adult occupational attainment, 95% CI [.24, .30] and 11 per cent of variance in adult mental health and well-being, 95% CI [.09, .13]. According

Figure 2: NCDS/BCS pathways to career development and well-being (N=6221/6632).

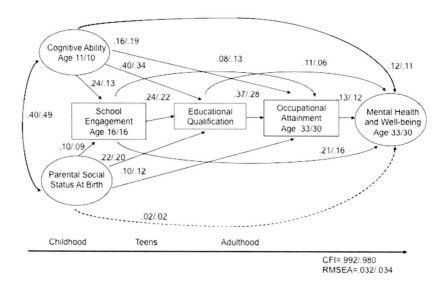

Figure 2 shows the standardised path coefficients of the structural equation model that may be squared to obtain the variance shared by adjacent variables.

to Cohen (1992), the f2 values of .02, .15, and .35 are termed small, medium, and large, respectively.

In both cohorts all paths in the model were statistically significant, except for the path between family social status and the latent variable of mental health and well-being, which was not significant. In both NCDS and BCS70 cohorts, parental social status was associated significantly with childhood cognitive ability. Although the association was strong, it did not explain more than 20% of the variation in cognitive ability in NCDS and not more than 25% in BCS70.

There was a significant association between parental social status and childhood cognitive ability, which became stronger for the later born cohort ($z=6.37$, $p<.001$). These two variables also had a direct association with occupational attainment. Childhood cognitive ability was significantly associated with school engagement in both cohorts, and parental social status was associated with school engagement in both cohorts. The findings suggest that parental social background affected young adult mental health and well-being mainly through its association with educational qualification and occupational attainment. There was a direct association between teenage school engagement and adult mental health and well-being. We furthermore find significant and independent direct effects of childhood cognitive ability on adult career attainment and mental health and well-being.

Cohort Differences
Cohort differences in path coefficients were tested using *t*-tests. Results showed that there were cohort differences in the pathways linking childhood intelligence and school engagement ($z=10.82$, $p<.001$), suggesting that in the later born cohort high cognitive ability is not necessarily associated with high school engagement. There was a decrease in the associations between childhood cognitive ability and educational qualification ($z=4.60$, $p<.001$), and between educational qualification and occupational attainment ($z=5.31$, $p<.001$) in BCS70 cohort, suggesting that in the later born cohort, childhood cognitive ability had a reduced role in shaping educational attainment, which in turn, had a reduced effect on occupational attainment in the later born cohort.

Conclusion

We find that parental social status and childhood cognitive ability have a direct influence on educational achievement and adult career outcomes, which consequently affect adult mental well-being. The findings are in agreement with other studies based on the British cohort studies suggesting that parental social status, childhood cognitive ability, and education are all significant determinants of adult social status attainment (Breen and Goldthorpe, 2001; Bynner, 1998; Richards, Power, and Sacker, 2008; Richards and Sacker, 2003). Furthermore, there is support for the hypothesis that the influence of social background and cognitive ability on adult attainment and mental wellbeing is partly mediated via school engagement, which in turn also shows a significant direct association with adult career attainment and mental well-being, independent of parental social background and childhood cognitive ability. Using the lifecourse model and developmental-contextual framework this study adds towards a better understanding of social inequalities in adult attainment and health, examining the role of both structural as well as individual factors in a changing socio-historical context. Using data from two large, prospective and population-representative samples in the UK enabled us to assess generalisability of patterns across different samples. In both cohorts, the same model could be fitted to the data, indicating stability of our findings.

The association between parental social status and childhood cognitive ability has increased for the later born cohort, indicating increasing social inequalities in academic attainment with young people from less privileged backgrounds achieving less well academically (Breen and Goldthorpe, 2001; Feinstein and Bynner, 2004; Schoon and Polek, 2011).

The relative weak associations between family social status and school engagement may indicate that the determinants of school engagement might include other factors than those included in the model, such as school environment, peers, and teacher expectations, which might play a more salient role in influencing young people's levels of school engagement, offering potential leverage for interventions (Eccles and Midgley, 1989; Eccles and Roeser, 1999; Eccles and Roeser, 2009). It could however also suggest that young people are generally motivated at school, independent of their social background.

There has been an interesting shift between cohorts, as in the 1970 cohort high cognitive ability is less strongly associated with school engagement than in the 1958 cohort. This might suggest increasing school disengagement among bright young men and women in the later born cohort (Schoon, 2008, 2010b; Steedman and Stoney, 2004), which occurs before educational choices are realised. Engaging young people in the school environment, making the school context relevant to their life planning and educational /occupational choices, might be one mechanism to increase the realisation of individual potential and reduce social inequalities in attainment and wellbeing. Aiming to engage young people who have become disaffected with school, it is important to take into account their education histories, as the experience of childhood disadvantage can influence levels of academic attainment, which in turn influences later achievements (Gregg and Machin, 2001; Schoon et al., 2002), but also the attitudes of children towards learning (Horgan, 2007), and their adult wellbeing. It is important to create opportunities for achievement, possibly through activities outside the class room, which can help children to develop confidence in learning and in their own capabilities.

The findings also suggest that in the later born cohort the associations between childhood cognitive ability and educational qualification and between educational qualification and occupational attainment were decreased, suggesting that educational achievement and occupational attainment of young people in the later born cohort were less influenced by their ability tests scores they had in their childhood. The findings thus lend support to the assumption that the most privileged have benefited from the expansion of further education, not the most able (Galindo-Rueda and Vignoles, 2005; Schoon, 2010a). In interpreting these findings, it has to be kept in mind that adult outcomes have been assessed at slightly different ages in the two cohorts, reflecting a three year difference in the point of measurement, and that childhood cognitive ability tests used in NCDS and BCS70 were different. The differences in path coefficients linking cognitive ability to later outcomes may thus partly due to the different tests used in the different cohorts.

Limitations and future research

This study is based on a large, fairly representative sample of the UK population that was followed from birth into the adult years. As with all research using cohort studies, this work is constrained by having to make best use of available data. For example, childhood cognitive ability was assessed with different test instruments in the two cohorts. Using a latent variable approach, however, it is possible to make comparisons at the conceptual level, especially since the instruments captured both verbal and nonverbal aspects of general cognitive ability. The available data has also restricted the scope of potential mechanisms we can examine.

Another limitation is the attrition of respondents over time. It may be that missing data at the individual level and at the variable level has affected the validity of the results. Response bias at the individual level would tend to underestimate the magnitude of the effects of social family background on future development since sample attrition is greatest amongst individuals in more deprived circumstances. Our results may thus be a conservative estimate of the long term influence of social inequalities experienced during childhood. Missing data at the variable level may also be non-random. The FIML approach has been adopted as a 'best effort' technique for dealing with these problems, but bias in our model estimates may still be present.

Nonetheless, this study is one of the first to show the long-term effects of school engagement on young people's career development and mental well-being, in addition and above the influence of family social status and childhood cognitive ability, using evidence from two nationally representative cohort studies. Whilst family background and childhood cognitive ability are more difficult to change, factors such as school engagement and educational achievement are more readily malleable (Eccles, 2004; Fredricks, Blumenfeld and Paris, 2004; Wang and Holcombe, 2010). Schools may help pupils to enhance their motivation to pursue their interests and develop their talents. Equal opportunity policies may help young people, especially those from social-economic disadvantaged families, to obtain higher qualifications and thus to increase their employment prospects and subsequently their levels of mental health and well-being. Future research may examine other factors such as school environment (e.g. teacher-pupil relationships, peer friendship, and class climate etc.) and family influences (such as parental mental health, family types, and parenting styles) on school engagement and adult inequalities in attainment and wellbeing in more detail.

Acknowledgements

The analysis and writing of this article were supported by grants from the UK Economic and Social Research Council (ESRC): RES-594-28-0001. Data from the Cohort Studies were supplied by the ESRC Data Archive. Those who carried out the original collection of the data bear no responsibility for its further analysis and interpretation.

Table 1: Pearson correlations among family background, childhood cognitive ability, school engagement, qualification and occupational attainment, and mental health and well-being in the 1958 cohort (NCDS).

	Variables	Mean SD	1	2	3	4	5	6	7	8	9	10	11
1.	Gender	.51 (.50)	—										
2.	Parental social class	2.27 (.99)	-.017	—									
3.	Father ageleft school	15.48 (1.86)	.002	.453	—								
4.	Mother ageleft school	15.47 (1.50)	.017	.345	.533	—							
5.	Verbal scores (cognitive ability)	23.37 (8.86)	.114	.254	.247	.223	—						
6.	Non-verbal scores (cognitive ability)	21.99 (7.15)	.018	.253	.248	.220	.787	—					
7.	School engagement	17.96 (4.54)	.081	.151	.134	.116	.250	.235	—				
8.	Academic and vocational qualifications	2.46 (1.35)	-.059	.314	.295	.269	.501	.483	.392	—			
9.	Occupational attainment	2.71 (1.21)	.014	.245	.223	.185	.365	.340	.252	.484	—		

	Variables	Mean SD	1	2	3	4	5	6	7	8	9	10	11
10.	Psychological distress	2.32 (2.92)	.141	-.100	-.085	-.062	-.166	-.179	-.182	-.202	-.160	–	
11.	Sense of control over one's life	2.60 (.76)	-.008	.088	.084	.062	.143	.150	.156	.194	.188	-.391	–

Note: Variables were scored such that a higher score indicated being female, a more professional occupation for the parent and higher age parents left school, a higher verbal and non-verbal cognitive ability scores, a higher school engagement score in teen, highest academic and vocational qualification, and more professional occupation in early adulthood, more professional occupation in early adulthood, higher scores on psychological distress and higher level of sense of control over one's life.

Table 2: Pearson correlations among family background, childhood cognitive ability, school engagement, qualification and occupational attainment, and mental health and well-being in the 1970 cohort (BCS).

	Variables	Mean SD	1	2	3	4	5	6	7	8	9	10	11	12	13
1.	Gender	.51 (.50)	—												
2.	Parentalsocial class	2.30 (.98)	.003	—											
3.	Father agleft school	15.46 (1.13)	.004	.444	—										
4.	Mother ageleft school	15.43 (1.05)	-.001	.353	.472	—									
5.	Word similarities (Cognitive ability)	28.49 (4.21)	-.094	.253	.225	.242	—								
6.	Word definitions (Cognitive ability)	10.57 (4.97)	-.108	.293	.258	.279	.647	—							
7.	Recall of digits (Cognitive ability)	22.55 (4.23)	.039	.107	.108	.105	.296	.313	—						
8.	Matrices (Cognitive ability)	15.90 (5.29)	.047	.210	.196	.209	.435	.441	.291	—					
9.	School engagement	11.44 (2.26)	.076	.112	.088	.090	.111	.132	.037	.123	—				

	Variables		1	2	3	4	5	6	7	8	9	10	11	12	13
10.	Academic and vocational qualifications	2.71 (1.30)	.002	.282	.263	.255	.349	.376	.196	.335	.292	—			
11.	Occupational attainment	2.86 (1.09)	.078	.250	.217	.210	.284	.309	.184	.280	.251	.448	—		
12.	Psychological distress	3.43 (3.42)	.089	-.086	-.050	-.070	-.085	-.096	-.069	-.123	-.180	-.126	-.111	—	
13.	Sense of control over one's life	2.67 (.66)	.029	.105	.072	.084	.131	.133	.083	.149	.150	.178	.195	-.442	—

Note: Variables were scored such that a higher score indicated being female, a more professional occupation for the parent and higher age parents left school, a higher verbal and non-verbal cognitive ability scores, a higher school engagement score in teen, highest academic and vocational qualification, more professional occupation in early adulthood, higher scores on psychological distress and higher level of sense of control over one's life.

Table 3: Measurement of the latent variables in the model in NCDS and BCS cohorts.

	Men			Women		
	Unstandardised estimate	Standardised error	Standardised estimate	Unstandardised estimate	Standardised error	Standardised estimate
1958 cohort						
Parental social status	1.000	0.069	0.584	1.000	0.084	0.588
RGSC	1.791	0.046	0.797	2.155	0.060	0.756
Father's education	1.185	0.017	0.660	1.498	0.017	0.657
Mother's education	1.000	0.031	0.904	1.000	0.015	0.918
Childhood cognitive ability	0.774		0.874	0.774		0.862
Verbal tests	1.000		-0.544	1.000		-0.730
Non-verbal tests	0.318		0.614	0.212		0.617
Mental health and well-being						
Mental distress						
Sense of control over one's life						
1970 cohort						
Parental social status	1	0.051	0.623	1	0.053	0.614
RGSC	1.32	0.043	0.723	1.331	0.044	0.7
Father's education	1.098	0.097	0.644	1.084	0.089	0.62
Mother's education	1	0.093	0.401	1	0.087	0.407
Childhood cognitive ability	1.873	0.116	0.599	1.744	0.106	0.567
Recall of digits	1.929	0.033	0.773	1.888	0.018	0.776
Matrices	2.424		0.81	2.3		0.816
Word similarities	1		-0.527	1		-0.622

	Men			Women		
	Unstandardised estimate	Standardised error	Standardised estimate	Unstandardised estimate	Standardised error	Standardised estimate
			1970 cohort			
Word definitions	0.315		0.847	0.219		0.719
Mental health and well-being						
Mental distress						
Sense of control over one's life						

Chapter 14

'Activating events' in adult learners' lives: Understanding learning and life changes through a retrospective lens

Karen Evans and Edmund Waite

Introduction

The concept of career trajectories is typically used in work on transitions of young adults into the labour market, providing ideal type segmented routes that can be used to understand a variety of personal histories (Evans and Heinz, 1994). In adult life, routes diverge, experiences diversify still further and multiple new contingencies come into play (Ecclestone et al (2010); Alheit and Dausien (2002); Biesta et al (2011). In researching adults' life and work experiences, initial career trajectories take on historical significance. This chapter discusses the relationships between adult employees' individual behaviours in relation to learning (which we see as manifestations of their learning and career orientations) and the opportunities afforded to them through their workplaces. We focus on workers at the lower end of the earnings distribution to highlight the diversity of 'pathways' and social processes by which people come, through youth and adult experiences of various kinds, to the 'destinations' of lower graded jobs. We also show how these 'destinations' are merely staging posts in highly differentiated occupational and personal learning careers. The implications for lifelong learning are great: they require a rethinking of existing education and training institutions and the interaction between labour-market changes and aspects of personal and family life.

In previous work, Evans and Heinz (1993, 1994) and Evans et al (2000) identified 'transition behaviours' as patterns of activity that young people in England and Germany adopt in attempting to realise their personal interests and occupational goals through occupational and educational opportunity structures. Transition is a process that starts, for young adults, with educational achievement, occupational 'choice' (however restricted) applying for and taking up jobs as well as establishing independent personal and family lives. These processes continue in adult life with activities undertaken with the aims of maintaining employment, changing employment, balancing work and family life, finding personal fulfilment. They may be considered transitional where they involve changes in the adult's orientations to learning and career. Behaviours in relation to learning are the patterns of activity that people adopt in relation to learning opportunities available to them, in this case workplace programmes involving the development of 'adult basic skills' and varying degrees of opportunity to learn through new workplace and life experiences. These do not indicate enduring personal attributes such as personal flexibility, rigidity etc., but they do indicate complex sets of adults' motivations, beliefs and attitudes towards learning and their own capabilities to achieve in and through learning. These orientations can change according to specific experiences of success or failure, opportunities or setbacks at any stage. Orientations towards work and career, similarly, comprise complex sets of motivations, beliefs and attitudes rooted in actual life experiences. Using this framework allows an elucidation of experiences that are transitional for the adult employee in the sense of changing their learning or work/ career orientations and allows a comparison with what actually happens in their work and personal lives after engagement in new learning. It also facilitates a retrospective view of where, in the eyes of learners, these experience have come from and how they have been rooted in their earlier lives.

The significance of 'basic skills' in the lifecourse

Schoon and Silbereisen (2009) and Schoon (2010b) have shown that traditional templates are changing and that there is a polarisation of experiences in youth into fast versus slow transitions, calling for a more process-oriented rather than age- or situation-fixed approach to account for variations in role combinations at specific life phases. It is argued that future labour markets might accentuate this polarisation as the changing nature of job requirements calls for higher level skills, on the one hand, and increasing demand for jobs deemed to be low-skilled, on the other—especially regarding jobs in the retail trade and in personal-care services (Karoly 2009). It is now generally held that a single training period before entry into the labour market will no longer be sufficient, and future workers have to be prepared for continuous learning, and for upgrading of knowledge and skills, or 'reskilling' throughout their working life.

Since the launch of the national 'Skills for Life' strategy in 2001, the UK government has invested heavily in a drive to improve literacy, numeracy and ESOL provision, an important dimension of which has been the funding to support the development of 'basic skills' through programmes in and through the workplace. Research into ways in which workplace learning programmes designed to develop 'basic skills' have influenced the career orientations and trajectories of employees at the lower end of the earnings distribution, has shed light on the realities of learning in the lives of these adults. Longitudinal survey research combined with in-depth interviews repeated on three occasions over a period of eight years (2003-2011) has shed light on shifts in career orientations and attitudes towards learning as adults participate in learning in adult life, particularly learning that is accessed through their workplaces. Specific personal, institutional and macro factors come into view as these adults make connections between their present and past learning. Repeat interviews reveal how personal and retrospective accounts of adult workers' learning themselves develop and change over time. How do these personal accounts of learning connect with earlier life experiences in childhood, youth and early adulthood? How are they shaped by the contingencies of their present situation and their longer term horizons?

Adults learning in and through work: a social-ecological, life-course view

The ways in which adults learn in and through the workplace are rooted in educational trajectories and their complex intertwining with social institutions (of labour market, workplace, community) and social roles (of employee, citizen, family member) at different stages of the life-course. The usefulness of a social ecology metaphor for understanding these processes is that it provides a way into understanding the complexity of factors that impact directly or indirectly on education and lifelong learning without losing sight of the whole. Every contextual factor and every person contributing or influenced is part of a complex ecology, a system of interdependent social relationships that is self-sustaining. The application of social ecological approaches range from macro-level policy analysis (Weaver-Hightower 2008), to the adoption of the 'learning individual' as the unit of analysis, in social psychological research (Bronfenbrenner, U. (1979) or, more recently, in the context of life-course research (e.g. Biesta and Tedder 2007). Biesta et al argue that people do not act *in* structures and environments—they act through them. This resonates with conceptualisations of agency as bounded rather than structured (Evans 2002). In both youth and adult life, the beliefs people have in their ability to change their situation by their own efforts, individually or collectively, are significant for the development of skills at work and beyond (Evans 2002). These beliefs change and develop over time and according to experiences in the labour market, family and wider community. The ability to translate these beliefs into action is achieved rather than possessed (Biesta and Tedder, 2007) and capabilities are limited by bounds that can be loosened (Evans 2002, 2007).

The research

The UK research has undertaken structured interviews with 564 employees in 55 UK organisations from a variety of sectors (including transport, food manufacturing, engineering, health and local government) as well as with the relevant managers and tutors at the selected sites. Each worker-learner was also assessed early on in the course. Follow-up structured interviews and literacy assessments were undertaken in order to trace developments in literacy levels and working practices over time. In addition, three phases of in-depth interviews (referred to as Time 1, Time 2, and Time 3/ final follow-up interviews) have been undertaken with a sub-sample of 66 learners from 10 sites as well as with their relevant managers and tutors. Research informants have been asked to reflect on their experiences, looking back on influences and events. In this way 'types' can be reviewed against individual interpretations of where people think they are coming from, are going to and how they make sense of their experiences in the context of their present employment and life situation. From the vantage point of the follow-up interviews conducted in 2010/11[29], nine cases are considered in-depth (see Table1). These have been selected as 'telling cases' rather than representative ones, although each case does reflect dominant themes and dimensions found in the wider sample.[30]

Table 1: Profiles of selected cases.[31]

Bill Williams (b.1961)	has been working as a front-line operative at Coopers (a food manufacturing company in the north-east of England) since leaving school. Bill completed *learndirect* (online learning) literacy and numeracy courses at the company's learning centre which until recently has been registered as an official *learndirect* centre.
Mike Philips (b. 1953)	has been working at HLN Manufacturing (a large engineering company specializing in the manufacture of parts for cars) for the past 30 years, most recently as a forklift driver. He left school at 15 with no qualifications. He was one of 8 learners that took part in a 'Skills for Life' course at HLN..
Abdul Nazif (b.1971)	was brought up in Nigeria and received an education in both English and Arabic. He has been working as a caretaker (looking after council-owned accommodation) at Thorpton Council since 1999.

---

29 Companies and learners were followed up under the Economic and Social (ESRC) LLakes Centre Award RES-594-28-0001from 2008 to 2011.
30 See Evans et al., (2009) and Wolf and Evans 2011 for an account of the use of mixed methods.
31 Pseudonyms are used throughout, both for employees and their companies.

Mike Swan (b.1973)	has worked at the Weapons Defence Establishment (WDE) since leaving school at the age of 16. He took part in an 'ICT and English' course consisting of one and a half hour sessions over 22 weeks at the company's learning centre.
Mary Gallagher (b. 1960)	was brought up in Ghana where she received an elementary education before undertaking vocational training in embroidery. She moved to the UK with her husband and studied at an FE college for one year but had to leave the college when her son was born. She worked as a cleaner at Thorpton Local Authority where she was given the opportunity to undertake a 'Communications and Literacy' course (paid outside working hours).
Ralph Welsey (b. 1953)	left school at 17 with a few 'CSEs and O Levels' and has been working for Weapons Defence Establishment (WDE) since 1992 as a 'craft auxiliary' which mainly entails labouring work.
Lin Yeung (b.1956)	was brought up and educated in Hong Kong before moving to the UK shortly before her 18th birthday. She worked in her family's restaurant in London for 20 years before becoming a cleaner at Thorpton Council in London. She undertook a 'Literacy and Computers course' for 2 hours a week over 16-17 weeks during working hours.
Dinah Koroma (b. 1976)	received her school education in Nigeria before moving to the UK. Her work as a care worker in Manning Council entailed looking after elderly residents at a care home.
Alberto Lopez (b.1971)	gained a college degree in mechanical engineering at Portugal before coming to the UK in response to adverse employment opportunities. His job as a 'warehouse executive' at Orbit Packaging (an SME packaging company) entailed 'picking and packing.' His primary motivation for undertaking an ESOL course at Orbit Packaging was to improve his general English language skills.

Educational experiences in early life and youth: shifting learning orientations

Longitudinal, mixed methods research uncovers the multiple interacting factors shaping the adult life course such as those that occur between education, within family life and within a work career. The in-depth interviews with adult workers illuminated how the enduring effects of early educational experiences are brought into the present and acted on in family and working life.

As in the case of the broader sample of employees who have been interviewed in the initial phase of the research (see Wolf and Evans, 2011), the majority of these individuals spoke about their early educational experience in largely negative terms, and often with regret. In referring to these experiences, learners revealed a shift in learning orientations since childhood. Mike Swan admitted that "I didn't really try that hard, and it didn't really interest me … I look back and think well I should have done a bit better really, … I know I could have." Bill Williams similarly referred to a shifting attitude to learning since childhood: "at school you have to go. I was only sixteen when I left school. I'm forty-three now. I just got older and dafter, some people say wiser … you start to realise now that these things are worth teaching at school, you try to instil into your child they're not just teaching you these things to make life boring, they're teaching you because you need them in the future".

Similarly, Mike Philips made a point of encouraging his own children to study seriously at school and they had subsequently gone on to study at university: "there was only me in our house, that had got no qualifications or certificates or anything. I mean even our dog had got a pedigree, so I thought it's time to catch up." Abdul Nazif, who was educated in English and Arabic, admitted "I failed every class … because I couldn't spell properly." He also bemoaned the truncated nature of his education: "I regret not going to college and coming out the other end." Mary Gallagher enjoyed her experience at school but regrets that she received only an elementary education in Ghana as a result of her parents' insistence that she undertake vocational training at an early age in response to economic pressures: "I did like school, yes. But you know when you are young, everyone wants you to do this, do that so I went to the wrong direction." Ralph Welsey also enjoyed the experience of being at school but left with no qualifications.

Dinah Koroma had suffered from a disrupted education as a result of immigration to the UK from Nigeria: "I did enjoy my primary school, and my Sunday school but I did not finish my education before I came to this country." Similarly, Lin Yeung received a reasonable junior school education in Hong Kong in Cantonese (and some English) but was not able to complete secondary school qualifications as a result of her family's immigration to the UK. Of the highlighted learners, Abdul Lopez had the most positive early learning experiences in so far as he enjoyed his time at school and had proceeded to achieve a higher education degree in mechanical engineering.

The diversity of early experiences is already apparent in these cases, together with commonalities in the later realisation of what had been missed. They reflect the larger sample, in which many cases of those born and schooled in the UK recorded that early experiences of education had generated little interest and the value of learning had not been realised until the person had moved beyond initial schooling. In other cases, often including migrants to the UK, early experiences of learning had been enjoyed but had either not been interrupted or had not translated into hoped-for outcomes in the labour market. In these cases new avenues were being sought.

Accessing learning via the workplace fits life situations

The location of adult learning courses in the workplace during working hours played an important role in allowing adults to act upon these changing realisations of the value of learning and shifts in their learning orientations since childhood.

Mary Gallagher underlined the benefit of workplace courses in allowing employees to engage in learning without causing disruption to work and family commitments; Mike Swan similarly underlined the convenience and accessibility of workplace learning: "To be honest I think the advantages are if it's in the workplace it's nearer, and because it's on company time people are probably more willing to do it. Rather than go off somewhere to do it".

In addition to underlining the convenience of learning through the workplace courses, Ralph Welsey mentioned that learning in the workplace was less intimidating: "I'd be nervous I think apprehensive (about attending a college) … I haven't been in the classroom situation leading to any qualifications since I was about seventeen. Thirty-six years ago." In Time 2 follow-up interviews, Ralph revealed that he felt far more confident about engaging in further learning in a college since the workplace course had acted as a bridge to learning in more formal educational institutions: "Because I've done the initial step really I would have said it's a good introduction for anybody really".

Bill Williams recounted the obstacles he had faced when previously studying the Greek language (in pursuit of personal, leisure interests) at an evening college and contrasted this with the ease and accessibility of studying online through a company ('Coopers') learning centre. Mike Philips had also previously been deterred from engaging in further learning as a result of the geographical and time constraints associated with studying at a college. Albert Lopez also highlighted the convenience of workplace learning and revealed that he would not be prepared to study in a college.

For Lin Yeung, the workplace provided a more 'relaxed' learning environment: "In the college it seems that it is more tense". Lin Yeung particularly appreciated the chance to engage in informal conversation and banter with her colleagues which provided an important antidote to the isolation from native English speakers she had encountered in her work as a cleaner as well during her previous employment in her family's Chinese restaurant.

In Kersh et al., (2012) we have shown how the semiotic significance of the spatial dimension of workplace SFL (Skills for Life) provision proves to be extremely important in this context. The workplace often symbolises an environment that is perceived as different from a classroom-like setting where the learner might have had negative prior experiences. In addition, the workplace may offer rewards such as improved career prospects (for example promotion), which provide an additional incentive for taking an SFL course. Developing confidence in the workplace is another crucial stimulus. Although workplace SFL provision aims to boost skills relating to economic productivity and is focused quite narrowly on one spatial environment—the workplace—the learners' motivations are much broader and relate to a wider range of differing environments. Apart from using their newly acquired skills in the workplace learners can also recontextualise their skills to other contexts, for example to their family environments.

How do earlier learning, life experiences and current work connect in 'career development'?

In this section we build further on the Evans and Heinz (1993) and Evans et al., (2000) classifications to conceptualise the career development of the highlighted adults in terms of the following categories: 'progressive' (e.g. promotion), 'upwards drift' (e.g. skills development within existing role), 'horizontal development' (undertaking the same role with no major changes to literacy and numeracy skills requirements), 'downwards drift' (less use of literacy and numeracy and other skills requirements), 'interruption' (e.g. redundancy).

The career trajectories of Bill Williams, Mike Philips, Lin Yeung and Alberto Lopez can be characterised as 'horizontal development'. Bill remained as a front-line operative at Coopers throughout the timeframe of the research (moving from the role of 'seasoning technician' on the production line to the role of 'packaging technician' involving packing cases of crisps over a period of eight years). Bill's main reason for signing up for the *learndirect* courses in Maths and Literacy at Coopers was that he was "just curious … I mean I left school with no qualifications to speak of, CSE [Certificate of Secondary Education] things, which are probably in museums now …". The literacy courses have helped him with writing letters and the maths courses have improved his capacity to help his child with homework but have not impacted substantially on the workplace.

Mike Philips' main motivation for undertaking a Skills for Life course at HLN manufacturing was, "For general interest, general knowledge, and to improve

Table 2: Trajectories, work orientations and adult learning: changes over time.

		Mike Swan (WDE)	Ralph Welsey (WDE)	Mary Gallagher (Frizlands)	Lin Yeung (Frizlands)	Dinah Koroma (Manning Council)
Job role at Time1, T 2 and 3		Machine Tool Fitter (T1 and 2), Trainer (3)	Machine Tool Fitter (all stages)	Cleaner (T1) Care worker (T2 and T3)	Cleaner (T1, 2 and 3)	Care Worker
Summary of career trajectory	Progressive, Upwards Drift, Horizontal Development, Downwards Drift, Interruption	Progressive	Upwards Drift	Progressive	Horizontal Development	Upward Drift
Work Orientations at Time 1, Time 2 and 3	'Content with Current role' 'Reconciled to Current Role' 'Struggling to Overcome Barriers' 'Stand-by Opportunism' 'Aspirational'	'Stand-by Opportunism' (T1) Aspirational (active) (T2 and 3)	'Content with Current Role' (T1) Stand-by Opportunism (T2, 3)	'Stand-by Opportunism' (T1) Aspirational (active) (T2 and 3)	Aspirational (passive) (T1-2) Reconciled to Current Role (T3)	Aspirational (active) (T1,2, 3)
Uses of Literacy in workplace at Time 1, Time 2 and Time 3	H- M- L (high,medium, low)	M-H-H	M-M-H	L-H-H	L-L-L	H H H
Further Learning	'Job-related';'SFL';'Personal Interests';'No Further Learning'	ICT, Job-related	Job-related	SFL and Job-related (re-training)	No Further Learning	NVQ Social Care
Impact of SFL on career	Negligible Impact, Facilitative, Transformative	Transformative	Facilitative	Transformative	Negligible	Facilitative
Wider impact of SFL course (outside work)	'Attitudinal''Interests' 'Family Support' 'Link to Further Learning' 'Use of Literacy at Home' 'ICT at Home'	'Attitudinal' 'ICT at Home'	'ICT at Home'	'Attitudinal' 'Family Support'	'Attitudinal' 'Link to Further Learning'	'Use of Literacy at Home'

		Abdul Nazif (Frizlands)	Bill Williams (Coopers)	Mike Philips (HLN Manufacturing)	Alberto Lopez (Orbit Packaging)
Job role at Time1, T 2 and 3		Caretaker (T1, 2 and 3)	Front-line Operator (T1, 2 and 3)	Forklift Driver (T1 and 2). Redundancy (T3)	Warehouse Worker (T1, 2 and 3)
Summary of career trajectory	Progressive, Upwards Drift, Horizontal Development, Downwards Drift, Interruption	Upward Drift (Time 1, 2 and 3)	Horizontal Development	Horizontal Development Interrupted	Horizontal Development
Work Orientations at Time 1, Time 2 and 3	'Content with Current role' 'Reconciled to Current Role' 'Struggling to Overcome Barriers' 'Stand-by Opportunism' 'Aspirational'	Aspirational (passive) (T1,2, 3)	Content with Current role (T1,2, 3)	Content with Current Role (prior to company closure)	Aspirational (passive) (T1, 2 and 3)
Uses of Literacy in workplace at Time 1, Time 2 and Time 3	H- M- L (high,medium, low)	LLL	LLL	L-L- NA	L-L- L
Further Learning	'Job-related','SFL','Personal Interests','No Further Learning'	Job-related	SFL (T2).	ICT Personal Interests	No Further Learning
Impact of SFL on career	Negligible Impact, Facilitative, Transformative	Facilitative	Negligible	Negligible	Negligible
Wider impact of SFL course (outside work)	'Attitudinal''Interests' 'Family Support' 'Link to Further Learning' 'Use of Literacy at Home' 'ICT at Home'	'Use of Literacy at Home' 'Interests'	'Interests' 'Family Support'	'Attitudinal' 'Interests' 'Link to Further Learning'	'Attitudinal'

myself. I think as long as you're stimulated by learning different things, seeing different things then you'll always stay active … and as long as your brain is alert I'm sure you'll get no problems". Mike Philips reported that the participation on the workplace course had boosted his confidence and encouraged him to embark on further learning. After the 'Skills for Life' course, Mike Philips proceeded to undertake two computer courses at Level 1 and Level 2 at HLN manufacturing which were organised by the company's union learning representatives at the company's newly built learning centre. Following the closure of HLN manufacturing, Mike Philips is currently unemployed. He reveals that he is finding it difficult to find another job as a result of the economic downturn and the lack of employment opportunities in the Walsall area. Mike reveals that the computer course has had the primary longer-term effect on his life in allowing him to pursue hobbies and facilitate his job search: "I am able to use internet and receive emails now as part of my everyday life".

Lin Yeung's participation on a SFL course at Frizlands swimming pool initially helped her develop her informal English language communication skills, thereby allowing her to interact more easily with colleagues; "because of the course … I can join in the conversation … so when we are having a break … I do have a bit of confidence to chat to them … I think it's good to help me with my confidence". She harboured plans at Time 1 interviews to move to a job in the retail sector which would entail what she regarded as more challenging work. Her experience of studying on the workplace course at Barking encouraged her to apply for a literacy course at a local college in order to facilitate her career opportunities through the development of her English language communication skills. However, she had to abandon the course at an early stage as a result of family commitments.

A shift in Lin Yeung's work arrangements also meant that she had less opportunity to develop her English language skills through communication with colleagues: 'I haven't got much time to communicate with them, it's mainly you know a few word and that's it. Alberto Lopez undertook an ESOL course at Orbit Packaging in order to improve his English in general as well as facilitate workplace communication. Although his warehouse job entailed 'picking and packing boxes' and had minimal literacy requirements, the ESOL course allowed Alberto Lopez to communicate more easily with colleagues: it had an, "important effect on work and communication … It helped my understanding". Alberto Lopez was also able to make use of his improved literacy in his home life. From the beginning of Time 1 interviews onwards, Alberto

Lopez expressed the intention of gaining promotion to a post that would entail supervisory responsibilities. Although Alberto Lopez moved to a new company in Northampton he was still engaged at the time of the final interview in similar types of packaging work with minimal literacy requirements (e.g. reading lists of received items). He has done no further training (apart from a forklift truck driving certificate).

The career development of Ralph Welsey, Dinah Koroma and Abdul Nazif may be described in terms of 'upwards drift' trajectory. Ralph Welsey worked as a 'craft auxiliary' at WDE which mainly involved workshop labouring work. Ralph Welsey's main motivation for undertaking the workplace courses at WDE was to develop his ICT skills; he attached little significance to the literacy component of the course. The levelling out of management structures at WDE entailed an increasing delegation of responsibilities to Ralph Welsey's grade of employment. During the course of the final follow-up interview, Ralph Welsey revealed that his job has been 'evolving' as a result of the positive working environment in his section. He attached considerable significance to the support of managers who had helped him learn new skills informally (e.g. by demonstration) and had given him scope to develop his skills on an experimental basis; "I was given time to learn things myself on the computer—to fiddle around on the computer". The original 'ICT and literacy' course has had a longer-term impact on his working practices as a result of his regular usage of these skills: "the old memory plays up … If you are not using your skills regularly it is surprising how quickly you lose it".

Dinah Koroma's experience of undertaking a literacy and ICT course at Manning Social Services was related directly to her job as a care worker, looking after elderly residents at a care home in Camden. Her job involved an increasing use of literacy in writing care plans. By the time of the final follow-up interview, Dinah Koroma was still a care worker in an old people's home. She has undertaken her National Vocational Qualification (NVQ) in social care and was hoping to start a degree course in social work the following year, funded through the local authority.

Abdul Nazif had been working as a resident care-taker since 1999. In his current job he needs to keep an account of incidents in the buildings. He has had self-acknowledged problems with literacy throughout his recent working life. He found the course provided a welcome reprieve from the daily work routine. This learning opportunity had helped Abdul with certain aspects of literacy such as spelling but he feels that the course was not sufficiently long enough to have a major impact and had only partially remediated past 'damage': 'putting something good into something that's spoilt for so long it's not going to make it right, so much damage already, Malcolm (the tutor) did a great deal of work on me, but it didn't really put the picture right.'

Although Abdul Nazif was still undertaking the same role (care-taker) at the time of the final follow up interview his career trajectory can be described as 'upward drift' as he has continued development of his literacy skills through informal methods (e.g. the writing down of key phrases in a notebook as a well as the writing of poetry and lyrics to relieve the tedium of work). He continued to regard the development of his English language skills and computer literacy as important for fulfilling his wish to be promoted to the role of estate officer but family and other commitments have so far prevented him from implementing his goal of undertaking a further literacy course at a local college. At the time of the final interview he was continuing to develop his writing and computer skills through informal methods: "I am learning for myself as I go along".

Whereas the impact of these workplace adult learning courses on the career trajectories of Lin Yeung, Abdul Nazif, Bill Williams and Keith Hughes was 'negligible' and for Ralph Welsey, and Dinah Koroma, it was 'facilitative', participation in SFL workplace courses that had a 'transformative' impact on the careers of Mike Swan and Mary Gallagher.

As will be explored in more detail in the next section, Mary Gallagher revealed that the process of undertaking a 'Communications and Literacy' course at Thorpton council gave her the confidence to leave her job as a cleaner and embark on a new career as a care-worker in a psychiatric hospital.

The course was also important in giving her the confidence to embark on further learning in the form of a NVQ Level 2 in care work and additional courses in aspects of health, safety and elderly care through her current employer. The course has also had wider benefits in allowing Mary to help her son with his homework. Mary Gallagher continued to develop her literacy skills through the writing of care plans for elderly patients as well as handover notes between shifts. She also developed her literacy skills informally through the everyday practice of filling in forms as well as through observing and learning from the care plans of more experienced colleagues. She has also benefited from observing colleagues' interaction with the elderly patients: 'I watch them talking to clients … how they treat them.'

Having undertaken the 'ICT and literacy' course at the Weapons Defence Establishment, Mike Swan was promoted from machine tool fitter to Works Supervisory Officer which involved increased use of ICT in order to undertake risk assessments. Looking back at the course, he reveals that :"... it mainly gives more confidence to try and improve, try other courses as well, work and things like that". He has proceeded to undertake an IT level 2 course at the Weapons Defence Establishment and a computer programming NVQ Level 1 course at a nearby college. Both of these courses were provided by the company in order to support his transition to the new post.

Although at Time 1 interviews Mike Swan had attached minimal significance to the literacy component of the course since he felt it had minimal relevance to his working practices, subsequent changes to his career led him to view the course differently at Time 2 interviews:"I realise that it (the literacy component of the course) was quite an important part ... before I wasn't really writing too much, and now obviously I use it a lot more, do more handwriting as well as on the computer". Participation on the 'ICT and literacy' course has also impacted on Mike Swan's life outside work in so far as he subsequently bought a computer at home and disseminated the skills he initially acquired on the course to his partner. As a result of participation on the course, Mike Swan has also been able to undertake a more supportive and involved role in his daughter's education. By the time of the final interview, Mike Swan had been promoted to a training post and was now in charge of training sixteen apprentices.

Taken together, these qualitative findings are consistent with the patterns identified in Reder's (2009) work, based on the analysis of large scale data sets. Engagement in literacy practices tends to increase in early adult life, and is related to combinations of maturational effects and changes in life experiences and activities. Among those who participate in adult basic skills programmes, Reder found that participation is often broken up into multiple episodes, and often involves varying amounts of 'self-study'. The evidence[32] also tentatively suggested that better jobs that may engage a broader range of workers' literacy skills are likely to support the development of proficiency, a suggestion supported by the above case analyses and the wider findings of the present research (see Evans and Waite, 2010) and Wolf and Evans, 2011).

---

32 Statistical modelling has shown a 2-step process is taking place. Both programme participation and selfstudy positively impact on engagement in literacy practices and this in turn may lead to increases in literacy proficiency, according to Reder's 2009 findings. The most direct and immediate impacts of participation are evident for literacy practices than for literacy proficiency. The latter appears in the longer term to be positively affected by participation.

How do career orientations change in adult working life?

The complex sets of adults motivations, beliefs that constitute 'career orientations' can be conceptualised on the basis of the following categories: 'content with current role'; 'reconciled to current role'; 'struggling to overcome barriers'; 'stand- by opportunism'; 'aspirational'. The category 'content with current role' signifies a satisfaction with current employment status as well as a preference not to be promoted or experience change in the workplace. 'Reconciled to current role' denotes an acceptance of current employment status which may also be shaped by a lack of employment and training opportunities within the organisation (thereby making promotion prospects unlikely) as well as by a lack of opportunity to undertake training outside of work (e.g. as a result of family commitments).

'Stand-by opportunism' denotes not only an attitude of satisfaction with current employment status but also a willingness to take advantage of any learning or career advancement opportunities that may become available. Such an attitude is therefore based on the reasonably optimistic premise that the work environment is sufficiently favourable to foster the potential for such opportunities to materialise. 'Aspirational' career orientations signifies a wish for promotion or career advancement. 'Active Aspirational' as opposed to 'passive aspirational' attitudes entail actively taking up any learning or work opportunities that may become available. If such opportunities are not available such a disposition entails active measures to embark on more challenging work-such as further learning outside work or departure from the organisation.

Although Bill Williams, Mike Philips, Lin Yeung, Alberto Lopez experienced a 'horizontal' career trajectory after engagement on the workplace Skills for Life course these were underpinned by differing career orientations. From Time 1 interviews onwards, Bill Williams was fully contented with his current job role; "I've only got sixteen years to go until I'm sixty ... at my age and my qualifications I'm getting double the minimum wage ... I'm relatively happy in what I do ..." This deeply engrained attitude to the workplace may be attributed to a combination of Bill's socio-economic background (outlined above) and school qualifications as well as employment opportunities in the local area (an area of high unemployment in the north-east of England). Such attitudes were further consolidated by the impact of the economic downturn which has prompted Bill to place an even higher value on his employment at Coopers; 'you can't pick and choose in this day and age'. Mike Philips was also fully reconciled to his job as fork-lift driver until he experienced redundancy as a result of closure of the site. During the course of LLAKES interviews, Mike Philips revealed that he was drawing on his experience of the workplace ICT course at GKN in order to pursue hobbies as well as facilitate his search for a new job. In contrast to colleagues of a similar age from HLN manufacturing who had become reconciled to long-term unemployment or early retirement, Mike still maintained hope of finding further employment despite the adverse economic opportunities in the local economy.

By contrast, Lin Yeung whose career trajectory may similarly be described as 'horizontal' expressed 'aspirational' attitudes at Time 1 and Time 2 before becoming 'reconciled to her current role' by the time of the final follow-up interviews. During the course of Time 1 interviews, Lin Yeung revealed that participation on the SFL workplace course had encouraged her to sign up for an English course at a nearby college.

> Because if that course didn't come up I was just relaxed you know, I would not go for further learning, now because I learnt something which I want to improve a bit more, encourage me to go a bit further.

Lin's participation in further learning was related to her wish to move into more 'challenging' work.

> I hope that it can give me more confident ... to write a letter easily or to fill in forms, to write a report so that, hopefully they can help me in the future if I need to go for a job.

At Time 2 interviews, Lin Yeung revealed that she had dropped out of the English course since family commitments had made it difficult to attend the college in the evening. As noted in the previous section, she also expressed frustration with the lack of opportunities to develop her English language communication skills in the workplace: "I haven't got the chance to talk to people and ... also it seems that I don't have to use my brain that much, honestly." During the course of the final follow-up interviews, Lin Yeung revealed that she was fully reconciled to her job as a cleaner and no longer harboured plans to embark on more challenging work or further learning: "It would be difficult to go on another course. I don't have enough time. The job and family takes up too much time".

Lin's participation on the SFL workplace course at Frizlands therefore initially acted as an 'activating event' which launched her on the path of further learning with a view to embarking on a more challenging career. However, the difficulty of attending college in the evening together with adverse working conditions culminated in a shift from 'aspirational' career orientations to a reluctant reconciliation with current employment status.

Despite following a 'horizontal' career trajectory which involved packaging in warehouses in Orbit Packaging and then Northampton, Albert Lopez retained aspirational motivations throughout the duration of the research projects. At Time 2 interviews, Albert Lopez admitted to being frustrated with his work situation.

> … I'm like in a swamp you know, water doesn't run anywhere … there's no life here do you understand … I'm willing to learn something new … it doesn't matter how long doing the same thing like a machine, you are human you … you want to work for challenge for learning something.

By the time of the final (2010/11) interviews, Albert Lopez had moved to a new job in Northampton that also involved packaging work in a warehouse. The 'upward drift' career trajectories of Ralph Welsey, Dinah Koroma, Abdul Nazif were also underpinned by differing career trajectories.

During the course of Time 1 interviews, Ralph Welsey did not harbour thoughts of promotion or have high expectations of a fulfilling work experience.

> My job now serves its purpose. I've got no interest in it … it's just I come in here and I go home.

However, he expressed a willingness to take advantage of any opportunities to develop within his role in keeping with the career orientation that we term 'stand-by opportunism'. During Time 2 interviews, Ralph Welsey revealed that increasing responsibilities, largely of an administrative nature, had been delegated to his post. However, he also expressed disappointment that these responsibilities were not accompanied by increased pay.

Obviously it's more interesting than sweeping up, but then ... at what point do you say I'm doing this additional work and I think I should be earning more and I'm not. And that's going to start eating away, its not worth doing ...

During the final follow-up interview, Ralph Welsey revealed that the process of delegating responsibilities (as part of a general 'levelling out' of management responsibilities) had increased and was now accompanied by a commensurate pay rise which had provided a boost to his morale: 'I would not be talking to you now if I had not been given a pay increase. It is vital to your motivation-otherwise you feel you are being 'done by'.

The experiences of Ralph Welsey underline the key significance of broader institutional support for career development:"at the lower end of the grade scale, you have to be in a situation where the door opens a bit for you as well. You can't just push the door open yourself. It is a two way thing." In terms of the longer-term impact of the course,"for me, it was a foothold, a way of moving up. At my age, it was the only way of moving up."

From Time 1 interviews onwards Dinah Koroma maintained a long-term goal of training to be a social worker. The ICT and literacy course together with working conditions in a care home have nurtured these 'aspirational' goals throughout this time-scale, although the council has not yet presented her with the chance to train as a social worker.

Abdul Nazif has similarly retained 'aspirational' career goals despite experiencing the disappointment of not being promoted to the role of estate manager:"I think I've always been ambitious. I've always wanted to move on and make something of the job." Abdul highlighted the relevance of further learning to his career prospects but conceded that personal circumstances had hitherto prevented him from attending a college.

it's my responsibility. I shouldn't be expecting anyone to do that, I should actually use my wages, pay for it and get the English higher and to move forward in life ... I've got a daughter who's nine and nothing is cheap ... difficult to buy, a lot of problems, the car is a lot to run, kids need things all the time ... The more I can work earn now the better, so I want to better myself ... get a job in an office where they pay more, but I have to learn what it takes to make that money.

In different ways, workplace learning activities have acted as 'activating events' that have triggered new sets of career attitudes and motivations. Rather than radically altering or realigning career attitudes and motivations, the workplace courses served as 'tipping points' that nudged some employees towards embracing 'career orientations' that entailed a broadening of their career horizons and a galvanising of their willingness to take on more challenging work. In the cases of Mary Gallagher and Mike Swan, the cumulative long-term effect of this shift in career orientations has had a 'transformative' impact on their respective career trajectories.

The workplace basic skills NVQ course at Barking gave Mary Gallagher the confidence to leave her job as a cleaner and retrain as a care worker: "You know, I was working as a cleaner. If it was not for the course … I couldn't have done any better. But because of the course that helped me to take that … I can do better … I go somewhere else. Not the same as a cleaner all the time." Reviewing the longer-term impact, Mary reiterated that the course has had a major effect in broadening her career horizons beyond the domain of cleaning. In a similar way, Mike Swan views, retrospectively and from a longer-term vantage point, the 'ICT and literacy' course as being important, "that was the kick-start. It got me thinking and kick-started me to do lots of other things". Looking back on the course, he sees that the literacy component was also helpful because he now needs to write more frequently: "the course at Newbury college was all assignment based so the other course helped in terms of punctuation and so on …". As part of his current job he uses computer for teaching resources, management system (keeping timesheets of apprentices) as well as undertaking risk assessments. He expresses a strong loyalty to the company and acknowledges institutional support for his career development: "I have been given a lot of support from the company".

These cases challenge dominant perceptions of the 'dead-end' nature of low waged work and overly deterministic notions of life trajectories that lead from low qualifications in youth to long-term low skilled work and under-employment in adult life. Our qualitative findings are consistent with the findings of Gorard and Rees (2002), who have also shown, through quantitative analysis, that determinants of later participation in learning reflect the circumstances of adult life and the access people have to learning, including through their work.

Discussion

The metaphor of a social ecology of learning is helpful in allowing us to explore the interaction of these factors through taking account of the relationships between the affordances of the workplace (or those features of the workplace environment that invite us to engage and learn), the types of knowledge afforded by literacy and numeracy learning (including knowing how and 'knowing that you can') and the agency or intention to act of the individual employee, reflected in their diverse motivations. These are triangular relationships and mutually interdependent sets of interactions. There are affordances for learning in all workplace environments. Some are more accessible and visible than others. The intention of employees to act in particular ways in pursuit of their goals and interests, whether in their jobs or personal lives, makes the affordances for learning more visible to them. The know-how associated with literacy practices such as report-writing or finding better ways of expressing oneself, and the confidence of 'knowing that you can' often develop as the person engages with the opportunity. The process of making the affordances for learning more visible itself can generate some employees' will to act and use those affordances, and new knowledge results. In the shifting attitudes to learning, the changing levels of know-how and the confidence that comes from 'knowing that you can' both stimulate action and the seeking out of affordances within and beyond the workplace in the form of further opportunities.

Both Mike Swan and Ralph Welsey benefited from a favourable work environment at the Weapons Defence Establishment. Mike Swan was able to capitalise on the growth of confidence and increased willingness to take on more challenging work-a shift from 'stand-by opportunism' to 'aspirational' career orientations-in the form of promotion within his section of the company. The promotion allowed him to develop his newly acquired skills and reinforce his confidence which has subsequently led to further promotion to the post of trainer. The organisational 'levelling out' of management responsibilities at WDE has also allowed Ralph Welsey to gradually develop ICT and administrative skills which, combined with a commensurate pay rise, has had a positive effect on his morale and attitude to work. Ralph's further development of these skills has depended heavily on support from colleagues as well as informal learning.

Dinah Koroma has also been able to further develop her writing and ICT skills through her everyday work as a care worker. Whereas the majority of SFL workplace courses were generic in nature and were not effectively tailored to the workplace (Wolf et al., 2010), the SFL course at Manning Social Services effectively responded to the need for increased report- writing amongst care-workers.

By contrast, Lin Yeung, Abdul Nazif, Alberto Lopez and Mary Gallagher were faced with working environments that did not afford readily available opportunities for skills utilisation and promotion. The differing responses to such institutional constraints underline the significance of personal dispositions in social ecological patterns of behaviour. Faced with the lack of opportunity to express 'voice' in the workplace, Mary Gallagher opted for 'exit' (Hirschman, 1970), leaving her job as a cleaner in order to pursue a new career as a care worker. Lin Yeung, on the other hand, has carried on her work as a cleaner and has experienced a shift from what we term 'aspirational' to 'reconciled to current role' career orientations as a result of the lack of opportunities for skills development and promotion in the workplace together with practical obstacles to further learning outside the workplace as a result of family commitments. Abdul Nazif has managed to develop his skills informally despite not fulfilling his longer-term goal of becoming an estate officer, whereas Alberto Lopez continues to be frustrated by the polarisation between his career goals and the unchallenging nature of work in a warehouse.

The importance of taking account of the interaction between personal features (some of which are deeply rooted in family and socio-economic background), institutional conditions and the broader macro environment is highlighted in the case of Bill William's contentment with current role over the long-term. Such attitudes were shaped by early educational and social influences as well as considerations relating to high levels of unemployment in the local economy. Mike Philips reconciliation to his current job role at HKN was similarly shaped by socio-economic and educational background (e.g. lack of qualifications) together with the bleak employment opportunities in the local region. The longer-term impact of the course in allowing Mike Philips to respond to redundancy and facilitate the search for more employment highlights the inter-weaving of personal and career-oriented outcomes of workplace SFL provision.

The experiences of these highlighted individuals (as in the case of the broader sample of learners) underlines the advantages of these types of workplace provision in providing an accessible and convenient opportunity for learning that also tends to be less prone to the more intimidating associations of formal educational environments for learning. Such provision has a significant impact in responding to employees' shifting learning orientations since childhood and in allowing individuals to address the legacy of previously negative educational experiences. However, the impact of such provision on the career attitudes and trajectories of employees is likely to be eroded over time unless the broader organisational setting supports the ongoing practice and development of skills and provides pathways for career development that are responsive to shifting career orientations.

While learning needs to be seen as an integral part of practice rather than as something that is added on, attention needs to be paid to the environment as a whole—for example, the work environment affects how far formal learning can be a positive trigger for further learning and *vice versa*. The affordances of the workplace (or those features of the workplace environment that invite us to engage and learn) are enhanced or limited according to the wider ecologies embedded and reflected in the employment relationship and the wider social dynamics of family and community.

Conclusion

This chapter starts to fill in the broad brush sketch of how adult lives unfold, through a textured account of what adult life at work means in practice for people whose life trajectories lead them to enter it at the low wage, low-graded end of the labour market. Their retrospective views underline the significance of earlier experience but they also problematise attempts to solve the problems of 'disadvantaged' youth through front-loaded education and training. Shifts towards more positive orientations to learning often emerge in adulthood out of life experiences and they change with contingencies and roles in adult life.

Evans and Niemeyer (2004) have previously shown how learning programmes designed to support young people who are at risk of becoming detached from education, training and labour market opportunities are unlikely to succeed unless they engage young people actively and in ways that are 'situated' in relation to their life and work contexts. In this chapter we have shown how the salience of these criteria continues into the adult years. Learning that is situated practically involves engagement in actual work practices and workgroups, access to programmes of activity, and the time and space provided for learning. To be situated socially, culturally and biographically involves the adjustment of learning contexts to learners' interests and experiences, links between activities and chains of support, and the acknowledgment of social and emotional dimensions of learning. Various configurations of learning that are well situated within workplace settings may considerably facilitate adults' engagement and motivation.

Exploration of employees' personal accounts of adult learning shows how specific workplace experiences and activities can act as 'activating events' in so far as they have the potential to not only trigger new 'learning orientations' (values, attitudes towards learning) but may also forge new 'career orientations'. These frequently entail greater confidence and willingness on the part of employees to develop in new domains of the workplace. However, the impact of these shifting orientations on career trajectories, and the degree to which such changes can be sustained over time depends on personal and institutional factors as well as the broader political and economic environment. Positive impacts on career attitudes and trajectories of employees are likely to be eroded unless the broader institutional setting actively supports the ongoing practice and development of skills and pathways for career development.

Part 5: Wider international perspectives on youth, working life and wellbeing

Chapter 15

Young adulthood in Australia and New Zealand: Pathways to belonging

Johanna Wyn

Introduction

Young people's trajectories through education and into employment have been a focus in youth research for over a quarter of a century, reflecting global social and economic changes in labour markets. The focus on education to employment trajectories also reflects the nexus between youth studies and youth policy, a space in which normative assumptions about age and normative patterns of life have become taken for granted. The idea of youth transitions has almost become synonymous with 'school-to-work' trajectories, to the exclusion of other significant areas of life such as wellbeing, relationships with people and place and leisure. There has to date been very little research that explores the flows of influence across these areas of young people's lives. Wellbeing, leisure and personal relationships are often relegated to side issues to the main game of education and employment; their influence on education and employment patterns and decisions all but ignored.

This chapter takes up the challenge of building on the insights of approaches to youth research that take a predominantly 'transitions' lens. I argue that it is timely to rethink what has been gained from this approach over the last twent-five years, and to reflect on what has been lost from sight. I argue that the metaphor of transitions has limitations, including a tendency to universalise and naturalise phases of the life course. These tendencies can create a form of blindness to local conditions and to the changing nature of local and global environments. There is a dual element to transitions that is ironically often lost from sight within a 'transitions' approach, because of its focus on the trajectories of individuals according to predetermined markers of progress.

Moving away from the metaphor of transitions, I suggest that the idea of belonging enables youth researchers to integrate economic change (i.e. school to work) with other dimensions of life, including wellbeing and relationships to people and place. Belonging is a descriptive term that invites the researcher (and policy maker) to map and understand how young people put together the complex elements of life that enable them to be connected, included, well, to participate and to be economically stable. Decisions about education and employment are one element in the quest to belong—but they are not the only element.

The idea of belonging is implicit in a lot of recent 'boundary crossing' youth research, including the intersections of youth cultures and transitions research (Furlong, et al., 2011) and research that focuses on the intersections between locality and biography (Hall et al., 2009; Massey, 2008; Kraack and Kenway, 2002). These approaches open up an understanding of the resources that young people draw on to build their lives, and the ways in which changing conditions impact on life chances. Hall, Coffey and Lashua (2002) argue that youth transitions need to be understood in relation to young people's relationships to place. Their research shows how narratives of transformation redevelopment and regeneration of a rural community interact with young people's biographical transformations. This work identifies the importance of understanding the connectivities between young people and place. Similarly, Kraak and Kenway have analysed the relationships between place and young men's identities and work in a rural town in Australia (Kraack and Kenway, 2002). They show how structural changes to the rural economy have stripped away traditional resources (especially work) for the performance of male identities.

This chapter focuses on young people in Australia and New Zealand, against the backdrop of the neoliberal policy reforms of the 1980s and beyond. I argue that these policy reforms, as well as the global economic changes that they were responding to, have significantly impacted on the ways in which young people can belong. In both Australia and New Zealand, the economic benefits of investing in education were slow to materialise. Across the young population in both countries, gaining post-secondary educational qualifications is associated long-term with greater security of employment (Rea and Callister, 2009; Andres and Wyn, 2010). What is of interest is what happens in between the steps of education and work.

In the following sections I firstly provide a very brief description of the context of young people's lives in Australia and New Zealand, focusing especially on the impact of the neoliberal policy interventions that began in the 1980s and that continue to impact on young people's lives. Next I explore some of the limitations implicit in a transitions approach to researching young people. I argue that the metaphor of transitions tends to reify externally imposed sequential steps onto young lives, obscuring the interconnections between education, employment, location, personal relationships and wellbeing. Drawing on the idea of belonging, I set out some of the benefits of understanding education and employment decisions as nested within wider concerns and goals of young people to belong. The chapter then provides some examples of research on young people in Australia and New Zealand that illustrates this approach. I conclude that new approaches are needed to address chronic patterns of inequality. The same groups of young people have been marginalised from education and employment for over a quarter of a century. Although education and employment are key elements in addressing inequality, the pathways through these cannot be fully understood without acknowledging their significance for belonging.

The context of young lives in Australia and New Zealand

Young people living in Australia and New Zealand have access to common cultural practices and resources, especially through digital communications. Yet their lives are inflected by diversity that is both within and between these countries. Even the effects of common government policies are mediated by place.

Young people's relationship with places and landscapes is increasingly being recognised—as youth researchers acknowledge that young people's transitions need to be understood in the context of local conditions and historical traditions. This includes understanding the specific ways in which the local is transcended through globalising processes. In Australia, even in the most remote locations, young people are connected to ideas and people in other places through digital communication technologies. Young Indigenous Australians living in remote communities for example are physically isolated but nonetheless connected to national and international cultures through digital communications (Blanchard et al., 2008, Kral, 2010). These global communication flows are not simply one-way. Digital communications give young people in remote locations access to global, commercially produced cultures as well as giving them a platform to 'speak out' to a global audience, constructing contemporary stories about their culture and their lives that enable them to express their traditions in new ways Kral (2010).

Australia is a vast continent with islands in the Tasman Sea, the Pacific and the Indian Ocean. Its population of 22.7 million is concentrated in cities on the eastern coast. New Zealand is an island country located in the Pacific Ocean, consisting of two main islands and many smaller islands with a population of 4.4 million. Both countries are migrant societies, established as British colonies in the late 1700s and early 1800s. In fact, New Zealand was part of the Australian colony of New South Wales until 1841. The Indigenous people of New Zealand, the Maori, signed a treaty (the Treaty of Waitangi) with their invaders, recognising Indigenous land rights. No treaty was signed between the invaders of Australia and the Aboriginal people, and the rights to land of Indigenous Australians are still contested. These and many other locational and historical circumstances mean that there are important differences between Australia and New Zealand. Nonetheless, as I have argued previously, (Wyn and Harris, 2004), young people in Australia and New Zealand share some common circumstances. They have grown up in English-speaking countries in the Pacific that were colonised during the 1800s. Young people in Australia and New Zealand are shaping their lives in the context of significant changes to many aspects of life that the preceding generation took for granted. I now turn to these common aspects of contemporary social change.

Neoliberal frameworks

Neoliberal discourses, circulating through global policy networks including the Organisation for Economic Cooperation and Development (OECD, 1996), since the early 1990s have had a powerful impact on young people's lives in Australia and New Zealand. Education and labour market policies have a particularly strong impact on young people. These policies are still shaped by concerns that emerged in the late 1970s, about the threat to societies that did not realise the transformation from a reliance on primary and manufacturing industries to globally connected new economies based on service and knowledge industries. Located in the Asia Pacific region, Australia's and New Zealand's economies both faced the challenge of competition for cheap labour if they did not transform their economic bases. Educational policy documents of the late 1980s and early 1990s stressed the need for post-industrial economies to create and draw on new kinds of human capital, requiring ever higher levels of education and ever wider educational participation (Delors, 1996; OECD 1996).

In economic terms, the education, labour market and workplace policies that were put in place in Australia and New Zealand at this time represented an historic shift from Keynesian to monetarist policies. Keynesian policies were based on the assumption that governments have responsibility for society, including the quality of that intangible but important element—the social fabric (Mizen, 2004). This was expressed across the industrialised world through policies that sought to be socially inclusive and to provide for universal entitlements by citizens to health care, education, and welfare benefits. The shift to monetarist policies in the 1980s rested on neoliberal discourses of individualism and emphasised self-responsibility and the constitution of the self as a project of self-realisation as a continuous process in which people make free and rational choices in order to transform and improve themselves. Markets would determine the shape of society, and rather than collective identifications (such as occupation or religion), and individual consumption, lifestyle and leisure activities were seen as anchors for identity, replacing traditional sources, such as employment. Almost imperceptively, citizenship has shifted from being a set of rights and form of participation to the exercise of consumption.

Researching the impact of these changes on young New Zealanders, Nairn, Higgins and Sligo describe young people born after 1984 as 'the children of Rogernomics' (Nairn et al., 2012). This term emphasises the influence of policies of Roger Douglas, minister for finance in New Zealand's Labour government in the 1980s. Their research with young New Zealanders paints a picture of a 'neoliberal generation' whose sense of purpose and identity was forged during economic and social policy reforms that transformed New Zealand's economy and society. It also transformed the way that young people looked at their lives. For example, Nairn and her colleagues argue that young New Zealanders have in one sense embraced the idea that individuals must be responsible and entrepreneurial and accept that investing in education will benefit them in the future. Their research shows how this discourse becomes somewhat dissembled as young people face the realities of local labour markets that fail to deliver the economic benefits of their investment in education. Nairn, Higgins and Sligo show how the 'children of Rogernomics' invest in a huge amount in identity work—the work of making themselves into responsive, flexible, neoliberal subjects—making do with the resources available in their local contexts (Nairn et al., 2012).

The neoliberal reforms in New Zealand and Australia opened up each of the countries to global marketplaces and competition. In New Zealand, the Labour Government introduced ruthless reforms in 1983 and 1984, drawing on Douglas' approach to economic policy. The reforms were aimed at establishing closer economic ties with Australia and a restructuring of the economy, making competition a tool for economic management. As Nairn and her colleagues acknowledge, the direction of the neoliberal reforms undertaken in New Zealand in the 1980s were similar to those being implemented in the UK and Australia, but the severity of the policies in New Zealand had dramatic results. Many commentators argue that the benefits of the restructuring did not materialise for many New Zealanders, and that social problems resulting from social exclusion multiplied (Kelsey, 1999; Thrupp, 2001).

For both young Australians and young New Zealanders, uncertainty of employment was a key characteristic of the socio-historical conditions that this generation faced, as a direct outcome of policies that aimed to bring about significant reforms to labour markets and workplaces (Rea and Callister, 2009). The structural changes brought about by neoliberal policies, of which labour market and workplace reforms are a part, have resulted in the acceleration of temporal norms and expectations, resulting an 'unprecedented degree of permanent temporal pressure' (Rosa, 2005: 455). This temporal pressure does not mean that participants achieve life goals early. To the contrary, the speeding up of life has the opposite effect. It means that opportunities for shared leisure and regular social contact and support became more fragmented and contingent, because there are fewer common times. An analysis of the trajectories of young Australians and Canadians suggests that the unprecedented degree of temporal pressure highlighted by Rosa (2005) was one of the factors associated with the tendency for young people in the 1990s to marry and become parents later than the previous generation (Andres and Wyn, 2010).

In Australia in particular young people's capacity to establish stable lives was reduced by workplace reforms that created job uncertainty and reduced workers' rights. The time spent in education, combined with labour market policies that increased job uncertainty and labour market precariousness meant that young people found it difficult to achieve the goals of modest affluence and security that they held in their early twenties. The high levels of uncertainty and insecurity created by these trends and policies were reflected in low rates of marriage and low fertility for the Australians, when compared with their Canadian counterparts. Low fertility was officially recognised by the Australian Howard government of the 1990s by the introduction of a baby bonus—a payment to all mothers on the birth of their child. These social conditions also corresponded with a trend for the young Australians to assess their mental (and physical) health as poor (Wyn and Andres, 2011).

Young people's struggles to make their education pay in precarious and changing labour markets and the state of their social and mental health are important features of their generation. More needs to be known, for this generation and successive generations, about how their decisions about their education and employment were made in relation to their sense of and possibilities for belonging—in social and physical locations. Placing education and employment in its social and physical context is especially important in times of increased economic insecurity, precisely because the links between education and employment are less reliable. The following section argues that it is timely to move to conceptual frameworks that enable the lens to view education and employment as strategies—not transitions—in the struggle to make a life.

The idea of transitioning

Transition is a metaphor, a heuristic device that sociologists, youth researchers and policy-makers have relied on consistently since the early 1980s, when the youth labour market 'collapsed'. Indeed, the gradual disappearance of low-skill jobs that had traditionally been the destination for young people who did not complete their secondary education was one of the realities that drove the closer links between education and labour market policies in the 1980s. By the 1990s, even for graduates of post-secondary and higher education, the transition into employment was prolonged (Andres and Wyn, 2010).

Within youth studies, which has close links with policy, there has emerged a tendency to identify normative, standard or even desired patterns of transition from education to employment and then to position this particular transition as the central feature of young people's lives. The domination of economic transition to the exclusion of other dimensions of life has been previously noted by Cohen and Ainley (2000) and Hall, Coffey and Lashua (2009), and in my own previous work (Wyn and Woodman, 2006; Wyn, Lantz and Harris, 2012). Criticisms of the use of the transition metaphor include its tendency to naturalise the social phases of childhood, youth and adulthood, creating the notion of standard, universal transitional stages or steps. The underlying assumption that youth transition is a 'natural' process is perhaps most clearly illustrated through the failure to recognise socio-historical nature of the adulthood into which successive generations of young people are supposed to transition. Addressing this issue, Blatterer (2007) and many others have questioned the basis of the distinction between youth and adulthood, throwing doubt on the ontological possibility of a linear trajectory through the life course.

The slippage into bio-social assumptions is unhelpful because it obscures the ways in which biographies (and phases of life) are constructed in place and time. It elevates some patterns of life to a 'standard' or norm against which non-standard patterns are seen to be a problem. Perhaps it is for this reason that in Australia and New Zealand, policies that have been aimed at increasing the participation in education and employment of 'marginalised' groups have been spectacularly unsuccessful. For over a quarter of a century, youth policies, framed by the 'problem' of youth transitions from school to work, and informed by increasingly sophisticated technologies for measuring and tracking educational and workforce participation, have failed to generate policies that can shift the chronic pattern for young people from poor families, young Indigenous people and young people from rural and remote communities to have the highest rates of school non-completion and unemployment, and the poorest health outcomes (Foundation for Young Australians, 2011; OECD, 2011; Rea and Callister, 2009).

Alongside the legacy of transitions-based youth research, there is a tradition within the sociology of youth to understand how individual biographies are shaped by socio-historical conditions and to demonstrate how the meaning of both youth and adulthood is given through prevailing social and economic relations of society (Allen, 1968; Finch 1986; Mizen 2004; Blatterer 2007). Some have attempted to nuance a transition approach with a more socio-historical approach that recognises locational, cultural and temporal elements (Bagnall, 2005). However, even if this is possible, it is difficult to ignore the weight of tradition that has been accumulated around 'transitions'.

In a move to return to sociological frameworks that bring social and historical context, place and culture to the fore, the concept of belonging provides a new frame for understanding the constraints and possibilities taken up by young people, the trajectories that they forge, and the strategies that they use to be well.

Belonging

The idea of belonging builds on the connections being forged in youth studies across the traditional transitions/culture conceptual divide. This divide has been noted previously by Cohen and Ainley (2000). They critiqued the trend within youth studies to render aspects of life beyond school and work as 'factors' that impacted on this 'central' dimension of transition. More recently Furlong, Woodman and Wyn see a convergence between cultural and transition approaches to youth research, as youth researchers address the challenge of recognising that both culture (and lifestyle) and structured forms of reproduction that operate through systems of education and employment influence young lives (Furlong et al. 2011).

Furlong et al. note that understanding young people's lives in a context of social change has been an impetus for this conceptual convergence. This point is underscored by Hall, Coffey and Lashua (2009), who make a case for revisiting the question of young people's relationship with location. They borrow from conceptual traditions within geography, anthropology and architecture to 'advance a sociological argument for the consideration of continuity and everyday registers of meaning as a way of understanding change—both to place and in young people's lives' (2009: 547). Their study of the intersecting nature of biography and landscapes in the south-east of Wales explores the double dimensions of change (social and personal) that are washed out in conventional understandings of transition as a series of steps. They find that change is characterised by a continuity of sequences in which both lives and places are connected. Their work demonstrates the complex connections between place, history and individual lives that make up the changing process of belonging— both materially, locationally and in terms of identity.

Youth research that is framed by a transitions approach tends of necessity to focus on set points—transition points. These are often points that are pre-determined by policy (for example, leaving school, getting a job, leaving home). Hall, Coffey and Lashua refer to this as 'serial vision', a series of episodes that are joined up in accounts to give a sense of sequence. They argue that real lives are lived in between these spaces (Hall et al., 2009). I agree, and would argue that as researchers we may miss important details about how lives are lived in real time and in places if we fail to 'record the life that goes on between events and happenings—in place and biography' (Hall et al., 2009: 559).

This has been achieved in studies that attempt to move beyond the confines of traditional approaches to researching youth transitions. For example, researching young New Zealanders, Nairn et al. (2012) asked young people to record an 'anti-CV' (*curriculum vitae*) as a way of moving beyond the 'set piece' CV that records achievements according to predetermined (and largely adult) notions of significance stages and achievements. Instead, the anti-CV enabled the research participants to put together a portfolio in the form of photographs, images and notes, of the things that were important to them and that conveyed who they were. These portfolios tended to convey a strong sense of place, incorporating the physical landscape into their portrayal of their lives. In other work, Nairn et al. (2003) employed youth peer researchers to gain an insight into how young people occupied their space in a rural and regional town in New Zealand. The results reveal a very different picture from the conventional youth research wisdom that youth are not welcome, victimised and excluded from public space (White, 1996). Instead, what Nairn and her colleagues reveal is the ways in which young people strive to belong. Their photographs and stories provide an insight into what place—physical and social—means to them. They conclude:

> Most importantly, we demonstrate how binaries such as rural/urban, inclusion/exclusion, while providing the means for initial categorisation, do not adequately describe the complexities and contradictions of the everyday worlds of young people in rural and urban environments. The parallels between the young people's experiences in both rural and urban locations does not suggest a unitary childhood experience across the rural/urban divide, but rather reinforces the artificiality of this particular divide. The differences within each data set from Alexandra and Dunedin remind us of the diversity of young people's experiences within any one site/space or any one type of environment. There is no unitary public, or for that matter private, rural or urban childhood.
>
> (Nairn et al., 2003: 38)

Research that shifts the focus away from pre-established markers of transitions and steps towards adulthood provides a very different view of young lives. The 'spaces between events and happenings' that Hall, Coffey and Lashua refer to are largely filled with the everyday ways in which people belong (Harris et al., 2007), in relation to place and family. The next section explores this in more depth.

Place, family, connectedness

Participants in the Australian *Life Patterns* longitudinal research program, who are now aged in their late thirties, throw new light on the significance of belonging, through an exploration of the role that place and family play in their life decisions. These participants were in the vanguard of the new mass education sector—tertiary education. Their experiences, from the time of leaving secondary school (in 1991) onwards, are revealing of the things that happen 'between the spaces' of normative transition points in life. Participants who lived in rural areas were especially conscious of the normative 'narrative' about transition because they perceived it to be an urban-based narrative that positioned them as 'other' or non-metropolitan. Their decisions about post-secondary education were usually framed differently from their metropolitan peers, because a) the rural-based young people had far fewer local post-secondary education options and b) many were focused on gaining qualifications that would be relevant in non-metropolitan settings (Cuervo and Wyn, 2012). This means that they have tended to be explicit about the role of both family and place in their decisions about education, work and life.

The centrality of place and relationships in decision-making about study and work is illustrated by Anne, who lived in a rural area in Victoria, about 200 kilometres north of Melbourne, the capital city of Victoria. She did a Bachelor of Arts in sociology and psychology at regional campus, because she wanted to remain 'in the country'. Anne said:

> I'm a country girl at heart, so I chose—actively chose that. I didn't want to be in Melbourne. It was important for me to—I know the town, so it's great. [Regional city's] a great place, so it's a really nice place. I was familiar with it, I knew where it was, it's close to home. I was quite comfortable doing that as opposed to Melbourne.

She married in her final year of her degree, when she graduated, she got a job in human resources in a government department in the regional centre near the town she grew up in. In 2011 she was living in the same town with her husband and three children. This is where she feels she and her family belong, because of ties to family and the landscape. As Anne says:

> My children never got to meet their grandfather, but they know that. They know that he planted those trees and they're still there now. So throughout everything that changes in the world, that's something that's still there thirty-five years later. So intergenerational, that's right.

She wants her children,

> … to know where they came from, so to know some of their history and to know what was important to their mum and dad and what was even important to their grandmother and grandfather, some of that intergenerational stuff. They mightn't get it, it might take them another twenty years before they understand some of that stuff, but yeah.

Clearly family is central to Anne's narrative about her life and work, as it was with a majority of the participants in our study. However, family is often ignored or marginalised in research on young people's transitions through education and employment. Family relationships are a key source of support for young people during their final years of secondary school and beyond, and this support is often mutual (Wyn, Lantz and Harris, 2012). In talking about the relevance of family and place in their lives, the participants in our research are providing a map of the ways in which they are connected—to the past, in the present and to an imagined future.

The idea of belonging enables the ways in which young people are connected to be more visible. It highlights processes of social inclusion by emphasising the strategies that young people use to belong. Belonging and connectedness are also closely related to wellbeing. For example, health researchers use connectedness as an indicator of wellbeing. The Australian Institute of Health and Wellbeing found that families living in neighbourhoods characterised by greater community investment, trust and organisational affiliations tend to function better and safe neighbourhoods are associated with better psychological wellbeing and educational achievement of young people. Research shows a direct association between a young person's level of social support and the number of health risk factors they exhibit (AIHW, 2007: 105). The idea of belonging provides a framework for mapping how young people manage to be well as they navigate their own individual lives in changing times and circumstances.

Conclusion

This chapter argues that our understanding of young people's lives, including the nature and meaning of their trajectories and pathways, can be advanced by moving beyond a 'transitions' approach that gives what is perhaps undue priority to education and employment trajectories. It draws on recent thinking in geography and cultural studies as well as the more traditional youth transitions research to focus on young people and belonging. This approach shifts the focus from normative transition points to the spaces in between these points, where family, leisure, wellbeing and a being connected often drive their decision-making. Education and work are significant elements of their lives, but these elements are framed by young people's sense of who they are and where they belong.

Drawing primarily on research in New Zealand and Australia, the analysis has implications for youth research in other countries. A climate of economic uncertainty tends to weaken the nexus between education and work and heighten the significance of local connections, and of the strategies that young people use to belong—often despite education and labour market conditions.

The chapter notes that in Australia and New Zealand, the documentation of patterns of transition from education to employment reveals that for over twenty-five years the same groups of young people: those living in poor communities, in rural communities and Indigenous young people, fail to make optimal transitions. Yet policies based on a transitions approach have failed to make a difference to these patterns. It is suggested that a shift of perspective, onto patterns of belonging, offers a more productive approach to research and policy on young people's lives. Understanding what education and work mean in the wider context of young people's lives provides a more effective platform for addressing the needs of the most disadvantaged.

Chapter 16

'Ring of fire or a puff of (commentators') smoke?': Youth, unemployment and transitions in Gauteng, South Africa

David Everatt

Property is not the sacred right. When a rich man becomes poor it is a misfortune, it is not a moral evil. When a poor man becomes destitute, it is a moral evil, teeming with consequences and injurious to society and morality.

Lord Acton

Introduction

Following the Arab Spring revolutions in northern Africa and the Middle East in 2011, many South African commentators and politicians cast more or less anxious eyes (depending on their political perspective) towards the mass of unemployed young people—overwhelmingly African—that were spatially displaced by apartheid and are now seen, as young people everywhere appear ineluctably to be seen, as the 'idle threat' of the 1970s and 1980s (Freedman, 1988). Worse, they are cast as the harbingers of a new revolution in newly- democratic South Africa. Because of on-going racially-based spatial displacement that has outlived apartheid, youth—African youth, let us be clear—are seen to form a 'ring of fire' surrounding the wealthy core of Johannesburg and Tshwane (formerly Pretoria). The core cities may have become more non-racial, but the peripheries—the townships created by apartheid and the informal settlements that mushroomed after the demise of apartheid—are near-uniformly African. The 'ring of fire' terminology is deliberately laden with latent threat, taken as it is from the arc of volcanoes and fault lines crossing the Pacific basin that led to the devastating Japanese earthquake and tsunami of 2011.

This article will argue that there is truth to the notion that the inequality that marked South Africa under apartheid, and which has become worse under democracy, is unsustainable here, as it proved to be in North Africa and the Middle East. There is also truth to the notion that the race-based residential segregation imposed by apartheid and sustained—primarily for the poor—under democracy, has created a 'ring' of poor people living in and around the wealthy spine of cities that run down Gauteng Province. Gauteng is the economic powerhouse of the country that contributes thirty-four per cent to national Gross Domestic Product (GDP) but is simultaneously the smallest province with the largest population in the country. However, where this article takes issue with the commentators who have been so quick to warn that South Africa's 'Tunisian moment' is imminent, is their insistence on pointing to 'youth'—this undifferentiated, threat-laden lumpen—as the 'problem'.

South Africa has profound challenges of rectifying the race-based damage of apartheid, in every sphere of life from the economy and education to psychosocial and other areas. But if the country faces one overriding challenge, it is not 'youth' or 'jobless youth' or 'the distressed generation' or any other way in which people have tried to describe youth while implicitly singling them out as the key threat to South African stability and democracy. The real threat remains inter-and intra-race inequality, which is growing steadily, leaving the poor—even in a wealthy province like Gauteng—locked out of the economy. Young people, such as those in the Occupy movement, may well be those brave and idealistic enough to challenge the status quo—the inherently unstable status quo—but this will be because of what is wrong with the system, not because of something that is 'wrong' with youth.

Youth as threat

'Jobless youth a 'ticking time bomb' for SA', headlines warned readers of the Business Day newspaper, quoting Zwelinzima Vavi, head of the Congress of South African Trade Unions (COSATU), part of the ruling tripartite alliance (alongside the African National Congress (ANC) and South African Communist Party (SACP)) (Jobless youth …, 2011). Vavi's speech combined the jobless growth of South Africa under democracy and the catastrophic youth unemployment figures, on-going racialised inequality and racialised residential segregation, and the same demographic pyramid where young people make up almost two- thirds of the South African population as in many North African and Middle Eastern societies, to conjure up what seemed an unavoidable conclusion—it must happen here too!

The parallels appeared so demographically and economically obvious that the outcome—a youth-driven revolution—seemed equally inescapable. This also provided Vavi, and others, with a convenient stick with which to beat the ruling ANC they regarded as insufficiently focused on redistribution (or, for those from the right, an ANC too focused on redistribution). Indeed, as this chapter was being written, the University of Cape Town Press published a book entitled Youth violence: sources and solutions in South Africa, a title seemingly guaranteed to sell by playing on deep-seated societal fears of youth as irredeemably violent and destabilising, on which Vavi also drew (Ward, van der Merwe and Dawes, 2012). After all, if young people could take on the might of apartheid with stones and petrol bombs—and win—what might they be capable of under democracy? Look what young people had done in London, let alone Egypt or Tunisia or Jordan and other Middle East countries. Once again youth—by which commentators mean African, male, urban young people— were little more than a violent uprising waiting to happen.

Others, of differing political persuasions, may have disputed the causes but not the predicted outcome. The younger brother of former President Thabo Mbeki, Moeletsi Mbeki, a noted commentator and business-person, argued that the ANC had become so intellectually and morally bankrupt that 'Tunisia Day' was not far off—both he and Vavi (Mbeki, now in the private sector, was also a former COSATU spokesperson), pointed to the large number of 'service delivery protests' in support of their arguments (Nicolson, 2011). According to Mbeki:

> The result is a war that the ANC has created between itself and its own people. More and more South Africans are living outside the economy and on the fringes of social life, often in sub-human conditions.
> People no longer see this as justice. And the state now has to prepare itself for a confrontation with the poor. But what our leaders are forgetting is that the SA population is very politicised, because of our recent past, and this is a struggle they can now fight with the vote.   (Forde, 2012)

Mbeki was closer to the point—that 'the poor' would not sit back watching the national bourgeoisie enrich itself endlessly, at their expense; the issue was inequality, not youth. Others argued that the ANC only paid lip-service to democracy, and had created its own monster—corruption—that was driving protest and leading to 'it's own Tunisia and Egypt style revolution'. Jay Naidoo,[33] a former government minister-turned-businessperson (and another former head of COSATU) and commentator, wrote bluntly:

33 See for example de Vos P. 'A recipe for impunity' writing on his blog, Constitutionally Speaking, May 28th 2011.

South Africa's political and social issues are only a microcosm of what's happening throughout the world. The blatant disregard for our world's youth and their lack of voice is fuelling the fire for future revolutions, not only in South Africa, but in many countries where youth feel invisible. This lack of voice is only reinforcing hopelessness and encouraging violence, the very behaviour that we are witnessing in the Middle East and North Africa.   (Naidoo, 2011)

Here the threat entwines 'the poor' and 'the youth' as one undifferentiated mass, waiting for 'their turn'. These comments, from people of somewhat different political perspectives, triggered a flood of blogging, social media twittering and class chattering, all of which ultimately focused on two things: that little had improved for 'the masses of the people' since 1994 (or, 'the ANC is corrupt', leading to the same outcome); and that leading the violent threat facing us all were ... the youth. The hopeless, disconnected, alienated, irredeemably violent, youth.

The purpose of this chapter is to try and understand the values and attitudes of young people living in Gauteng, particularly young Africans—the harbingers of the 'fire' that will 'ring' Johannesburg, Tshwane and other wealthy enclaves. In so doing, the chapter also highlights the challenges of applying transitional perspectives in developing and transitional societies such as South Africa. To do so, the chapter draws heavily on the results of a just-completed,[34] 17,000 sample survey of Gauteng Province, the country's economic heart and most populous province—and the province identified as including a wealthy core (including the most costly real estate in Africa) surrounded by the supposed 'ring of fire' of unemployed and angry youth on the verge of rising up against the new ruling order. In other words, we want to know what young people believe and how they live, and use that as a test for the accuracy or otherwise of the headline-grabbing claims of imminent revolution—as well as the notion that the revolution will be youth-led because of something immanent to young people.

Youth then and now

In just twenty years, South African youth—particularly African, urban youth—have gone full circle, from a 'lost generation' to 'partners in development' and back to the denizens of the 'ring of fire' on the margins of society threatening

---

34 The data here are the 'first cut' from the survey, and final figures (after final cleaning) may differ by a percentage point here and there.

revolution. During the 1970s and 1980s, when young people boycotted school in favour of 'liberation first, education later', were imprisoned in their thousands, left the country to join the exiled ANC or stayed home and joined affiliates of the United Democratic Front (UDF) and other struggle organisations, were tortured and brutalised, it was common to talk of a 'lost generation', an epithet first applied to the youth of 1976 who triggered the Soweto Revolt. In the midst of a liberation struggle and low intensity war, there seemed little point in worrying about pejorative cohort labelling.

All of that changed in 1990, when political prisoners were released and political movements unbanned. A movement was initiated to mobilise young people across racial and political boundaries, supported by policy research (to generate realistic policy proposals for the new democratic government). Led by Christian churches, the movement began working on the notion of 'marginalised youth' in 1991, almost as soon as the political transition from apartheid to democracy began. The purpose was to identify what damage had been done to young people as they took on the leading 'foot soldier' role in the struggle against the massive and brutal security apparatus of the apartheid state, so as to inform post-apartheid policy-making. The working assumption was that while any cohort would include some people who were beyond the pale, the overwhelming majority of young people were ready to play their part in building the 'new' South Africa, albeit with support. The movement pushed the notion of integrated youth development, arguing that young people required support and inputs in multiple areas, often simultaneously, whether psychological or educational or social or economic and so on.

The notion of 'marginalised youth'—and the policy programme meant to help draw them back into the mainstream—was consciously meant to challenge the then still common notion of a 'lost generation'.[35] For the churches sponsoring the initiative, this had a very charged content—to write off an entire generation as 'lost'—that is, beyond redemption—particularly one that had sacrificed so much, was scripturally untenable and ethically and morally unpalatable. At a policy and political level, the same held true: how could young men and women, many barely teenagers, who took on armoured cars with stones and bottles, be discarded as 'lost'? Political activism was a sign of their engagedness, not their 'lost' status. This is as true of Occupy and similar movements now as it was of the anti-apartheid struggle then. The difference, of course, is that South Africa is

35 See Everatt D. and Orkin M., (1992) Growing up tough: results of a national survey of youth, Community Agency for Social Enquiry (mimeo); and for less concern with the notion, see Van Zyl Slabbert F., Malan C., Olivier J and Riordan R., (eds) (1994) Youth in the new South Africa, Pretoria: HSRC Press.

now led by the ANC, in alliance with COSATU and the SACP, and perceptions of threat have changed accordingly.

Classic transitional theory would not necessarily work for those youth who had been active in the struggle—those, for example, tortured in detention, or who took up arms to defend their communities in self-defence and self-protection units as the ANC and its rival, the Inkatha Freedom Party, engaged in low- intensity warfare in the interregnum. Many would not return to school and then enter the labour market—but surely the democratic state would have more to offer than 'go to school' or 'become a plumber/painter/electrician'? Surely there would be a significant 'democracy dividend' due, following the integrated approach proposed by the marginalised youth movement? For a brief moment, as the National Youth Development Forum took shape, youth of many different parties joined, and a moral consensus about the needs of young people seemed possible. ANC and COSATU leaders supported the adoption of a policy programme at the 'marginalised youth' conference of 1993, and it looked as if all the political heavy-weights (many youth would be voting in 1994 ...) would indeed support integrated youth development. Expectations ran high.

But it was not to be. Mandela called on the youth to return to school; the unions began responding to the demands of their members not non- members (e.g. calling for investment in *adult* basic education as a post-apartheid priority), and soon the youth were being pushed back to the margins, while old men in suits made decisions for them. Young people were expected to assume their appropriate cultural position—allowed to attend a meeting, but disallowed from speaking unless invited so to do, by their (male) elders. By 1996, twenty years since the 1976 uprisings led by youth, as government rushed through a badly drafted 'National Youth Commission Act' (with a remarkable definition of youth that stretched from fourteen to thirty-five years-old), optimism had largely evaporated. Youth may have played a singular role in bringing about the end of apartheid; but they lacked the sustained organisational power to ensure that their demands were met.

The Reconstruction and Development Programme (RDP), the ANC (1994) election manifesto, was launched with great fanfare as the first democratic general election approached. In its own words, the RDP was 'an integrated, coherent socio-economic policy framework. It seeks to mobilise all our people and our country's resources toward the final eradication of apartheid and the building of a democratic, non-racial and non-sexist future.' The RDP was the result of intensive lobbying and horse-trading inside the ANC alliance. Sectors developed policy and programme formulations, and then had to secure support for them through the six drafts of the RDP that were circulated and debated (and fought over) inside the alliance. The youth sector had the advantages of detailed baseline data, agreed policy positions, and an organisational basis; in short, the sector seemed well-positioned to secure significant commitments from the soon-to-be ruling party.

In 1993, there were some eleven million young people aged between sixteen and thirty, who were (then) defined as youth. Adding the youth and children, the size grew to seventy-one per cent by 2001. Youth (aged fouteen to thirty-five) comprise forty-one per cent of all South Africans, followed by children (up to eighteen years-old) at thirty per cent. This leads to an obvious point, namely that virtually every South African policy is (i.e. should be) a youth policy. When it finally appeared, the RDP was 147 pages long, and covered an enormous range of topics from education to policing to nutrition. 'Youth Development' appeared in the Human Resource Development section where it was given a total of six paragraphs, covering a page and a half. It was offered as a sub-section of 'Arts and Culture' and came immediately after 'Sport and Recreation'. Youth had been reverted to a familiar position: give them soccer fields and they'll be happy.

At government level, the RDP stated merely that 'appropriate government departments must more forcefully represent youth interests' (ANC, 1994). By 1994, the shape of South Africa had been settled in terms of policy and institutional arrangements. Youth fared poorly: a national youth service initiative was the only policy proposal in the RDP, a Council the only institution for championing youth development, and integrated youth development was entirely absent. Youth were a target group for public works programmes and the like—alongside women, people with disabilities, people from poor rural areas, and so on—but beyond that, nothing.

The RDP set the tone for the next seventeen years of democracy. Was there a democracy dividend, beyond the obvious (and not to be under-emphasised) change in rights and freedoms? Without repeating the bulk of South African youth studies 1990-2011, the simple answer is 'no'.[36] Youth development—

---

36 For a potted history by this author, see the following; other youth-related literature has tended towards more specific areas such as HIV and AIDS, or risk-taking, or education, and so on; Everatt D., (2007) Youth and the democracy dividend in South Africa: where's our share?! in Africa Insight (37) 3 September 2007; Everatt D,. (2001) Youth in South Africa 1994—2001 and beyond in Helve H. and Wallace C., (eds) Youth, Citizenship and Empowerment, London: Ashgate; Everatt D., (2000) From urban warrior to market segment? in Youth in South Africa 1994-2000, Development Update (3)2.; Everatt D., (1995) 'School eject or reject?' Contextualising 'out-of-school youth' in the new South Africa. Prospects XXV(3): 451-468, International Bureau for Education/UNESCO (Geneva, November 1995 edition).

the content of which is taken for granted if in fact is widely disputed—gets occasional airings by officials, but solutions are scanty at best—talk of public works programmes with short-term employment opportunities, or small training schemes—as if all young people aspire to be plumbers, painters or electricians. At the other extreme, it is translated into large loans to 'entrepreneurs' to move them into the formal economy, via the Umsobomvu Youth Fund, which was soon swallowed by a new structure, once a new ANC term of office began. Structures morph and change, with two constants: one, on-going complaints about limited budgets, and secondly, on-going elite capture by members of the ANC Youth League (ANCYL). With the odd, honourable exception, all government-funded youth structures seem primarily to serve as sinecures for aspirant youth politicians; but structures are all that the ANC government has offered youth since 1994.

In addition, annual ritual penance is paid to 'the youth' come Youth Day (in commemoration of the June 1976 uprisings). But 'the youth' in these instances often actually means 'we who were youth then' (be it the 1976 uprising or the resistance movement of the 1980s) not 'the youth of today'. The latter are caustically written off in conversation and occasionally in public outbursts as 'born frees', the generation who had everything handed to them on a plate because of the sacrifices of those who went before and were, by definition, more self-sacrificing, less selfish and, of course, now more deserving. The youth of today have become, yet again, in pejorative terms, *the youth of today*—a burden, an enigma, a visually bizarre, tattooed, pierced, aurally grating, slang-riddled, disrespectful, smoking, drinking, risk-taking ungrateful generation who do not give automatic respect merely because of age—in other words, they have many of the attributes that were so valued in the anti-apartheid struggle—but now, with the ANC in charge, they are once again a threat. The only question that seems to be at issue is how idle or violent that threat may prove to be.

As in 1990, 'the youth' in South African parlance refers to black, urban youth—not an age cohort, not 'teenagers', nor young whites or Indians or (in most instances) coloured, three of the four 'official race groups' in post-apartheid South Africa. Rural youth are near-absent, as are young women, as are white, coloured and Indian young people. Author Hein Marais had noted in 1993 that

> ... 'youth' are being converted into latter-day savages: demented, destructive, demonised. The images are archetypal, primal—the stuff of

thousand year-old myths and sweaty nightmares. Of beasts outside the
city gates, shadows that swing along the end of the bonfire ...

(Marais, 1993)

Those words described the fears of a population watching a violent war
between the ANC and the Inkatha Freedom Party. The political violence died
away, but youth were re-stigmatised during the seventeen years of South African
democracy. Democracy itself was part of the problem—young people were seen
as having 'too many rights', and the banning of corporal punishment at school,
the availability of abortions to young women without parental consent (under
certain circumstances) and other human rights advances were seen to have made
the 'born frees' ungovernable—that is, not amenable to adult discipline. Their
loose morality and sexual abandon was associated with the terrible onset of HIV
and AIDS, providing some awful 'proof' of their moral weaknesses.

Young people are aware of the space given them by the new rights regime, as
one pointed out in a focus group during 2011:

> We always hide behind the democracy. If a young person today does
> something wrong at home and needs to be punished, we start hiding
> behind democracy and our rights.
>
> (African, male, 18-25, Nelson Mandela Authority, suburbs)[37]

This is the problem with youth—they are agents, they learn how to play the
system, they don't do what they're told, they don't automatically respect age or
authority, and are far from passive. That is exactly why they are often forces for
progressive change—because they question *status quos*, wherever they are, and are
more willing to take risks in support of their ideals. Which may explain why the
post-democracy dividend for youth, in attitudinal terms anyway, is a deep adult
resentment—and an academic one to match. For some youth, as they became
better qualified, moved easily into professional circles, and joined the nascent
(and much disputed analytically) 'black middle class'—and with the changing
class positions, came changing vote preferences.[38] 'The youth vote' became much
more fluid, and far closer to the classic 'floating voter', than any older African

37 Focus group commissioned by the Gauteng City-Region Observatory and Ahmed Kathrada Foundation
    for a project on non-racialism. The full transcript (of 18 groups) is available at www.gcro.ac.za.
38 See for example Everatt D., (2011) Class formation and rising inequality in South Africa: What does
    this mean for future voting patterns? in Mbeki M. (ed.) *Advocates of Change: How to Overcome Africa's
    Challenges*, Johannesburg: MacMillan.

voters—hence the anger at the 'born frees' who used their freedom to vote non-ANC or not vote at all. On the other hand, youth are at the receiving end of a backlash against their enjoyment of the fruits of democracy (to over-state the case somewhat, but suggestive of the attitudes that drive it)—the youth are lazy, spoiled and unworthy of democracy in the eyes of many elders.

Many academics either overtly or implicitly reflect similar attitudes. One academic recently noted that 'The passivity of many jobless adolescents is striking'[39] when looking at persistent black youth unemployment. It did not seem to be relevant that twenty years of structural racism in the post-apartheid education system and job market (part of the inheritance left by apartheid), which has held black youth unemployment at staggeringly high levels, might suggest a systemic fault. Far easier to blame the youth. Another, apparently seeking some sort of adjectival middle-ground, wrote of unemployed youth in South Africa as 'The distressed generation?', the question mark perhaps saying more about author than subject, given her conclusion that 'the damaging consequences [of long-term structural unemployment] are too ghastly to contemplate' (du Toit, 2003).

It is in this context, where youth are again an 'idle threat', taking South Africa dangerously close to its 'Tunisia day', that we turn to look at youth themselves, at least insofar as they can be discerned from survey data.

Spatial issues

Before turning to the survey, however, the dot density map below uses data from the 2001 Census—the last for which data are publicly available at the time of writing—and shows how apartheid spatial planning ensured that people (of all ages) of different races, even by 2001, were still largely living in the ghettoes designed for them under apartheid. In the map, each dot represents a hundred people, and in typically South African fashion, they have been coded by race—white people are white dots, while African, Indian and coloured people are black dots. The concentrations of black dots show the townships zoned for 'non-whites' by the apartheid regime—and their post-apartheid resilience.

---

39 Jeremy Seekings quoted in *Re-thinking South Africa's 'Youth Policy' approach*, Centre for Development and Enterprise, draft report, p.17.

Figure 1: Population by race in Gauteng (source: Census 2001, Statistics South Africa).[40]

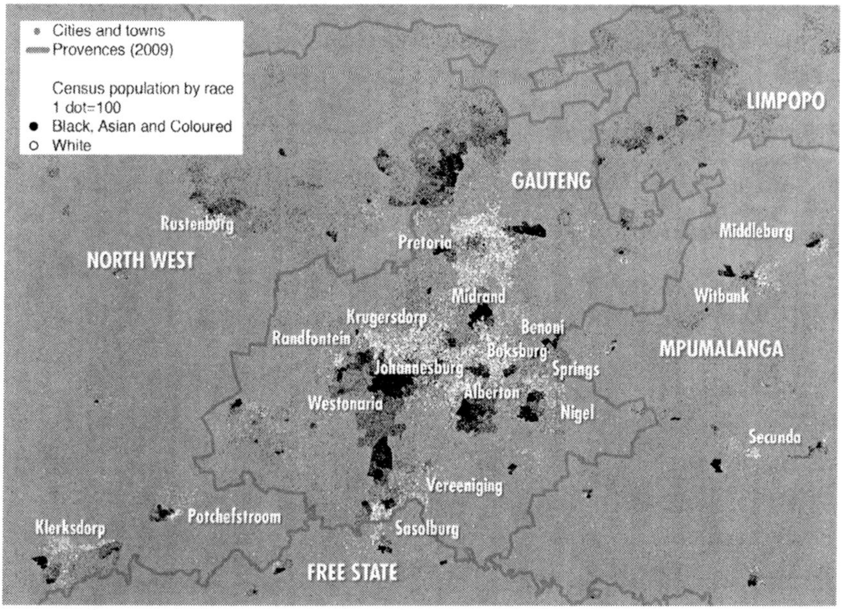

The persistence of racial segregation—in no small part explained by the exceptionally high price of suburban housing in Gauteng (OECD, 2011b)—is immediately apparent, as is the density of former townships, where people were packed into areas with very strictly controlled borders. We can assume that this will have changed somewhat by the time that Census 2011 data are released, but the persistence of high housing prices coupled with the global recession will not have helped speed up racially integrated residential patterns.

Secondly, the black population in Gauteng scarcely makes a 'ring'—rather, there is an on-going move from the periphery to the centre. Population estimates from Statistics South Africa suggest that the population of the province grew by 1,278,211 between 2001 and 2007, a 13.6 per cent increase. This is far from evenly spread; the province is shrinking in some places (mainly on the periphery), and bulging in others (the three big cities that form the provincial spine). The imbalance—large metropolitan governments alongside smaller municipalities—is by design:[41] incorporating Soweto into Johannesburg after 1994, for example,

---

40 My thanks to Chris Wray for his remarkable skills at generating beautiful maps.
41 Government of South Africa (1998) *The White Paper on Local Government*, March 1998; see also Wooldridge D., (1998) *Metropolitan government: choices for South Africa*, paper commissioned by the Local Government White Paper Committee.

was a natural mechanism for redistribution of wealth and services previously skewed under apartheid, and it has been maintained as an efficient mechanism of delivering bulk services (including Free Basic Services) at an efficient scale, as the province seeks to remove the inequitable legacies of apartheid.

Figure 2: Population distribution by age

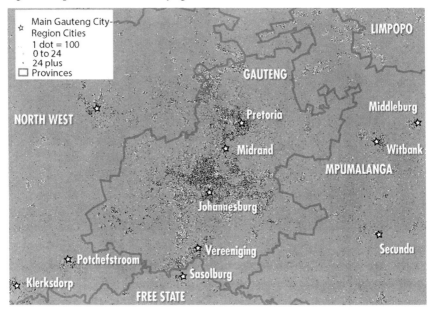

(Source: Census 2001, Statistics South Africa).

But this also poses a set of challenges—differing levels of economic activity and opportunities for employment creation, differing tax bases, differing revenue bases from which to provide services, and so on. It is unclear whether or not policy-makers predicted the speed and scale—or unevenness—of Gauteng's population growth. As South Africa urbanises, so does Gauteng, and more people move away from smaller (and poorer) municipalities and into the very large metropolitan centres. We re-ran the dot density map to show the population aged 0-24 (in white dots of 100) and those 25+ (in black dots, see Figure 2)—and as the map makes clear, there is no 'ring' of (revolutionary) 'youth' around middle-class city-dwellers, neat-sounding as the image may be. In a country with the lowest elderly dependency ratio of all city-regions on the database (OECD 2011b), we should not be surprised to find that children and youth are everywhere.

The danger of this is that youth simply swing from a 'ring of fire'—which has at least the comfort of being 'out there' somewhere—to a more Thatcherite notion of 'the enemy within'. Youth demographics—in terms of where they live—do not differ markedly from those of older people. If we turn to the recent 'Quality of Life' survey, which interviewed 17,982 people across the province (yielding an error bar of 0.7 per cent),[42] we find that 35 per cent of the population lives if the City of Johannesburg—rising from a low of 32.2 per cent among 16-19 year-olds through 34.8 per cent among 20-24 year olds, and peaking at 37 per cent for 25-29 and 35-39 year olds, with a statistically insignificant 1 per cent dip in the cohort between them. The same is true of the cities of Tshwane, and of Ekurhuleni—the point being simply that youth are distributed across the province in similar proportion to adults. In Gauteng there tend to be more working age people, and fewer older people, than in some rural provinces, where people 'go home' when they retire; but within Gauteng, youth are at the heart of the province in large numbers, and distributed around it in similar ways to the rest of the population.

It is also worth noting that South Africa's demographics do not look like those of Gauteng. Where whites comprise 9 per cent of the national population, they comprised 22 per cent of Gauteng's population in 2001, and the 2012 survey had a 15.4 per cent white sample (the latter in part because of access problems). Africans make up some three-quarters of the population in Gauteng, and of them, only 70 per cent were born in the province, so there are particular dynamics at work here, both in terms of spatial distribution, demographics and mobility. In a province that generates a third of national GDP, nestling in a broader city-region that generates 43 per cent of GDP, young people in Gauteng or the broader Gauteng City-Region are located in a very specific space, the economic heartland of the country, with virtually no in-province rural spaces or hinterland.

If there is a 'ring' around the province, it is primarily the neighbouring provinces, many of which contain *bantustans*—the areas selected by the architects of apartheid, into which black South Africans were herded, precisely because such areas were economically unviable and people would have to migrate and sell their labour (but not become permanent urban residents). As such, the province—indicated by the map, figure 3—does represent a light-coloured oasis of prosperity in a rather larger, dark area of poverty—which in turn helps

42 The sample, error bar and age/race comparators are: Survey (17 982)–0.7 per cent, youth 16-24 (3 019)–1.8 per cent, youth 16-30 (5 790)–1.3 per cent, African 18-21 (1 424)–2.6 per cent, African 22-24 (1 168)–2.9 per cent, African 25-30 (2 470)–2.0 per cent.

explain why, in a country with a falling birth-rate,[43] the population of Gauteng grows at a rate of some 2.9 per cent per annum.

Figure 3: Poverty levels in and around Gauteng.

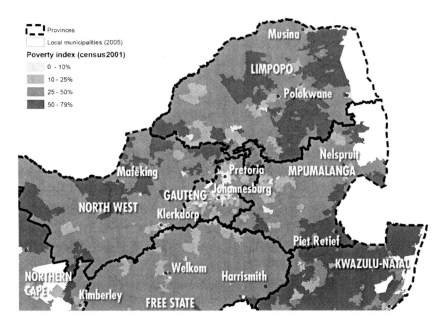

The data suggest that while the compelling image of a 'ring of fire' surrounding wealthy Gauteng might have some salience—the 'ring' is made up of the core voters of the ruling ANC, poor African voters, of all ages. Clearly this is less easy to use as a rallying cry than pointing the finger at youth. Youth are almost always regarded as a threat, a potentially subversive cultural grouping that rejects adult authority, and because of their common lack of major debt (such as house or car payments) and consequent lack of 'a stake in the system' are also regarded as the least credit-worthy members of the labour force, and are the least likely to be employed in the formal sector. But are the prophets correct? Do young people hold views that set them on a collision course with the current trajectory of post-apartheid development? We now pause briefly to look at the values and attitudes of young people in Gauteng, in order to try and better answer some of these questions.

---

43 National Planning Commission, (2011) *National Development Plan 2030*, Pretoria: The Presidency.

Youth—age cohort or revolutionary cadre?

The problem with youth is that they look and sound just like adults—but suffer far worse at the hands of an economy that is amongst the most unequal on earth. This is highlighted by the fact that young people in Gauteng (and across the country) are better educated than their elders, the product of both a modernising society and the fruits of democracy (education is one area where there has been something of a 'democracy dividend'). In Gauteng, for example, 2.7 per cent of respondents had no formal education at all—that amounts to some 300 000 people without any education at all—of whom less than one in twenty-five is aged below twenty-four. Another 13.3 per cent of the Gauteng population had only completed their primary schooling, making most functionally illiterate—again, some 95 per cent of these citizens are aged above 24 years of age. At the upper end—the tertiary level of education—the sample average stood at 19.6 per cent. The equivalent figure for 20-24 year-olds (the figure for 16-19 year olds is obviously skewed) was 17.3 per cent, with a number still studying; rising to 19.9 per cent among 25-29 year-olds. So while things may even out at the top, they are deeply uneven—measured by age—at the base. No wonder these (better) educated youth seem to represent a threat to some of their un-or under-educated elders.

This is thrown into sharp relief by economic statistics.

It is predictable (and positive) that the youngest cohort is primarily in 'other'—because most of them should be students or scholars—and so their

Figure 4: Economic status by age (Source: 2011 GCRO 'Quality of Life' survey).

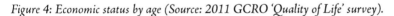

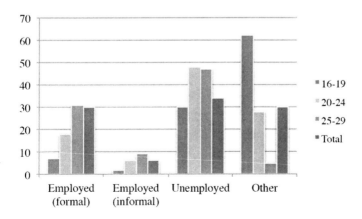

low economic participation rates are not a surprise. But move up one cohort, to those aged between 20 and 24 years of age, less than a fifth (18 per cent) have found formal sector employment, plummeting to just 6 per cent working in the informal sector—and one in two (48 per cent) unemployed. A high proportion (28 per cent) are in the 'other' category, so still studying amongst other activities; and when we look at those aged 25-29, we see 'other' has dropped to 5 per cent but unemployment has stayed high at 47 per cent—while both formal and informal sector employment have grown. Unemployment for the sample as a whole stood at 30 per cent, illustrating quite how hard young people find it to enter the economy—formal or informal.

These figures for all youth also hide the racial differentiation that continues to cut across most aspects of South African society.

The graph below shows the African/white contrast, which of course is the easiest way of illustrating the racial divisions within the South African politico-economy—but it is fair to say that only when looking at all four race groups (as officially recognised in the country) that we get a sense of how far these two groups are outliers. Figures for Indians are often better than for whites, while coloured youth look far more like African youth figures.

All those qualifying remarks notwithstanding, African youth—like African adults—are bearing the brunt of an unequal economy, exacerbated by a global

Figure 5: Employment status by race and age (Source: 2011 GCRO 'Quality of Life' survey). chpt 16.5.psd

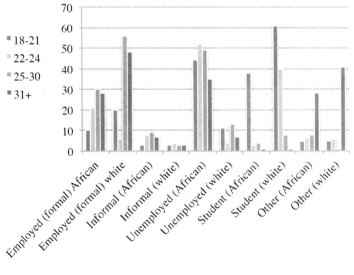

recession. Economics also often dictates the extent to which young people can stay in education—which is not free—as well as those who can 'afford' to be non-working by choice rather than circumstance (part of 'other' are those who describe themselves as 'housewives', for example). Just looking at the 'unemployed' set of columns, we see the basis of the fears about the 'ring of fire' and/or uprising, namely around half of all young Africans in Gauteng are out of work. For whites, the figure barely makes it into double-digits.

A crisis? Without question, but it is the same crisis that was found in 1992/3, and repeatedly since then, in successive youth studies. The issue at stake here is not merely whites clinging onto economic privileges, though that may be part of the story. Underlying these figures, and driving the crisis, is the growing inequality in South Africa, both inter-and intra-racial. (OECD, 2011b) Freedom represented the victory of the 'national bourgeoisie', and although the ANC professed to believe in a two-stage revolution—first a nationalist victory, then a socialist revolution—the party seems quite comfortable stuck in phase one, where those in the ANC's charmed circle do markedly better than those—of all races—beyond its reach. One result—young African people, the sneered at 'born frees' who did not earn their freedom through struggle and suffering—are being made to pay for their 'lack of sacrifice' by the signal failure of the state, controlled by the ANC, to even contemplate real redistribution.

As a result, poverty is unequally shared, not just across race lines—though we use them here—but across rural/urban (within African), across class lines (within/among African) and across all four race groups. Hunger is rare for white youth and their families, but 21 per cent of African respondents (of all ages) told us that in the 12 months prior to being interviewed, children in the household went unfed due to lack of money to buy food. The same was true for 12 per cent of coloured respondents, 7 per cent of Indian and 3 per cent of white respondents. Thus where 18 per cent of all respondents in Gauteng had seen children in their household go without food due to lack of money, this was overwhelmingly the experience of African respondents.

Economics also informs how people live—we have already seen its impact on where they live. But given the impressive delivery record of the Gauteng provincial government, 9 in 10 young people live in formal dwellings, with 12 per cent of 20-24 year-olds living in informal structures—often an unavoidable first stop in creating a new household, as young people leave the small 'matchbox' township houses of their parents and build a shack on the way to starting their own new household. Informal dwelling is however most common among those aged between 25 and 39, where it averages 13 per cent; and then drops to a tiny 2.4 per cent for those aged 65 or over. To emphasisie the point, the youth look and live like the rest of Gauteng's population; often doing better than their elders.

Young and old are equally likely to belong, or not, to a civil society organisation. Non-memebership does not automatically drive alienation of anomie. The survey scores were similar for all age cohorts and did not vary by non-membership.

Figure 6: 'Politics is a waste of time' (showing 5-point scale as 3-point) (Source: GCRO 'Quality of Life' survey 2011). chpt 16.6.psd

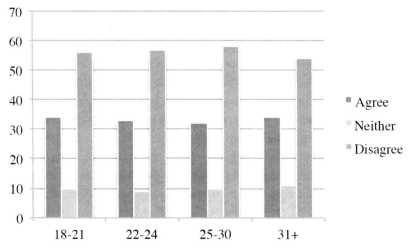

For example, we posed a Likert item that stated: 'Politics is a waste of time' as a means of identifying politically disaffected respondents—surely 'revolutionary youth' would be disaffected by then post-apartheid settlement? The answer, simply, is 'no'—or, more accurately, no more or less than any other age cohort. Respondents of all ages roundly rejected the statement.

It seems that young people, if anything, have greater faith in the efficacy of politics than their elders, though only by a matter of degree.

Asked if they strongly agreed, agreed, neither agreed nor disagreed, disagreed or strongly disagreed with the notion that 'the country is going in the wrong direction', we did find high levels of agreement—but again, they were equally shared by young and old.

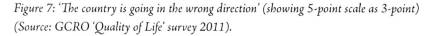

Figure 7: *'The country is going in the wrong direction' (showing 5-point scale as 3-point) (Source: GCRO 'Quality of Life' survey 2011).*

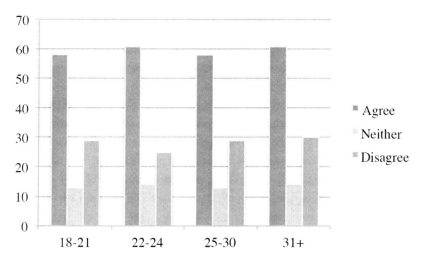

So there is widespread concern about the general direction post-apartheid South Africa is following, shared evenly across all ages. There is a shared view that politics is an efficacious means of effecting change, although while evenly shared, there is also an evenly shared scepticism—a third of all age cohorts reject this notion. And in some cases, young people are more open-minded than older respondents. When asked a 3-way question about 'foreigners'—which really means 'black African foreigners' who were the victims of a xenophobic outbreak in 2008 that saw 62 die—an average of 28 per cent of youth (across the 18-24 cohort) agreed that 'all foreigners should be sent home'—rising to 34 per cent in the 31 or over cohort. Almost a quarter (23 per cent) of the youth cohort agreed that all foreigners should be left to live freely in South Africa—true of 20.5 per cent of those aged 31 or over, with the rest agreeing that only 'legal' foreigners should be allowed to remain in South Africa.

Despite their terrible economic situation—if we recall, Mohamed Bouazizi's act of self-immolation triggered a demonstration in Sidi Bouzid in Tunisia because of corruption, authoritarianism, high unemployment, the lack of freedoms, and human rights abuses—young people are, if anything, more satisfied with their life 'overall' (as at the end of 2011). Thus where 16.8 per cent of the 16-19 cohort expressed dissatisfaction with their lives, and where presumably the roots of malcontent may lie, this rose slightly to 22 per cent and 25 per cent respectively for 20-24 year-olds and 25-29 year-olds and stayed at similar levels for the sample as a whole, dropping only among those aged 65 or over. Moreover, if we look at the positives—those who told us they were satisfied with their lives (and avoided the 'neither satisfied nor dissatisfied' mid-point chosen by many older respondents) we find that 71 per cent of 16-19 year-olds said so, the highest of any age cohort in the sample barring retirees (at 72 per cent). This dropped slightly to 65 per cent for 20-24 year-olds, and again to 59 per cent for those aged 25-29.

Finally, within the 'Quality of Life' survey is a 52-variable quality of life matrix that measures quality of life across ten 'dimensions' (including health, connectivity, work, security, socio-political, infrastructure, family, community, dwelling and a global satisfaction measure). The index scores people between 0 and 10, and the sample average in 2011 was 6.25. It is worth noting that 18-21 year-olds scored highest of all, at 6.30, dropping to 6.23 for those aged 22-24. There are racial differences, as we'd expect:

Table 1: Quality of Life scores (African/white by age cohort) (Source: GCRO 'Quality of Life' survey 2011).

Race/age cohort	Overall QoL score (sample mean: 6.25)
African 18-21	6.20
White 18-21	6.97
African 22-24	6.12
White 22-24	7.12
African 25-30	6.16
White 25-30	7.16
African 31+	6.07
White 31+	6.88

Life remains better in Gauteng for white youth—and older respondents—than for Africans. Every cohort of whites has a higher—in some cases far higher—quality of life than their African counterparts (we have excluded Indian and coloured youth from the analysis). So while racial lines of division continue to run through the youth as through adults, there are lines dividing all youth from adults, regardless of race.

Conclusion

Mohamed Bouazizi's self-immolation in the Tunisian town of Sidi Bouzid, triggered mass protests against corruption, authoritarianism, and human rights abuses. Without the military to back him, President Ben Ali stepped down on 14 January 2011, setting off a season of protest that inspired hundreds of thousands of North Africans in Egypt, Algeria and Libya to take to the streets and fill public squares. Dictators seemed fragile, apparently falling in a domino-like sequence not seen since the Berlin Wall came crashing down. But the issues that drove the Arab Spring were not to do with inherently violent youth—quite the opposite, they were youth and adults wanting freedom, rights, legality, transparency, democracy—as well as an entry into the economic sphere. In South Africa, it would be difficult to mount an argument that youth and adults feel rightless, disrespect the constitution, or are preparing to rise up against a perceived dictatorship—no dataset would support any such analysis (and it is worth recalling that the ANC did succeed in recalling a sitting president in 2009). The similarity with South Africa lies in the twin facts of a large young population coupled with low participation by those youth in the economy. That remains a core challenge in South Africa today, as it was on the eve of democracy. The aim of this chapter has not been to set up a straw argument for the sake of knocking it down. Much of the data analysed here suggest that the ring of fire analogy may not be entirely wrong—but the target group is wrong. The 'problem' lies not with the youth, even though they clearly have some good reasons—most obviously economic—for being angry with the *status quo*. Rather, the 'ring of fire' really comprises the sea of poverty that encircles the province of Gauteng on all sides. With population growth already higher than all other provinces as a result of the magnetic pull of this critical national economic space, the need to develop the surrounding areas is self-evident. Whether the Arab Spring is likely to percolate to the south of the continent or not is not clear: but if it does, it will be as a result of the poverty and inequality that continue to afflict democratic South Africa—not because 'the youth' have encircled the *laager* of privilege with a 'ring of fire' they will unleash upon the denizens of Gauteng.

Chapter 17

School to work transition and youth views on labour in Japan

Tomokazu Makino

Introduction

Japan's unemployment rate in the 1980s was at the two per cent level. Although the number was higher for age group fifteen to twenty-four years-old, on average it was 4.6 per cent. Japan's labour system at the time, and the school to work transition system supporting it, was well regarded both in Japan and abroad. Even more recent studies share this view (Brown, Green and Lauder, 2001).

Japan's economy, however, entered a long period of stagnation after reaching its peak in the late 1980s and early 1990s, a period known as the 'Bubble Economy'. In the period following, known as the 'Lost Decade', labour conditions in Japan underwent great change. The unemployment rate rose from 2.1 per cent in 1990 to 5.4 per cent in 2002, and for the age group ifteen to twenty-four years-old, from 4.3 per cent to 10.1 per cent.

Despite the worsening situation, the statistics can still be regarded quite positive in comparison to other countries. However, the rapid increase of the unemployment rate over a short span of time brought major changes in views towards Japan's school to work transition system. There was a lot of discourse seeking to identify reasons for the deteriorating situation and measures to counter it. There were arguments (and counter-arguments) pointing out the system's flaws and the psychology of Japan's youth regarding unemployment or changing jobs. In other words, how youth viewed labour was seen as the primary cause for problems with the school to work transition system.

The aim of this chapter is to look at Japan's school to work transition system over the last twenty years, as well as youth views and values regarding labour in Japan. In particular, by surveying various studies and statistics, I will look at what social science studies have managed to elucidate since the 'Lost Decade', as well as the messages and responses to them that have been disseminated to society. The topic of school to work transition may appear to have been fully studied already, but what is different about this chapter is that it takes the above perspective to study several aspects that are usually studied separately, such as changes in the school to work transition system, and youth values, to put together an integrated story.

From high school to work

During the period of high economic growth in the 1960s, companies looking for unskilled labour were in fierce competition over junior high school graduates (known as 'golden eggs') due to labour shortages. A study of this topic alone would be meaningful. However, in 1974, the ratio of students advancing to high school was over ninety per cent, and to junior college or university almost forty per cent. Today, the latter number is closer to sixty per cent. Below, I discuss the present- day topic of school to work transition for high school and university students.

It is well-established that school to work transition for high school students was supported by a unique system in Japan whereby high schools mediated the job search process of their students, as elucidated by Kariya (1991). Where a high school student found employment, it was influenced by whether the school had been able to successfully place a student there in the past (track record) and the school's academic rank. From the perspective of companies, this was a system of 'designated schools' to which job postings were made known. With the goals of providing job search guidance to inexperienced students, preventing job opportunities from only being offered to specific students, and preventing already established networks from collapsing if the system were more free, the schools managed to balance supply and demand by only allowing approved students to apply for certain jobs, and disallowing students from applying for multiple positions at the same time (one-student-one-application system). Students would find out about their predecessors who found jobs in the companies of their choice, then work towards becoming worthy of the school's recommendation to the company by improving their academic performance and skills. This three-way (company-school-student) approach is what formed the foundation of the internationally well-regarded school to work transition system for the most part of the 1960s to 1980s.

School introductions to jobs have continued since then, too, but there have been several changes to the process. The most basic change is that the ratio of job openings to applicants has fallen. According to a survey by the Ministry of Health, Labour and Welfare (MHLW), using the number of job-seeking new high-school graduates per year as the denominator and the total number of job openings posted by companies as the numerator, the job opening to applicant ratio has quickly fallen below one job per applicant in 1999 after reaching its peak in 1992 at 3.08. Despite temporarily recovering, it fell again at the end of the economic depression in the 2000s, and in 2012 is at 0.68 (all statistics as of July that year). The number of job seekers is also on a sharp decline, with more students advancing to university and giving up on entering the job market after observing the harsh job market. This figure has been going down since reaching its peak in 1986 at 617,761, and in 2012 is at 186,820. Despite this fall in the number of jobseekers, the ratio of job openings to applicants is low. The situation is particularly dire in rural areas. In 2011, of the 47 prefectural governments in Japan, only six municipalities had a job opening to applicant ratio over 1, mostly municipalities with large cities (with Tokyo the highest at 1.92). The situation in Tohoku and Kyushu are particularly bad, with 0.18 in Tohoku's Aomori Prefecture, 0.26 in Kyushu's Kumamoto Prefecture, and the country's lowest at 0.17 in Okinawa Prefecture.

According to the School Basic Survey of the Ministry of Education, Culture, Sports, Science and Technology (MEXT), in 2011, of the 160,272 high school graduates looking for jobs, about 60 per cent found employment in one of two job types: 40.0 per cent in 'manufacturing personnel' (i.e. factory workers) (51.6 per cent of males) and 18.1 per cent as 'service industry personnel' (30.7 per cent of females). The job types that students find attractive for their stability and that used to have strong potential for actually being realised—'professional/ technical personnel,' 'clerical personnel' and 'sales personnel'—garnered no more that 7.0 per cent, 9.7 per cent and 8.6 per cent respectively. The types of jobs that high school students are pursuing today do not require a high level of knowledge, skill or experience (Kumazawa, 2006). Further, companies putting out job postings for high school graduates are increasingly small and medium sized enterprises. Jobs at big companies and technical or administrative work are more available for university, rather than high school graduates. Companies are concerned about the lack of basic skills these days, and are increasingly avoiding high school graduates.

High school students, instead, look to part-time jobs, which offer more interesting work, and in some cases, more income. According to the MHLW's Survey on Employment Trends (Ministry of Health, Labour and Welfare, 2010), 63.1 per cent of males and 72.0 per cent of females aged nineteen and below who started work are entering part-time jobs (setting the parameters at those employed within that year and including students going on to further studies). Until the mid-1990s, these figures were around fifteen per cent. The favourable job postings that teachers used to utilise to control and motivate students to study are few in number, and available only to students with the highest grades. Consequently, many high school students go into part-time work instead (Kosugi, 2005).

With students losing faith in the system for obtaining jobs through school, offering job-seeking guidance has also become less meaningful for teachers, even appearing to be pointless. Supporting unenthusiastic students in the job-seeking process has become an extra effort for them. The guidance of teachers in recommending companies is no longer in step with the youth culture of respecting what the student wants to do, which is also fuelled by the recent social trend of respecting one's journey to 'find oneself' (Yajima and Mimizuka, 2005).

From university to work

I could explain here the historical background of the school to work transition system in terms of university graduates. But unless you live in Japan, the job-search process currently in place will probably have the most impact.

It is important in the beginning to clarify the general trends. According to the 2011 School Basic Survey, found showed that of 552,794 university graduates, 340,378 (61.6 per cent) found full-time work and 19,146 (3.5 per cent) found temporary work. In 1990, when the peak of the market was more favourable to job seekers where students could choose a company to join, these figures stood at 81.0 per cent and 0.8 per cent. They continued to worsen between the 1990s and early 2000s, peaking in 2003 at 55.0 per cent and 4.6 per cent. Despite recovering in the late 2000s, the numbers are again getting worse. However, students finding work as 'professional/technical personnel,' 'clerical personnel' and 'sales personnel' occupy 33.5 per cent, 32.1 per cent and 21.3 per cent of the total, showing a clearly different situation to that of high school students.

Regarding the process explained below, I must first explain that this was established in the 1990s. Every year, RECRUIT Works Institute calculates the total number of job openings targeting university graduates and the ratio of job openings per applicant (the number of people recruited by private companies throughout Japan who are scheduled to graduate university (undergraduate or graduate school)). As with the changes in the ratio of high school students finding jobs, since the 1991 peak of 2.86 jobs per applicant, the number has fallen. It fell to 0.99 in 2000 and recovered somewhat around 2005 with favourable conditions in the manufacturing industry, but with the economic crisis in the late 2000s, it has again fallen, and in 2012 stands at 1.23. Under these circumstances, school to work transition for university graduates is a harsh process, equal to, or even surmounting the experience of high school and university entrance exams. To this day, there are all kinds of hurdles that students must clear—the written exam for which they must reach the cutoff point, the stressful interview where they are asked overbearing questions, and the 'self-analysis' and 'entry sheet' they must fill in, which will be explained in detail below. The individualisation, or liberalisation of the job search process that followed with the scrapping of the 1997 recruitment agreement between companies and schools, which determined when the recruitment season would begin, and the advancement of the information age are also important factors underlying these changes.

So let's look at the current situation, using the job process for liberal arts graduates (mostly in universities in large cities) from autumn 2010 through to 2011 as an example. The academic year in Japan begins in April, but in October, the end of summer break is marked by the sudden onslaught in universities of students donning dark suits—third year students beginning their job search. Signs for guidance sessions and seminars about the job search are posted everywhere, and students join these enthusiastically, at numbers even more than those at academic events.

Guidance sessions often cover themes such as the types of work executed in the various industries, and the types of recruits being sought. The ones most often conducted, however, teach job search techniques, such as how to ascertain which industries or companies to focus on (of particular importance is the 'self-analysis,' a uniquely Japanese method for screening companies to which they apply), how to correctly fill in an 'entry sheet' (also a uniquely Japanese form for applying to companies), and how to effectively promote themselves at an interview. Youths with basically no work experience other than part-time work must look back on their life thus far and identify the type of work they deeply feel they want to do. Only a minority can actually do whatever they identify from this soul searching. This is, of course, because the jobs that everyone is interested in are inundated with applicants. The entry sheet is something students must write very carefully and inventively to promote themselves in response to very standard questions such as 'What did you involve yourself in during your university days?' Students devote themselves to filling out these application materials and submit them to various companies. These days, students send entry sheets to an average of 30 companies (although in a 2011 interview, I spoke to a student who had applied to 85). Additionally there are the web portals offering company information and recruiting seminar schedules through which application guidelines can be easily accessed. The importance of these websites has been highlighted since around 2000. These days, bookshops are full of manuals on how to self-analyse. Also involved in the process are speculations of the apparel industry on what suits or shoes to sell to job-seekers, and consultancies targeting confused students. In other words, school to work transition for university students is turning into a big business.

So students begin the job search process in early autumn, and after guidance sessions, seminars, and recruitment sessions, submit entry sheets in the winter season. Because this clashes with end-of-term report deadlines and tests, most third year students' schedule books are crammed with activities. Interviewing begins during the winter break, in February and March. If things go well, the student's schedule is packed with interview appointments. I spoke to one student who had as many as fifty company interviews (some students take pride in the number of entry sheets submitted, interviews granted, and offers obtained as evidence of their hard work in the job search process). It is common for multiple interviews to be conducted in one company's screening. Sometimes, it is with the company's human resources manager, but in many cases, as the process moves forward, company directors and presidents also attend. They may be one-on-one interviews, but not always. After this screening, an unofficial decision can be made by the company regarding whether or not to hire the student. The more well-known the company is, the lower the chance of success due to the large number of applicants. It is not uncommon to have odds of one in several hundreds. The peak for decisions being made is between April and May during the students' fourth year of university.

Many people probably regard this recruitment system, a much-accepted practice in Japan, as very unique (i.e. that the Japanese tend to put a lot of energy into competing with each other on the same playing field). Although unique, this school to work transition process poses no problems if all goes smoothly, but several problems with the system have been identified in recent years. For example, with many companies conducting recruiting sessions according to the schedule above, it is not easy for students who get a late start in the game to catch up. Being unable to be on the same playing field as others in the fall of one's third year of university later becomes a huge disadvantage. Furthermore, this recruitment system, known as the 'simultaneous recruiting of new graduates,' is, as the name suggests, based on the idea of recruiting new graduates, making it very difficult for students who repeat a year or who have graduated in a previous year to participate in. Students risk being viewed negatively due to the fact that they were unable to get a job at the same time as everyone else. Some students even hold back on graduating because of how tough it can be for non-new graduates to get a job. The schedule explained above is typical of big cities, such as Tokyo and Osaka, but if students in rural areas wish to apply for jobs there (and companies in big cities obviously have more job openings), they face the burden of transportation costs to attend recruitment sessions and interviews, and lack information to share among friends.

Problems with the current job search system have been covered above, and there are many issues being debated, but I would like to mention three more aspects. First, the job search process often hinders study. Because many teachers understand how difficult finding a job can be, it is difficult for them to reproach or punish students who use it as an excuse to miss class. The early job search process has been an established schedule for a long time, and although a reform bill was passed in the autumn of 2011 to attempt to delay it to allow students to concentrate more on their studies, the outcome is still unclear.

Secondly, I mention a problem with the 'simultaneous recruiting of new graduates' system. Why does it have to target new graduates only? In the past, many companies conducted on the job training (there was more leeway for this back then), which is why they sought out new graduates, who they anticipated would have a high capacity to be trained from scratch. This is understandable. These days, however, many companies are looking for recruits who are already prepared to step up to the plate, but they expect students with no work experience to be ready for this. This poses a dilemma. If it is this readiness they are looking for, they should be able to cast a wider net to include all kinds of people, and not look only to new graduates to fill their needs (that said, mid-career recruiting is on the rise). However, the school to work transition system, which focuses on the recruitment of new graduates, remains unchanged (including in terms of the tremendous impact the first job taken on by a new graduate has on his/ her future career).

Third, there is contradiction in discourse related to the job search process. There is pervading discourse that self-help (i.e. self-analysis and application documents, as well as self-promotion during the interviews) is a determining factor in the process, and this continues to impose great pressure on students. And yet a more basic factor that cannot be overlooked is the impact of a university's academic rank and social prestige. Besides, it is a trend of the economic system to prescribe the recruitment process at a macro level. We can also see this in connection with changes in the unemployment rate and job opening to applicant ratio mentioned thus far. If a student's effort to secure a position or find employment in the sector or company he/she desires is futile, it cannot be said to completely be his/her fault. However, most discourse puts the blame on the student's failure to self-help (Makino, 2012). There were often news reports and advertisements in 2010 and 2011 about students buying iPhones to be able to book spots in recruitment sessions immediately online (there is a maximum capacity), and using Twitter and Facebook to promote themselves to human resource personnel. This may again become a resource for criticizing students on their efforts, it they fail to purchase an iPhone to make the job search process easier, or fail to promote themselves in social media.

Keywords and debates regarding youth labour

The school to work transition process described above became the subject of debate from the 1990s to 2000s, but youth employment has recently come under debate from a variety of perspectives. The social sciences have taken on the role of discussing the issue, particularly to refute the 'youth bashing' described below. The reader may already be familiar with other writing on this topic, but below is a brief overview regarding how social science studies in Japan have analysed labour issues since the 'Lost Decade.'

The term 'parasite single' is one clue to understanding both negative and positive aspects regarding youth labour and life course in recent years. The concept was created by family sociologist Yamada (1999) to refer to unmarried youth who continue to live with their parents after graduation, and rely on them for basic living needs, as well as unmarried youth who just enjoy this lifestyle. Yamada analysed the increase of the number of 'parasite singles' from the perspective of interdependency in Japanese families, and discussed the social and economic impact of the phenomenon. The word 'parasite' however, has been used on its own and become a typical expression used in 'youth bashing.' One part of Yamada's argument—that Japan's youth cannot lead independent lives—and the economic impact of this in particular have been raised.

The word *freeter* is a combination of Japanese and English words to refer to people who do not take on full-time jobs and work freely instead, and was first coined during the economic boom. Though not a standard definition for this term, if we take the description in the MHLW's White Paper on the Labour Economy of part-time workers and those looking for part-time work between 15 to 34 years-old, there were 1.83 million such people in 2010. In 2003, when the number peaked at 2.17 million, the meaning of the term *freeter* shifted from its original meaning to refer to youth who avoid entering the harsh world of full-time employment and choose an easy way to earn a living (Tachibanaki, 2004).

The term 'NEET' ('Not in Education, Employment or Training') emerged in England in the late 1990s to describe the situation of youth who are unable to access unemployment assistance and are regarded as a long-term social cost. In Japan, however, the term has come to refer to people who do not work or youth who have no wish to work, again becoming a term used in 'youth bashing' (Honda, Naito and Goto, 2006).

The word *hikikomori* (social withdrawal) refers to people who are unable to maintain links with school, community, and sometimes family, due to something being wrong with his/her physical or mental condition, interpersonal relations, failure on the job or similar facctors (Takenaka, 2009). There are said to be several hundreds of thousands of youth with this condition. Although only a small minority in this group have committed shocking crimes— for example the illegal confinement of a young girl, or the homicide resulting from a hijacking a bus—*hikikomori* have been portrayed negatively, as weird, spoiled by their parents, and as non-economic generating burdens. While the general public's understanding of *hikikomori* in recent years has continually increased, researchers and supporters of *hikikomori* still need to work to spread awareness of the phenomenon.

The above is a broad overview of concepts regarding youth employment that emerged from the 1990s to 2000s, through which the reader may find a similarity among the various terms mentioned. Each was used, in some ways even as a catch line, in the context of describing youth who are not in full-time employment, or who are unable to work, to indicate the cause as immaturity or mental incomprehensibility. This was related to the focus on mental incomprehensibility brought on by youth subcultures and shocking juvenile crimes at the time.

There are, however, many opposing arguments. Following the decline in company recruitments after the economic depression in the 1990s, many people fell into the *freeter* or NEET categories because they had no other choice. In 1995, Keidanren's (Japan Federation of Economic Organisations) *Shin Jidai no Nihonteki Keiei* (*Japanese Management in the New Age*) pointed out that because companies must survive in an increasingly fluctuating and globalising economy, they must actively use non-regular workers, which would lower costs. To back this up, the Worker Dispatch Law was revised from the end of 1990 to 2000 to expand the types of work that allowed fixed-term employment contracts and to extend the contract period's upper limit. The gap in treatment between regular and non-regular employees in Japan is huge. Non-regular employees are in a way being used by companies as an adjustment valve to survive the increasingly fluctuating markets of today. It is the youth—the generation of new hires—that are taking on this role. Further, the youth taking on non-regular work who then are pushed out of such jobs and stop working are viewed very negatively, making it difficult for them to re-enter the labour market.

Even people with regular employment can no longer hope for wage hikes, and are having a tough time, working longer hours than ever before regardless of age. One's job is easily threatened if the person dislikes working long hours. Many companies do make efforts to improve their labour conditions, but in general, it is harder these days to steadily follow one's desired life course. Is it thus not surprising that the youth are moving back in with their parents to reduce the risks even just a little bit, or for more people to marry late (if at all), or for the birth rate to be low? Does there not need to be some sort of social response to this? Such questions are posed to counter criticisms of the youth (Genda, 2005; Kumazawa, 2006), and are increasingly points begging for government awareness, with some aspects increasingly being addressed in policy making.

Youth views on labour today

As discussed, there are various debates regarding Japan's school to work transition system and youth employment. How do today's youth feel about working these days? A number of surveys present a very different picture to those that deem today's youth immature and incomprehensible.

Let's begin by considering the Japan Productivity Centre's (JPC) long-term Survey on the New Recruit's Perception of Work (since 1969). One question asks, 'Are you work-oriented or private life-oriented'? Around 1990, more people said they were private-life oriented, but since 2000, the two have been competing. Although not specifically directed at youth, the 2005 World Values Survey (Dentsū and Nippon Research Centre, 2008) noted that from an international perspective, the Japanese place great importance in work in their daily life (78.1 per cent responded that it was bad for work to lose importance, a figure much higher than other countries). According to the Survey on the New Recruit's Perception of Work, we can observe a greater awareness of the importance of work (which we can say is uniquely Japanese), even among the youth that appear to prioritise their private life.

In response to the question in the same survey, 'Do you wish to stay with your current company for a long time?' more respondents since 2000 have responded, 'I want to stay until I retire' or 'Yes, for now.' According to a student survey conducted from 1987 by sociologist Katagiri (2009), 32.4 per cent of students in 1997 said 'people should not change jobs' compared to 38.4 per cent in 2002 and 52.7 per cent in 2007, showing a steep rise support for this view. Katagiri also reported that as the years have passed, more and more students say that their life goal is 'to have a peaceful life,' with less responding, 'to have an affluent life,' 'to enjoy life as I please,' or 'to make the world a better place.' Katagiri points out, somewhat critically, that university students of late have lost their independence, spirit of challenge, and the optimism that supports these, and prioritise acting in tune with the people around them and stability. Yamada (2009) goes one step further to describe this as the 'conservatisation' of the youth. Some studies do not automatically perceive the valuing of acting in sync with others or of stability as negative and attempt to understand the relationship between these phenomena (Asano, 2006; Iwata et. al., 2006), but some studies point out the difficulties for today's youth of living within the restraints of limited, close interpersonal relations (Doi, 2008), or blame the 'cowardice' of today's youth and conclude that this can be seen as far as in the decline of their drives for consumption and sex (Miura and Harada, 2009), or continue to deem the youth 'low risk-oriented,' in that they are taking the safe way out.

Educational sociologist Honda (2010) uses data from the National Survey of Social Stratification and Social Mobility (since 1955) to report that what the youth prioritise in work tends to be 'work that they are interested in' or 'work through which they can display their skills.' Similar views on labour in youth can be observed from the Cabinet Office and JPC surveys mentioned above. As described in discussing the school to work transition of university students, the sense among youth of wanting to engage in work that they are interested in is a shared feeling. In today's harsh labour environment, only a handful of people can find work through which they do not take risks yet enjoy. It is also uncertain whether they can make enough money to live on and eventually raise a family. Today's youth face various work-related dilemmas.

So what sociological studies in Japan have shown is that youth views on labour today are by no means about immaturity or incomprehensibility, and that the dilemma they face is strongly related to the social and economic situation. Awareness of this is spreading, but there is still no end to the 'youth bashing'; that today's youth lack initiative and do not take risks, have too much faith in big companies, are self-centered, and avoid communication and close themselves off from people they consider different. Although such arguments are not completely wrong, they would be more meaningful if the social situation giving rise to such views were touched upon, as well as what today's youth see (or are able to see) from where they are located in this dilemma, and how this differs from previous generations.

Recent policies, debates and the future of the school to work transition process

We can review recent school to work transition-related policies in a similar way to the above-mentioned 'youth bashing' and its counter arguments. That is, by attributing failure to find a job to fault on a personal level, to the empowerment of the individual to deal with this, and a critique of this approach.

Career education was one popular measure taken in the 2000s. In the Central Council for Education's report *Improvements to Transition from Elementary/ Secondary Education to Higher Education* (1999), the first official document to mention the term, 'career education' was explained as 'Education that in addition to giving students knowledge and skills about good attitudes towards work and career, teaches them to understand their individuality and nurtures their skills and views on labour to allow them to take the initiative in choosing their path.' Although a great variety of practices fall under 'career education,' of particular importance has been the development of views on labour and self-understanding (Kumazawa, 2006; Honda, 2010).

Many sociologists and economists have criticised the emphasis on consciousness building. The reason is quite simple and overlaps with what has been previously mentioned. Regardless of how much they develop job consciousness, if there are no jobs, or labour conditions as a whole are deteriorating, the reward for such efforts is not as expected. In fact, there are critiques of the discourse seeping in attributing success in the job search to personal effort, and nurturing immediate adaptation.

Of course, school to work transition is a process that adjusts to society. What is proposed as an alternative to career education, which focuses on consciousness building, is the improvement of vocational education (Kumazawa, 2006; Honda, 2009). The OECD average ratio of general education graduates among high school graduates is 49 per cent, to which Japan's ratio is 72 per cent. This is the third highest among OECD member countries following New Zealand at 77 per cent and Canada at 76 per cent (OECD, 2011c). Despite previous arguments, this tendency to value general education is the result of the longtime practice of steadily recruiting new graduates. But now that we cannot overlook problems in the school to work transition system, more active vocational education is necessary. One specific example is, at the introductory level, to provide more factual information to students, such as the significance of different types of work, job satisfaction and job difficulties, labour laws, statistical trends, and useful resources and services. These measures are more difficult to establish than simply raising consciousness about the kind of work students are interested in, and they do not catch on in schools very easily. But if we consider the fact that tough conditions for workers in today's fluctuating economy will continue, vocational education is an important measure to take, regardless of any short-term changes in business conditions.

Let's also review the plans to reform the school to work transition system (See OECD, 2009a). The Youth Independence/Challenge Plan released by the government in 2003 details several ground breaking services and shows a trend towards offering comprehensive support. This includes Japan's version of the Dual System (education/job-training program for *freeters* and unemployed youth), Job Café (a one-stop service centre for young job-seekers) and Youth Independence Camp (a vocational training camp for youth who have lost their enthusiasm in the job search process). In 2008, the Job Card system began, by which card holders record their academic and job histories on cards that serve to support their vocational training and job search. Kosugi (2010) argues that it is necessary to establish a framework for socially appreciating the careers and skills of non-regular workers, and the Job Card system is an attempt in this direction. In the 2000s, the ratio of junior high school, high school and university students undertaking work experience and internship programs is also rising steadily. However, although these measures are being implemented, youth unemployment is continuing to become more and more serious. With difficulties faced around the world, improving the situation will not be simple.

The 1990s to 2000s is identified as a period in Japan when various social problems (e.g. regarding education or crime) and life course events and issues were most understood not within social contexts but as resulting from internal problems (psychologisation) (Mori, 2000; Makino, 2012). Intertwined with this, the period saw the spread of neoliberal discourse strongly asserting self-effort and self-responsibility. As we have discussed, problems in school to work transition for youth is often raised as a problem of lack of self-responsibility due to mental immaturity. Sociological counter arguments have been made and various measures carried out amidst a flurry of psychologistic and sociological discourse. Recently, one well-known company has made it clearly known that it will hire university graduates up to three years after their graduation under its new graduate recruitment system. It is not yet known what the outcome will be in terms of who they recruit, whether other companies will follow suit, and whether there will be any change in the recruitment of high school students. But at last, having made it past the psychologistic 1990s and 2000s, we can see indications of change in companies, too. If the social sciences are to back these changes even more, it will be by providing evidence about labour. A careful study of the outcomes and changes that are beginning to result from government measures will clarify their adequacy and help steer future discourse in the right direction.

Chapter 18

Russian youth in the labour market: Education, employment, work transitions and well-being

Julia Zubok

In modern rapidly changing societies, the problems of work transitions, trajectories and life chances and their effects on well-being take on a new actuality. In recurring economic crises, young people more than other social groups suffer from recession, falling standards of living, mass unemployment, and volatility in the labour market. Economic instability and social uncertainty are the main factors in changes in life transitions in all spheres.

In a broad sense transition covers various shifts, from one sector to another, from one form of activity to another, and spatial shifts connected with migration from rural to urban locations. (Fahey and Gale, 2005). In a more concrete sociological sense the transitions of youth represent certain changes of young people's social status towards the achievement of social maturity, at the same time recognising its social subjectivity. This idea is expressed in the Jordan Human Development Report (UNDP, 2000), which places emphasis on the series of transitions from adolescence to adulthood, from dependence to independence, and from being recipients of society's services to becoming contributors to national economic, political, and cultural life. Viewed in this context, becoming independent is one of the most significant aspects of youth. Moving from the childhood home to one's own place, letting go of one's parents and acquiring a spouse, and making choices after one's compulsory education regarding continuing education and career moves are all part of one of the most dramatic life changes a person experiences. The transition perspective articulates the issue of when and how young people achieve the status of becoming fully operational members of society—and thereby acquire citizenship in all its dimensions (UNDP, 2000).

As it is clarified in the World Youth Report 2003, 'It is possible in many societies to identify four distinct aspects of young people's movement from dependence to independence, as follows: (a) leaving the parental home and establishing new living arrangements; (b) completing full-time education; (c) forming close, stable personal relationships outside of the family, often resulting in marriage and children; and (d) testing the labour market, finding work and possibly settling into a career, and achieving a more or less stable livelihood.... This characterisation applies to both developed and developing countries; demonstrating the capacity to contribute to the economic welfare of the family is a key stage in the journey to adulthood. These transitions are interconnected; leaving home and setting up one's own personal economy require an independent source of income, and to reach this stage a young person generally has to have acquired qualifications and to have succeeded in demonstrating his or her skill in the labour market or some equivalent subsection of society. The relevant issue in these sorts of interpretations of youth is that the general problem of transitions relates specifically to the process of becoming independent', (UN, 2003, 6).

With regard to the labour sphere the transitive processes are associated with the development of occupational interests and the necessary training to enter a profession; start of work, finding of a job in the acquired specialty, employment and professional mobility; material security and well-being.

Motivation is the most important qualitative characteristic of youth transitions. At the individual level motivation reflects personal orientations of young people, in structured and interrelated personal needs, interests, values and attitudes. These orientations determine the general direction of transitions. That is why 'within these transitions between sectors, societal groups and geographical location, the research focus may be on changes in economic position and/or attitudes', (Fahey and Gale, 2005, 3).

At the individual level and in the everyday life context the transition is expressed in the desire to achieve (or surpass) the status of a 'significant other' who provides a kind of benchmark or reference point. Achievement brings satisfaction and contributes to self-assertion in the status of an adult. Lack of implementation of life plans, on the contrary, leads to frustration and even to infantilism or to extreme desires to achieve their goal at any cost. Meanwhile, in acquiring the form of upward or downward mobility, models of the transition as a socially determined phenomenon bear the imprint of the socio-historical and socio-cultural features of the social environment in which the transition is carried out. So, under conditions of economic stability youth transitions were smooth and mostly linear processes of *filling of social niches* (Evans and Furlong, 1997). Internalisation of the whole range of significant patterns in the status-role structure of adult society guaranteed successful development. Such a model of transition was, to the full extent, carried out in Russian society during the Soviet period of its history. Attitudes to young people as an object of education, up-bringing and ideological influence dominated the transition. From this standpoint, youth participation in public life was naturally considered as a preparatory, institutionally controlled stage of transition to the future of adult life. Therefore, the main task was seen in terms of the impact of society on young people with the purpose of societal education and purposeful formation of their social image. The effectiveness of this influence was considered from the positions of learning of necessary value-normative components and ways of activity. So, the youth policy was seen as the implementation of the paternalistic role of the state under conditions of generally stable functioning of the society. The socio-economic climate of that time in general contributed to the fact that the transitions were predictable and the nature of stratification levelled the transitions of the majority of young people making them more or less common. It cannot be said that this approach met resistance from young people. The large majority of youth groups with conformist orientations and those who needed compensatory and social support to overcome certain disadvantages were satisfied with this approach. The policy focused on the real problems of young people, although in a relationship with the forms and methods of their specific state regulations. On the one hand this type of relation limited manifestations of the one's own activity and self-determination by holding the young person in a clearly defined framework. On the other hand, necessary conditions for the successful transition were guaranteed by the state.

Owing to economic changes and unemployment the transitions of young people in different countries have become complicated. Extended education, unemployment, the constant need for professional retraining are common features. The very same transition has become full of conflicts arising from unresolved contradictions between youth and the globalising of the market economy. As a result the model and image of the transition has been associated with *social bridges*, paving the *social paths* (Evans and Furlong, 1997). Moving along these paths young people come into adult life, facing essential problems and difficulties that are intensified by different types of contradictions between young people and local/global society.

Together with acceleration of the pace of socio-economic changes and growing instability, youth transitions continued to change. All the achievements of young people, especially in the labour sphere are largely the result of the influence of social forces, outside of the control of young people. One of the main characteristics of the transition of young people has become a status inconsistency—uneven in the intensity and success of progress in different spheres of life, not so much dependent on individual aspirations, but on the determining influence of structural factors, primarily social class, gender, ethnicity, education and the labour market. At the same time they acquire new forms of expression combined with the factors of globalisation and local economic conditions. 'In the course of making school-to-work transitions social class, gender and ethnic divisions among young people widen, deepen and are consolidated ... These divisions are then reproduced ...' (Roberts, 2003, 19) (see also Konstantinovskiy, 2000). It means that youth transition has gradually lost its linear shape and became a changeable and a variable social trajectory.

The further growth of instability and uncertainty, typical for the most of contemporary societies, has brought new changes into the mechanism of youth transitions. They are mostly determined by the combination of the individual abilities and recourses to resist different types of global risks and *to navigate* or thread a way through the *waves of uncertainty* (Evans and Furlong, 1997; see also Kovacheva, 2000). This supposes young people's ability to define goals, the starting and the end point and the route, which are turned into particular trajectories. But many paths and trajectories exist among the different groups of young people, reflecting significant social and cultural differentiation.

Although these patterns were investigated more than a decade ago, this process remains and can now be viewed against the background of a new world crisis. 'Transitional labour markets are marked by the emergence of new opportunities, prospects and hopes, on the one hand, and by a decreasing demand for labour, higher levels of joblessness, and spells of long-term unemployment, on the other hand. These factors affect young people's transition to adulthood and represent a serious challenge for society and its stability. New windows of opportunity are important, and quite often new chances are seized by young people, but such opportunities are limited and may not compensate for the risks associated with substantially decreased social protection. The inability to find a job carries psychological costs, causes frustration and depression, and undermines motivation', (UN, 2007, 175).

This process expresses itself in its own way in different parts of Europe. 'The first and widely accepted fact about youth conditions in East Central Europe is that young people are making their life transitions at a time when the societies they live in are making societal transitions. If we want to analyse youth transitions in the region we have to study the interplay of these problematic transformations' (Kovacheva, 2001, 1) (see also Roberts and Fagan, 1999).

In the post-Soviet period in Russia the interaction between young people and society was reshaped through the processes of liberalisation, in ways that were connected with the expansion of the zone of independence from the former social restrictions, norms, values and samples of morality. The traditional mechanisms of the institutional regulation (the state, the family, education, training and labour collectives, political structures, etc.) of young people's lives— their consciousness and behaviour—sharply weakened. The typical unified methods of the former system for the formation of the new generation through the exercise of purposeful influence were rejected. Society no longer put in front of youth any tasks or ideological requirements. Young people spontaneously and independently mastered the changing social reality. In fact, in the 1990s young people throughout East Central Europe 'were thrown sharply away from the certainty of the previously firmly structured and strictly controlled transition patterns of the state-socialist societies into the sea of the risks and uncertainties of market regulated societies. At present they face the conflicting challenges of globalisation and nationalistic mobilisation, technological advancement and economic underdevelopment, individualisation and traditional military conflicts. The risks of the transition force young people to invent flexible strategies to move through education and training, work and leisure, family and peer relationships to uncertain destinations,' (Kovacheva, 2001, 1: see also Machacek, 1998; Zubok, 2005; Zubok, 2007; Zubok and Yakovuk, 2008). Liberalisation and the rejection of the unified model of the transition on the societal level caused changes in the methods of self-determination and self-actualisation of young people in different spheres of life. The ability to be flexible and to rationalise their personal interactions with social structures as well as readiness to change dynamically along with the changing social environment became probably the most important social competence of young people (Zubok, 2009; Zubok and Chuprov, 2009).

Further reduction of the institutional impact in the sense of regulation and support, expansion of the self-construction of biographies in connection with the appearance of a larger number of alternatives for individual development, confronted young people with the necessity of making independent choices both of life goals and ways of their implementation. This enhances the value of young people's subjective activity in the planning and organisation of their lives and actualises the need to develop their own life paths. It should be noted that many young people are quite successfully coping with this task, at least in the short term perspective. This, however, does not mean that society is completely indifferent to what is happening with younger generation. Through youth policy to some extent, directly or not and more or less successfully, society does make an impact on youth preferences and choice. And, by and large, young people are objectively interested in cooperation with the institutional structures dealing with the change in opportunities and conditions for their own development. But the choice, in the end, remains for the young people.

The motives behind choices made in the process of transition are determined by the peculiarities of the environment in which the choice is made, and by young people's own feelings of the future. The last is connected with their ability to overcome the boundaries of time and space in search of the new patterns of goals and solutions. In the context of rapid change, when there is 'a reduction in the present, i.e. shortening the length of time intervals in which we can count on a certain constancy of our relationships' (Lubbe, 1994, p. 94.) such action is an absolutely natural desire to look into the future in order to navigate. The ability to feel the new needs and to realise the choice in connection with the coming tomorrow, to transfer this invisible, but intuitively felt future into the present day and thus to construct one's personal life in accordance with the notions of what *will* be significant, important and valuable (skills, competencies, knowledge, etc.) is the essential mechanism of successful transition. Young people generate the social, political and technological innovations within society and often in a decisive manner violate the permissible limits and norms. And then there is a sort of transgression that takes place: look there, where no one has yet looked and understand that while a certain point is hidden, its presence is certainly felt (Zubok and Yakovuk, 2007, see also: Gardner, 1993; Janion and Rosiek, 1984; Kozielski, 2002). Entering into independent life the younger generation actively guess and learn new spaces and develop their own meanings and values. Intuitive feelings become the basis of social self-regulation of youth transitions under conditions of uncertainty. Their constant rethinking in response to changing conditions gives transitions spontaneity and unpredictability in direction and variability in the goals, as well as situational essence.

Therefore, youth transitions are determined not only by institutional influence, but also by the meanings and values given to them, by perception and interpretation. These may affect the forms of interaction chosen by young people during their transition (Miles, 2000). In this regard 'studying youth transition in the twenty-first century is still intellectually important. The role and effects of key transitions might be different to previous decades and social structures might be changing, however these changes should not simply be assumed and must be the subject of detailed empirical analyses' (Gayle, 2009, 8).

Principles of the empirical evaluation and data base

Approaches to the empirical analysis of youth transitions take into account the following peculiarities of interaction between young people and society.

First, the public system is the entirety of the relatively independent, but interconnected elements. Youth, as the part of a whole, makes transitions under the influence of the social conditions; at the same time youth makes its own contribution to the construction of a new reality and societal development. Sources for construction and development are both within the younger generation and outside—in the social environment. On the one hand, the inner driving forces such as motivation, knowledge, skills, and the activities of young people—are being formed and implemented under the influence of a wide range of social, political and socio-cultural determinants. Therefore, the nature of transitions depends on social conditions and understanding of transition made by different groups of youth is possible only in conjunction with the analysis of the more general processes taking place in society. On the other hand, young people have their own aspirations, social claims and ambitions, which are realised in their activities as a relatively independent self-developing group.

Second, the main feature of youth is connected with its role in production and reproduction of the social structure and relations. Therefore, the analysis of youth transitions is necessary to correlate with the nature of the reproduction mechanisms of the society.

Third, as a social group youth should be considered holistically in its different social and cultural expressions. Therefore, indicators that reflect its transitions should cover the complete process of its interaction with society.

The above features determine the basic principles of sociological research into the processes of transition of young people.

Changes in status and motivation of different youth groups divided by age, education, gender, region and settlements, backgrounds, types of activity and place in different sectors of the economy, profession and occupation are within the main focus of this research.

A data base is being accumulated as the result of on-going monitoring, through a series of studies conducted with a comparable methodology, aimed at tracking the social changes among youth in connection with the ongoing transformation process in the twelve regions of the Russian Federation (RF). This monitoring process allows the transitions of young people to be traced dynamically. The all-Russian territorial research sample is a representative model of the Russian population in the age from fifteen to twenty-nine years-old.

Monitoring started at the end of Soviet era in the year 1990. At its first stage, a questionnaire survey covered 10,412 young people with the main characteristics of the last generation of Soviet youth and tendencies of their changes under the influence of first signs of transformation (so called Gorbachev's perestroika), were recorded. At the second stage, (1994, N=2,612), research focused on changes of the qualitative characteristics of youth under the conditions of the collapse of the Soviet Union and the country's transition to market relations. The third stage (1997, N=2,500), studied the trends of development of the youth under the conditions of the continuing systemic crisis of Russian society, caused by privatisation and the liberal reforms (so called shock therapies). In the fourth stage (1999, N=2,004), the consequences of a default in August 1998 (destabilisation of the economy, growth of external debt, the bankruptcy of enterprises, and growth of inflation) have been analysed as a significant factor of transitions. At the fifth stage, (2002, N=2,012), the subject of research was the trends in youth transitions and development in connection with the strengthening of the state and centralising power that was announced after 2000 (Putin's first presidential term). In the sixth stage (2007, the sample was 1,200 young people) attention was given to the comparison of youth transitions in two different periods of the post-Soviet Russian society. This compared the period of total uncertainty of the 1990s with the period of relative stabilisation with notable efforts for construction of the new certainty within the same economic system, but another political environment. At the last—seventh stage, (2011, N=1301), the changes in status, consciousness and behaviour of young people under the influence of the global financial crisis and the attitude of young people to the different aspects of social reality have been analysed. Special attention is given to the mechanisms of the cultural transmission of fundamental values and stereotypes between youth and the parental generation and the impact that is made on young people's self-constructed lives and choices in transition. Accordingly the accumulated empirical data make it possible to track the fundamental and situational changes of the younger generation in Russia. Data from this monitoring are used for a more detailed analysis of changes in different aspects of youth transitions over this long period.

Changing transitions of Russian youth

The vector of changes among today's youth is largely predetermined by all the post-Soviet period of Russian transformation. During this period it has undergone a series of stages, each characterised by the imminent transition from certainty to uncertainty and *vice versa*.

There are at least four stages, when the vector of uncertainty is reversed. The first of these stages is the period immediately after the post-Soviet reforms, known as 'shock therapy'. The processes of escalation had been caused by the uncertainty of radical measures for the fundamental and rapid reconstruction of the very foundations of the socio-economic system, the transition from certainty of the planned economy to uncertainty of free unregulated market. This led to a dramatic decline in production, the degradation of a number of industries that provided the fundamental basis for economic and social development and last, but not least—a radical change in the nature of relations in the work sphere. Despite all the difficulties of that period, in the second half of the 1990s there were some signs of the adaptation of young people to the situation, which resulted in relative stability and certainty of new mechanisms of the market relations with more or less stable, usual practice in the work sphere.

This phase ended with the 1998 economic default, the new stage of income decline and industry collapse in Russia. This time all previously developed personal strategies were painfully destroyed, which then increased uncertainty

After the beginning of 2000s a new phase with emerging prospects for overcoming the complete uncertainty was delineated, typical for the 1990s. The transition began from a state of ruin and social anomie to an increase in living standards and social stability. At this stage, associated with the change of political power but continuity of the previous vector of economic policy, there emerged clear signs of economic stabilisation as the crisis and chaos no longer dominated. Some measures including so called 'National Priority Projects' for investment into the economy gave opportunities to solve some of the social problems and stimulate certain industries.

The increased certainty in the economic sphere was reflected in the stabilisation of the labour market, income growth of all groups of young people, relative independency in solving of their current problems and reduction of social tensions. And, although the progress in the economic and financial spheres of that time are inseparable from the global processes associated with the high cost of oil, Russia being one of the major exporters, and coupled with the political endeavours, it enabled policies to address social issues like: health, education, living conditions in the rural area and housing.

All this had a positive impact on the minds of young people, most of which are firmly focused on the consolidation, economic stability and balanced economic and social development. Incipient transitions from complete uncertainty to a search for new forms of certainty in all areas and above all, in economics, have made Russian transformation more gradual.

The perceived stabilisation of the economy has been tested by the global financial crisis, continuing from 2008 to the present economic recession, when it became clear, that the transition from the total instability and uncertainty to complete stabilisation did not mean at all the automatic resolution of existing contradictions. Uncertainty is still based on such macro social processes as the new stage of long-term reforms of education, structural changes in production, and growing differentiation of life chances which has determined the nature of youth transitions in the work sphere. Therefore, an understanding of transitive processes occurring among Russian youth today is possible only with a macro-view of the transitions in the Russian society in the post-Soviet period. In addition, today's youth are the children of the 'perestroika generation'. *Their* parents are witnesses of the collapse of the USSR, who gained the experience of surviving and self-regulation of spontaneous changes. In spite of the existing inter-generational conflict, parental influence on children remains quite strong.

Education growth trends

The uncertainty of the 1990s is reflected in the education of young people. In an effort to survive, young people at that time preferred to work instead of studying. Only twenty-five per cent of young people saw the links between gaining better qualification and the level of their education, only twelve per cent found strong connection between education and wages, and ten per cent of young people considered education as the factor of career promotion. So at the beginning of the transformation the majority of young people's attitude towards education was weakening.

Falling education levels (education completed at the time of the research) only began to change as a result of the relative stability in the country, which followed after the default of 1998 (Table 1).

Table 1. *Changes in the level of education of young people by age, 2002-2011 (in per cent)*

The level of education	2002		2006		2011	
	18-24	25-29	18-24	25-29	18-24	25-29
Non completed secondary education (lower 9 classes)	8.6	5.6	8.8	8.5	4.4	0.7
Complete secondary Education	41.1	19.7	37.3	15.5	34.4	13.6
Secondary vocational education	32.1	46.1	35.6	39.8	36.1	48.6
Higher and non complete higher education	18.2	28.3	18.3	35.6	24.6	36.4
Other types of education	0	0.3	0	0.6	0.5	0.7

Table 1 shows the positive growth trend in levels of youth education. In 2011, compared with 2002, the proportion of young people with incomplete secondary education significantly decreased. At the same time there has been as increase in the number of young people who have received specialised secondary, incomplete higher education and higher education. Of particular note is the positive growth of vocational education among young people, because of its sharp decline in the 1990s (in 1997 the proportion of young people with specialised secondary education was 29.4 per cent). This ensures the quality and growth of the contingent of entrants to higher education establishments. The 'rejuvenation' of higher education is evident. By 2011 the number of young people completing higher education doubled. This trend is due to several factors.

First, the fact that after the collapse of the economy and coping with privatisation strategies for surviving in the first half of the 1990s, when education has lost all significance for successful promotion and employment, a modern rebuilding of the economy and labour market began. The role of income-related redistribution of property, as well as the primitive forms of employment transition, associated mainly with small businesses, which allowed many young people not only to survive, but also to integrate into the new economic system, has been gradually decreasing. Industries have begun developing which require new knowledge and highly qualified professionals. Therefore, the demand for education objectively increased.

Second, young people who came after the privatisations and who did not manage to create capital with the help of small business, experienced a rapid disillusionment and started to focus more on education. Thus, in the mass consciousness there was a renaissance of the pre-reform education values, specific to the Russian mentality and in the minds of most young people the opinion that without education it is impossible to achieve prosperity. As for the current generation of youth, it has inherited these outlooks, but at the same time is facing new situations in the labour market when employment of almost any kind requires not only expertise, but also a high school diploma. Moreover, the work itself is not often characterised by complexity of tasks which would have been impossible without higher education. For example, it is common for the various managers in the stores, managers for the salons of mobile phones and even the cleaners in large companies to have undertaken higher education. In this case, the fact that the young person has spent several years inside the walls of the institution of higher education is for the employer a warranty of a sufficient set of social skills, which include the level of thinking and the level of general culture, and communication skills, as well as the attitudes towards work. Therefore, the preference in the labour market is usually given to those who have such a diploma.

Third the growth of education among young people under the twenty-four years old is associated with measures of students' deferment from the obligatory military service (conscription).

According to the percentage benefiting from higher education the current generation of youth differs favourably from the previous generations. At the same time every fourth young people aged 25-29 years (23.5 per cent) continues studying at the secondary education institutions and 58.8 per cent in the universities. Compared to 2002 the proportion of students aged 18-29 years living in various regions of the country is significantly changed. In 2002 there were 39.5 per cent students studying in universities located in regional centres, 10.8 per cent living in smaller cities and urban districts and 7 per cent in rural areas. By 2011, 28 per cent were living in regional centres, 45.1 per cent in the districts and 26.9 per cent in rural areas.

While the proportion of students among the residents of regional centres is significantly decreased, it is increased four-fold among the young people living in small towns and rural areas. This is a stable trend and for these youth higher education has provided a way to overcome the routine of rural life. However, a marked decrease in the number of students in regional centres is due to the specific educational mobility of different types of communities. If you come from small towns and rural areas and enter the universities located in these regional centres, then the residents of the regional centres themselves leave to study in megalopolises. From this point of view the unified state examination, introduced in Russian schools, expanded the possibilities for young people to enter Moscow, St. Petersburg and some other large city's universities. The level of education achieved by the present young generation is sufficient to provide training for the life and work. It also increases young people's ambitions in the labour market, however the latter does not always corresponds to the level of the ambitions. At the same time, the education, especially higher education remains unaffordable for many segments of the youth population.

The problem of access to education

To a large extent, this problem is related to the social stratification that exists in Russian society. In families with different levels of material well-being different influences are brought to bear on the life situations and the basic characteristics of young people's attitudes towards education. Let's consider the influence of the material conditions of life on the education of young people (Table 2).

Table 2. The level of youth education depending to the material conditions of life, 2011

Income position	Non completed secondary education (lower 9 classes)	Complete secondary Education	Vocational education	High and non complete high education
Low incomes	8.2	28.9	43.3	19.6
Medium-income	1.1	25.7	44.6	28.6
Financially secured	0	17.6	29.4	52.9

As Table 2 indicates, there is a clear dependence of education on the material conditions of life. The higher levels of education are accessible primarily for the financially secured young people.

A particular danger to society arises from the continuous extension of 'paid' (fee-charging) services in education. The analysis shows that the availability of paid education is significantly differentiated depending on the material conditions of the family. Even in a group of young people who are financially secured, it is not available for one in ten. Among the young people of medium incomes (by Russian standards), representing a majority of young people, the means for obtaining paid education are either not available (38.3 per cent), or they will have to deny themselves in many ways to afford it (53.7 per cent). For the vast majority of the low income stratum of youth (72.2 per cent) paid education is practically inaccessible. Therefore, most young people are of the opinion that the growth of paid services in education is inappropriate. Only 4.3

per cent believe that paid education is acceptable both in the secondary school and in the high school. 32.5 per cent of young people accept the possibility of fee charging only for the higher education, but not for secondary schools. And 63.2 per cent are of the opinion that education, both in higher and secondary school, should be free.

The inaccessibility of education negatively affects the motivations for its acquisition.

Instrumentalisation of the education motives

In many ways, the quality of education depends on the motives for its acquisition. The changes in the motivational structure of youth have their origins in the 1990s and reflect the consequences of default in 1998. The self-regulation process of young people that followed this period was reflected in its relation to education and to knowledge. In 2011 in the age group of 18-24 years-old, a belief in the value of education as an end in itself. Education is important as good knowledge, but not just as diploma was held by 41 per cent and for 25-29 year olds education was a terminal value for 36.4 per cent. For comparison, in 2002 among the 25-29 year olds its value was higher—59.4 per cent.

In other words there is a tendency towards a significant reduction of terminal values with the respect to education. However, the share of the instrumental values of education significantly increases with the age. Attention is drawn to a very low percentage of respondents who bind the meaning of education to the knowledge acquired. Every second person in the 25-29 age group (47.9 per cent) believes that knowledge is just a means of solving problems and 48.6 per cent of young people believe that money can replace knowledge. That means that the process of instrumentalisation has spread to the cognitive values held by young people.

At the same time, with the backdrop of the constantly reproducing instrumental attitudes towards education that were typical for the post-Soviet period, in 2011 there was a sharp jump of this trend. This kind of 'spike' in the proportion expressing instrumental education values indicates the presence of a very powerful negative factor, apparently related to the next step in the reforming the education system and the inclusion of Russia in the Bologna educational process.

First, this adopted modernisation of education is not based on the traditions of Russian education and does not take account of the Russian mentality. Second, the meaning of the reforms is often not understood by young people, and third, they do not feel a direct connection between success in further education and life trajectories, which affects the efficiency and modernisation of education itself and the quality of educational preparation.

Consequently, the instrumentalisation of the dominant motives of education in general adversely affects the careers of young professionals at its very initial stage.

Searching for the first job

Meanwhile, a high level of formal education determines the inflated claims for the first job. Today's young people are more demanding both with regard to job content and the working conditions; they are also oriented to high wages. The current state of production does not always meet these requirements. Therefore, in 2011 36.3 per cent the youth worked in full compliance with their specialty; 27.4 worked in a related or similar area; 29.7 per cent on a completely different specialty. For the remaining 6.6 per cent the relationship was difficult to define. As it can seen, every third young professional did not work directly in the specialty, received in the university. For the comparison in 2002 50.1 per cent young professionals worked in full compliance with the given specialty, with 25.2 per cent working in a different specialty. Although the opportunity to find jobs in their field is not always dependent on the quality of training and is often determined by labour market situation, it remains important to trace how the work in the specialty is related to the professional qualities of young professional.

The presence of such kind of association is confirmed in the consideration of terminal values of knowledge and work. So, the terminal value of knowledge distinguishes 58.3 per cent of young professionals, working in accordance with the given specialty. And the attitude to work as a terminal value in the group working in accordance to the speciality obtained with a university degree is three times higher than among those working in another specialty.

So, our analysis shows, first, that professional qualities acquired during their studies is the condition for successful connection between education and professional career of young professionals. These include, above all, the attitude to education, to knowledge and character of values of labour. Therefore, the search for the first job is largely hampered by the low level of these qualities, which itself is associated with the situational attitude of youth towards education and knowledge. Second, the high expectations that have formed in current generation of Russian youth, focused with regard to certain standards of consumption, are in conflict with the labour market, which often does not provide the success in the first job search.

Changing of work motivation under conditions of unstable economy

The transition to a market economy could not fail to affect the change of motivation of young people. In essence, young people's attitudes towards the work and professional ethics, depends on the direction of this change. Analysis of motivation as an important indicator of the direction of youth transitions in the sphere of work shows the extent to which changes in motivation, including social needs, interests and values of employed young people, is consistent with the nature of modern market economy. The needs reflect the dissatisfaction with unfulfilled desire to work; interests and values reflect the modes of labour activity regulation.

Since 1990 there has been an overall positive trend in youth orientation towards work. This is evidenced by a consistent increase in the number of answers 'do not know how to live without employment,' appropriate to higher level of needs for work in itself. In 2002, the proportion of young people who felt a high level of needs for employment reached 27 per cent. However, a marked decline in 1994 and 1997 of this proportion of respondents indicates that under conditions of social uncertainty of the first half of 1990s and the period of default, these needs were pushed out by situational interests. Fluctuations were experienced by the group of young people with low work needs, identified on the basis of agreement with the statement 'would not work if was financially secured.' This group in 1990 consisted of 16 per cent in 1994–12.5 per cent in 1997–11.3 per cent in 1999–14.3 per cent and in 2002–15.4 per cent.

The decline of this group occured in a period of relative stabilisation, when work brought satisfaction, not only as a source of income but also as a form of self-realisation. And *vice versa*, it increased sharply in the period that followed just after the financial default, along with an increase in uncertainty, as the results of young people's efforts at work were reduced to zero by hyperinflation and the economic recession. The severity of this situation did not strengthen, but destroyed labour motivation in its basic elements—desire and readiness to work. This relationship remains valid at present time. Meanwhile, an analysis of the control question showed that in the minds of youth the work concept is differentiated between work in general and 'interesting work', in particular. Most of young people (55.8 per cent) feel the need for interesting work and not the need for work as it is.

Thus it is revealed that Russian youth, traditionally, from the Soviet era, focused on the content of work: the work should be interesting and creative. But, although for the period of market reforms in Russia the motivational structure was confirmed (in a latent form) for the earnings, stable orientation can be traced for maintenance of work. Young people care enough as to how the earnings will be provided. Against this background, significant changes took place in values as an important component of motivation. Beginning from 1997 the instrumental value of work that defines its meaning in terms of means of realising other goals, significantly increased. This increase in instrumental motives is noted in connection with the growth of social uncertainty in the first half of the 1990s, during the period of default and at the beginning of the global financial crisis. Thus, a high level of need in the labour is accompanied by the growth of instrumental values of work. The situation of continuing uncertainty in economic and labour relations, as well as the erosion of ethical values, which lasted throughout the post-Soviet period, determined the change of work ethic among young people, in ways which acted on personal self-determination (Table 3).

Table 3. Changing of notions about the personal factors of self-determination, 1990-2007 years.

Personal self-determinination factors	Distribution of responses (C)							
	1990		1999		2002		2007	
	C	R	C	R	C	R	C	R
Industrious	4.31	3	5.45	3	5.75	3	5.45	5
Professional skill	5.03	1	5.94	1	5.97	1	5.88	1
Enterprising	3.32	6	5.39	4	5.64	5	5.60	2
Money, material possessions	4.22	4	5.57	2	5.80	2	5.51	4
Useful links	4.16	5	5.51	5	5.68	4	5.55	3
Honesty, integrity	4.98	2	5.03	6	5.05	6	5.02	6

C—the average coefficient rate on seven-point scale. R–Rank.

As it is seen from Table 3, on the one hand, according to respondents' self-perceptions, professionalism has consistently taken a leading role in self-determination of youth. There has however been a marked reorientation of the youth in relation to the work: enterprise, as a factor in personal self-determination, moved from the sixth place (in 1990) to the second place (in 2007) place. Money and material goods noticeably played less of a role. This held until 2002. Apparently, this was a consequence of increasing social certainty in the country and some stabilisation of the material situation of youth in the pre-crisis period. On the other hand, for 'useful contacts' there was a move to the third position. So in personal self-determination of youth, Russian specific factors associated with the strong informal and corporate relations were important. In some cases, especially at the stage of entering to the labour market, they can play a significant role. In these circumstances, the overall thrust of the motivation of young people, both in terms of education and labour, has become instrumental.

Therefore, despite significant positive changes towards greater respect for labour, it would be premature to conclude that these changes reflect more positive dynamics in the motivations of young people in this area. Rather, it reflects the contradiction between the objective need for a modern work ethic and the policy actually carried out in respect of employment of young people. As a result, in 2007 compared to 2002 there was a significant decrease, in absolute terms, in the share of respondents who emphasised hard work, professionalism and entrepreneurial spirit as factors contributing to the understanding of him/her as a personality. The weighted average on the seven-point scale value of hard work have declined from 5.75 in 2002 to 5.45 in 2007, professionalism–respectively from 5.97 to 5.88, enterprise–from 5.64 to 5.60. These trends largely reflect the consequences of increasing the country's promotion of enrichment while in the minds of young people overestimated consumer models are retained against a background of the depreciation of fair and honest labour, as a source of prosperity.

The contradiction between ethical orientations and standards of living leads to increasing of the uncertainty and social tensions in the consciousness of young people. As a consequence, in his/her mind it changes the idea of the modern ethics of labour. Rationalism, which lies at the basis of modern society, loses some of its major components in the views of Russian youth. This is confirmed by answers to the question about the importance of professionalism, integrity and decency of work as such, for the modern man.

Thus, the weighted average of the importance of professionalism in 2002 was equal to 6.11 points and 5.99 in 2007; good work–6.29 and 5.51, respectively, honesty and other moral qualities 5.78 and 5.58. In the case of conservation of these trends, the image of modern society will be less tied in the minds of Russia's young people to achievements in labour and more and more to low-cost ways to accelerate the achievement of momentary quick success.

Thus, for the entire post-Soviet period there have been changes in the motivation of young people, that indicate a very slow process of formation, in people's minds, of a modern ethic of work. This, on the individual personal level, is geared towards short-term goals, but there are extremely negative impacts on the development of economic relations in general.

Factors of youth employment

The level of youth employment in Russia is determined by the following factors. First, by the level of education and the attitude to it, as considered above, and second, by the influence of gender-specific factors: for men—military service by conscription, for women—birth of children, and thirdly, by the regional specific factors of the labour market. In addition, the employment indicators are significantly affected by a geographic distribution of educational institutions and enterprises. Their remoteness from the place of residence in the large areas of Russia often remains an obstacle to obtaining education and work. In this regard, there are big regional differences in youth employment. In the age group of 20-24 year olds the proportion of people employed in manufacturing ranges from 74 per cent (Chukchi Autonomous District) to 15 per cent (Republic Ingushetia) and the proportion of students from 11 per cent (Chukchi Autonomous District) to 62 per cent (Moscow). The lowest percentage of students and working young people aged 18-24 years is observed in the Caucasian republics—the Republic of Dagestan, Karachaevo-Cherkessia and the Republic of Ingushetia. In many ways, this it is also linked the high levels of social tension in these regions.

One of the main obstacles of the young people's integration into sphere of work is the overall level of youth unemployment. According to the Labour Department employment statistics in 1992 it amounted 38.1 per cent, in 1995–35.8 per cent, in 1996–34.5, in 1997–31.8 per cent, in 1998–32 per cent, in 1999–34.5 per cent, in 2002–32 per cent As it can be seen, despite the downward trend, young people persistently account for a third part of the total number of unemployed. In a crisis of 2008 youth unemployment figure was kept at 32 per cent by reducing the payments rather than by full time employment. But it remains very high and according to some estimates exceeds the average level of youth unemployment in the EU (see for example ILO, 2011b).

The unemployment was spread among vocational school graduates, colleges and universities. According to the Ministry of Education in 2009 about 100,000 graduates could not find a job. The most acute social problem is the transition of young people from material production to other spheres of work.

Reducing employment in the sphere of material production

In the years after the start of market reforms, employment of young people in the sphere of material industrial production as been steadily declining. In 1990 approximately 80 per cent of working youth were occupied in branches of industrial production, in 1994–a little more than 60 per cent, and in 1999–44.2 per cent. The decline of youth employment in material production sectors continued even in the pre-crisis period; 41. 4 per cent worked in this sphere in the year 2002 and 39.8 per cent in 2007. Although the tempos of youth's transition from the sphere of material production to other spheres were slowed, in comparison with 1990s, nevertheless this trend could not be regarded as satisfactory. On the one hand it is connected with the enlargement of employment in new forms of properties and sites, which widened the youth possibilities to choose the working place. From the other hand it has already led to the great decreasing of non-rent enterprises in this sphere of productivity. Youth employment has moved mostly towards the spheres of finance and trading and has not notably shifted to new branches connected with new technologies.

Another noticeable trend is redistribution of youth employment from the state sector of the industry into the non-state sector. In 1994 youth employment in the state sector of economics decreased to 1.5 times, compared with 1990, to 63.9 per cent. This trend continued thereafter, but with slowed tempos. In 1997 youth employment in the state sector was equal to 58 per cent of the whole population of working youth. For the period from 2002 to 2007 it decreased more than halved, from 41 per cent to 17.5 per cent. In the pre-crisis (2008) year 76.9 per cent of youth, occupied in the production industry worked in joint-stock companies. This positively affected their individual incomes and well-being, as payment in non-state sector is higher than in the state sector. However, the weakening of the potential of the state sector, especially the local enterprises negatively influenced the economic situation in the regions, where there are a significant number of enterprises with the state form of ownership. This has negatively affected young people. The low level of economic development of these regions has limited their opportunities for self-realisation.

The contradictions of youth self-realisation
opportunities in the sphere of work

Analyses of self-realisation opportunities point to the reason why young people have moved away from jobs in material production. The dynamic of changes in the basic opportunities is indicated in Table 4.

Table 4. Evaluation of opportunities for self-realisation of youth in material production, 1990-2007 years.

Opportunities	Distribution of evaluation (C)			
	1990	1997	2002	2007
improve skills	4.46	4.01	4.58	4.52
increase wages	3.29	3.15	3.86	3.83
make business	–	2.55	2.76	2.70

C-Coefficient on the average seven-point scale.

Comparative data shows, first, there is a contradiction between the relatively high evaluation of training opportunities and low scores for evaluation of opportunities for wage increases. In 1990, in varying degrees 37.8 per cent had an opportunity to improve their skills, and 28.1 per cent their wages. In 2007 the possibility of self-realisation has increased significantly, but the ratio remained the same: 53.9 per cent had the opportunity to improve their skills and 36.1 per cent their wages. In other words, the possibility of high-quality labour force growth is not supported with the appropriate level of wages. Russia remains one of the countries with the lowest levels of remuneration in the sphere of work.

Second, there is an extremely low evaluation of opportunity to make one's own business, i.e. youth entrepreneurship in industry. And it not big business that is spoken about here, but any kinds of small establishments and different forms of self-employment prior to crisis and economic recession. Consequently, there is a marked decrease in the above qualitative indicators of the professional status of youth in material production as well as narrowing opportunities for self-regulation in the situation of an unstable labour market.

Third, there is a direct connection between opportunities for self-realisation and levels of social uncertainty. It is no accident that markedly reduced self-assessments were given by youth in 1997 and 2007 i.e. the years prior to default and the financial crisis, respectively. In general, it is recognised that most indicators for youth in the sphere of material production for the period of post-Soviet reforms have worsened. The implications of these trends have affected the state of the country's industry. In 2010 measures to strengthen a number of leading companies in engineering and the defence industry has been implemented. But the shortfall of skilled labour force, due to the outflow of youth from material production in previous years, will take many years to rectify.

Moving from material production into the service sector

The non-production, service sphere includes employment in brokering, trading, logistics and distribution, banking and social services. If in 1990 the employment in this sector amounted to about 9 per cent of the total number of young workers, in 1999 it had almost doubled, reaching 17.2 per cent, mainly due to transitions from the sphere of material production. Then the pace of movements into this area decreased, but the general trend continued. In 2002 the employment rate was 20.6 per cent and in 2007–22.7 per cent of young Russians. About 80 per cent of young people working in the field of distribution and exchange work in the private sector. The moving of youth into this sphere can be attributed to perceptions of more features that enhance well-being, compared to industrial production.

Moreover, since 2002 youth is moving from the state sector to non-state more actively. In 2002 17.5 per cent of all working in this area were employed in the state sector and 75 per cent in the non-state sector, and in 2007, respectively 7.9 per cent and 82.5 per cent. This reflects a general tendency to reduce the role of the state in this area.

As a positive trend, the growth of the qualitative characteristics of young people working in the service sectors. The level of secondary education of young people employed in this sector has increased from 17.2 per cent in 2002 to 24.3 per cent in 2007 and of specialised secondary education from 43.3 per cent up to 45.7 per cent. The skill level (average on the seven-point scale) has also risen from 4.77 to 4.99. The positive trend of changes in this area is also demonstrated by all the other parameters.

Social services refers to the economic sphere that is associated with health care, rehabilitation centres, legal, notary, law enforcement, housing and utilities and public services, social security and insurance.

In 1990 about 11 per cent of the total number of young workers was employed in the field of social services. By 1999 there were already 22.7 per cent. In 2002 this sector amounted 23.5 per cent of young workers.

However, in 2007 there was a marked decrease to 17.8 per cent. The decrease was mainly due to reduction in the proportion of youth employment which declined during this period from 65.3 per cent to 55.5 per cent in the state sector. At the same time data show that there has been some improvement in the characteristics of young people working in the field of social services. The proportion of those with incomplete higher education and higher education increased from 18 per cent in 2002 to 21.8 per cent in 2007 and the level of qualification has also increased from 4.68 to 4.73 on the seven-point scale.

All this shows the positive impact of this trend both on the youth and on the development of the service sphere of the Russian economy under conditions of market relations.

Material well-being and consumption

The financial position of young people is both the most important factor and indicator of the success of social advancement of youth. It reflects the extent to which the consumption of material goods contributes to cultural and physical development of young people, the restoration of their internal forces.

At the empirical level, the financial situation is assessed on the basis of objective indicators—incomes, housing conditions, and the subjective ones—perception of quality of life and satisfaction with it.

From 1990 to 1994 the quality of life of young people remained extremely low. Every third (32.1 per cent) of young people were constantly in need and barely making ends meet. Moreover, the needy were from all categories of youth.

The taken measures to increase income in the period from 2002 to 2007 positively impacted on the financial situation of young people. The incomes of youth trebled compared to 2002. Despite the fact that the increased incomes were largely absorbed by higher inflation and a slowly growing in retail prices, we should note a marked increase in quality of life among youth. This is confirmed by subjective assessments of young people (Table 5).

Table 5. Changing of the own evaluation of living standards by youth, 1994-2007

Estimates of the living standards	Answers of respondents in per cent				
	1994	1997	1999	2002	2007
I barely make ends meet. The money I earn is hardly enough for food	11.2	13.8	10.6	8.6	3.8
I have enough money only for food and cheap clothing	26.1	29.4	34.9	31.0	16.8
My income is only enough to eat and dress decently. Expensive things I can't afford	29.0	24.3	28.4	31.1	28.0
I have enough money for good clothes, and some things of long term use. However, the expensive stuff is outside of my possibilities	20.0	13.0	15.4	15.8	21.3
I can afford some expensive things. However, I do not have enough to afford buying a car or a holiday abroad	8.6	13.1	8.5	11.0	21.9
I can afford a modest holidays abroad and inexpensive car, but buying own apartment is impossible	2.2	3.9	1.9	2.1	6.7
I have no financial problems. I can afford almost anything I wish, including an expensive car, apartment, etc.	0.5	0.6	0.2	0.3	1.6

Percentage of young people, judging their own standard of living as low ('I could hardly take my ends meet,' 'my money is enough only for food and cheap clothing), since 1994 continually decreased from 37.3 per cent in 1994 to 20 6 per cent in 2007. At the same time there has been increase of the part of young people with an average, by Russian standards, quality of life ('my income is enough to eat properly and dress,' 'I have enough money and good clothes, and some things are affordable,' 'I can afford some fairly expensive household items, but the purchase of a car is not available for me', from 57.6 per cent in 1994 to 71.2 per cent in 2007. And although the proportion of young people with a quite high standard of living is not great ('I can afford a modest holiday abroad and inexpensive car,' 'I can afford whatever I want'), it has increased–from 2.7 per cent in 1994 to 8.3 per cent in 2007.

The number of young people in need has also decreased. Young people in Russia are less likely to experience financial difficulties. Thus, the proportion of young people constantly or frequently experiencing financial difficulties diminished by 2.5 times–from 48.6 per cent in 1994 to 19.6 per cent in 2007.

Thus, an overall trend of poverty reduction among young people is observed. But one-fifth of young people does not see the possibility of solving their financial problems and differentiation in living standards among Russian youth remains extremely high.

The characteristics of the material conditions of young people impact on consumer orientations and the means of their implementation. On the one hand, there is a growing desire of young people for independent living, to be separated from their parents and to gain their own homes. On the other hand, the acquisition of their own homes has been and remains inaccessible for young people because of its extremely high cost in comparison with the incomes of young people, minimal proportion of economic housing of its general construction, high interest rates on loans, and the insignificance of government housing programs for different categories of youth. This is one of the deepest problems which lacks effective solutions today. In the period from 1994 to 2002 the proportion of youth living with their parents increased from 57.4 per cent to 69 per cent. It was only by 2007 that it declined slightly to 66.7 per cent. Despite the implementation of priority national project 'Available and comfortable housing', the percentage of youth living separately from their parents in their own apartment or house has dropped from 20.6 per cent in 2002 to 15.5 per cent in 2007.

At the same time, the number of youth renting a room or part of it was growing (from 5 per cent to 9.1 per cent), as well as of those living in dormitories or with relatives (from 3.7 per cent in 2002 to 4.9 per cent in 2007). The absence of effective state youth policy in this area is becoming an obstacle to one of the essential transitions of young people to independent life.

Thus, despite the fact that a number of indicators revealed positive trends in the financial position of the Russian youth, it is apparent that there are low standards of living for the majority of young Russians. The significant positive changes which took place in the stabilisation period, with a marked increase in social certainty, were very short-lived. All in all, the evidence is reflecting both the unsustainability of the apparent signs of economic stabilisation and some spontaneity of various stages in the socio-economic development of Russian society.

Conclusions

The situation among Russian youth and their counterparts in different parts of the world clearly indicates that not only the concept of transition itself remains relevant, but those approaches that have been developing in the last two decades have not lost their relevance. Characteristics and metaphors which at a theoretical level were given to youth transitions still adequately reflect its main distinctive features. Meanwhile, the mechanism of the transition continues to change due to the interaction of global and local living conditions of young people. It reflects dynamic acceleration of the pace of changes and obsolescence of not just traditional, but also newly arising patterns of social interactions.

Analysis of Russian youth transitions provides significant evidence in favour of the thesis that the nature and direction of the transition of young people in the sphere of work are directly related to the situation in the society. The terms and conditions of certainty and uncertainty, as well as the situation of their transitions differently influence young people, their social positions and orientations. Youth tends to achieve the most positive results at the phase of relative stability and certainty. In turn, the state transition to a new phase of uncertainty destabilises these positive trends. Socio-economic sources of uncertainty are manifested in poor education, inability to find an adequate use of their specialty, the obstacles encountered in the job search, the restriction of opportunities for self-realisation, the strain of mobility and limitations in the improvement of young people's living standards, They are also manifested in practices of rationalisation that reduce labour motivation and destroy work ethic. All this makes young people vulnerable not only in the labour market, but ultimately in other spheres of life.

However, in the transition from uncertainty to certainty the internal forces of young people are activated and encourage motivation towards self-regulation and self-organisation. Due to these internal self-organisation mechanisms, young people manage to overcome the difficulties of transition both in the society and their individual lives. The restoration from time to time of the former positions of youth indicates better than anything else the self-regulation mechanisms in action and their positive impact. On the one hand such self-regulation becomes the main factor of individual or group successful transitions, on the other hand they provide self-reproduction of the society or its segments. The identified growth of positive trends in various spheres of production and in young people's lives emphasises young people's innovative potential as the most creative element of one's self-regulation. Therefore, the creation of conditions for self-regulation, self-organisation and self-actualisation of young people could determine the effectiveness of youth policy with regard both to their transitions and to ways of overcoming the global or local economic crisis.

Chapter 19

School to work transition in India

Vinod Chandra

In an increasingly global market appropriate technology and equipped labour play a significant role in production processes in both agriculture and the industrial sector of economy. Especially in developing countries, such as India, where surplus manpower is available, unskilled labour is unable to gain access to full and productive employment in a competitive job market. Realising the seriousness of the issue, the Millennium Development Goals (MDG) also emphasised the need to achieve 'full and productive employment and decent work for all, including women and young people'. India, as one of the signatories of the MDG, has moved forward to achieve this goal and set up the 'National Council on Skill Development' (NCSD) on July 1, 2008. The main objective of the National Council on Skill Development is to promote sector action for skill development. The Prime Minister of India Dr. Manmohan Singh, who is also the chairman of NCSD, has said in its fourth meeting on January 19, 2012, that 'India can reap the demographic dividend of a young population provided that the young citizens of the country are educated and possess the skills required for earning a decent livelihood, and reaching higher levels of achievement in their personal and professional lives. We have the serious challenge of providing quality education and skills to about eighty-five per cent of the people aged between fifteen and fifty-nine years-old, who acquire less than twelve years of education. A social and economic policy of inclusive development cannot ignore the fact that a significant proportion of India's citizens are forced to take up unskilled work because they lack the education and skills required for taking up economically and professionally rewarding employment.'

It becomes important, in this context, to undertake an examination of young people's transitions to work. Indian youth constitute forty per cent of the population. The Indian school education and higher education system is aimed to equip them for obtaining decent work, suitable economic returns and dignity of their labour in the job market. It is pertinent to see whether the Indian youth, coming out of the education system particularly from secondary education, is competent enough to be absorbed into the competitive labour market. Are they suitably skilled for the job which is available to them? Are the youth successful in obtaining productive employment? Are they able to integrate into the labour market? What are the career aspirations of young school leavers and how are they linked with employability in various employment sectors? What are their experiences of transition from school to work?

What is school-to-work transition?

School to work transition is a relatively new concept for Indian youth. The job training, apprenticeship programmes, competency and skill based training programmes are new programmes introduced by schools and university-colleges. Young people from fifteen to twenty-four years-old generally face new socio-economic life chances. They have to utilise their skills based on their initial primary and secondary level education and training which helps them to become productive members of the society. The school to work transition basically banks upon the philosophy of interconnectedness of school learning and challenges in work life. During school life young people learn many life skills apart from the course curriculum. These life skills are decision making, creative thinking, problem solving, effective communication skills and coping with emotions and stress. Technical training and life skills training are keys to success in the workplace.

For youth in the age group of fifteen to twenty-four, an important consideration is their education and skills development through vocational education. They are also worried about economic inactiveness which leads them to search for suitable jobs. Their entry to the labour market is another major event in their life. They start to seek occupational matches with their aspirations. They are also concerned about their stability in employment and obtaining adequate income as salary.

It is sometimes very difficult to analyse the pathway of transition from school to work because some young people undertake economic activity during their school life. They may undertake part-time paid jobs during their schooling or sometimes they may find paid jobs after school hours and sometimes they need to migrate out of their communities. Some school leavers are discouraged from undertaking jobs or discouraged from even searching for a job. Some secondary school leavers attend industrial training programmes of various trades and of various crafts. So following the track of secondary school leavers is very difficult as they may or they may not undertake paid work. The World Development Report 2007 (pp. 5-9) has summarised five major transitions faced by youth. They are learning for life, transition to work, healthy adolescence, forming families and exercising citizenship. The first two transitions outlined in WDR focus on the education sector. The learning for life and school to work transition are closely interconnected with issues such as healthy adolescence and family circumstance. In developing countries like India, learning for life and the transition from school to work are very significant as the whole focus is to earn through paid employment and support the family with an independent economic standing. In the phase of globalisation this transition process has emerged as an important phenomenon as there is a demand for skilled labour and there is a scarcity of skilled manpower available to meet the demand of the global market. During the transition period, youth are trapped by both demand and supply. Therefore, transition of youth from school to work is an area of great concern for social scientists and policy makers.

The present chapter is organised in two sections, each based on specific dimensions of transition from school to work in India. The first section of the chapter focuses on macro-level issues and policies. The status of secondary and higher education is discussed with the intention to find out the gaps or strengths of the education system in India. The discussion is further linked with the situation of vocational training and skill development among young people in India. The second section of the chapter focuses on the empirical realities of school to work transition. Two studies are referred to in order to examine the situation of school to work transition. The results of an empirical study entitled *Youth in India: Situation and Needs 2006-2007* conducted by the International Institute for Population Sciences (IIPS) and Population Council, published in 2010, is used to analyse the situation. The results of second empirical study entitled *Occupational and career aspirations of school leavers of Lucknow and Allahabad Youth* (Chandra and Tiwari, 2009) conducted by the author himself, are used for further analysis.

I
Situation of Secondary Education in India

In a comparison of East Asia and Latin America, global competitors of the Indian economy, India's gross enrolment rate (GER) at the secondary education level is very low. It is just forty per cent in comparison to East Asian countries which have average seventy per cent and Latin American countries which have average eighty per cent. Access to secondary education in India is not very encouraging as at the secondary level (which is class 9 and 10) the gross enrolment rate

(GER) is fifty-two per cent while at the senior secondary level (class 11 and 12) it is just twenty-eight per cent, with a combined GER of forty per cent (2005). Total secondary enrolment (lower secondary and higher secondary) in 2004 was 37.1 million students with 65 per cent (24.3 millions) in lower secondary and 35 per cent (12.7 millions) in senior secondary. The major reasons for the poor enrolment and access to secondary education are:

    i.   Insufficient school infrastructure,

    ii.   Lack of trained teachers,

    iii. High cost of secondary schooling which families are unable to afford,

    iv. Insufficient alternative opportunities for secondary education for school leavers

    v.   Attitude towards the social and economic benefits of secondary schooling.

Despite the poor level of enrolment in secondary education, significant growth in this area has been noticed over the last decade. The data at the secondary level show that enrolment is increasing and the situation is not as dismal as it was before year 2000. In 2009, a total of 48.26 million students were enrolled at secondary level (constituted from class 9 to 12) while only 28 million were enrolled in the year 2000. So, there is substantial rise in the enrolment figure.

Table 1 Enrolment in Schooling in India (in Millions)

Year	Primary	Middle	Total Secondary (class 9 to 12)	Total School Education (class 1 to 12)
2000	113.6	41.3	28	182.9
2001	113.8	42.8	27.6	184.2
2002	113.9	44.8	30.5	189.2
2003	122.4	46.9	33.2	202.5
2004	128.3	48.7	35	2122
2005	130.8	51.2	37.1	219.1
2006	132.1	52.2	38.4	222.7

Source: Selected Educational Statistics–2005-06, Ministry of Human resource Development

Table 2 Enrolment in School Education in 2009 (In Millions)

	Primary to pre-Secondary (class 1 to class 8)	Senior Secondary (Class 11 and 12)	Total School Enrolment (class 1 to 12)
Boys	102.67	9.83	129.40
Girls	92.41	7.83	113.95
Total	195.09	17.66	243.35

Source: Selected Educational Statistics–2009, Ministry of Human resource Development

In a report produced by the World Bank on Secondary Education in India in 2009 it is argued that this rise in the number of enrolments has two possible reasons. The first is the government of India's major focus on elementary education since 2001 through Sarva Siksha Abhiyan (SSA). This is a massive scheme funded by the government and the World Bank to not only increase the literacy level of India but to provide universal and compulsory elementary education to all. A sizeable number of beneficiaries of this scheme complete their upper primary education (which is education up to class 8) and reach secondary level education. Since 2001 the number of students has increased in secondary education by an estimated five per cent per year as a result of the compulsory elementary education. The second possible reason is that due to new economic circumstances in the twenty-first century India, household income is on the rise and the size of families has decreased. So, secondary education has become easily affordable. Looking at the pull factors, a globally competitive labour market requires more educated and technically skilled labour. In this way, families are more comfortably pushing their children to secondary education so that they may be equipped for taking up the challenging jobs.

In the World Bank Report, projections suggested 'an increase in absolute demand for secondary education between 2007/08 and 2017/18 of around 17 million students per year, with total enrolment growing from 40 to 57 million students'.

Problem of dropouts in secondary education in India

The official data on drop-out rates at secondary level from 1995-96 to 2005-06 shows that there is a decrease of eight per cent in drop-out rate from class 1 to class 10 (see Table 3 below). However, the drop-out rate in primary school has reduced significantly from forty-two to twenty-nine per cent in the same period.

Table 3 Trends in drop-out rates (per cent) in secondary level in India, 1995-2006

Year	Secondary Education (1 to 10)		Total
	Boys	Girls	
1995-96	66.7	73.7	69.6
1998-99	64.5	69.8	66.7
1999-00	66.6	70.6	68.3
2000-01	66.4	71.5	68.6
2001-02	64.2	68.66	66.0
2002-03	60.7	65.0	62.6
2003-04	61.0	64.9	62.7
2004-05	60.4	63.9	61.9
2005-06	–	–	61.62

The major reasons for drop-outs in secondary education are that students were not interested in their studies, parents were not interested in further studies for their wards, students were unable to cope with the demands of schooling and students needed to work for wages to supplement the family income. Their participation in other economic activities was also a reason and some, students, especially female students, had also to attend to the domestic chores.

Situation of higher education in India

During the eleventh five year plan (2007-2012), the government has taken very bold steps to improve the Gross Enrolment Ratio (GER) by introducing various structural changes in the Higher Education system, which was primarily based on the pre-independence Indian model of higher education introduced by British government. The United Progressive Alliance (UPA-II) led government introduced private sector investment into higher education and consequently a number of private universities have been established in various states through specific state legislation. Indian higher education system is one of the largest higher education systems with 43 central universities, 227 state universities, 18 private universities, 105 deemed universities, 41 institutions of national importance and 5 institutions established by various state legislatures, a total of 436 higher education institutions (universities) in the academic year 2009-10. Apart from these institutions there were 25,938 colleges of higher education which includes 14,321 colleges of arts, fine arts, social work, science and commerce; 2,894 colleges of engineering, technology and architecture; 2,074 medical and para-medical colleges; 3,357 colleges of education and teacher training; 3,292 colleges of other disciplines and 1,914 polytechnics in year 2009-10. A total 20.74 million were enrolled in these higher institutions.

Table-4 Number of Higher Education in India in December 2011

1	Central university	43 (7%)
2	State university	297 (47%)
3	Private university	100 (16%)
4	Deemed university	129 (20%)
5	Institution of national importance and other university level institution established under state legislature	65 (10%)
6	Total	634

Source: Higher Education in India at a glance, Brochure published by University Grants Commission, New Delhi in March 2012.

Growth in higher education in India

Recently (in March 2012) the University Grants Commission (UGC), government issued a brochure *Higher education in India* at a glance in which the vital statistics pertaining to higher education in India were published. The statistics shows that India has total 564 universities and 33,020 colleges recognized by UGC with total 169.76 million student enrolment in the year 2012. If we see the overall growth of higher education in India, as per the UGC data the number of universities has increased from 27 in 1950-51 to 564 in 2010-11, the number of Colleges from 578 to 33,020, the number of students enrolled in higher education has gone up from 100,000 to 16.97 million (Table 5.) The increase in the enrolment ratio from 1 per cent in 1950 to 10 per cent in 2007 and 12 per cent in 2010 should speak volumes about the expansion of access to higher education in India.

Table-5 Growth of Higher Education in India since Independence

Year	Colleges for General Education	Colleges for professional Education	Universities/ Deemed University/ Institute of National Importance
1950-51	370	208	27
1960-61	967	852	45
1970-71	2285	992	82
1980-81	3421	3542	110
1990-91	4862	886	184
2000-01	7929	2223	254
2004-05	10377	3201	364
2010-11	(Total colleges for both general and professional Education) 33020		564

Source: UGC Report 2005-06; UGC's Brochure–Higher Education in India at a Glance (2012); Ministry of Human Resource Development—Statistics of Higher and Technical Education 2005.

Identifying the gap in enrolment in secondary and higher education

A comparative analysis of the enrolment data and drop-outs from elementary education to higher education suggests that a total 195.09 million students were enrolled in elementary school education in 2009 (from class 1 to 8) which reduced to only 48.26 millions in secondary level education. This shows that there is substantial fall among elementary school goers (from class 1 to 8) and 146.83 million student do not pursue their secondary education. Furthermore, out of 48.26 million secondary school attendees only 16.97 million students proceeded to higher education. So, total 31.36 million students have discontinued their studies after completing their twelve years of formal education. This suggests that altogether 178.19 million students have completed their five to twelve years of formal education in schools in India are available for jobs market.

Table 6 Total Enrolment from School Level to Higher education in India during 2009 to 2010

Indicators	Total Enrolment in 2009 in Millions	Total Enrollment in 2010 in Millions
School Education (from Class 1 to 8)	195.09	—
For Secondary level (Class 9 to 12)	48.26	—
School Education (Class 1 to 12)	243.35	—
Higher Education (Undergraduate and above)	—	16.97 millions

Situation of vocational training in India

The government of India has initiated various programmes for vocational training through Industrial Training Institutes (ITI) and Industrial Training Centers (ITC) offered by the Directorate General of Employment and Training (DGET) under the ministry of Labour and Employment. The DGET is the apex body for development and coordination at the national level for programmes relating to vocational training. It formulates policies, lays down standards, trade testing, and certification and monitors training programmes and matters connected with the field of vocational training. Both school leavers and school drops-out attend these ITIs and ITCs and develop their skills for various occupational trades. At the state level, the department of labour operates numbers of training programmes as well. At the same time vocational education is offered through schools 10 plus 2 level (10 plus 2 level can be replaced by senior secondary level) under the ministry of Human Resource Development. Although the central government of India and the state governments in India try to meet the requirements for skilled and trained labour of technologically advanced industrial units, the major challenges of skill development initiatives revolve around the issue of the huge youth population. The youth population is much larger than the places available in the vocational training centres. To realise the need for skill development among the young people aged fifteen to twenty-four, the government has initiated various skill development programmes in association with private partnerships under the National Council for Skill Development.

The history of vocational education in India goes back to the 1960s when the Kothari Commission on Educational Reforms in 1966 proposed that twenty-five per cent of students should enter the vocational stream. Later on, the Kulandaiswamy Committee Report had pitched this number at fifteen per cent to be achieved by the year 2000. However, at present only about five per cent of students of class 10 to 12 standard are in vocational streams. The National Sample Survey Organization NSSO data also informs us that only five per cent youth of age nineteen to twenty-four years old have passed through vocational education.

Table 7 Total capacity of ITIs and ITCs in India

State	No. of government ITIs	Seating capacity	No. of private ITCs	Seating capacity	Total ITIs and ITCs	Total capacity
Northern Region	705	107,986	1,116	107,937	1,821	215.923
Southern Region	338	85,916	2,427	2,64830	2,765	350,746
Eastern Region	193	46,586	696	111,357	889	157,943
Western Region	761	167,662	670	61,610	1,431	229,272
Total	1997	408,150	4,909	545,734	6,906	953,884

Vocational training programmes at secondary school were only introduced in 1976-77 in a few states due to financial constraints, but these states could not achieve the basic objectives of the programme. Later on, the government introduced a scheme called Vocationalisation of Secondary Education during 1997-98. Since then around 6,000 institutions at plus two level of education have introduced the programme. This was followed by the ITIs and polytechnics in India. The DGET offers a variety of training courses catering to the requirements of different industrial sectors through a network of ITIs and ITCs. The total number of ITIs and ITCs was 8,014 at March 2010. Table 7 shows the number of vocational training institutions in India which have total capacity of 953 thousand places to train students. This is an insufficient to meet the demand for places.

We have already noticed that a large number of youth of age fifteen to twenty-four are unable to attend their secondary education after completing eight or ten years of education in school due to socio-economic constraints. On the other hand, the education they receive in school may not be useful for obtaining a decent job for a sustainable livelihood with quality of life. The majority of them try to enter the world of work without the required skills and competencies to compete in the labour market. As a result they are always subject to exploitation by their employers or they remain unemployed or underutilised. This marginalisation of the youth is a serious problem in India.

Employment situation of 15-24 year-old Indian youth

The National Family Health Survey-3 (NFHS-3) 2005-06 data provide important information about employment among fifteen to twenty-four year-old youth. Table 8 shows the percentage of employed youth, men and women, by selected background characteristics. Overall sixty-four per cent of male youth and twenty-seven per cent of female youth were employed at the time of survey. There were three per cent male and seven per cent female who were not employed at the time of survey but were employed sometime in the twelve months preceding the survey. In comparison to rural youth, urban youth are less likely to be employed mainly due to high drop-out rate.

II
Transitions from school to work: some empirical facts

Very few studies have come forward to assess the situation of transition from school to work in India. The most important study was from the International Institute for Population Sciences (IIPS) and Population Council Transition to work roles among youth in India, (2010). This study was taken up in six states, Andhra Pradesh, Bihar, Jharkhand, Maharashtra, Rajasthan and Tamil Nadu. The study included a representative survey of both male and female youth of age fifteen to twenty-four in rural and urban areas, from 2006 to 2008 with a sample of 50,848. The majority of youth were found to be unprepared for employment as they did not fulfil job requirements for technical knowledge and skills, they were poorly educated and were not equipped with vocational skills. Only forty-two per cent males and thirty per cent females had completed secondary education. The shocking fact that came to light despite the best efforts made by government and non-government organisations to boost elementary education, was that one in twelve males and one in four females were illiterate and had never attended any formal schooling. The study also found some differences between states in the educational level of youth.

Table—8 Per cent Distribution of Youth Age 15-24 by Employment Status, 2005-06

Background characteristics	Women					Men				
	Employed in the last 12 months		Not employed in the last 12 months	Total	Number of Women	Employed in the last 12 months		Not employed in the last 12 months	Total	Number of men
	Currently employed	Not currently employed				Currently employed	Not currently employed			
Age 15-19 yrs	26.6	6.8	66.6	100.0	24812	47.4	3.0	49.5	100.0	13008
Age 20-24 yrs	28.1	6.7	65.2	100.0	22779	81.6	3.2	15.1	100.0	11989
Urban	19.9	2.3	77.8	100.0	14931	58.8	2.1	39.0	100.0	9435
Rural	30.7	8.8	60.5	100.0	32660	66.8	3.7	29.4	100.0	15561
No Education	36.2	11.0	52.8	100.0	12524	93.5	3.2	3.2	100.0	2440
< 5 years complete	36.6	9.8	53.7	100.0	3422	89.7	4.3	6.1	100.0	1896
5-9 years complete	26.5	5.9	67.5	100.0	18009	68.6	3.5	27.8	100.0	11200
10 or more years complete	17.8	3.2	79.0	100.0	13633	45.2	2.3	52.3	100.0	9452
Total age 15-24	27.3	6.8	65.9	100.0	47590	63.8	3.1	39.2	100.0	24997

Source: A profile of Youth in India: National family Health Survey -3, 2005-06, Published by Ministry of Health and family Welfare, Government of India and IIPS Mumbai

A range of vocational training programmes was offered by the government and non-government organisations in these states, but only one fifth male youth and a quarter of female youth had ever attended the vocational training. Another study by Circle for Child and Youth Research Cooperation in India (CCYRCI) found that of 600 urban youth in Lucknow and Allahabad city, only eighteen per cent youth had opted for vocational training after completing their class 10 examination. The data was gathered for this study during 2008-09 through a purposely designed interview schedule. The IIPS study also found a significant variation in vocational training of rural and urban youth. Rural youth were less interested in taking up the vocational training than urban youth. Only sixteen per cent male rural youth had vocational training while thirty-two per cent male youth from urban areas opted for vocational training. One of the possible reasons for this variation is that rural youth get engaged in unpaid agricultural activities and other domestic chores at their place of residence in the villages and therefore do not get chance to attend the vocational training. An interesting fact was that the types of vocational training chosen by females were different from the vocational training chosen by males. The majority of females reported attending vocational training for tailoring, handicrafts, painting and embroidery, and secretarial skills such as typing and shorthand. Males reported attending training for auto mechanics, electrical works, fitter and cutter trade, computer hardware, mobile repairing etc.

The CCYRCI study explored whether the young people interviewed were interested in undertaking a vocational training course before taking any job. The study finds that more than sixty per cent of the sample said that they would have opted for vocational training if any incentives had been given to them and that they had been told about them. They had shown their ignorance about these training courses before taking up their jobs. The lack of information about skills development courses and training is one of the important reasons preventing young people attending vocational training in urban centres.

Almost similar findings came in the large survey-based study of IIPS. Their data shows that a large proportion of males (fifty-six percent) and females (sixty-eight percent) were interested in acquiring vocational skills. The study also demonstrated that males preferred training in computers, auto mechanics, electrical works and driving while females preferred the relatively traditional skills for women. Girls from urban areas sought training for vocations such as beauticians, nursing, and computer training. So, youth during this transition had shown the traditional gender-based division in work roles.

Young people's experience of their transition from school to work

It was not easy for many youth to undertake new work roles after their school education or even incomplete formal secondary education. The data show that they had been irregularly engaged in paid work in the last twelve months. In CCYRCI study it was found that most of the young people entered into their first job with an expectation of a decent atmosphere at work place and a handsome salary in return. However, they did not get what they had expected. On exploring further, it was informed that due to the lack of their suitable technical knowledge and skills, the attitude of their employers caused despair and dissatisfaction in them and they gradually left the job.

Job dissatisfaction was one of the major reasons for leaving a job. During paid work young people faced much pressure from both family and employers. Their family wished them to continue their jobs while work conditions did not allow them to continue. This situation places them in a dilemma of whether to continue or discontinue. Therefore, some of them gave up their jobs after a small period of work. Hence, the transition to work roles is fraught with many challenges.

In CCYRCI study, a boy, eighteen years-old, had narrated the story of his first job in Lucknow city at a local printing press:

> When I joined my job in the printing press, I was so excited as I had never ever seen such a big press and a large scale printing. The manager at the press was initially very kind and was helping me to learn the job. But after a month or so, I had realised that he was giving me menial jobs in the press such as stacking the papers, arranging printed sheets for binder, sometimes he used to send me to his clients to collect cheques or manuscript, and the like jobs … while I was interested in computer processing and machine man's job … I thought that he will introduce me to those jobs … but time passed and he started ill-treating me rather than giving me a job of my interest. Gradually, I started losing my interest in the work that was allotted to me … After consistent motivation given by one of my friends I gathered enough courage to speak to my manager. I had requested the manager to give me machine man's job or computer job in the press. After listening to me he answered me bluntly that since you are not trained and your English proficiency is also not good you cannot get a job of your choice. He also asked me to leave the job if I

am not happy. I was in a fix what to do. Finally I decided to give up the job and so I did ...

This is not the only case where it has been found that youth were pushed back to unemployment due to lack of proper training and professional skills. Due to lack of skills they have been treated as cheap labour too. The untrained youth are not getting due economic return for their labour.

The data in CCYRCI study also shows that fifteen to twenty-four year-olds also spend lot of their time in urban centres searching for jobs but usually they require specialisation and qualifications. Most young people, lack the specialised skills and therefore, it is very difficult to get a job of their choice. Sometimes they will spend six to twelve months looking in the job market. Lack of 'employability' and lack of entrepreneurial attitude are the major reasons given for youth unemployment. Young people are available for work and employment but they are not employable. The issue of 'skill deficiency' and 'employability' has been a serious concern in the recent debates of professional bodies such as NASSCOM (National Association of Software and Service Companies) and CII (Confederation of Indian Industries).

Young people spend much time looking for suitable jobs and try different kinds of jobs. When they get a job, they may undertake it for a short period but keep searching for a more suitable job. The moment they get more suitable job they leave their previous job. This period is to be considered as job search period and due to lack of skill it is extended in the majority of cases. In this period of transition youth get different kinds of support from their families such as emotional support and financial support.

Conclusion

In an assessment of job descriptions and their educational and professional requirements, about fifty per cent of the jobs in India require an educational qualification below matriculation such as ITI or certificate programme, but also require more enabling abilities and soft skills such as communication skills, decision making skills, skills required for developing interpersonal relationship, time-management skill, stress management skills etc. About thirty per cent of jobs require secondary educational qualifications such as polytechnic or diploma programmes. However, about ten per cent jobs require a qualification of degree level from universities and colleges and less than five per cent jobs require qualifications of post graduate degree level. A large mass section of youth comes from the first and second group of employment. About three quarters of youth may be seen to be engaged at the low and middle levels of skill needs. They are frugally educated and many are hardly literate (dropouts at the elementary level of education). They need specific skills and training/orientation in their jobs. They generally come from deprived and poor sections of society. These youth need training support to make them ready for jobs and work roles offered by the competitive labour market.

The Indian job market has had a perpetual complaint about a compatibility gap between the work roles of youth in job market and their profile of skills and knowledge. Nevertheless, it has managed to adjust under the erstwhile closed market conditions. After globalisation, the job market perspective has changed. The spirit of competition is driving the precept of excellence and makes stringent demands on compliance with globally competitive standards in products and services. It was thought that the country was poised to cross the threshold of poverty sooner than anticipated due to the expected benefits of expanded global markets, but as globalisation has progressed, the crisis of skilled labour force has started unfolding. The changed conditions in the job market warrant urgent restructuring of government policies for the secondary and tertiary education system. Skill development through vocational education is required to cope up with the opportunities and challenges of employment in the new economic order. In many cases, it is not poverty or lack of formal education that torments the youth; it is relative state of skill deprivation that pushes them back in the job market. The interventional solutions lie in building up those skills and capabilities that empower all youth to seize their own employment opportunities and demonstrate their competitive abilities.

Part 6:   Commentary

Chapter 20

The importance of resources in work transitions in late-modern contexts

James Côté

Introduction

The chapters in this book converge on several themes, most notably the struggles young people experience in their attempt to find meaningful work that pays a living wage. Many of the chapters explore the importance of the personal resources needed to overcome structural obstacles associated with class, ethnicity/race, and gender, and how many young people pay a price in terms their personal well being.

Most of the societies studied in these diverse chapters constitute late- modern societies, albeit in various 'stages' of economic development. These types of societies present challenges to new members not found in early forms of modernity or premodern, tradition communities. In addition to the forms of structural obstacles found in earlier types of societies, the transition to work has itself become a structural obstacle that can arrest, divert, and channel young people, with consequences for their well being. The pathways taken around and/or through these obstacles are based not only on young people's ascribed characteristics, like gender and ethnicity, but also their 'achieved' characteristics, like educational credentials and personal agency. What also differs from traditional societies is that the transition to full employment can now itself be an obstacle associated with 'youth,' as the age of 'economic maturity' has risen throughout modernity (Neugarten and Moore, 1968), accelerated by the collapse of the youth labour market three decades ago.[44] This changing position of youth lengthened 'transition to adulthood' (Côté and Allahar, 1996, 2006).

---

44 The social age of economic maturity can be defined at the point at which the bulk of an age group is fully participating in productive contributions to their community; it is affected by the need of the community for the productive contribution of a given percentage of its members, which amounts to about 100% in traditional societies, but is significantly lower in late-modern societies (because of developments like technological advances that displace jobs and labour policies that favour structural unemployment in order to keep wages low). An adequate indicator of this concept is the participation rate in the labour force by age, although this estimate does not capture those who are voluntarily not engaging in paid labour,

At the same time, in various ways, the above chapters describe cultural and national variations in the ways in which young people agentically manage the various elements of their subjective–, interactional–, and social-identities (cf. Côté, 1996). Strategic management of these identities involves developing, managing, and executing a 'portfolio' of resources suitable to the contexts available to them in their society of origin or orientation (as Bynner describes in his chapter).

However, the relevance of personal resources in relation to structural obstacles is one of the biggest points of contention in this area of research, as the various positions taken by the authors in this volume reveal. Some researchers argue that structural obstacles and power relations can make the exercise of strategic agency difficult, or even that a 'resources approach' naively serves the more ruthless aspects of neoliberalism (see Sukarieh and Tannock, 2011, for a critique of this general approach), calling for young people to conform to alienating conditions.

This critique appears to be shared to some degree by several of the authors in this volume (e.g., Everatt, Makino, Ranta, McGrellis and Holland). Nevertheless, the evidence against an extreme structuralist position is mounting, and many of the chapters in this book present evidence that a nuanced and contextually specific structure-agency position needs to be developed if we are to understand the range of outcomes in the current transition to work as found in the variety of late-modern societies around the world (e.g., Bynner, Evans and Waite, Schoon and Schulenberg, Lähteenmaa, Edwards and Weller, Svynarenko, Helve, Reynolds, Cheng and Schoon, Zubok). Below, I present a typology that helps to sort out the issues of structure and agency in work transitions that goes beyond a simplistic polarity between 'society makes them fail' and 'it's all their fault if they don't succeed,' as this dichotomy is sometimes expressed in common language.

In the spirit of this more nuanced approach, an underlying premise of many of these chapters is that certain context-specific resources are particularly important in societies where many roles and statuses are no longer strictly ascribed and where opportunities for upward social mobility exist. This decline in ascription by its very nature requires people to structure their own lives in certain ways, and the resulting individualisation of the life course requires forms of identity-based agency (cf. Côté and Schwartz, 2002). For example, in late-modern

like homemakers, and those in the agrarian sector who are not counted as wage earners. Participation in education beyond the post-compulsory age is another possible indicator of the delay in economic maturity, to the extent that the rate exceeds the need in the economy for highly skilled labour, which is estimated to be about 20% (Rifkin, 1995). Rates above this level suggest that a certain proportion of the youth segment is put 'on hold' in educational institutions until it is needed in the labour market (Côté and Allahar, 1996, 2006).

societies most occupations are less likely to be passed from one generation to the next, so each generation must take up its own planning process. However, in many regions and countries where there are opportunities for upward mobility the non-ascriptive opportunity structures may not adequately replace the ascriptive structures, leaving many people from less advantaged backgrounds with diminished material and emotional life chances. The diminished normative- and opportunity-structures in these societies is a concern because it can make identity formation more complex and precarious, sequestering young people from mainstream society with its attendant opportunities and benefits for longer periods than is desired by many of those young people (cf. Beck, 1992; Giddens, 1991). In understanding this extended sequestration, and the range of individual reactions to it, several studies in this volume adopt the notions of fast and slow tracks, and how each has certain liabilities beyond individual control (e.g., Evans and Waite; Schoon and Schulenberg). At the same time, in some countries the job opportunity structures are so poor in general, but especially for young people (as Everatt describes for South Africa, and Chandra does for India, and to some extent by Ngai for China), that the viability of agentic strategies are extremely limited. The structure-agency typology presented below helps to highlight these situations as well.

Sociologically, passing through or penetrating a given structural barrier requires that the person doing so understands the social-identity dynamics by which people are judged based on 'who they are.' For example, it has been long established in sociology that each social class or status group has its own symbolic codes in terms of language, attitudes, and habits (e.g., Bernstein, 1971; Bourdieu and Passeron, 1977). Learning and managing new codes requires an ability to properly manage identities and appropriately present oneself in those new contexts. These skills involve the executive personality (or subject) processes that Erikson (1968) called ego strengths, and others call agency (cf. Emirbayer and Mische, 1998). Additionally, it is crucial for the person to have a working knowledge of the contents of identities in differing situations for various audiences (e.g., knowledge of role expectations and how to meet them).

Changes in the educational requirements for entry into the labour force in various countries mean that for many young people the work transition is also a social class transition of upward mobility, the most difficult of which is from the working class to middle class (or blue collar to white collar work). At the same time, subsequent life in the middle class is not necessarily a problem-free one in terms of managing deeply ingrained behavior and language patterns, in the face of middle-class prejudices (cf. Ryan and Sackrey, 1996). Those who change social primary socialisation prepared them for their adult lives (this is illustrated in this volume by Innanen and Salmela-Aro and Evans and Waite). Those who begin new lives in different social contexts are acutely aware of many things that are taken for granted by those who have only known that one way of living. Indeed, late-modern societies are producing more people who have experienced a type of 'contradictory class-location' (e.g., Wright, 1982), or a bi-cultural dislocation (e.g., Hughey, 2008), and as have become mass phenomena sociologists are anxious to understand these new experiences. At the same time, those who are unable or unwilling to undertake status or class transitions need to be better understood, especially when the person appears to be 'self-handicapping' or that person's significant others are holding that person back by threatening to stigmatise or ostracise the person (see Reynolds in this volume). In these latter cases, several contributions to this volume examine 'identity horizons,' or their equivalent, namely, how broadly or narrowly the person conceptualises his or her future prospects (see Svynarenko, as well as Helve, for this model of identity applied to Finnish youth).

A sociological model that emerges from several chapters this volume is similar to a model developed in psychology—developmental contextualism (Lerner and Kauffman, 1985). In my own work, I have used such a model by studying longitudinally how Canadian university students' own personal efforts can help them to transcend or overcome structural barriers through specific forms of active educational engagements (Côté, 2005; Côté and Levine, 1997). In late modernity, although societies continue to present barriers associated with social class and other forms of disadvantage, in some societies educational institutions can be open enough in certain respects for some people to overcome those barriers by adapting their agentic efforts to compatible contexts. In other words, countries vary in terms of the role played by education in intergeneration inequalities (e.g., Blanden, Gregg, and Machin, 2005). At the same time, as the chapter by Salmela-Aro shows for the Finnish educational system, and the chapter by Innanen and Salmela-Aro illustrates for the Finnish workplace, both contexts can adversely affect the well being of some people in the form of depression and burn out. Even so, that research shows that those with more personal resources fair much better.

An example of a country where the nature of barriers appears to be changing is Canada. Recent research consistently finds that parental education level—and not income—is the strongest predictor of university attendance, with each year of parental university education increasing the likelihood by about five percentage points that a child will attend university (Finnie, Lascelles, and Sweetman, 2005).[45] According to Finnie et al. (2005), holding income constant, if their parents have just a high school education, in the early 2000s the likelihood of young males attending university was twenty-nine per cent; for young women it was thirty-seven per cent. However, this probability jumped to fifty-three per cent and sixty-five per cent, respectively, if at least one parent had some university education.

Tracked over time, there has been a significant increase in university graduation among 'first-generation' university students (i.e., students who are the first in their family line to attend). According to Turcotte (2011), between 1986 and 2009, the percentage of Canadian-born first-generation university graduates aged twenty-five to thirty-nine increased from twelve per cent to twenty-three per cent, compared with increases from 44.7 per cent to 55.8 per cent for those with a least one parent who had a university degree. Of course, parents from higher income backgrounds are more likely to obtain higher levels of education, but the point is that if we are to see education as the 'great equaliser,' in addition to addressing structural barriers, we need to focus on the personal resources associated with achieving higher levels of educations, and not necessarily income *per se*. And, while the wealthiest will probably always be more likely to see their children through higher levels of education, in some countries the difference between the most-and least-affluent is not as stark as some may think.

To use Canada as an example once more, in Canada social class and educational opportunities are not all or nothing comparisons; rather, although three quarters of children from families in the highest income quartile are likely to go on to a higher education (two and four-year institutions), just over one-half of those from the lowest quartile are also likely to do so (Zeman, 2007). For four- year universities alone, these figures are twenty-five per cent and forty-six per cent, respectively. But, as noted above, the reasons for this twenty-one per cent gap are not necessarily 'class issues' in Canada, but also matters of the 'educational capital' that parents transfer to their children.

---

45 An explanation for these findings is that parents with higher educations can give more appropriate advice and information and act as intellectual and emotional role models. Thus, children with more educated parents are more likely to grow up seeing higher education as part of who they are—their identity—and to not feel that the university environment is a foreign or hostile one to them. In other words, university-educated parents have more agentic identity resources to pass onto their children that are relevant to the university context, so their children are less likely to experience 'identity anxiety' and more likely to have broader 'identity horizons'.

All the same, we need to be aware of cases where educational systems are more clearly part of a class issue, as appears to still be the case in the UK. Blanden, Gregg and Machin (2005) report that in Britain only nine per cent of those from the lowest income quartile now complete a higher degree compared to forty-six per cent of those from the highest quartile. In comparing cohorts born in the late 1970s with those born in 1958, the wealthiest quartile increased its higher education completion rate from twenty per cent to forty-six per cent, while the poorest quartile increased its completion rate from six per cent to only nine per cent over the same period. They argue that this difference in educational attainment is responsible for most of the intergenerational inequality now found in Britain. Comparing the British figures with the Canadian ones discussed above, the poorest quartile in Canada is about three times more likely to attend university than its counterpart in Britain. Thus, what appears to be a clear class issue in Britain is not necessarily one in Canada.

Moreover, an examination of what happens among those who do attend Canadian universities finds that parental income largely 'washes out' when personal resource factors are taken into account.[46] For instance, my longitudinal research in Canada identifies 'person-context interactions' where students' motivations and behaviors can be all-important in determining how university settings are experienced and what benefits are derived from them (Côté and Levine, 1997, 2000). Specifically, this research suggests that those who approach their higher-education studies with the primary goal of enhancing their own personal and intellectual development experience these contexts and their mentors more favorably, regardless of their socio-economic background, and have better outcomes in terms of grades and learning. Inactive or perfunctory approaches are not associated with these positive experiences and outcomes, and excessive parental pressure can have negative effects, as can high levels of financial support from parents (i.e., students can be less engaged in their studies when their parents are paying for their education).

Structure and agency: A typology of resources

In clarifying which resources are most useful in context-transition and contradictory-location management, this line of research has the potential to

---

46 For instance, Frenette (2007) reports that in comparing the university participation rates of those from the lowest income quartile with those from the highest income quartile backgrounds, non-economic factors explained 84% of the gap (reading abilities, school grades, parental influences [like have a higher education themselves and encouraging their children to go on to a higher education], and high school quality). Financial constraints (like tuition costs) accounted for only twelver per cent of this gap (while parents' education accounted for twice as much).

help young people improve their life chances, including the economically and socially disadvantaged. In particular, this knowledge should be useful to those who do not have the benefit of an affluent background, and/or have parents who do not know how to pass on more intangible resources like effective impression management in higher-educational contexts. In advocating the exercise of agency, therefore, the intention behind this research is not to increase existing social-class advantage, or advocate some sort of neoliberal or Machiavellian agenda, but to help all young people better negotiate the confusing transitions in late-modern societies, including those young people who are without birthright or other socio-economic advantages. For those sociologists who are skeptical of the use of agency or other psychological concepts involving personal strengths, I remind them that those from disadvantaged backgrounds need to learn how to identify and mobilise their internal potentials if they are to improve their life chances, regardless of the type of society in which they live (e.g., capitalist, socialist, or communist). Structural changes that simply place people in positions for which they are ill equipped are not a viable solutions.

Nevertheless, while certain structural changes should still be our goal if we are to liberate the disadvantaged, and we must continue to identify structures that discriminate against people in harmful ways, structures are slow to change. Consequently, in the meantime we need to learn how to help people 'penetrate' structures that might otherwise constitute barriers for them (cf. Emirbayer and Mische, 1999[47]). This position resonates with conceptualisations of agency as bounded rather than structured (see the Evans and Waite chapter in this volume and note their quotation from Biesta and Tedder (2007), who 'argue that people do not act *in* structures and environments—they act through them').

In addition, we need to be wary of the tendency to try to 'save the working class from itself,' a common but misguided implicit preoccupation among some sociologists that can make matters worse rather than better. There is much to be respected in working class culture, and such attitudes can increase the stigma that the more affluent classes impose on the working class (cf. McQuaig and Brook, 2010). Ironically, this stigma constitutes a symbolic barrier that exacerbates the

---

47   In a similar view of agency and structure, Emirbayer and Mische argue that the potential for agency in a given individual depends both upon the specific qualities of that individual and the specific qualities of the context in which the individual is acting. Actors, by definition, function in contexts; as such, they are never free from structure, but also vary in terms of their ability to utilise and transform that structure. In this respect, Emirbayer and Mische endorse the position that agency 'consists primarily in the capacity of resource-equipped actors to act creatively through the transposition of existing schemas into new contexts' (p. 1005, emphasis added).

psychological need for identity management among the working class, potentially limiting their identity horizons.

Thus, faced with the challenges endemic to late-modern societies, young people more than ever need a repertoire of personal, social, and economic resources to manage various transitions and diverse contexts (cf. Côté, 2000, 2002; Côté and Levine, 2002). It is well established that those without adequate structural resources face greater risks for social and economic exclusion. But, as many of the chapters in this volume show, those without agentic resources are at risk, including the risk of diminished well being. Indeed, research using an empirical measure of identity-based agency finds that those who score higher on this measure are less prone to depression and anxiety, and are less impulsive (Schwartz et al., 2009, found that this relationship was the same across a multi-ethnic sample of 905 White, Black, and Hispanic American university students).

The two types of resources relevant to the structure-agency debate are illustrated in Table 1, which cross-tabulates agentic factors with structural ones and thereby provides an algorithm for estimating risks and benefits. Structural resources include parental affluence, ethnic group, and social capital networks, while agentic resources include the types of abilities and capacities discussed above and in the chapters in this volume, as well as well-being itself (e.g., mental health issues like depression make it more difficult to people to deal with the structural issues in their lives).

Table 1: A model of resources and the risks and benefits (– and +) associated with them.

		Agentic resources	
		High	Low
Structural resources	High	+/+	−/+
	Low	+/−	−/−

In general, this typology is useful in terms of evaluating the needs of people (of any age), as well as among disadvantaged subpopulations. To provide a general illustration of the algorithm, in Canada about twenty per cent of the population lives in or near poverty—an economic disadvantage associated with various risks. Additionally, as in many countries, at any one time some twenty per cent of the Canadian population struggles with some sort of mental health problem that seriously diminishes their well-being and ability to function in productive roles. If we enter these probabilities into the above table, at any given time only about two thirds of the population would be estimated to have 'sufficient' structural (economic) and agentic (mental health) resources for 'risk-free' functioning (.8

x .8 = .64, or 64 per cent, for the +/+ cell). The remaining one third of the population lacks one or both of these crucial resources for risk-free functioning (the two low/high cells have 16 per cent probabilities [.8 x .2], and the low/low cell has a four per cent probability [.2 x .2]).

To show how this typology would work for a more specific group of young people, we can focus on a disadvantaged community, such as an impoverished inner city area. For example, if the poverty rate is forty per cent for the area and the poor mental health rate is forty per cent (e.g., as a result of a local culture of heavy drug use), the estimate would be that only about one third of the population is adequately resourced (.6 x .6 = .36, or 36 per cent). Young people growing up in such areas would thus be at such a compounded risk. Or, to take Everatt's example of South Africa with a youth unemployment rate of about fifty per cent (a rate commonly found in many developing countries [ILO, 2006], and in the 'Black neighbourhood' studied by Reynolds in the UK), even if only twenty per cent of youth could be counted as having low agency, the proportion of the youth population that would be found in the most felicitous '+/+' cell is only forty per cent (.5 x .8), leaving an equal percentage of agentically capable youth in the precarious fast-track '+/−' cell (also .5 x .8).

In addition to providing a means of estimating population risks, this typology reminds us that young people are not homogeneous in their resource needs and that youth/adolescence theories/policies need to take this into account (cf. Ranta in this volume). This typology also helps us to understand a number of the transition concepts and trajectories discussed in the contributions in this volume, as illustrated in Table 2

Table 2: Factors influencing the chance of young people benefitting from prolonged transitions to work and the likely education-to-work trajectories.

		Agentic resources	
		High	Low
Structural resources	High	++ slow-track	−/+ mixed
	Low	+/− fast-track	−/− marginal

In more affluent countries with well-developed economies and relatively low unemployment rates, those who could be considered 'high' on both structural and agentic resources would be most likely to be taking the 'slow track' through higher educational institutions. Those with little of either type of resource would be more clearly subject to marginalisation, or what is now called social exclusion (the '–/–' cell). But for them, solutions to their problems requiring higher degrees of agency probably would not work, and we know of no easy way to 'confer' agency on people. My own research suggests that identity-based agency involves deep-seated personality attributes that are developed during childhood and early adolescence, not the age period associated with the transition to work (Côté, 1997, 2002). If this is the case, the problem of life-course transitions is exacerbated by the 'Matthew effect' (cf. Merton, 1968), namely, that those who begin the transition process with the most advantages ultimately do best in terms of outcomes because those advantages compound over time. The probability that the Matthew effect is in play makes it more urgent for us to understand how to help all children and adolescents develop the basis of identity-based agency.

Those in the other two cells would be more likely experience elements of these two contrasting situations. Those who are agentic but lack structural resources should be more likely to attempt 'fast track' trajectories, but they would also be more likely to encounter precarious employment situations for which their agentic capacities may not be able to compensate. Lastly, the subgroup of youth who have structural advantages but low levels of the agentic resources necessary to fully capitalise on those advantages, would be more likely to be mixing slow- and fast-tracks, with alterations between work and education that are perhaps not useful in finding secure, long-term employment. For example, poor school performances may limit occupational opportunities, and poor person-context fits in the cutting-edge jobs may make for spotty work histories in spite of their structural advantages (e.g., note that not all of the children of the wealthy go on to a higher education, and it is possible that for some low levels of agency in relation to educational contexts play a role).

Transitions through, and to, what?

Two issues pertaining to the intrinsic nature of transitions and the life course are raised in several of the chapters in this volume. The first pertains to whether young people are transitioning or passing 'through' something (youth? emerging adulthood?) to something else (adulthood?). These issues involve cutting-edge debates that merit comment here.

The extended transition to adulthood: A new developmental stage or denial of resources?

As Schoon and Schulenburg, as well as Ranta, note in their chapters, some psychologists have recently claimed that the period from the late teens through the twenties is a new *developmental stage* during which it is functional to postpone adulthood in order to better prepare for it. It is further claimed that the concept of *emerging adulthood* captures this delay of adulthood, and has five main features: identity exploration, trying out possibilities in love and work, instability, self-focus, and feeling in between (Arnett, 2000).

Reactions to the validity and value of this concept have been very polarised. Although some people are embracing the concept of *emerging adulthood* as defined by Arnett, especially younger psychologists and some journalists interested in pop psychology, many established psychologists are rejecting it, as are most sociologists. Many of those rejecting it find nothing wrong with the conventional terms 'youth' and 'early adulthood' to represent the period spanning the transition from adolescent dependency to adult independence, and its extension in the current era. For these scholars, there is scepticism about the need for new terminology to describe what appears most likely to be a response to a loss of certain employment opportunities for young people—a denial of structural resources by the wider society—causing prolonged transitions from school to work (e.g., Bynner, 2005; Hendry and Kloep, 2007).

Moreover, there is scepticism that the model proposed by Arnett (the person who coined the term) adequately matches the claims regarding the importance of what might constitute a new stage of human development. As the contributions to this volume show, there are no apparent thresholds differentiating adolescence from early adulthood; indeed, the same processes found in adolescence appear to merely extend into early adulthood—they become prolonged, not qualitatively different. Three related objections have been raised (cf. Côté and Bynner, 2008): First, there is little evidence that new forms of normative developmental change actually take place between adolescence and adulthood. The main problem is that Arnett is vague in terms of what exactly is supposed to be developing, and his five features (above) do not constitute the elements of a developmental stage.[48] A developmental stage must add something to development beyond

---

48 Based on a formulation by Snarey, Kohlberg, and Noam (1983), emerging adulthood would be a 'cultural age' like adolescence, because there is an emphasis 'on quantitative changes in age, mastery, performance, knowledge, rights, and responsibilities' (p. 328). In contrast, Erikson's identity stage constitutes a 'functional phase' because there is both a qualitative change in identity structure and a quantitative change in social status (from adolescence to adulthood) upon resolution of the stage. The fact that the identity stage now

simple change; if a set of experiences does not have predictable value-added consequences other than amorphous change over time, it cannot be considered developmental (Lerner, 2002).

Second, any beneficial effect of a prolonged transition to adulthood appears to be restricted to more affluent majority-member youth of certain affluent societies—those who have the financial resources to invest in their prolonged educations and personalised, leisure-oriented lifestyles (i.e., those in the +/+ cell of the structure-agency typology presented above who are blessed with both structural and agentic resources) and these appear to be the ones Arnett calls 'emerging adults'. If a 'developmental stage' is important enough for those from affluent backgrounds and majority cultural groups to experience, it must also be important for the disadvantaged and those from other cultural backgrounds to experience it. If not, we cannot consider it a stage of human development, for such stages should apply to the entire species.

And, third, Arnett has insisted that his own psychological model (of a stage that manifests in five activities/subjective states) adequately explains young people's motives for delaying their adulthood (i.e., he claims they 'choose' to do so), yet there is little support for his model as a normative phenomenon, independent of specific cultural contexts. As Ranta notes (this volume), it is 'impossible to group young adults into a homogeneous group, with a normative developmental pathway into adulthood irrespective of individual differences, varying resources and encountered challenges.'

Thus, many social scientists in a variety of fields do not believe there is much to be gained from using this concept as Arnett and his followers currently define it, and some prominent developmental psychologists do not accept that Arnett has presented sufficient evidence for his claim to have 'discovered' a new developmental stage.[49] Arnett's model carries with it untested developmental claims and unwarranted prescriptive implications (i.e., that people 'ought to' choose to delay adulthood). As Schoon and Schulenberg note in their chapter, the term 'emerging adulthood' itself is not objectionable, because it does help draw attention to the need to study the prolonged transition to adulthood, but the use of the term is currently hampered by Arnett's controversial model.

takes longer does not mean that emerging adulthood is a functional phase, because in a functional phase qualitative changes must take place if subsequent development is to take place. Finally, a 'structural stage' requires qualitative changes in the structural arrangements of a mental process like cognition or the ego, and Arnett's version of emerging adulthood certainly does not correspond with this.

49 Email communications with Richard Lerner and Laurence Steinberg, July 27, 2007.

Thus, while there is a broad consensus that the 'transition to adulthood' has become more prolonged in recent decades, it is most likely the result of the increasingly prolonged time it takes to secure a job that pays a living wage and thus provides the opportunity for self-determination, including the family of the person's choice. The crucial issue appears to be that the youth segment in many societies does not have adequate access to the necessary structural resources. This situation needs be addressed; at the same time, we need to learn how to nurture agentic resources for all children and youth, from both structurally disadvantaged or advantaged backgrounds. Arnett's *emerging adulthood* model simply normalises this delay and signals to policy makers that nothing needs to be done to address the structural and agentic issues identified in this volume.

The end of adulthood?

When we look below the surface of the 'language of certainty' employed in discussing matters of the life course, just as there is uncertainty about what young people 'pass through,' there is also uncertainty concerning what young people 'pass into.' The chapter by Wyn raises this issue, and it is implicit in several others. But, to gain a sense of where we are currently and where we are headed in the future in terms of how the life course will change over time, it is useful to look to the past.

An etymological analysis of the English word 'adulthood' shows how the concept evolved. For example, the word 'adult' first appeared in the Oxford English Dictionary (OED) in 1656, but it is instructive to note that it is derived from the Latin *adolescent*, which is the present participle of *adolescere* (to grow up, mature). *Adolescere* is the inceptive verb of *adolere* (to make grow), while *adultus* (grown) is the past participle. The term 'adolescent' was brought into English usage in the 1400s, a half century earlier than the word 'adult,' while the term 'adulthood' did not appear until 1870 (Côté, 2000; Merser, 1987). The term 'youthhood' appears periodically from the 1600s through 1800s (Jones, 2009; Oxford English Dictionary, 2001), and has only recently been resurrected by Mørch (1995) and Côté (2000).

This etymological analysis suggests that current age distinctions are the result of the massive social, economic, and technological transformations of traditional societies into modern ones over the past several hundred years. These transformations altered social institutions and, as these institutions changed, so did people's lives: people were healthier and lived longer, and adults were less likely to raise large numbers of children. These changes led to the formation of age groups whose members were similar to each other but distinct from members of other age groups. Thus, people of different ages became different in terms of social roles and responsibilities, as well as in social expectations about cognitive and emotional attributes (Mintz 1993).

According to Merser (1987), the relatively recent appearance of a word to describe adulthood suggests that people needed something to depict the new social conditions they faced, especially increasing uncertainty and the need to make life-altering choices. In traditional societies, most people had little choice in how their lives played out. Instead, regardless of their age, people were bound by duties and obligations to fulfill ascribed family and community roles and statuses (as argued above, identities were ascribed more than achieved). Young and old alike were expected to work for a common welfare of their community enterprises, regardless of their own preferences. However, as Merser argues, the rise of uncertainty and the consequent need to know more about the world in order to make choices gave new meaning to the notion of 'maturity' and widened the gap between those with little experience (children) and those with more experience (adults). This process was hastened by the decline of absolute religious authority and the rise of secular authority, which meant that increasingly, people were seen as responsible for their own destinies and choices.

Jordan (1978) explored the changing meaning of adulthood in the United States over this same time period. In his search of the archives from early English settlers to the U.S., Jordan found little evidence that people held images of different stages of the life course. Instead, he found references to the roles and duties assigned to husbands, wives, children, and servants. Within these roles there was no reference to growth, maturing, or psychological needs and preferences. Among Puritans, for example, people were compelled to know their existing conditions, not to change their conditions. Jordan argues that the decline of patriarchy made way for binary ideas about personality characteristics such as maturity-immaturity and mastery-dependence. Increasingly, family members other than the dominant male gained status and rights, so people were defined less in terms of their roles and duties and more as individuals with needs and potentials. What Merser and Jordan are describing are essentially the roots of the individualisation of the life course.

In addition, Jordan argues that in the past, concern over gender roles overrode age roles in the sense that the dominant images were of manhood and womanhood as distinct but complementary states. Accordingly, it was more important to distinguish males from females than to distinguish children from adults. Over time, this changed with age roles and distinctions gaining importance in relation to gender distinctions. In other words, in early American history, it appears that women and men had more in common with those of the same sex regardless of age; over time adult men and women came to have more in common with each other than with children of the same sex.

Complementing these trends was a fall in both fertility and mortality rates. With fewer children to raise, each child could receive more attention. At the same time, more parents lived to see their children leave their homes. Therefore, a period of the life course without dependent children became common and people could turn attention to themselves and reflect on their psychological states and needs. Jordan argues that with the rise of the social sciences in the twentieth century, a technical language emerged that labeled the life stages of childhood, adolescence, and adulthood as 'real', rather than as historically produced and changeable cultural experiences.[50]

Still, cultural constructs embedded in language can have real consequences in people's lives. When we continue with the assumption that the current historical period corresponds with late modernity, we need to recognise the possibility that the life course period currently referred to as youth is prolonged due to an inadequacy in economic opportunities for self-sufficiency in conjunction with an inadequacy of social institutions to provide a normative structure for a shorter transition to adulthood (Côté, 2000). The late-modern citizen thus faces identity challenges beyond those of traditional societies in the sense that the tasks associated with achieving full-societal membership and becoming a fully-functioning participant in the society are not only ill-defined, but the economic means of securing those roles are often precarious.

In addition to the confusions about how the strategise the challenges posed during the 'youth period', the 'adult period' poses additional challenges for the individual. In spite of the reification of the concept, a consensus about exactly what constitutes 'adulthood' in late-modern societies is difficult to find both in the academic literature and among the public (Côté, 2000). This may be due in part to the declining normative structure and the associated erosion of the markers to confer adult status that characterised the lives of recent generations (completing education, adopting work roles, independent living, marriage, and parenthood), and in part to adult status increasingly becoming a psychological

---

50 In this context, Jones (2009) remarks that had the term 'youthhood' prevailed instead of 'adolescence', we might not have such a conflation of terminology. As history changes the experiences of the different phases of the life course, given our need to label patterns of experience, we could simply think in terms of the lengthening and shortening of these phase as historical circumstances change.

state based on the culmination of individual preferences associated with the individualisation process. It is perhaps because of the diminished normative support for these markers of adulthood that there is such a concern currently among researchers about 'transitions.' But, placed in historical context, the markers of early-to late-modern societies should not be mistaken as universal ones, for in traditional societies, the education-to-work transition did not exist for the vast majority of the population, which led to agrarian lives where work roles began in childhood and simply became more demanding with age.

The psychological side of contemporary adulthood can be understood in the necessity for people to engage in self-development, a task that requires the formation of a self-identity with two essential functions: integration into society and differentiation of the self from other selves. It traditional societies, where identities are largely ascribed, people are not expected to form such self-identities on their own to a great extent: their integration is established by merit of their ascribed social identities, and the psychological and social differentiation from others is minimised. In late-modern societies, the formation of an individualised self-identity requires people to make choices as to 'who they are' as adults in terms how they fit in (or what Wyn refers to as 'belonging' in this volume), and what gives them some mark of uniqueness. This does not mean that a 'state of adulthood' is entirely a relative matter of individual preference, but rather that more onus is placed on individuals to match their preferences from among a wide array of potentially validating communities and life-style options. In light of these issues, it is not readily apparent how to establish viable anchor-points for conceptualizing adult identity formation that would withstand critical scrutiny concerning what might be seen as an arbitrary and biased definition of adulthood.

One solution to this impasse is to note that, just as traditional communities do, modern communities and their members have certain 'needs' to be fulfilled by mature members. From this pragmatic standpoint, several guideposts can be adopted for defining 'endpoints' of youth and 'beginnings' of adulthood that are not tied to the social markers underpinning the 'transitions' approach that is coming under increasing scrutiny for its lack of universality. Most generally, with respect to what others would need, or expect, from adults in their day-to-day lives, and what communities need in terms of relatively predictable day-to-day functioning, we can ask how adults would be specifically identified as follows:

+ what do children and students need from adults in their lives?;
+ what do (responsible) employers look for in (full-time) adult employees?;
+ and what do partners/spouses need in intimate partners?

Using these criteria, we can then ask the pragmatic question, 'how would we know adults when we saw them?' Some reasonable answers would include: ◆ they would be flexible but not in continual flux;

- ◆ they would be willing to assume and maintain responsibilities that are more important than their own immediate personal gratifications;
- ◆ they would be willing to maintain their current courses of action for the foreseeable future;
- ◆ their lives would be embedded in communities and important to others;
- ◆ and their lives would be centered on making productive contributions to society.

What are described above are essentially citizenship roles that bind communities together and these roles can be undertaken regardless of age or the number of social markers passed. In this sense, the way forward would be to understand how late-modern citizens of all ages can be properly resourced so that they can not only traverse the precarious passage through education to productive roles including employment, but to do so in social responsible manner that is of benefit to not only themselves but their community/society—for the common welfare as is the case in traditional societies.

References

Abbott, A., (2001) *Time Matters: On Theory and Method*, Chicago: University of Chicago Press.

Abele, A. and Spurk, D., (2011) The dual impact of gender and the influence of timing of parenthood on men's and women's career development: Longitudinal findings, *International Journal of Behavioral Development* [online], 35.

Abercrombie, N., Hill, S. & Turner, B.S. (2006) *The Penguin Dictionary of Sociology*, London: Penguin Books.

Adkins, L., (2005) Social capital: The anatomy of a troubled concept, *Feminist Theory*, 6 (2): 195-211.

African National Congress (ANC) (1994) *The reconstruction and development programme*, Johannesburg: Ravan Press, www.nelsonmandela.org/omalley/index.php/site/q/03lv0 2039/04lv02103/05lv02120/06lv02126.htm [Accessed 12 February, 2013].

Ahola, K., and Hakanen, J., (2007) Job strain, burnout and depressive symptoms: A prospective study among dentists, *Journal of Affective Disorders,* 103: 103-110.

Ahola, K., Honkonen, T., Virtanen, M., Aromaa, A. and Lönnqvist, J. (2008). Burnout in relation to age in adult working population, *Journal of Occupational Health* [online], 50, joh.sanei.or.jp/pdf/E50/E50_4_08.pdf [Accessed 14 April, 2012].

Alexander, C., (2007) Imagining Cohesive Societies in M. Wethereall, M. Lafleche and Berkeley, R (eds) *Identity, Ethnic Diversity and Community Cohesion*, London: Sage.

Alheit, P. and Dausien, L., (2002) The Double Face of Lifelong Learning: two analytical perspectives in a learning revolution. *Studies in the Education of Adults*, 34: 3-22.

Allen, S., (1968) Some Theoretical Problems in the Study of Youth, *The Sociological Review* 16(3): 319-31.

Allianssi, The Finnish Youth Co-operation, (2006) *Nuorista Suomessa. Tietoa nuorista, heidän asemastaan, elinoloistaan ja nuorisotyöstä [About adolescents in Finland. Information on youth, their status, life styles and youth work]*, Research report.

Andres, L., and Wyn, J., (2010) *The making of a generation: The children of the 1970s in adulthood*, Toronto: University of Toronto Press.

Arbuckle, J. L., (1996) Full information estimation in the presence of incomplete data, in Marcoulides, G. A., and Schumacker R. E., (eds.) *Advanced structural equation modelling*, pp. 243-277, Mahwah, NJ: Lawrence Erlbaum Associates, Inc.

Arbuckle, J. L., (2009) *Amos Version 18.0 User's Guide*, Amos Development Corporation.

Archambault I., Janosz M., Fallu, J. S., and Pagani, L. S., (2009) Student engagement and its relationship with early high school dropout, *Journal of Adolescence*, 32(3): 651-670.

Archambault, I., Janosz, M., Morizot, J., and Pagani, L., (2009) Adolescent behavioural, affective, and cognitive engagement in school: Relationship to dropout, *Journal of School Health,* 79(9): 408-415.

Arnett, J. J., (2000) Emerging adulthood: A theory of development from the late teens through the twenties, *American Psychologist*, 55: 469-480.

Arnett, J. J., (2006) Emerging adulthood in Europe: A response to Bynner, *Journal of Youth Studies*, 9(1): 111-123.

Arnett, J. J., (2007) Emerging adulthood, a 21st century theory: A rejoinder to Hendry and Kloep, *Child Development Perspectives*, 2(1): 80-82.

Arnett, J.J., (2004) *Emerging adulthood: The winding road from the late teens through the twenties,* Oxford: Oxford University Press.

Arnett, J.J., (2011) *Homepage* [online], www.jeffreyarnett.com/articles.htm [Accessed 8 August 2011].

Arnett, J.J., Kloep, M., Hendry, L. and Tanner, J.L., (2011) *Debating emerging adulthood,* Oxford: Oxford University Press.

Arnot, M., David, M. and Weiner, G., (1999) *Closing the gender gap,* Cambridge: Polity Press.

Arulampalam, W., Gregg, P. and Gregory, M., (2001) 'Unemployment ccarring', *The Economic Journal,* 111: 577-584.

Asano, T., (ed.) (2006) *Kenshō wakamono no henbō: Ushinawareta jūnen no ato ni (Studying the metamorphosis of the youth: After the lost decade),* Tokyo: Keisō Shobō.

Ashton, D. and Bynner, J. (2011) Labour Market Training and Skills: practice and policy, Chapter 5 in Wadsworth, M. and Bynner, J., *A Companion to Life Course Studies,* London: Routledge.

Aunola, K., Stattin, H. and Nurmi, J-E., (2000) Adolescents´ achievement orientations, school adjustment, and externalizing and internalizing problem behaviors, *Journal of Adolescence* [online], 29(3), www.springerlink.com/content/nrk7h2206254w1p7/fulltext.pdf [Accessed 25 January].

Australian Institute of Health and Welfare (AIHW), (2007) *Young Australians, Their Health and Wellbeing 2007,* Cat no. PHE 87, Canberra: Australian Institute of Health and Welfare.

Autio, M., (2006) *Kuluttajuuden rakentuminen nuorten kertomuksissa [The construction of consumerism in young people's narratives],* Helsinki: Suomalaisen Kirjallisuuden Seura SKST 1066, Nuorisotutkimusseura, Nuorisotutkimusverkosto, julkaisuja 65.

Bagnall, N., (ed.) (2005) *Youth Transitions in a Globalised Marketplace,* New York: Nova Science Publishers.

Bakker, A. B., and Demerouti, E., (2007) The job demands-resources model: State of the art, *Journal of Managerial Psychology,* 22: 309-328.

Bakker, A.B., Demerouti, E. and Euwema, M.C., (2005) Job Resources Buffer the Impact of Job Demands on Burnout, *Journal of Occupational Health Psychology* [online], 10(2), igitur-archive.library.uu.nl [Accessed 25 January].

Banks, M., Breakwell, G., Bynner, J. Emler, N., Jamieson, L. Roberts, K., (1992) *Careers and identities,* Buckingham: Open University Press.

Banks, M.H. and Ullah, P., (1988) *Youth unemployment in the 1980s: Its psychological effect,* Beckenham: Croom Helm.

Barham, C., Walling, A., Clancy, G., Hicks, S. and Conn, S., (2009) Young people and the labour market, *Economic and Labour Market Review,* 3(4): 17-29.

Beck, U. and Beck-Gernsheim, E., (2002) *Individualization: Institutionalized individualism and its social and political consequences,* London: Sage.

Beck, U., (1992) *Risk society. Towards a new modernity,* London: Sage Publications.

Behrens, M. and Evans, K., (2002) Taking control of their lives? A comparison of the experience of unemployed young adults (18-25) in England and the new Germany, in *Comparative Education,* 38(1).

Bentler, P. M., (1990) Comparative fit indexes in structural models, *Psychological Bulletin,* 107: 238-246.

Bernstein, B. B., (1971) *Class, codes and control,* London: Routledge and K. Paul.

Biesta, G. and Tedder, M., (2007) Agency and Learning in the Lifecourse: Towards an Ecological Perspective, *Studies in the Education of Adults*, 39(2): 132-149.

Biesta, G., (2011) *Improving Learning through the Life Course: Learning Lives*, Abingdon: Routledge.

Bildt, C. and Michélsen, H., (2002) Gender differences in the effects from working conditionson mental health: a 4-year follow-up. *International Archives of Occupational and Environmental Health* [online], 75, www.springerlink.com/content/f1wea13jghny0h79/fulltext.pdf [Accessed 26 January].

Billari, F. C., (2001) The analysis of early life courses: Complex descriptions of the transition to adulthood, *Journal of Population Research,* 18: 119-142.

Birch, E., and Miller, P. W., (2007) The influence of type of high school attended on university performance, *Australian Economic Papers,* 46: 1-17.

Blanchard, M., Metcalf, A., Degney, J., Herrman, H., and Burns, J., (2008) Rethinking the Digital Divide. Findings from a study of marginalised young people's information and communication (ICT) use, *Youth Studies Australia*, 27(4): 35-42.

Blanden, J., Gregg, P. and Machin, S., (2005) *Intergenerational Mobility in Europe and North America*: A report supported by the Sutton Trust, London: Centre for Economic Performance.

Blatterer, H., (2007) *Coming of Age in Times of Uncertainty*, New York: Berghahn Books.

Blossfeld, H. P., (2005) *Globalization, uncertainty and youth in society*, London: Routledge.

Bourdieu, P. and Passeron, J. C., (1977) *Reproduction in education, society and culture*, Beverly Hills, CA: Sage.

Bourdieu, P., (1980) *The logic of practice*, Stanford: Stanford University Press.

Bourdieu, P., (1986) The forms of capital, in Richardson, J.E. (ed) *Handbook of theory for research in the sociology of education*, Westport, CT: Greenwood Press.

Bourdieu, P., and Wacquant, L., (1992) *An Invitation to Reflexive Sociology*, Chicago: The University of Chicago Press.

Brann-Barrett, M., (2010) Same landscape, different lens: variations in young people's socio-economic experiences and perceptions in their disadvantaged working-class community, *Journal of Youth Studies*, 14 (3): 261-278.

Brannen, J. and Lewis, S., Nilsen, A., and Smithson, J., (eds) (2002) *Young Europeans, Work and Family Futures in Transition*, London: ESA/Routledge.

Brannen, J. and Nilsen, A., (2005) Individualisation, choice and structure: a discussion of current trends in sociological analysis, *The Sociological Review* 53(3): 412-428.

Breen, R. and Goldthorpe, J. H., (2001) Class, mobility and merit-the experience of two British birth cohorts, *European Sociological Review,* 17(2): 81-101.

Brewer, M., Muriel, A., Phillips, D. and Sibieta, L., (2009) *Poverty and Inequality in the UK,* London: Institute of Fiscal Studies.

Briggs, D., (2010) 'True stories from bare times on road': Developing empowerment, identity and social capital among urban minority ethnic young people in London, U.K, *Journal of Ethnic and Racial Studies*, 46 (3).

Brockmann, M., (2011) Knowledge skills and competence in the European labour market: What's in a vocational qualification? in Clarke, L., Brockman, M., Winch, C., Hanf, G., Méhaut, P. and Westerhuis, A., (eds.) *Knowledge skills and competence in the European labour market*, Abingdon: Routledge.

Bronfenbrenner, U., (1979) *The Ecology of Human Development: Experiments by Nature and Design,* Harvard University Press, Cambridge.

Brown, P. Green, A. and Lauder, H., (eds.) (2001) *High skills: Globalization, competitiveness, and skill formation*, Oxford University Press.

Browning, C., Feinberg, S., and Dietz, R., (2004) The paradox of social organisation: Networks, Collective Efficacy and Violent Crime in Urban Neighbourhoods, *Social Forces*, 83(2): 503-534.

Brückner, H., and Mayer, K. U., (2005) De-standardization of the life course: What does it mean? And if it means anything, whether it actually took place? in Macmillan, R., (ed.) *The Structure of the Life Course: Standardized? Individualized? Differentiated?* (pp. 27-54). Amsterdam: Elsevier.

Buchmann, M. C., and Kriesi, I., (2011) Transition to Adulthood in Europe, *Annual Review of Sociology*, Vol 37: 481-503.

Burgess, S., Propper, C., Rees, H. and Shearer, A., (2003) The class of '81: the effects of early-career unemployment on subsequent unemployment experiences, *Labour Economics* 10(3): 291-311.

Butler, N., Despotidou, S., and Shepherd, P., (1997) *1970 British Cohort Study (BCS70) ten year follow-up: A guide to the BCS70 10-year data available at the Economic and Social Research Unit Data Archive*, London: Social Statistics Research Unit, City University.

Buunk, B. P. and Schaufeli, W. B., (1993) Professional burnout: a perspective from social comparison theory, in Schaufeli, W. B. Maslach, C. and Mareks, T., (eds.) *Professional burnout: recent developments in theory and research* [online], Washington DC: Taylor and Francis.

Bynner, J. and Evans, K., (1994) Building on cultural traditions: problems and solutions, in Evans, K. and Heinz, W.R., (eds.) *Becoming adults in the 1990s*, London: Anglo German Foundation.

Bynner, J. and Parsons, S., (2002) Social Exclusion and the Transition from School to Work: The case of Young People Not in Education, Employment or Training NEET, *Journal of Vocational Behaviour*, 60: 289-309.

Bynner, J., (1998) Education and family components of identity in the transition from school to work, *International Journal of Behavioural Development*, 22: 29-53.

Bynner, J., (1999) New routes to employment: Integration and exclusion, in Heinz W.R., (ed.) *From Education to Work: cross national perspectives*, Cambridge: Cambridge University Press.

Bynner, J., (2005) Rethinking the youth phase of the life course: The case for emerging adulthood, *Youth and Society,* 8(4): 367-384.

Bynner, J., (2010) Youth Transitions and Changing Labour Markets: Germany and England in the late 1980s, *Historical Social Research (Historische Sozialforschung), 35,* (2): 76-98.

Bynner, J., Elias, P., McKnight, A., Pan, H. and Pierre, G., (2002) *Young people's changing routes to independence*, York: Joseph Rowntree Foundation.

Bynner, J., Reder, S, Parsons, S. and Strawn, C., (2008) *The digital divide: Computer use, Basic skills and Employment: A comparative study in Portland, USA and London, England,* NRDC report, Institute of Education, London.

Byrne, M. B., (1994) Burnout: testing for the validity, replication, and invariance of causal structure across elementary, intermediate, and secondary teachers, *American Educational Research Journal,* 31(3): 645-673.

Callender, C. and Jackson, J., (2005) Does the Fear of Debt Deter Students from Higher Education? *Journal of Social Policy,* 34: 509-540.

Carole, F.E. and Pastore, F., (2002) Youth participation in the labor market in Germany, Spain and Sweden, in Hammer, T., (ed) *Youth unemployment and social exclusion in Europe. A comparative study*, London: The Policy Press.

Carver, C.S., Scheier, M.F. and Weintraub, J.K., (1989) Assessing coping strategies: A theoretically based approach, *Journal of Personality and Social Psychology* [online], 56(2), www.psy.miami.edu/faculty/ccarver/documents/p89COPE.pdf [Accessed 26 January].

Central Council for Education, (1999) Im*provements to Transition from Elementary/ Secondary Education to Higher Educati*on, www.mext.go.jp/b_menu/shingi/chuuou/ toushin/991201.htm [Accessed 12 February, 2013].

Chandra, V. and Tiwari, A., (2009) *Occupational and career aspirations of school leavers of Lucknow and Allahabad Youth*, published report by Circle for Child and Youth Research cooperation in India (CCYRCI), Lucknow.

Cheung, S. Y., and Heath A., (2007) 'Nice Work if You Can Get It': Ethnic Penalties in Great Britain, *Proceedings of the British Academy*, 137: 507-550.

Clay, A., (2009) Keepin' it Real, Black Youth, Hip-Hop Culture and Black Identity, *Review of Educational Research*, 79: 946-968.

Cohen, J., (1992) A power primer, *Psychological Bulletin*, 112: 155-159.

Cohen, P., and Ainley, P., (2000) In the Country of the Blind? Youth Studies and Cultural Studies in Britain, *Journal of Youth Studies*, 3(1): 79-95.

Coleman, J. C., (1989) The focal theory of adolescence: A psychological perspective, in Hurrelman, K. and Engel, U., (eds.) *The social world of adolescents: International perspectives* (pp. 43-56), Berlin: Walter de Gruyter.

Coles, B., Godfrey, C., Keung, A., Parrott, S. and Bradshaw, J., (2010) *Estimating the life-time cost of NEET: 16-18 year olds not in Education, Employment or Training*, University of York, php.york.ac.uk/inst/spru/pubs/1776/.

Collinson, M., (1996) In search of the high life: drugs, crime, masculinity, and consumption, *British Journal of Criminology*, 36(3): 428-44.

Commission for Racial Equality (2005) *Commission for Integration and Cohesion: A Response by the Commission for Racial Equality* London: Commission for Racial Equality.

Conger, R., Conger, K., and Martin, M. (2010), Socioeconomic Status, Family Processes, and Individual Development, *Journal of Marriage and the Family*, 72(3), 685-704

Cook, T. D., and Furstenberg, F. F., (2002) Explaining aspects of the transition to adulthood in Italy, Sweden, Germany, and the United States: A cross-disciplinary, case synthesis approach, *Annals of the American Academy of Political and Social Science*, 580: 257-287.

Côte, J. and Bynner, J., (2008) Exclusion from Emerging Adulthood: UK and Canadian Perspectives on Structure and Agency in the Transition to Adulthood, *Journal of Youth Studies*, 11 (3): 251-268.

Côté, J. E. and Allahar, A., (1996) *Generation on Hold: Coming of Age in the Late Twentieth Century*, New York: New York University Press.

Côté, J. E. and Allahar, A., (2006) *Critical Youth Studies: A Canadian Focus*, Toronto: Pearson Education.

Côté, J. E. and Bynner, J., (2008) Changes in the transition to adulthood in the UK and Canada: The role of structure and agency in emerging adulthood, *Journal of Youth Studies*, 11(3): 251-267.

Côté, J. E. and Levine, C., (1997) Student motivations, learning environments, and human capital acquisition: Toward an integrated paradigm of student development, *Journal of College Student Development*, 38: 229-243.

Côté, J. E. and Levine, C., (2000) Attitude versus aptitude: Is intelligence or motivation more important for positive higher educational outcomes? *Journal of Adolescent Research*, 15: 58-80.

Côté, J. E. and Levine, C., (2002) *Identity Formation, Agency, and Culture*, Hillsdale, NJ: Lawrence Erlbaum.

Côté, J. E., (1996) Sociological perspectives on identity formation: The culture-identity link and identity capital, *Journal of Adolescence*, 19: 419-430.

Côté, J. E., (1997) An empirical test of the identity capital model, *Journal of Adolescence*, 20: 421-437.

Côté, J. E., (2000) *Arrested adulthood: The changing nature of maturity and identity*, New York: New York University Press.

Côté, J. E., (2002) The role of identity capital in the transition to adulthood: The individualization thesis examined, *Journal of Youth Studies*, 5(2): 117-134.

Côté, J. E., (2005) The identity capital model, in C. Fisher and R. Lerner (Eds.), *Applied Developmental Science: An Encyclopedia of Research, Policies, and Programs (ADSE)*, Thousand Oaks, CA: Sage.

Côté, J. E., and Levine, C. (2002). *Identity formation, agency, and culture: A social psychological approach*, Mahwah, NJ: Erlbaum.

Côté, J. E., and Schwartz, S. J., (2002) Comparing psychological and sociological approaches to identity: Identity status, identity capital, and the individualization process, *Journal of Adolescence*, 25: 571-586.

Côté, J. E., Skinkle, R. and Motte, A., (2008) Do perceptions of costs and benefits of post-secondary education influence participation? *Canadian Journal of Higher Education*, 38(3): 73-93.

Côté, J., (1996) Sociological perspectives on identity formation: the culture-identity link and identity capital, *Journal of Adolescence*, 19: 417-428.

Cote, J., and Bynner, J. M., (2008) Changes in the transition to adulthood in the UK and Canada: the role of structure and agency in emerging adulthood, *Journal of Youth Studies*, 11(3): 251-268, www.tandfonline.com.

Côté, J.E. and Levine, C.G., (2002) *Identity, Formation, Agency and Culture*, London: Lawrence Erlbaum.

Covington, M. V., (2000) Goal theory, motivation, and school achievement: An integrative review, *Annual Review of Psychology*, 51: 171-200.

Cuervo, H., and Wyn, J., (2012) *Young people in rural places*, Melbourne: Melbourne University Press.

Cunnien, K. A., MartinRogers, N. and Mortimer, J. T., (2009) Adolescent work experience and self-efficacy, *International Journal of Sociology and Social Policy*, 29: 164-175.

Curran, P., and Hussong, A., (2009)

Davie, R., Butler, N., and Goldstein, H., (1972) *From Birth to Seven*, London: Longman.

Dearden, L. Goodman, A. and Saunders, P., (2003) Income and Living Standards, in Ferri, E. Bynner, J. and Wadsworth, M.E., (eds.) *Changing Britain: Changing lives: three generations at the end of the century*, pp 148-193, London: Institute of Education.

Deary, I. J., Taylor, M. D., Hart, C. L., Wilson, V., Davey-Smith, G., Blane, D., and Starr, J. M., (2005) Intergenerational mobility and mid-life status attainment: influences of childhood intelligence, childhood social factors, and education, *Intelligence*, 33: 455-472.

Delors, J., (1996) *Learning: The treasure within*. Report to UNESCO of the International Commission on Education for the Twenty-first Century. Paris: UNESCO.

Demerouti, E., Bakker, A., Nachreiner, F., and Schaufeli, W., (2001) The job demands-resources model of burnout, *Journal of Applied Psychology*, 86: 499-512.

Dentsū and Nippon Reserch Centre, (2008) *Sekai shuyōkoku kachikan databook (World values databook)*, Tokyo: Dōyūkan.

Department for Education (2011) *NEET Statistics, Quarterly Brief Quarter 2*, London: DfE

Department of Enterprise, Trade and Investment (2010) www.detini.gov.uk/deti-stats-index/deti-stats-index-2.htm [Accessed 11 August 2011].

Department of Health, Department for Education and Skills, (2004) *National service framework for children young people and maternity services: the mental health and psychological well-being of children and young people: standard 9*, London: HMSO.

Doi, T., (2008) *Tomodachi jigoku: 'Kūki wo yomu' sedai no survival (Friend hell: Survival of the generation that reads between the lines)*, Tokyo: Chikuma Shobō.

Douglas, J. W. B., (1964) *The home and the school*, London: Panther Books.

du Bois-Reymond, M. and Stauber, B., (2005) Biographical turning points in young people's transitions to work across Europe, in Helve, H. and Holm, G., (eds.) *Contemporary youth research, local expressions and global connections*, Hants: Ashgate.

du Bois-Reymond, M., (1995) Future orientations of Dutch youth: The emergence of a choice biography, in Cavalli, A. and Galland, O., (eds.) *Youth in Europe*, London: Pinter.

du Toit, R., (2003) *Unemployed youth in South Africa: The Distressed Generation?*, paper presented at the Minnesota International Counseling Institute, 27 July-1 August 2003, p.20, intranet.hsrc.ac.za.

Eccles, J. S., and Midgley, C., (1989) Stage/environment fit: Developmentally appropriate classrooms for early adolescents, in Ames, R., and Ames, C., (eds.) *Research on motivation in education*, vol. 3, pp. 139-181, New York: Academic Press.

Eccles J. S., (2004) Schools, academic motivation, and stage-environment fit, in Lerner, R. M., and Steinberg, L., (ed.), *Handbook of Adolescent Psychology*, (2nd ed), pp.125-53, Hoboken, NJ: Wiley.

Eccles, J. S., and Wigfield, A., (2002) Motivational beliefs, values, and goals, *Annual Review of Psychology* 53:109-3

Eccles, J., (2011) Gendered educational and occupational choices: Applying the Eccles et al. model of achievement-related choices, *International Journal of Behavioral Development* [online], 35(3).

Eccles, J.S. and Roeser, R.W., (2009) Schools, academic motivation, and Stage-Environment Fit, in R.M. Lerner and L. Steinberg (eds.), *Handbook of Adolescent Psychology*, (3rd eds.), pp. 404-434, Hoboken, NJ: Wiley.

Eccles. J.S. and Roeser, R.W., (1999) School and community influences on human development, in Boorstein, M.H., and Lamb, M.E., (eds.), *Developmental Psychology: An Advanced Textbook*, (4th eds), pp. 503-554, Hillsdale, NJ: Erlbaum.

Ecclestone, K., Biesta, G. and Hughes, M., (eds.) (2010) *Transitions and Learning through the Life Course*, Routledge, Abingdon.

Edwards, R., (2002) Introduction: conceptualising relationships between home and school in children's lives, in Edwards, R., (ed.) *Children, Home and School: Regulation, Autonomy or Connection?*, London: Routledge Falmer.

Edwards, R., Franklin, J. and Holland, J., (2003) *Families and Social Capital: Exploring the Issues Families and Social Capital,* ESRC Research Group Working Paper No. 1, London: South Bank University, www.lsbu.ac.uk/ahs/downloads/families/familieswp1.pdf [Accessed 31 January 2012].

Elder, G. H., (ed.) (1985) *Life course dynamics: Trajectories and transitions,* Ithaca, NY: Cornell University Press.

Elder, G. H., Jr. and Johnson, M. K., (2003) The life course and aging: Challenges, lessons, and new directions, in Settersten, R. A., Jr., (ed.) *Invitation to the life course. Toward new understandings of later life,* Amityville: Baywood.

Elder, G. H., Jr. and Shanahan, M. J., (2006) The life course and human development, in Lerner, R. M. and Damon, W., (eds.) *The handbook of child psychology,* sixth ed., Vol. 1, Hoboken, New Jersey: John Wiley and Sons.

Elder, G. H., Jr., (1998) The life course and human development, in Damon, W. and Lerner, R. M., (eds.) *Theoretical models of human development. Handbook of child psychology,* Vol. 1, Hoboken, New Jersey: John Wiley and Sons.

Elder, G., Johnson, K., and Crosnoe, R., (2004) The emergence and development of life course theory in J. T. Mortimer and M. J. Shanahan (eds.) *Handbook of the Life Course,* New York: Springer.

Elder, G.H., (1999) *Children of the Great Depression: 25th Anniversary Edition,* Boulder, Co.: Westview Press.

Elder, Glen H., Jr. (2002) Historical Times and Lives: A Journey Through Time and Space. in Phelps, E., Furstenberg, F. Jr., and Colby, A., *Looking at Lives: American Longitudinal Studies of the 20th Century,* New York: Russell Sage Foundation.

Elliott, C.D., Murray, D. and Pearson, L., (1978) *British Ability Scales,* Windsor: National Foundation for Educational Research.

Elliott, J., and Shepherd, P., (2006) Cohort profile of the 1970 British Birth Cohort (BCS70), *International Journal of Epidemiology,* 35: 836-843.

Ellwood, (1982) Teenage Unemployment: Permanent Scars or Temporary Blemishes, in Freeman R. B. and Wise, D. A., (eds.) *The youth Labor Market Problem: Its Nature Causes and Consequences,* pp 349-390, Chicago: University of Chicago Press.

Elovainio, M., Kivimäki, M. and Vahtera, J., (2002) Organizational justice: evidence of a new psychological predictor of health, *American Journal of Public Health* [online], 92.

Elovainio, M., van den Bos, K., Linna, A., Kivimäki, M., Ala-Mursula, L., Pentti, J. and Vahtera, J., (2005) Combined effects of uncertainty and organizational justice on employee health: testing the uncertainty management model of fairness judgments among Finnish public sector employees, *Social Science and Medicine* [online], 6, igitur-archive.library.uu.nl/fss/2006-0216-200104/bos_2006_combined-effects.pdf [Accessed 26 January].

Emirbayer, M. and Mische, A., (1998) What is agency? *American Journal of Sociology,* 103, 962-1023.

Equality and Human Rights Commission (2010) *How Fair is Britain?* Report, London

Erikson, E. H., (1968) *Identity: Youth and crisis.* New York: Norton.

Eronen, S. and Nurmi, J-E., (1999) Social reaction styles, interpersonal behaviors and person perception. A multi-informant approach, *Journal of Social and Personal Relationships,* [online], 16 (3).

Eronen, S., (2000) *Achievement and social strategies and the cumulation of positive and negative experiences during young adulthood* [online], Department of Psychology. University of Helsinki. Research Reports, 22. Helsinki: University Printing House, www.doria.fi/bitstream/handle/10024/3718/achievem.pdf?sequence=2 [Accessed 26 January].

Eronen, S., Nurmi, J-E. and Salmela-Aro, K., (1997) Planning-oriented, avoidant, and impulsive social reaction styles: a person-oriented approach, *Journal of Research in Personality*, [online], 31.

Ervasti, H., Venetoklis, T., (2010) Unemployment and subjective well-being: an empirical test of deprivation theory, incentive paradigm and financial strain approach, *Acta Sociologica*, 53:119.

Euro Statistics, (2009) epp.eurostat.ec.europa.eu/cache/ITY_OFFPUB/KS-EI-08-001/EN/KS-EI-08-001-EN.PDF, [Accessed 21 May 2011].

European Commission (2009) Youth unemployment. Five million young people unemployed in the EU27 in the first quarter 2009, *News release, 109/2009*, 23 July 2009 epp.eurostat.ec.europa.eu/cache/ITY_PUBLIC/3-23072009-BP/EN/3-23072009-BP-EN.PDF [Accessed 21 May 2011].

European Commission (2012) *Youth unemployment statistics data 2011*, eurostat.ec.europa.eu.

European Commission, (2010) *Europe 2020: A European strategy for smart, sustainable and inclusive growth,* Brussels: European Commission, ec.europa.eu/commission_2010-2014/president/news/documents/pdf/20100303_1_en.pdf [Accessed 21 May 2012].

Eurostat statistics (2011) epp.eurostat.ec.europa.eu, xxxxxx???? [Accessed 21 May 2011].

Eurostat statistics, (1997) *Youth in the European Union: From education to working life*, Luxembourg: Eurostat.

Eurostat statistics, (2010) 51 million young EU adults lived with their parent(s) in 2008, *Statistics in focus*, 50/2010, Population and social conditions. Marta Choroszewicz and Pascal Wolff.

Evans K. and Heinz, W., (1993) Studying Forms of Transition: methodological innovation in a cross-national study of youth transition and labour market entry in England and Germany, *Comparative Education*, 29(2): 145-158.

Evans, K. and Furlong, A., (1997) Metaphors of Youth Transitions: Niches, Pathways, Trajectories or Navigations, in Bynner, J., Chisholm, L. and Furlong, A., (eds.) *Youth, Citizenship and Social Change,* Aldershot: Ashgate.

Evans, K. and Heinz, W., (1994) *Becoming Adults in England and Germany*, London and Bonn: Anglo-German Foundation.

Evans, K. and Niemeyer, B., (eds) (2004) *Reconnection: Countering Social Exclusion through Situated Learning,* Dordrecht: Springer.

Evans, K. and Waite, E., (2010) Stimulating the Innovation Potential of 'Routine' Workers through Workplace Learning, *Transfer: European Review of Labour and Research*, 16(2): 243-258.

Evans, K. Behrens, M and Kaluza, J. (2000) *Learning and work in the risk society,* Palgrave Macmillan: Basingstoke.

Evans, K., (2002) Taking control of their lives? Agency in young adult transitions in England and the new Germany, *Journal of Youth Studies*, 5: 245-271.

Evans, K., (2007) Concepts of bounded agency in education, work, and the personal lives of young adults, *International Journal of Psychology*, 42(2): 85-93.

Evans, K., (2009) *Learning Work and Social Responsibility*, Dordrecht: Springer.

Evans, K., Rudd, P., Behrens, M., Kaluza, J., and Woolley, C., (2003) *Taking control: Young adults talk about the future in eduation, training and work*, Leicester: Youth Work Press.

Evans, K., Schoon, I. and Weale, M., (2010) *Life chances, learning and the dynamics of risk throughout the life course,* Centre for Learning and Life Chances in Knowledge Economies and Societies [online], www.llakes.org.uk [Accessed 31 January 2012].

Evans, K., Waite, E. and Admasachew, A., (2009) Enhancing 'Skills for Life'? Adult Basic Skills and Workplace Learning, in Bynner, J. and Reder, S., (eds) *Tracking Adult Literacy and Numeracy: Lessons from Longitudinal Research,* London and New York: Routledge.

Everatt, D., (2011) Class formation and rising inequality in South Africa: What does this mean for future voting patterns? in Mbeki M., (ed.) *Advocates of Change: How to Overcome Africa's Challenges,* Johannesburg: MacMillan

Fadjukoff, P., (2007) *Identity formation in adulthood,* Jyväskylä: University of Jyväskylä.

Fahey, S. and Gale F., (2005) *The introduction to Youth in Transition. The challenges of generational change in Asia.* Gale, F. and Fahey. S. (eds.) Regional Unit for Social and Human Sciences in Asia and the Pacific, UNESCO, unesdoc.unesco.org/images/0014/001417/141774e.pdf.

Fangen, K., Fossan, K. and Mohn, F.A., (eds.), (2010) *Inclusion and Exclusion of Young Adult Migrants in Europe,* Surray: Ashgate.

Farrington D.P., Gallagher, B., Morly, L., St Ledger and West, D.J., (1986) Unemployment, school leaving, and crime, *British Journal of Criminology,* 26: 335-356.

Feinstein, L., and Bynner, J., (2004) The importance of cognitive development in middle childhood for adulthood socioeconomic status, mental health, and problem behaviour, *Child Development,* 75(5): 1329-1339.

Fernet, C, Gagné, M. and Austin, S., (2010) When does quality of relationships with co-workers predict burnout over time? The moderating role of work motivation, *Journal organizational Behavior* [online], 30, onlinelibrary.wiley.com [Accessed 26 January].

Ferri, E., Bynner, J. and Wadsworth, M., (2003) *Changing Britain, changing lives: Three generations at the turn of the century,* London: Institute of Education.

Field, J., (2003) *Social Capital,* London: Routledge.

Fimian, M., and Cross, A., (1986) Stress and burnout among preadolescent and early adolescent gifted students: A preliminary investigation, *The Journal of Early Adolescence,* 6: 247-267.

Finch, J., (1986) Age in Burgess, R. (ed) *Key Variables in Social Investigation,* London: Routledge, Kegan, Paul.

Finn J. D., Rock, D. A., (1997) Academic success among students at risk for school failure, *Journal of Applied Psychology,* 82: 221-234.

Finnie, R., Lascelles, E., and Sweetman, A., (2005) *Who goes? The direct and indirect effects of family background on access to post-secondary education,* Ottawa: Statistics Canada, Analytic Studies Branch Research Paper Series.

Finnish Medical Society Duodecim, The, and the Academy of Finland, (2010) *Nuorten hyvin-ja pahoinvointi [Adolescence well-being and ill-health], Konsensuskokous 2010, 1-3 Februrary,* Espoo, Finland.

Fogelman, K., (1976) *Britain's 16-year-olds,* London: National Children's Bureau.

Folkman, S., (2008) The case for positive emotions in the stress process, *Anxiety, Stress, and Coping* [online], 21(1), www.tandfonline.com/doi/abs/10.1080/10615800701740457 [Accessed 26 January].

Forde, F., (2012) Moeletsi Mbeki: ANC has created a war, *Africa Report* 15/12/2011, www.theafricareport.com/Politicians/moeletsi-mbeki-anc-has-created-a-war.html [Accessed 31 January 2012].

Foundation for Young Australians, (2011) *How Young People are Faring 2011*, Melbourne: Foundation for Young Australians.

France, A., (2007) *Understanding youth in late modernity*, Buckingham: Open University Press.

Fredricks, J. A., Blumenfeld, P. C., and Paris, A. H., (2004) School engagement: Potential of the concept, state of the evidence, *Review of Educational Research*, 74: 59-109.

Freedman D., (1988) *The Idle Threat-Unemployed Youth*, International Labour Organisation.

Frenette, M., (2007) *Why are youth from lower-income families less likely to attend university? Evidence from academic abilities, parental influences, and financial constraints*, Analytical Studies Branch Research Paper Series. Ottawa: Statistics Canada, Catalogue Number 11F0019MIE-Number 295.

Furlong, A. and Cartmel, F., (1997) *Young People and Social Change: Individualization and Risk in Late Modernity*, Buckingham: Open University Press.

Furlong, A. and Cartmel, F., (2007) *Young people and social change: New perspectives*, second ed., Berkshire: Open University Press.

Furlong, A., Woodman, D., and Wyn, J., (2011) Changing times, changing perspectives: reconciling 'transition' and 'cultural' perspectives on youth and young adulthood, *Journal of Sociology*, 47(4): 355-370.

Furstenberg, F. F., (2001) Adolescence, Sociology of, in Smelser, N. J. and Baltes, P. B., (eds.) *International encyclopedia of the social and behavioral sciences*, Oxford: Elsevier.

Gabel, S., (2011) Ethics and values in clinical practice: whom do they help? *Mayo Clinic proceedings* [online], 86(5).

Galindo-Rueda, F. and Vignoles, A., (2005) The declining relative importance of ability in predicting educational attainment, *Journal of Human Resources*, 40(2).

Gardner H., (1993) *Creative Minds*, New York: Basic Books.

Gayle V., (2009) *Youth Transitions-Future direction for data, methods and theory. International Conference on Youth Transitions*, 11 12 September, University of Basel www.staff.stir.ac.uk/vernon.gayle/documents/gayle_v8_001.ppt.

Ge, X., Lorenz, F. O., Conger, R. D., Elder, G. H., and Simons, R. L., (1994) Trajectories of stressful life events and depressive symptoms during adolescence, *Developmental Psychology*, 30: 467-483.

Genda, Y., (2005) *Hataraku kajō: Otona no tame no wakamono dokuhon (Working too much: Reader about youth for adults)*, Tokyo: NTT Shuppan.

Giddens, A., (1984) *The constitution of society. Outline of the theory of structuration*, Oxford: Basil Blackwell.

Giddens, A., (1991) *Modernity and self identity: Self and society in the late modern age*, Cambridge: Polity.

Giddens, A., (2001) *Sociology*, fourth ed., Cambridge: Polity.

Gillies, V., (2000) Young People and Family Life: Analysing and Comparing Disciplinary Discourses, *Journal of Youth Studies* 3(2): 211-228.

Glass, D. C. and McKnight J. D., (1996) Perception control, depressive symptomatology, and professional burnout: a review of the evidence, *Psychology and Health*, 11(1): 23-48.

Global Employment Trends for Youth: 2011 update, (October 2011) International Labour Office-Geneva: ILO issuu.com/futurechallenges/docs/wcms_165455

Golembiewski, R., (1989) A note on Leiter's study: Highlighting two models of burnout, *Group and Organization Management*, 14: 5-13.

Goodman, L. A., (1974), Exploratory Latent Structure Analysis Using Both Identifiable and Unidentifiable Models, *Biometrika*, 61(2), 215-231.

Gorard, S. and Rees, G., (2002) *Creating a Learning Society? Learning Careers and Policies for lifelong learning,* Bristol: The Policy Press.

Goujard, A., B., Petrongolo and J. V. Reenen, (2011) The Labour Market For Young People, in Gregg, P. and Wadsworth, J. *The Labour Market In Winter,* Oxford: Oxford University Press, 39-54.

Goulbourne, H., (1989) The Contribution of West Indian Groups to British Politics, in Goulbourne, H., (ed.) *Black Politics in Britain,* London: Avebury.

Goulbourne, H., Solomos, J., Reynolds, T. and Zontini, E., (2010) *Transnational Families: Ethnicities, Identities and Social Capital,* London: Routledge.

Graber, J. A. and Brooks-Gunn, J., (1996) Transitions and turning points: Navigating the passage from childhood through adolescence, *Developmental Psychology,* 32(4): 768-776.

Green, A. and Janmaat, J., (2011) *Regimes of Social Cohesion: Societies and the Crisis of Globalisation,* Basingstoke: Palgrave.

Green, A., Preston J. and Janmaat, J.G., (2006) *Education, Equality and Social Cohesion: A Comparative Analysis,* Basingstoke: Palgrave Macmillan.

Greenglass, E., (1991) Burnout and gender: theoretical and organizational implications, *Canadian Psychology,* 32(4): 562-574.

Gregg, P. and Tominey, E., (2004) *The wage scar from youth unemployment, Centre for Market and Public Organisation* Working Paper Series No. 04/097, University of Bristol.

Gregg, P. and Wadsworth, J. (2011) Unemployment and Inactivity. in Gregg, P. and Wadsworth, J. *The Labour Market In Winter,* Oxford: Oxford University Press, 22-38.

Gregg, P., and Machin, S., (2001) Childhood experiences, educational attainment and adult labour market performance, in Vleminckx, K., and Smeeding, T., (eds.) *Child Well-Being, Child Poverty and Child Policy in Modern Nations,* Bristol: The Policy Press.

Grob, A., (2001) Youth to adulthood across cultures, Transition from, in Smelser, N. J. and Baltes, P. B., (eds.) *International encyclopedia of the social and behavioral sciences,* Oxford: Elsevier.

Guerrero, T. J., (2001) *Youth in transition. Housing, employment, social policies and families in France and Spain,* Hampshire: Ashgate.

Haavisto, I., (2010) *Työelämän kulttuurivallankumous,* EVA:n arvo-ja asennetutkimus 2010, EVA, www.eva.fi/wp-content/uploads/2010/04/tyoelaman_kulttuurivallankumous. pdf, [Accessed 21 May 2012].

Hagestad, G. O., (2003) Interdependent lives and relationships in changing times: A life-course view of families and aging, in Settersten, R. A., Jr., (ed.) *Invitation to the life course. Toward new understandings of later life,* Amityville, New York: Baywood.

Hakanen, J. Bakker, A. B. and Schaufeli, W. B., (2006) Burnout and work engagement among teachers, *Journal of School Psychology* [online], 43, curriculumstudies.pbworks. com/f/Burnout+and+work+engagement+-+Hakanen,+J.pdf [Accessed 26 January].

Hakim, C., (1996) *Key Issues in Women's Work,* London: Athlone.

Häkkinen, I. and Uusitalo, R., (2003) *The effect of student aid reform on graduation times: A duration analysis,* Working Paper, 8, Uppsala: Uppsala University, Department of Economics.

Häkkinen, I., (2004) *Working while enrolled in a university: doe sit pay?* Working Paper, 1, Uppsala: Uppsala University, Department of Economics.

Hall, T., Coffey, A., and Lashua, B., (2009) Steps and stages: rethinking transitions in youth and place, *Journal of Youth Studies,* 12(5): 547-561.

Hammer, T., (ed.) (2003) *Youth unemployment and social exclusion in Europe. A comparative study*, London: The Policy Press.

Hansen, K., (2008) *Youth and the City in the Global South*, Indiana: Indiana University Press.

Harris, A., Wyn, J., and Younes, S., (2007) Young People and Citizenship: An Everyday Perspective, *Youth Studies Australia*, 26(3): 18-26.

Havighurst, R. J., (1948) *Developmental tasks and education*, New York, New York: Longman.

Hayes, C., (2011) Huge increase in Northern Ireland suicides since the end of the Troubles, *Irish Examiner*, 2 February. www.irishcentral.com/news/Huge-increase-in-Northern-Ireland-suicides-since-the-end-of-The-Troubles-115093799.html [Accessed 11 August 2011].

Heath, A., (2008) The Second Generation in Western Europe: Education, Unemployment and Occupational Attainment, *Annual Review of Sociology*, 34:153-179.

Heath, S., (2007) Widening the gap: Pre-university gap years and the `economy of experience', *British Journal of Sociology of Education*, 28: 89-103.

Heinz, W. R., (2009) Structure and agency in transition research, *Journal of Education and Work, Special issue: Continuity and change in 40 years of school to work transitions*, 22: 391-404.

Helsingin Sanomat (2010a) Yli puolet suomalaisnuorista elää kädestä suuhun [Over half of Finnish young adults live from hand to mouth] 17 February, www.hs.fi/talous/artikkeli/Yli+puolet+suomalaisnuorista+elää+kädestä+suuhun/1135252979194

Helsingin Sanomat (2010b) Omin eväin, *Helsingin Sanomat*, 8 August.

Helsingin Sanomat [Finnish newspaper] (1999), Euro-tilastot [Euro Statistics], www.hs.fi 19 March, A 14.

Helve, H and Bynner, J., (eds.) (2007) *Youth and Social Capital*, London: the Tufnell Press.

Helve, H. and Bynner, J, (eds.) (1996) *Youth and Life Management*, Helsinki: Helsinki University Press.

Helve, H., (1993) *The World View of Young People. A Longitudinal Study of Finnish Youth Living in a Suburb of Metropolitan Helsinki*, Annales Academiae Scientiarum Fennicae, Ser. B, Vol. 267, Helsinki: Gummerus.

Helve, H., (1996) Values, world views and gender differences among young people, in Helve, H. and Bynner, J., (eds.) *Youth and Life Management. Research Perspectives*, Helsinki.

Helve, H., (2002) *Pitkittäistutkimus nuorisotutkimuksessa [Longitudinal studies in youth research]*, Finnish Youth Research Society, 21 November.

Helve, H., (2002). *Arvot, muutos ja nuoret (Values, Change and Youth)*, Helsinki: University of Helsinki Press.

Helve, H., (2007) Social capital and minority identity, in Helve, H., Bynner, J. (eds.) *Youth and Social Capital*, England and USA: the Tufnell Press.

Helve, H., (2012) Transitions and shifts in work attitudes, values and future orientations of young Finns, in Hahn-Bleibtreu, M., and Molgat, M., (eds) *Youth Policy in a Changing World: From Theory to Practice*, (pp.135-158), Germany: Budrich.

Helve, H., Lähteenmaa, J., Päivärinta, T., Päällysaho, K.,Saarikoski, H., Virtanen, P., (1997) *Nuorten elämänpolkuja lama-Suomessa. (Life paths of young people living in recession-hit Finland)*, Helsinki: Youth Research Society.

Henderson, S., Holland, J. McGrellis, S, Sharpe, S., Thomson, R., (2007) *Inventing Adulthoods: a biographical approach to youth transitions*, London: Sage.

Henderson, S., Holland, J. McGrellis, S, Sharpe, S., Thomson, R., (2012) Storying Qualitative Longitudinal Research: Sequence, Voice and Motif, in Timescapes Special Issue of *Qualitative Research*, Vol 12.

Hendry, L. B. and Kloep, M., (2007a) Conceptualizing emerging adulthood: Inspecting the Emperor's new clothes? *Child Development Perspectives, 1*(2): 74-79.

Hendry, L. B. and Kloep, M., (2007b) Redressing the Emperor!-Rejoinder to Arnett, *Child Development Perspectives, 1*(2): 83-85.

Hirschman, A., (1970) *Exit, Voice, and Loyalty: Responses to Decline in Firms, Organizations, and States,* Cambridge, MA.: Harvard University Press.

Hofer, S. M., and Piccinin, A. M., (2009) Integrative Data Analysis Through Coordination of Measurement and Analysis Protocol Across Independent Longitudinal Studies, *Psychological Methods,* 14(2): 150-164. doi: 10.1037/a0015566

Holland, J. and Thomson, R. (2009), Gaining Perspective on Choice and Fate: Revisiting critical moments, *European Societies,* 11(3), 451-469 [Special Issue: At a crossroads: Contemporary lives between fate and choice, eds by Anna Bagnoli and Kaisa Ketokivi].

Holland, J., (2007) Fragmented youth: social capital in biographical context in young people's lives, in Edwards, R., Franklin, J. and Holland, J., (eds) *Assessing Social Capital: Concept, Policy and Practice,* Newcastle: Cambridge Scholars Publishing.

Holland, J., (2007) Inventing adulthoods: Making the most of what you have, in Helve, H. and Bynner, J., (eds)*Youth and Social Capital,* London: the Tufnell Press.

Holland, J., (2009) Change and continuity in young people's lives: biography in context, in Mancini, J.A. and Roberto, K.A., (eds) *Pathways of Human Development: Explorations of Change,* Lanham MA: Lexington Books.

Honda, Y. Naitō, A. and Gotō, K., (2006) 'NEET' tte iuna! (Don't call me a NEET!), Tokyo: Kōbunsha.

Honda, Y., (2009) *Kyōiku no shokugyō teki igi: Wakamono, gakkō, shakai wo tsunagu (The significance of education in employment: Linking youth, school and society),* Tokyo: Chikuma Shobō.

Honda, Y., (ed.) (2010) *Rōdō saishin 1: Tenkanki no rōdō to 'nōryoku' (Labour review 1: Work and competence in a transitional era),* Tokyo: Ōtsuki Shoten.

Horgan, G., (2007) *The impact of poverty on young children's experience of school,* York: Joseph Rowntree Foundation.

Hossain, N., Eyben, R. et al (2009) Accounts of Crisis: Poor People's Experiences of the Food, Fuel and Financial Crises in Five Countries, Brighton: IDS.

Hughey, M. W., (2008) Tripping the White fantastic: Navigating the politics of dislocation and bicultural authenticity in academe, in Rutledge, D. M., (Ed.) *Biculturalism, Self Identity and Societal Transformation (Research in Race and Ethnic Relations, Volume 15)* (pp.131-158), Bingley, UK: Emerald Group Publishing Limited.

Iacovou, M., (2002) Regional differences in the transition to adulthood, *Annals of the American Academy of Political and Social Science,* 580: 40-69.

Innanen, H., Juvakka, A. and Salmela-Aro, K., (2009) The role of achievement and social strategies and of work-life areas in job burnout, in Schwartzhoffer, R.V. (ed.), *Psychology of Burnout: Predictors and Coping Mechanisms,* New York: Nova Science Publishers.

Institute of Public Policy Research (IPPR) (2010) *Youth Unemployment and the Recession,* London: IPPR

Integrative Data Analysis: The Simultaneous Analysis of Multiple Data Sets. *Psychological Methods,* 14(2): 81-100

International Labour Organisation (ILO), (2006) *Global employment trends for youth*, Geneva: Author.

International Labour Organisation (ILO), (2011a) *Global Employment Trends: 2011* www. ilo.org/wcmsp5/groups/public/@dgreports/@dcomm/@publ/documents/publication/wcms_150443.pdf, [Accessed 21 May 2012].

International Labour Organisation (ILO), (2011b) *Global Employment Trends for Youth: 2011 Update*, Geneva: International Labour Organisation.

Irwin, S., (1995) *Rights of Passage: Social Change and the Transition from Youth to Adulhood*, London: UCL Press.

Irwin, S., (2005) *Reshaping Social Life*, London: Routledge.

Iwata, K. Habuchi, I. Kikuchi, H. and Tomabechi, S., (eds.) (2006) *Wakamono no communication survival: Shinmitsusa no yukue (Communication survival for young people: Where has intimacy gone?)*, Tokyo: Kōseisha Kōseikaku.

Janion M. and Rosiek S (eds.) (1984). *Osoby Transgresje*, Gdańsk: Wydawnictwo Morskie.

Joas, H., (1996) *The creativity of action*, Chicago, Ill: Univeristy of Chicago Press.

Jobless youth a 'ticking time bomb' for SA, Vavi warns', *Business Day* 07/0/2011.

Johnston, L., O'Malley, P., Bachman, J., and Schulenberg, J., (2010) *Monitoring the Future national survey results on drug use, 1975-2009. Volume I: Secondary school students* (NIH Publication No. 10-7584). Bethesda, MD: National Institute on Drug Abuse.

Jones, A., (2004) *Review of gap year provision*, London: DfES Publications, rgs.org/NR/rdonlyres/3147D7BD-5359-4387-BAC9-CEC80EC7D85F/0/AndrewJonesforDfES2003.pdf [Accessed 15 January 2012].

Jones, G. and Wallace, C., (1992) *Youth, Family, Youth and Citizenship*, Buckingham: Open University Press.

Jones, G., (2005) *Chinking and Behaviour of Young Adults 16-25: A Review*, London: Social Exclusion Unit, Office of Deputy Prime Minister.

Jones, G., (2009) *Youth*, Cambridge: Polity Press.

Jordan, W. D., (1978) Searching for adulthood in America, in Erikson, E. H., (ed.) *Adulthood* (pp. 189-199), New York: Norton.

Kamppinen, M., (2000) The transformation of time in the information society, *Foresight*, 2(2):159-162.

Kariya, T., (1991) *Gakkō, shokugyō, senbatsu no shakaigaku: Kōsotsu shūshoku no nihonteki mechanism (A sociology of school, employment and screening: Japanese mechanisms of high school recruitment)*, Tokyo Daigaku Shuppankai.

Karoly, L. A., (2009) The future at work: Labor-market realities and the transition to adulthood. in Schoon, I. and Silbereisen, K. R., (eds) *Transitions from school to work. Globalization, individualization, and patterns of diversity*, New York: Cambridge University Press.

Karvonen, S., (2006) *Onko sukupuolella väliä? Hyvinvointi, terveys, pojat ja tytöt. Nuorten elinolot-vuosikirja [Does sex matter? Well-being, health, boys and girls. Yearbook of the circumstances of the young]*, Helsinki: Nuorisotutkimusverkosto, Nuorisotutkimusseura, julkaisuja 71, Nuorisoasiain neuvottelukunta, julkaisuja 35, Sosiaali-ja terveysalan tutkimus-ja kehittämiskeskus.

Katagiri, S., (2009) *Fuantei shakai no naka no wakamonotachi: Daigakusei chōsa kara miru kono nijūnen, (Youth in an unstable world: Perspectives from a university student survey over 20 years)*, Kyoto: Sekai Shisōsha.

Kelsey, J., (1999) Life in the economic test-tube: New Zealand's 'experiment' a colossal failure, *Peace Movement Aotearoa Newsletter 1999*, www.converge.org.nz/pma/apfail. htm [Accessed 1 June 2012].

Kersh, N., Waite, E. and Evans, K., (2012) The Spatial Dimensions of Workplace Learning: Acquiring Literacy and Numeracy Skills within the Workplace,in R. Brooks, A. Fuller and J. Waters, (eds) *Changing Spaces of Education: New Perspectives on the Nature of Learning*, London: Routledge.

Kildal, N., (2001) *Workfare tendencies in Scandinavian welfare policies*, Geneva: International labour office, February 2001.

Kirves, J., Kivimäki, V., Näre, S. and Siltala, J., (2010) Sodassa kasvaneiden tunneperintö, in Näre, S. and Kirves, J. (eds.) *Sodan kasvattamat*, Helsinki: WSOY.

Kiuru, N., Aunola, K., Nurmi, J.-E., Leskinen, E. and Salmela-Aro, K., (2008) Peer group influence and selection in adolescents' school burnout: A longitudinal Study, *Merrill Palmer Quarterly*, 54: 23-55.

Kiuru, N., Leskinen, E., Nurmi, J. & Salmela-Aro, K., (2011) Depressive symptoms during adolescence: Do learning difficulties matter? *International Journal of Behavioral Development*, 35 (4): 298-306.

Kojo, M., (2010) Laajentunut nykyisyys: nuorten tulevaisuuteen suuntautuminen työn marginaalissa, *Nuorisotutkimus* 2/2010.

Konstantinovskiy D. L., (2000) *Youth in 90s self-actualisation in the new reality (in Russian)*, Moscow: Nauka.

Kortteinen, M. and Tuomikoski, M., (1998) *Työtön: tutkimus pitkäaikaistyöttömien selviytymisestä*, sarja: Hanki ja jää, Helsinki: Tammi.

Kortteinen, M., (1997) *Kunnian kenttä*, Tampere: Hanki ja Jää.

Kosugi, R. (ed.), (2005) *Freeters and NEETs*, Tokyo: Keisō Shobō.

Kosugi, R., (2010) *Wakamono to shoki carrer: 'Hi-tenkei' karano shuppatsu no tame ni (Youth and early careers: Departing from the atypical)*, Tokyo: Keisō Shobō.

Kovacheva, S., (2000) *Sinking or Swimming in the Waves of Transformation? Young People and Social Protection in Central and Eastern Europe*. Brussels: The European Youth Forum.

Kovacheva, S., (2001) *Flexibilisation of Youth Transitions in Central and Eastern Europe*, www.hwf.at/downloads/open_area/publications/forum_publications_05.pdf.

Kovalainen, A., (2004) Rethinking the Revival of Social Capital and Trust in Social Theory: Possibilities for Feminist Analyses of Social Capital and Trust, in Marshall, B.L. and Witz, A., (eds) *Engendering the Social: Feminist Encounters with Social Theory*, Maidenhead and New York: Open University Press.

Kozielski J., (2002) *Transgresja i kultura*. Warszawa: Wydawnictwo Akademickie Żak.

Kraack, A., and Kenway, J., (2002) Place, Time and Stigmatised Youthful Identities: bad boys in paradise, *Journal of Rural Studies*, 18: 145-155.

Kral, I., (2010) *Plugged In: Remote Australian Indigenous Youth and Digital Culture*, CAEPR Working Paper No 69/2010, Canberra: Centre for Aboriginal Economic Policy Research.

Krieger, N., Williams, D. R., and Moss, N. E., (1997) Measuring social class in US public health research: Concepts, methodologies, and guidelines, *Annual Review of Public Health*, 18(1): 341-378.

Kumazawa, M., (2006) *Wakamono ga hataraku toki: 'Tsukaisuterare' mo 'moetsuki' mo sezu (When young people work: Neither disposable nor burned out)*, Kyoto: Minerva Shobō.

Kuure, T., (2001) *Aikuistumisen pullonkaulat. Nuorten elinolot-vuosikirja [Bottlenecks of growing up. Yearbook of the circumstances of the young]*, Helsinki: Nuorisotutkimusverkosto, Nuorisotutkimusseura, julkaisuja 16, Nuorisoasiain neuvottelukunta, julkaisuja 19 ja Sosiaali-ja terveysalan tutkimus-ja kehittämiskeskus.

Kuure, T., (2006) Tuotettua epävarmuutta, in Hoikkala, T. and Salasuo, M., (eds.), *Prekaariruoska? Portfoliopolvi, perustulo ja kansalaistoiminta*, Nuorisotutkimusverkosto, Nuorisotutkimusseura, verkkojulkaisusarja, www. nuorisotutkimusseura.fi/julkaisuja/prekaariruoska.pdf [Accessed 21 May 2011].

Labour Force Statistics, (1997). September 3. 1997. Helsinki: Statistics Finland.

Lähteenmaa, J. and Kojo, M., (2010) not published paper held in *WORK-seminar of Academy of Finland*, spring 2010, Helsinki.

Landowski, E. (1991) *Passions sans nom: essais de socio-semiotique III*, Paris: PUF.

Langelaan, S., Bakker, A.B., van Doornen, L.J.P. and Schaufeli, W.B., (2006), Burnout and work engagement: do individual differences make a difference? *Personality and Individual Differences*, 40 [online].

Langston, C. A. and Cantor, N., (1989), Social anxiety and social constraint: When 'making friends' is hard, *Journal of Personality and Social Psychology*, 56(4): 649-661.

Lawler, S., (2008) *Identity: Sociological perspectives*, Cambridge: Polity Press.

Lawler. E. E., (2005) Creating high performance organizations, *Asia Pacific Journal of Human Resources* [online], 43(1).

Lazarsfeld, P., and Henry, N., (1968), *Latent structure analysis*, Boston: Houghton Mifflin.

Leccardi, C., (2006) Uncertainty, Temporality and Biographies in the New Century, in Leccardi, C., and Ruspini, E., (eds.) *A new youth?: young people, generations and family life*, Ashgate.

Lee, R., and Ashforth, B., (1993) A further examination of managerial burnout: Toward an integrated model, *Journal of Organizational Behavior*, 14: 3-20.

Leete, R. and Fox, J., (1977) Registrar General's social classes: origins and users, *Population Trends*, 8: 1-7.

Leiter M.P and Maslach C., (2004) Areas of work life: a structured approach to organizational predictors of job burnout, in Perrewe, P.L. and Ganster, D.C., (eds.) *Research in Occupational Stress and Well-Being* [online], Oxford: JAI Press/Elsevier Sciences Ltd. cord.acadiau.ca/tl_files/sites/cord/resources/Documents/21.pdf [Accessed 26 January].

Leiter, M. P. and Maslach, C., (2000) *Preventing burnout and building engagement. A complete program for organizational renewal*, San Francisco: Jossey-Bass.

Leiter, M. P., (1991) Coping patterns as predictors of burnout: the function of control and escapist coping patterns, *Journal of Organizational Behaviour*, 12.

Leiter, M. P., Gascón, S. and Martinez-Jarreta, B., (2009) Value congruence, burnout, and culture: similarities and construct of Canadian and Spanish nurses, in Antoniu, A-S., Cooper, C.L. Chrousos, G.P., Spielberger, C.D. and Eysenck, M.W., (eds.) *Handbook of managerial behaviour and occupational health*, UK: Edward Elger Publishers Ltd.

Leiter, M. P., Gascón, S. and Martinez-Jarreta, B., (2010) Making sense of work life: a structural model of burnout, *Journal of Applied Social Psychology* [online], 40(1), cord.acadiau.ca/tl_files/sites/cord/resources/Documents/23.pdf [Accessed 26 January].

Leiter, M., (1989) Conceptual implications of two models of burnout: A response to Golembiewski, *Group and Organizational Studies*, 14: 15-22, 394.

Leiter, M.P. and Maslach, C., (1999) Six Areas of worklife: a model of the organizational context of burnout, *Journal of Health and Human Resources Administration* [online],

21, cord.acadiau.ca/tl_files/sites/cord/resources/Documents/SixAreasOfWorklife1999. pdf [Accessed 28 January].

Leiter, M.P., Price, S.L. and Spence Laschinger, H., (2010) Generational differences in distress, attitudes and incivility among nurses, *Journal of Nursing Management* [online].

Lerner, R. M. and Kauffman, M. B., (1985) The concept of development in contextualism, *Developmental Review*, 5: 309-333.

Lerner, R., (2002) *Concepts and theories of human development*, 3rd ed., Mahwah, NJ: Lawrence Erlbaum.

Lindberg, M., (2008) *Diverse Routes from School, via Higher Education, to Employment. A Comparison of Nine European Countries*, Turku: Turun yliopisto, Koulutussosiologian tutkimuskeskuksen raportti 70.

Lubbe G., (1994) In Step With the Times. On the Reduction of Our Stay in the Present (in Russian). *Voprosy filosofii*, 4.

Luyckx, K., De Witte, H. and Goossens, L., (2011) Perceived instability in emerging adulthood: The protective role of identity capital, *Journal of Applied Developmental Psychology*, 32(3): 137-145.

Määttä, S., (2007) *Achievement strategies in adolescence and young adulthood* [online], Jyväskylä studies in Education, Psychology and Social research, 324. Jyväskylä University Printing House, jyx.jyu.fi/dspace/bitstream/handle/123456789/13319/9789513930455. pdf?sequence=1[Accessed 26 January].

Machacek, L., (1998) *Youth in the Processes of Transition and Modernisation in Slovakia*, Bratislava: SAS.

Macmillan, R., (2005) The structure of the life course: Classic issues and current controversies, in Macmillan, R., (ed.) *The Structure of the Life Course: Standardized? Individualized? Differentiated?* (pp. 3-26). Amsterdam: Elsevier.

Macmillan, R., and Copher, R., (2005) Families in the life course: Interdependency of roles, role configurations, and pathways, *Journal of Marriage and the Family*, 67(4): 858-879.

Macmillan, R., and Eliason, S., (2003) Characterizing the life course as role configurations and pathways: A latent structure approach, in Mortimer J. T. and Shanahan, M. J. (eds.) *Handbook of the life course* (pp. 529-554), New York: Plenum.

Maggs, J. L., Jager, J., Patrick, M. E., and Schulenberg, J., (2012) Social role patterning in early adulthood in the USA: Adolescent predictors and concurrent wellbing across four distinct configurations, *Journal of Longitudinal and Life Course Studies*, 3 (2): 190-210

Mäkikangas, A. and Kinnunen, U., (2003) Psychosocial work-stressors and well-being: self-esteem and optimism as moderators in a one-year longitudinal sample, *Personality and Individual Differences*, 35 [online].

Mäkikangas, A., (2007) *Personality, well-being and job resources* [online], From negative paradigm towards positive psychology, Jyväskylä studies in education, psychology and social research 320. Top of Form. Bottom of Form, jyx.jyu.fi/dspace/bitstream/handle/123456789/13334/9789513930110.pdf?sequence=1 [Accessed 26 January].

Makino, T., (2012) *Jiko keihatsu no jidai: 'Jiko' no bunkashakaigaku teki tankyū (The age of self-development: A cultural and sociological inquiry into 'self')*, Tokyo: Keisō Shobō.

Mannheim, K., (1972) *Essays on the sociology of knowledge*, London : Routledge & Kegan Paul, 1972.

Manninen, J. and Luukannel, S., (2006) *Maisterit ja kandidaatit työmarkkinoilla. Vuonna 2000. Helsingin yliopistossa alemman tai ylemmän korkeakoulututkinnon suorittaneiden sijoittuminen työmarkkinoille viisi vuotta tutkinnon suorittamisen jälkeen [University of Helsinki, university graduates in the labour market five years after graduation]*, Helsingin yliopisto: Koulutus-ja kehittämiskeskus Palmenia and Ura-ja rekrytointipalvelut.

Marais, Hein, (1993) The New Barbarians, quoted in Everatt D. (2004) 'Introduction' to *Creating a future: Youth policy for South Africa*, Johannesburg: Ravan press.

Marcia, J.E., (2002) Ego identity and personality disorders. *Journal of Personality Disorders*, 20: 577-596.

Marsh, C., (1986) Social class and occupation, in Burgess, R., (ed.) *Key variables in social investigation*, London: Routledge.

Marsh, H. W., Trautwein, U., Lüdtke, O., Köller, O., and Baumert, J., (2005) Academic self-concept, interest, grades, and standardized test scores: Reciprocal effects models of causal ordering, *Child Development*, 76: 397-416.

Martin, A. J., (2010), Should students have a gap year? Motivation and performance factors relevant to time out after completing school, *Journal of Educational Psychology*, 102: 561-576.

Martucelli, D., de Singly, F., (2009) *Le sociologies de l'individu*, Paris: Armand Colin.

Maslach, C. and Jackson, S.E., (1985) The role of sex and family variables in burnout, *Sex Roles* [online].

Maslach, C. and Leiter, M. P., (1997) *The truth about burnout: How organizations cause personal stress and what to do about it*, San Francisco: Jossey-Bass.

Maslach, C., (1993) Burnout: a multidimensional perspective, in Schaufeli, W. B., Maslach, C. and Mareks, T., (eds.) *Professional burnout: recent developments in theory and research*, Washington DC: Taylor and Francis.

Maslach, C., (2003) Job burnout: new directions in research and interventions, *Current directions in psychological science 12(5): 189-192*, [online].

Maslach, C., and Schaufeli, W. B. and Leiter, M. P., (2001) Job burnout, *Annual Review of Psycholog* [online].

Maslach, C., Jackson, S. E. and Leiter, M. P., (1996) *The Maslach burnout inventory (3rd ed.)*. Palo Alto, CA: Consulting Psychologists Press.

Maslach, C., Schaufeli, W., and Leiter, P., (2001) Job burnout: New directions in research and intervention, *Current Directions in Psychological Science*, 12: 189-192.

Massey, D., (1998) The spatial construction of youth cultures, in: Skelton, T. and Valentine, G., (eds) *Cool Places: Geographies of Youth Cultures*, London and New York: Routledge.

Masten, A., Desjardins, C. D., McCormick, C. M., Kuo, S. I. and Long, J. D., (2010) The significance of childhood competence and problems for adult success in work: A developmental cascade analysis, *Development and Psychopathology*, 22: 681-696.

McGrellis, S., (2005) Pure and bitter spaces: gender, identity and territory in Northern Irish youth transition, *Gender and Education*, 17(5): 515-529.

Mcknight, J.D., Glass, D.C., (1995) Perceptions of control, burnout, and depressive symptomatology: A replication and extension, *Journal of Consulting and Clinical Psychology*, 63: 490-494.

McNeish, W., and Loncle, P., (2003) State policy and youth unemployment in the EU: rights, responsibilities and lifelong learning, in López Blasco, A., McNeish, W. and Walther, A., (Eds.) *Young people and contradictions of inclusion: towards Integrated Transition Policies in Europe*. Bristol: Policy Press.

McQuaig, L. and Brook, N., (2010) *The trouble with billionaires*, Toronto: Viking Canada.

Merser, C., (1987) *'Grown-ups' A generation in search of adulthood*, New York: G. P. Putnam's Sons.

Merton, R. K., (1968, January 5) The Matthew effect in science, *Science*, 159: 56-63.

Miettinen, A., (2007) *Pätkätyön tulevaisuus?* E27, Helsinki: Väestöliitto, Väestöntutkimuslaitos.

Miles S., (2000) *Youth lifestyles in a changing world*, Buckingham: Philadelfia, University Press.

Ministry of Education and Culture (2012) *A development plan*, Reports of the Ministry of Education and Culture, Department for Education and Science Policy, Finland 2012:3. www.minedu.fi/export/sites/default/OPM/Julkaisut/2012/liitteet/okm03.pdf [Accessed 21 May 2012]

Ministry of Health, Labour and Welfare, (2010) *Survey on Employment* Trends. www.mhlw. go.jp/english/database/db-l/employment_trends_2010.html [Accessed 12 February, 2013].

Ministry of Human Resource Development (MHRD) (2010) *Selected Educational Statistics-School 2009-10*, Ministry of Human Resource Development official website mhrd. gov. in [Accessed 15 March 2012].

Ministry of Labour, (2006) *Industrial relations and labour legislation in Finland, Working Life Regulations*, 6/2006:33, Helsinki, www.tem.fi/files/18417/8015e_working_life_ relations.pdf [Accessed 10 June 2011].

Mintz, S., (1993) Life stages, in Cayton, M. K., Gorn, E. J., and Williams, P. W., (eds.) *Encyclopedia of American Social History Vol. III* (pp. 2011-2022), New York: Charles Scribner's Sons.

Miura, A. and Harada, Y., (2009) *Jōhōbyō: Naze wakamono wa yokubō wo sōshitsu shitanoka (Information disease: Why the youth have lost desire)*, Tokyo: Kadokawa Shoten.

Mizen, P., (2004). *The Changing State of Youth*. New York: Palgrave.

Modood, T., (2004) Capitals, Ethnic Identity and Educational Qualifications, *Cultural Trends*, 13(2):87-105.

Modood, T., (2007) *Multiculturalism*, Cambridge: Polity Press.

Moliner, C., Martinez-Tur, V., Peiro, J.M., Ramos, J. and Cropanzano, R., (2005) Relationships between organizational justice and burnout at the work-unit level, *International Journal of Stress Management*, 12(2): 99-116.

Mørch, S., (1995) Culture and the challenge of adaptation: Foreign youth in Denmark, *International Journal of Comparative Race and Ethnic Studies*, 2: 102-115.

Mori, S., (2000) *Jiko control no ori: Kanjō management shakai no genjitsu (The cage of self control: The reality of an emotional management society)*, Tokyo: Kōdansha.

Morrow, G.M., (2000) 'Dirty looks' and 'trampy places' in young people's accounts of community and neighbourhood: Implications for health inequalities, *Critical Public Health*, 10(2):141-152.

Morrow, V., (1999) Conceptualising social capital in relation to the well-being of children and young people: A critical review, *The Sociological Review*, 47(4):744-765.

Myllyniemi, S., (2004) *Nuorisobarometri 2004 [Youth Indicators 2004]*, in Wilska, T.-A., (ed.) *Oman elämänsä yrittäjät? [Entrepreneurial lives?]*, Helsinki: Nuorisotutkimusverkosto, Nuorisotutkimusseura, julkaisuja 44, Nuorisoasiain neuvottelukunta, julkaisuja 28, Opetusministeriö.

Myllyniemi, S., (2005) *Nuorisobarometri 2005 [Youth Indicators 2005]*, in Wilska, T.-A., (ed.) *Erilaiset ja samanlaiset*, Helsinki: Nuorisotutkimusverkosto, Nuorisotutkimusseura, julkaisuja 59, Nuorisoasiain neuvottelukunta, julkaisuja 31, Opetusministeriö.

Myllyniemi, S., (2009) Taidekohtia, *Nuorisobarometri 2009*. *(Youth Survey 2009)*, Nuorisotutkimusverkosto/Nuorisotutkimusseura, julkaisuja 97 (Youth Research Network / Youth Research Society). Helsinki: Yliopistopaino Oy.

Naidoo, J, (2011) The Coming 'Egyptian Moment' in South Africa, in *The Huffington Post* 17/3/2011.

Nairn, K., Higgins, J. and Sligo, J., (2012) *Children of Rogernomics: A neoliberal generation leaves school*, Dunedin: University of Otago Press.

Nairn, K., Panelli, R., and McCormack, J. (2003) Destabilising dualisms: Young people's experiences of rural and urban environments, *Childhood*, 19(1) pp. 9-42.

Neugarten, B. L. and Moore, J. W, (1968) The changing age-status system in Neugarten, B. L. (ed.) *Middle Age and Aging: A Reader in Social Psychology*, (pp. 5-21) Chicago: University of Chicago Press.

Nicolson G., (2011) Ring of Fire: Not so crazy a picture, in *Daily Maverick* 23/1/2012.

Nurmi, J-E, Salmela-Aro, K. and Haavisto T., (1995) The strategy and attribution questionnaire: psychometric properties, *European Journal of Psychological Assessment*, 11(2): 108-121.

Nurmi, J-E., Aunola, K., Salmela-Aro, K. and Lindroos, M., (2003) The role of success expectation and task-avoidance in academic performance and satisfaction: Three studies on antecedents, consequences and correlates, *Contemporary Educational Psychology*, 28(1), www.sciencedirect.com [Accessed 26 January].

Nurmi, J-E., Toivonen, S., Salmela-Aro, K. and Eronen, S., (1996) Optimistic, approach-oriented, and avoidance strategies in social situations: three studies on loneliness and peer relationships, *European Journal of Personality*, 10: 1-19.

Nurmi, J.-E., and Salmela-Aro, K., (1997) Social Strategies and Loneliness: a prospective study, *Personality and individual differences*[online].

Office for National Statistics, (2009) NOMIS official labour market statistics [online], www.nomisweb.co.uk [Accessed 26 August 2009].

Office for National Statistics, (2011) Labour market statistics bulletin: December 2011 [online], www.ons.gov.uk/ons/rel/lms/labour-market-statistics/december-2011/statistical-bulletin.html [Accessed 18 January 2013].

Office of Population Censuses and Surveys (OPCS) (1980) *Classification of occupations 1980*, London: Her Majesty's Stationery Office.

Onatsu-Arvilommi, T. and Nurmi, J-E., (2000) The role of task-avoidant and task-focused behaviors in the development of reading and mathematical skills during first school year: A cross-lagged longitudinal study, *Journal of educational psychology*, 92: 478-491.

Organisation for Economic Cooperation and Development (OECD), (1996) *Lifelong learning for all*. Paris: OECD.

Organisation for Economic Cooperation and Development (OECD), (2009a) *Jobs for Youth: Japan*, Paris: OECD Publishing.

Organisation for Economic Cooperation and Development (OECD), (2011a) *Employment Outlook 2011*, Retrieved from www.oecd.org/employment/outlook [Accessed 1 June 2012].

Organisation for Economic Cooperation and Development (OECD), (2011c) *Education at a Glance 2011*, Paris: OECD Publishing.

Organisation for Economic Cooperation and Development (OECD), (2011c) *Territorial Review of the Gauteng City-Region*, OECD, Paris.

Orr, D., Gwosc, C., Netz, N. (2011) Social and Economic Conditions of Student Life in Europe, *Eurostudent IV 2008–2011*. Bielefeld: W. Bertelsmann Verlag GmbH & Co. KG, ww2.sozialerhebung.at/Ergebnisse/PDF/EIV_Synopsis_of_Indicators.pdf

Orr, M., (1999) *Black Social Capital: the politics of school reform in Baltimore, 1986-1998*, Kansas: University of Kansas press.

Osgood, D. W., Ruth, G., Eccles, J. S., Jacobs, J. E., and Barber, B. L., (2005) Six paths to adulthood, in Settersten, R. A., Furstenberg, Jr., F. F. and Rumbaut, R. G., (eds.) *On the frontier of adulthood. Theory, research and public policy* (pp. 320-355). Chicago: The University of Chicago Press.

Otero-López, J.M., Santiago, J.M. and Bolaño, C.,C., (2008) An integrating approach to the study of burnout in university professors, *Psicothema* 20(4): 766-772, www. psicothema.com/pdf/3553.pdf [Accessed 26 January].

Ousley, H., (2001) *Community pride, not prejudice: Making diversity work in Bradford*, Bradford: Bradford Vision.

Owen, D., (2006) Demographic Profiles and Social Cohesion of Minority Ethnic Communities in England and Wales, Special Issue: Ethnicity and Social Capital, *Journal of Community, Work and Family*, 9(3): 251-272.

Paakkunainen, K. and Aaltojärvi, P. (eds.) (1995) *Nuorten työpaja - sosiaalinen peli, palkkatyö vai varasto?* Nuorisotutkimusseuran tutkimus: 2, Helsinki: Nuorisotutkimusseura.

Paakkunainen, K., (1997) Political scepticism and political groupings among unemployed youth: comparison between Finland and Germany, in Helve, H. and Bynner, J., (eds.) *Youth and Life management*, Helsinki: Univerisy of Helsinki Press.

Paakkunainen, K., Aaltojärvi, P. (eds.) (1995) Nuorten työpaja - sosiaalinen peli, palkkatyö vai varasto? Nuorisotutkimusseuran tutkimus: 2, Helsinki: NuorisotutkimusseuraΩ

Päällysaho, K. (1997): Nuorenako yrittäjäksi? Selvitys helsinkiläisnuorten yrittäjyyden alkutaipaleesta, in Helve, H., Lähteenmaa, J., Päivärinta, T., Päällysaho, K., Saarikoski, H., Virtanen, P. (eds): *Nuorten elämänpolkuja lama-Suomessa*, Nuorisotutkimusseuran julkaisuja 3/97, Helsinki: Nuorisotutkimusseura.

Palanko-Laaka, K., (2005) *Määräaikaisen työn yleisyys, käytön lainmukaisuus ja lainsäädännön kehittämistarpeet*, Helsinki: Työministeriö, työhallinnon julkaisu 359.

Parekh, B., (2000) *The future of multi-cultural Britain*, London: Runnymede Trust.

Park, C.L. and Folkman, S., (1997) Meaning in the context of stress and coping, *General Review of Psychology*, 1(2): 115-144.

Parker, P., and Salmela-Aro, K., (2011) Developmental processes in school burnout: A comparison of major developmental models, *Learning and Individual Differences*, 21: 244-248.

Pines, A. M., Aronson, E., and Kafry, D., (1981) *Burnout: From tedium to personal growth*, New York: Free Press.

Platt, L., (2005) The Intergenerational Mobility of Minority Ethnic Groups, *Sociology*, 39(3): 445-461.

Plewis, I., Calderwood, L., Hawkes, D., and Nathan, G., (2004) *National Child Development Study and 1970 British Cohort Study, Technical Report: Changes in the NCDS and BCS70 populations and samples over time*, London: Institute of Education, Centre for Longitudinal Studies.

Pohl, A., and Walther, A., (2007) Activating the disadvantaged. Variations in addressing youth transitions across Europe, *International Journal of Lifelong Education*, 26(5):533-553.

Power, A, and Tunstall, R., (1997) *Riots and Violent Disturbances in Thirteen Areas of Britain*, Joseph Rowntree Trust, Social Policy Research Findings (116), London.

Power, C., and Elliott, J., (2006). Cohort Profile: 1958 British birth cohort (National Child Development Study), *International Journal of Epidemiology*, 35: 34-41.

Powers, S. I., Hauser, S. T. and Kilner, L. A., (1989) Adolescent mental health, *AmericanPsychologist*, 44: 200-208.

Price, L. and Spence, S.H., (1994) Burnout symptoms amongst drug and alcohol service employees: gender differences in the interaction between work and home stressors, *Anxiety, Stress and Coping*, 7(1): 67-84.

Pulkkinen, L. 2006, The Jyväskylä Longitudinal Study of Personality and Social Development in L. Pulkkinen, J. Kaprio & R.J. Rose, (eds) *Socioemotional development and health from adolescence to adulthood*, New York: Cambridge University Press, pp. 29-55.

Pulkkinen, L. and Kokko, K., (2010) *Keski-ikä elämänvaiheena [Middle-age as a stage of life]*, Jyväskylä: Jyväskylän yliopisto.

Purvanova, R.K. and Muros, J.P., (2010) Gender differences in burnout: A meta-analysis, *Journal of Vocational Behavior* [online], 77: 168-185. www.sciencedirect.com [Accessed 26 January].

Putnam, R., (2000) *Bowling alone: The collapse and revival of American community*, New York: Simon and Schuster.

Quintini, G. and Martin, S., (2006) *Starting well or losing their way? The position of youth in the labour market in OECD countries*, OECD, Social, Employment and Migration Working Papers n°39.

Raffo, C. and Reeves, M., (2000) Youth transitions and social exclusion: Developments in social capital theory, *Journal of Youth Studies*, 3(2): 147-166.

Räikkönen, E., Kokko, K., and Pulkkinen, L., (2012) Patterns of adult roles, their antecedents and psychosocial wellbeing correlates among Finns born in 1959, *Journal of Longitudinal and Life Course Studies*, 3 (2): 211-227.

Rea, D., and Callister, P., (2009) *The nature of Young People's Transitions in NZ*, Institute of Policy Studies Working Paper 09/10: Wellington: Victoria University of Wellington

Reder, S., (2009) The Development of Literacy and Numeracy in Adult Life, in Reder, S. and Bynner, J., (eds) *Tracking Adult Literacy and Numeracy Skills: Findings from Longitudinal Research*, London: Routledge.

Reifman, A., Colwell, M. J. and Arnett, J. J., (2007) Emerging adulthood: Theory, assessment and application, *Journal of Youth Development*, 2(1), *Review of Psychology*, 53: 109-132.

Reynolds, T. and Briggs, B., (2008) *Rights and Wrongs: An Evaluation of the RAW Leadership Programmes*, London: Involve.

Reynolds, T. and Miah, N., (2007) *Black Asian and Minority Ethnic Employment Skills*, London: Borough of Lambeth.

Reynolds, T., (2004) Families, Social Capital and Caribbean Young People's Diasporic Identities, Families and Social Capital, *ESRC Research Group, Working Paper Series, No 11*, London South Bank University.

Reynolds, T., (2006a) Bonding Social capital within the Caribbean Family and Community, *Community, Work and Family*, 9(3): 273-290.

Reynolds, T., (2006b) Caribbean Young People, Family Relationships and Social Capital, *Ethnic and Racial Studies*, 29(6): 1087-1103.

Richards, M. and Sacker, A., (2003) Lifetime antecedents of cognitive reserve. *Journal of Clinical and Experimental Psychology*, 25: 614-24.

Richards, M., Power, C., and Sacker, A., (2009) Paths to literacy and numeracy problems: evidence from two British birth cohorts, *Journal of Epidemiology and Community Health*, 63: 239-44.

Richer, S., Blanchard, C. and Vallerand, R. J., (2002) A motivational model of work turnover, *Journal of Applied Social Psychology*, 32(10), onlinelibrary.wiley.com [Accessed 26 January].

Rifkin, J., (1995) *The end of work*, New York: G.P. Putman's Sons.

Roberts K, Tarkhnishvili L, Voskanyan A and Tholen J., (2005) Waiting for the market: young adults in Telavi and Vanadzor, *Journal of Youth Studies*, 8(3): 313-330.

Roberts, K. and Fagan, C. (1999) Old and New Routes into the Labour Markets in Ex-communist Countries, *Journal of Youth Studies*, 2(2).

Roberts, K., (2003) Problems and Priorities for the Sociology of Youth in Bennett, A., Cieslik, M. and Miles, S. (eds.) *Researching Youth*, Basingstoke: Palgrave.

Roberts, K., Clark, S. C. and Wallace, C., (1994) Flexibility and Individualisation: A Comparison of Transitions into Employment in England and Germany, *Sociology*, 20: 31-54.

Rosa, N., (2005) The speed of global flows and the place of democratic politics, *New Political Science*, 27(4), 445-459.

Rose, N., (1999) *Governing the soul. The shaping of the private self*, London: Free association books.

Ross, A., Schoon, I., Martin, P., and Sacker, A., (2009) Family and Nonfamily Role Configurations in Two British Cohorts, *Journal of Marriage and the Family*, 71(1): 1-14. onlinelibrary.wiley.com

Runnymede Trust, (2007) *School Choice and Ethnic Segregation: Educational Decision-making among Black and Minority Ethnic Parents*, London: The Runnymede Trust.

Rutter, M., Tizard, J., and Whitmore, K., (1970) *Education, health and behaviour*, London:

Ryan, J. and Sackrey, C., (1996) *Strangers in paradise: Academics from the working class*, Boston: South End Press.

Ryan, L., Sales, R., Tilki, S. and Siara, S., (2008) Social networks, social support and social capital: Polish migrants in London, *Sociology*, 42(4): 672-690.

Ryan, R. M., and Deci, E. L. (2001) To be happy or to be self-fulfilled: A review of research on hedonic and eudaimonic well-being, *Annual Review of Psychology*, 52; 141-166.

Saarela, P., (2002) *Nuorisobarometri 2002 [Youth Indicators 2002]*. Helsinki: Nuorisoasiain neuvottelukunta, julkaisuja 24.

Saarenmaa, K., Saari, K. and Virtanen V., (2010) *Opiskelijatutkimus 2010. Korkeakouluopiskelijoiden toimeentulo ja opiskelu (Student Survey 2010. University students living and studying)*, Opetus-ja kulttuuriministeriön julkaisuja 2010:18. Helsinki: Yliopistopaino / Universitetstryckeriet.

Sacker, A., and Cable, N., (2010) Transitions to adulthood and psychological distress in young adults born 12 years apart: constraints on and resources for development, *Psychological Medicine*, 40(2): 301-313.

Salmela-Aro, K. & Upadyaya, K., (2012) Schoolwork engagement inventory. Energy, dedication and absorption (EDA), *European Journal of Psychological Assessment*, 28(1): 60-67.

Salmela-Aro, K. and Helve, H., (2007) Emerging adulthood in Finland. In Arnett, J. (ed.) *Routledge international encyclopedia of adolescence*, New York, New York: Routledge, Taylor and Francis Group.

Salmela-Aro, K. and Nurmi, J.-E., (2005) Motivaatio elämänkaaren siirtymissä, in Salmela-Aro, K. and Nurmi, J.-E., (eds.) *Mikä meitä liikuttaa. Modernin motivaatiopsykologian perusteet,* Jyväskylä, Finland: PS-kustannus.

Salmela-Aro, K. and Nurmi, J.-E., (2007) Self-esteem during university studies predict career 10 years later, *Journal of Vocational Behavior,* 70, www.sciencedirect.com [Accessed 26 January].

Salmela-Aro, K. and Tynkkynen, L., (2012) Gendered pathways in school burnout among adolescents, *Journal of Adolescence* 35(4): 929–939.

Salmela-Aro, K., (2009) Personal goals and well-being during critical life transitions: The four C's-channeling, choice, co-agency and compensation, *Advances in Life Course Research,* 14: 63-73.

Salmela-Aro, K., (2011) Stages of Adolescence, in Brown, B. and Prinstein, M., (eds) *Encyclopedia of Adolescence,* Elsevier.

Salmela-Aro, K., Ek, E., and Chen, M., (2012) *Mapping pathways to adulthood in Finland,* Advances in Life Course Research, 16(1): 25-41

Salmela-Aro, K., Kiuru, N., and Nurmi, J.-E., (2008) The role of educational track in adolescents' school burnout: A longitudinal study, *British Journal of Educational Psychology,* 78: 663-689.

Salmela-Aro, K., Kiuru, N., Leskinen, E. and Nurmi, J. E., (2009) School burnout inventory (SBI), reliability and validity, *European Journal of Psychological Assessment,* 25 (1): 48-57.

Salmela-Aro, K., Kiuru, N., Nurmi, J.-E. and Eerola, M., (2011) Mapping pathways to adulthood among Finnish university students: Sequences, patterns, variations in family-and work-related roles, *Advances in Life Course Research,* 16: 25-41.

Salmela-Aro, K., Savolainen, H., and Holopainen, L., (2009) Depressive symptoms and school burnout during adolescence: Evidence from two cross-lagged longitudinal studies, *Journal of Youth and Adolescence,* 38(10): 1316-1327.

Salmela-Aro, K., Tolvanen, A. and Nurmi, J.-E., (2009) Achievement strategies during university studies predict early career burnout and engagement, *Journal of Vocational Behavior,* 75(2), www.helsinki.fi/collegium/english/staff/Salmela-Aro/achstrjvb.pdf [Accessed 26 January].

Salmela-Aro, K., Tolvanen, A. and Nurmi, J.-E., (2011) Social strategies during university studies predict early career work burnout and engagement: 18-year longitudinal study, *Journal of Vocational Behavior,* 79(1), www.sciencedirect.com [Accessed 26 January].

Sandefur, G. D., Eggerling-Boeck, J., and Park, H., (2005) Off to a good start? Postsecondary Education and early adult life, in Settersten, R. A., Furstenberg, Jr., F. F. and Rumbaut, R. G. (eds.) *On the frontier of adulthood. Theory, research and public policy* (pp. 356-395), Chicago: The University of Chicago Press.

Savicki, V., (2002) *Burnout across thirteen cultures: stress, and coping in child and youth care workers,* Westport, CT: Praeger.

Schaefer-McDaniel, N.J., (2004) Conceptualizing social capital among young people: Toward a new theory, *Children, Youth and Environments,* 14(1): 140-150.

Schaufeli, W. B., and Enzmann, D., (1998) *The burnout companion to study and practice: A critical analysis (Issues in Occupational Health),* London: Taylor and Francis.

Schaufeli, W. B., Martinez, I., Pinto, A. M., Salanova, M., and Bakker, A., (2002) Burnout and engagement in university students: A cross-national study, *Journal of Cross-Cultural Psychology,* 33(5): 464-481.

Schaufeli, W.B. and Bakker, A.B., (2004) Job demands, job resources, and relationship with burnout and engagement: a multi-sample study, *Journal of Organizational Behavior* [online], 25(3), igitur-archive.library.uu.nl/fss/2006-0807-200738/schaufeli_04_jobdemands.pdf [Accessed 26 January].

Schaufeli, W.B. and Enzmann, D., (1998) *The burnout companion to study and practice: A critical analysis,* London: Taylor and Francis.

Schaufeli, W.B., Leiter, M.P., Maslach, C. and Jackson, S. E., (1996) Maslach Burnout Inventory-General Survey (MBI-GS), in Maslach, C., Jackson, S. E. and Leiter, M. P., (eds.) *MBI Manual* (3rd ed.), Palo Alto, CA: Consulting Psychologists Press.

Scheier, M.F., Carver, C.S. and Bridges, M.W., (2001) Optimism, pessimism, and psychological well-being, in Chang, E.C. (ed.) *Optimism and pessimism. Implications for theory, research, and practice,* Washington, DC: American Psychological Association.

Schnapper, D. (1981) *L'epreuve du chomage,* Paris: Gallimard.

Schoon, I. and Polek, E., (2011), Pathways to economic well-being among teenage mothers in Great Britain. *European Psychologist* 16(1), 11-20.

Schoon, I. and Silbereisen, K. R., (eds) (2009) *Transitions from School to Work: Globalisation, Individualisation and Patterns of Diversity,* New York: Cambridge University Press.

Schoon, I., (2008) A transgenerational model of status attainment: the potential mediating role of school motivation and education, *National Institute of Economic Research,* 205: 72-82.

Schoon, I., (2010a) Childhood cognitive ability and adult academic attainment: Evidence from three British cohort studies, *Journal of Longitudinal and Life Course Studies,* 1(3): 241-258. www.llcsjournal.org.

Schoon, I., (2010b) Planning for the future: Changing education expectations in three British cohorts, *Social Historical Research,* 35(2): 99-119.

Schoon, I., and Silbereisen, K. R., (eds.). (2009), *Transitions from School to Work: Globalisation, Individualisation, and Patterns of Diversity,* New York Cambridge University Press.

Schoon, I., Bynner, J., Joshi, H., Parsons, S., Wiggins, R. D., and Sacker, A., (2002) The influence of context, timing, and duration of risk experiences for the passage from childhood to midadulthood, *Child Development,* 73(5): 1486-1504.

Schoon, I., Kneale, D., Jager, J., and Chen, M., (2012) Becoming adults in Britain: What is a successful transition? Changing transition experiences and associated levels of wellbeing, *Journal of Longitudinal and Life Course Studies,* 3 (2): 173-189

Schoon, I., Martin, P., and Ross, A., (2007) Career transitions in times of social change, His and her story, *Journal of Vocational Behaviour,* 70: 78-96.

Schoon, I., Ross, A., and Martin, P., (2009) Sequences, patterns, and variations in the assumption of work and family related roles. Evidence from two British Birth Cohorts, in Schoon, I. and Silbereisen, K. R., (eds.) *Transitions from School to Work: Globalisation, Individualisation, and Patterns of Diversity* (pp. 219-242), New York: Cambridge University Press.

Schulenberg, J. and Schoon, I., (2012). The transition to adulthood across time and place. Introduction to special section, *Longitudinal and Life Course Studies,* 3(2), 164-172.

Schulenberg, J. E., and Maggs, J. L., (2002). A developmental perspective on alcohol use and heavy drinking during adolescence and the transition to young adulthood, *Journal of Studies on Alcohol,* 54-70.

Schulenberg, J. E., Bryant, A. L., and O'Malley, P. M., (2004) Taking hold of some kind of life: How developmental tasks relate to trajectories of well-being during the transition to adulthood, *Development and Psychopathology*, 16(4): 1119-1140.

Schwartz, S. J., Côté, J. E., and Arnett, J. J., (2005) Identity and agency in emerging adulthood: Two developmental routes in the individualization process, *Youth and Society*, 37: 201-229.

Schwartz, S. J., Zamboanga, B. L., Weisskirch, R. S., and Rodriguez, L., (2009) The relationships of personal and ethnic identity exploration to indices of adaptive and maladaptive psychosocial functioning, *International Journal of Behavioral Development*, 33(2): 131-144.

Secondary Education in India: Universalizing Opportunity, (2009) Human Development Unit South Asia Region, January 2009, The World Bank

Seligman, M.E.P. and Csikszentmihalyi, M., (2000) Positive psychology: An introduction, *American psychologist*, 55(1), www.bdp-gus.de/gus/Positive-Psychologie-Aufruf-2000.pdf [Accessed 26 January].

Seligman, M.E.P., (1991) *Learned optimism*, New York: Knopf.

Sell, A., (2005) *Pätkätyöttömyys osana elämäntyyliä. Nuoria aikuisia pidentyvien siirtymien aikakaudella, Sosiologian pro gradu -tutkielma*, Helsingin yliopisto, Sosiologian laitos.

Sen, A. K., (1992) *Inequality Re-examined*, Cambridge (Mass): Harvard University Press.

Settersten, R. A., Jr., (2003) Propositions and controversies in life-course scholarship, in Settersten, R. A., Jr., (ed.) *Invitation to the life course. Toward new understandings of later life*, Amityville, New York: Baywood.

Shaheen, F. (2009) *Sticking Plaster or Stepping Stone? Tackling Urban Youth Unemployment* [online], London: Centre for Cities, www.centreforcities.org/assets/files/09-06-23%20Youth%20unemployment.pdf [Accessed 26 August 2009].

Shanahan, M. J., (2000) Pathways to adulthood in changing societies: Variability and mechanisms in life course perspective, *Annual Review of Sociology*, 26: 667-692.

Siegall, M. and McDonald, T., (2004) Person-organization value congruence, burnout and diversion of resources, *Personnel Review*, 33(3), www.emeraldinsight.com [Accessed 26 January].

Smith, J., (1999) Life planning: Anticipating future life goals and managing personal development, in Brandtstädter, J. and Lerner, R. M., (ed.) *Action and self-development. Theory and research through the life span*, Thousand Oaks, California: Sage.

Snarey, J., Kohlberg, L. and Noam, G., (1983) Ego development in perspective: Structural stage, functional phase, and cultural age-period models, *Developmental Review*, 3: 303-338.

Sondaite, J. and Zukauskiene, R., (2005) Adolescents' social strategies: Patterns and correlates, *Scandinavian Journal of Psychology*, 46(4), onlinelibrary.wiley.com [Accessed 26 January].

Song, M. and Parker, D., (2009) New ethnicities and the internet: belonging and the negotiation of difference in multicultural Britain, *Cultural Studies*, 23(4): 583-604.

Sonnentag, S. and Fritz, C., (2007) The recovery experience questionnaire: development and validation of a measure for assessing recuperation and unwinding from work, *Journal of Occupational Health Psychology*, 12(3).

Spence Laschinger, H. K., Wong, C. A. and Greco, P., (2006) The impact of staff nurse empowerment on person-job fit and work engagement/burnout, *Nursing Administration Quarterly*, 30(4): 358-367.

Stålsett, S.J., (2006) *Ethical dimensions of vulnerability and struggles for social inclusion in Latin America*, www.urbeetius.org/newsletters/23/news_23_stalsett.pdf [Accessed 21 January 2013].

Statistics Finland (1997) *Labour Force Statistics*, September 3. 1997. Helsinki: Statistics Finland

Statistics Finland, (2011b) *Statistical Yearbook of Finland 2011*, Helsinki : Tilastokeskus

Statistics of Finland, (1999) *Statistical Yearbook of Finland 1998*

Statistics of Finland, (2011a) *Education 2011* www.stat.fi www.stat.fi/til/opty/2009/ opty_2009_2011-03-15_tie_001_en.html [Accessed 31 January 2012].

Steedman, H. and Stoney, S., (2004) *Disengagement 14-16: Context and evidence*, CEP Discussion Paper No. 654.

Stettersten, J. R. A., (2007) The new landscape of adult life: Road maps, signposts, and speed lines, *Research in Human Development*, 4: 239-252.

Sukarieh, M. and Tannock, S., (2011) The positivity imperative: a critical look at the "new" youth development movement, *Journal of Youth Studies*, 14(6): 675-691.

Sulabha P, Sunita K, Shri Kant Singh and Vaidehi, Y. (2009) *A Profile of Youth in India, national Family health Survey (NFHS-3), India 2005-06*. Mumbai: International institute for population sciences; Calverton, Maryland, USA: ICF Macro.

Sulkunen, P. and Törrönen, J., (eds.), (1997) *Semioottisen sosiologian näkökulmia. (Points of view of semiotical sociology)*, Helsinki: Gaudeamus.

Sulkunen, P., (2009) *The saturated society: Governing risks and lifestyles in consumer culture*, London: Sage.

Sutela, H. and Vänskä, J. and Notkola, V., (2001) *Pätkätyöt Suomessa 1990-luvulla*. Helsinki: Tilastokeskus.

Suutari, M., (2002) Voices from the margins-three stories about unemployed young people. *Young*, 4/2002.

Tachibanaki, T., (2004) *Datsu freeter shakai: Otonatachi ni dekiru koto (Post-freeter society: What adults can do)*, Tokyo: Tōyōkeizai Shinpōsha.

Takanishi, R., (1993) The opportunities of adolescence-Research, interventions, and policy. Introduction to the special issue, *American Psychologist*, 48(2): 85-87.

Takenaka, T., (2009) *Hikikomori shienron: Hito to tsunagari, shakai ni tsunagu michisuji wo tsukeru (In support of Hikikomori: Creating a path linking people and society)*, Tokyo: Akashi Shoten.

Taris, T., Le Blanc, P., Schaufeli, W., and Schreurs, P., (2005) Are there causal relationships between the dimensions of the Maslach Burnout Inventory? A review and two longitudinal tests, *Work and Stress*, 19: 238-255.

The Finnish Centre for Pensions, (2011) *Pensioners and Insured in Finland: 80,000 persons retired on an earnings-related pension in 2009*. Helsinki, www.etk.fi/en/ service/earnings-related_pension_recipients/740/earnings-related_pension_recipients [Acessed 12 March 2012].

The Independent (2009) *Hoodies, Louts, Scums: How Media Demonises Teenagers*, 13 March.

The MONEE Project, CEE/ CIS/ Baltics, (2000), Florence: UNICEF Innocenti Research Centre.

Thomson, R., Bell, R., Henderson, S., Holland, S., McGrellis, S. and Sharpe, S., (2002) Critical moments: Choice, chance and opportunity in young people's narratives of transition to adulthood, *Sociology* 6(2): 335-354

Thomson, R., Henderson, S., and Holland, J., (2003) Making the most of what you've got? Resources, values and inequalities in young women's transitions to adulthood, *Educational Review*, 55(1): 33-46.

Thrupp, M., (2001) School-level education policy under New Labour and New Zealand Labor: a comparative update, *British Journal of Educational Studies*, 49(2): 187-212.

Tienda, M. and Wilson, J., (eds) (2002) *Youth In Cities: A Cross-National Perspective*, Cambridge: Cambridge University Press.

Toppinen-Tanner, S., Kalimo. R. and Mutanen, P., (2002) The process of burnout in white-collar and blue-collar jobs: eight-year prospective study of exhaustion, *Journal of Organizational Behaviour*, 23(5), onlinelibrary.wiley.com.

Turcotte, M., (2011, Winter) Intergenerational education mobility: University completion in relation to parents' education level, *Canadian Social Trends*: 38-44.

UK Social Exclusion Unit (1999) *Bridging the Gap: New Opportunities for 16-18 year-olds not in Education, Employment or Training*, London: The Stationery Office.

United Nations (UN) (2007), The World Youth Report, *Young People's Transition to Adulthood: Progress and Challenges*, www.un.org/esa/socdev/unyin/documents/wyr07_complete.pdf [Accessed 22 January 2013].

United Nations (UN), (2011) *World Youth Report. Youth Employment: youth perspectives on the pursuit of decent work in changing times*, New York, unworldyouthreport.org [Accessed 21 May 2012].

United Nations Children's Fund (UNICEF), (2000) *Young People in Changing Societies: Regional Monitoring Report No. 7* www.unicef-irc.org/files/documents/d-3029-What-UNICEF-is-doing-to-s.pdf [Accessed 21 December 2012].

United Nations Children's Fund (UNICEF), (2009) *Innocenti Social Monitor 2009: Child well-being at a crossroad. Evolving challenges in Central and Eastern Europe and the Commonwealth of Independent States*, www.unicef-irc.org/publications/562 [Accessed 21 December 2012].

United Nations Development Programme (UNDP) (2000), *Jordan Human Development Report 2000*, hdr.undp.org/en/reports/national/arabstates/jordan/nhdr_2000_jordan-en.pdf [Accessed 21 December 2012].

University Grants Commission (UGC) (2012) *Higher Education in India at a Glance*, University Grants Commission, New Delhi, oldwebsite.ugc.ac.in/pub/HEglance2012.pdf [Accessed 15 March 2012].

Van den Heuvel, M., Demerouti, E., Bakker, A.and Schaufeli, W., (2010) Personal resources and work engagement in the face of change, in Houdmont, J. and Leka, S. (eds.) *Contemporary Occupational Health Psychology*, West Sussex: John Wiley and Sons Ltd.

Veenhoven, R., (2004) Subjective measures of well-being, World Institute for Development Economics Research (WIDER), Discussion Paper No. 2004/07, Helsinki: United Nations University (UNU-WIDER).

Vertovec, S (2007) 'Super-diversity and is implications', Journal of Ethnic and Racial Studies, 29(6): 1024-1054.

Wadsworth M.E.J. and Bynner J., (2011) *A Companion to Life Course Studies: the social and historical context of the British birth cohort studies*, London: Routledge.

Wallace, C., (1987) *For Richer or Poorer: Growing up in and out of Work*, London: Tavistock.

Wallwork, E., (1991) *Psychoanalysis and ethics*, Yale University Press.

Walther, A., (2006) Regimes of Youth Transitions. Choice, flexibility and security in young people's experiences across different European contexts, *Young*, 14(1): 119-141.

Walther, A., and Pohl, A., (2005) *Thematic Study on Policy Measures for Disadvantaged Youth in Europe. Final report to the European Commission*, Tübingen: IRIS, ec.europa. eu/employment_social/social_inclusion/docs/youth_study_en.pdf [Accessed 21 December 2012].

Walther, A., Du Bois-Reymond, M., and Biggart, A., (eds.) (2006) *Participation in Transition. Motivation of Young Adults in Europe for Learning and Working*, Frankfurt a. M.: Peter Lang.

Wang, M. T., and Holcombe, R., (2010) Adolescents' perceptions of classroom environment, school engagement, and academic achievement. *American Educational Research Journal*, 47: 633-662.

Wang, M. T., Willett, J. B., and Eccles, J. S., (2011) The assessment of school engagement: Examining dimensionality and measurement invariance across gender and race/ethnicity, *Journal of School Psychology*, 49: 465-480.

Ward C.L., van der Merwe A., Dawes A., (eds) (2012) *Youth violence: sources and solutions in South Africa*, Cape Town: UCT Press.

Weaver-Hightower, M.B., (2008) An Ecology Metaphor for Educational Policy Analysis: A Call to Complexity, *Educational Researcher*, 37(3):153-167.

Weigert, A., Teitge, J. S., Teitge, D., (1986) *Society and identity: Toward a sociological psychology*. Cambridge: Cambridge University Press.

Weller, S. and Bruegel, I., (2009) Children's 'place' in the development of neighbourhood social capital, *Urban Studies*, 46(3): 629-643.

White, R., (1996) Racism, policing and ethnic youth gangs, *Current Issues in Criminal Justice*, 7(3): 302-313

Wilk, S.L. and Moynihan, L.M., (2005) 'Display rule 'regulators': the relationship between supervisors and worker emotional exhaustion,' *Journal of Applied Psychology*, 90(5): 917-927.

Willetts, D., (2010) *The Pinch: How the Baby Boomers Took Their Children's Future-and Why They Should Give It Back*, London: Atlantic Books.

Wilska, T.-A., (2001) The role of states in the creation of consumption norms, in Gronow, J. and Warde, A., (eds.) *Ordinary consumption,* London: Routledge.

Wilska, T.-A., (2004) *Oman elämänsä yrittäjät? Nuorisobarometri 2004 [Entrepreneurial lives? Youth Indicators 2004]*, Helsinki: Nuorisotutkimusverkosto, Nuorisotutkimusseura, julkaisuja 44, Nuorisoasiain neuvottelukunta, julkaisuja 28, Opetusministeriö.

Winefield, A.H. and Jarrett, R., (2001) Occupational stress in university staff, *International Journal of Stress Management* [online], 8(4), xa.yimg.com/kq/groups/13354653/431279762/name/Occupational+Stress+in+University+Staff.pdf [Accessed 26 January].

Wolf, A. and Evans, K., (2011) *Improving Literacy at Work*, Abingdon: Routledge.

Wolf, A., (2011) *Review of Vocational Education-The Wolf Report*, UK Department of Education, www.education.gov.uk/publications/standard/publicationDetail/Page1/DFE-00031-2011 [Accessed 25 May 2012]

Wolf, A., Aspin, L., Waite E., and Ananiadou, K., (2010) The Rise and Fall of Workplace Basic Skills Programmes: Lessons for Policy and Practice, *Oxford Review of Education*, 36(4): 385-405.

Woodman, D., (2009) The mysterious case of pervasive choice biography: Ulrich Beck, structure/agency, and the middling state of theory in the sociology of youth, *Journal of Youth Studies,* June, 12(3): 243-256.

World Development Report 2007 (WDR) (2007) The World Bank, Washington, DC, www-wds.worldbank.org/external/default/WDSContentServer/WDSP/IB/2006/09/13/00 0112742_20060913111024/Rendered/PDF/359990WDR0complete.pdf [Accessed 21 January 2013].

Wright, E. O., (1982) Class boundaries and contradictory class locations. In Giddens, A. and Held, D. (eds) *Classes, Power, and Conflict: Classical and Contemporary Debates* (pp. 112-129), Berkeley: University of California Press.

Wyn, J and Andres, L., (2011) Navigating Complex lives: a longitudinal, comparative perspective on young people's trajectories, *Early intervention in Psychiatry*, 33(Supplement 1): 1-5.

Wyn, J. and Harris, A. 2004. Youth Research in Australia and New Zealand, Young 12(3), pp. 269-287.

Wyn, J. and White, R., (1997) *Rethinking youth*, London: Sage.

Wyn, J. and Woodman, D., (2006) Generation, Youth and Social Change in Australia, *Journal of Youth Studies*, 9(5): 495–514.

Wyn, J., Lantz, S. and Harris, A., (2012) Beyond the 'transitions' metaphor: Family relations and young people in late modernity, *Journal of Sociology*, 48(1): 1–20

Yajima, M. and Mimizuka, H., (2005) *Kawaru wakamono to shokugyō sekai: Transition no shakaigaku, second ed. (Changing youth and work: Sociology of transition)*, Tokyo: Gakubunsha.

Yamada, M., (1999) *Parasite single no jidai (The age of the parasite single)*, Tokyo: Chikuma Shobō.

Yamada, M., (2009) *Naze wakamono wa hoshuka surunoka: Hantensuru genjitsu to ganbō (Why youth are becoming conservative: Reversal of reality and hope)*, Tokyo: Tōyōkeizai Shinpōsha.

Ylitalo, M., (2009) Nuorten kotitalouksien asema kulutuksessa [The status of young households in consumption]. *Hyvinvointikatsaus 1/2009 [The Welfare Review]*, Statistics Finland. Tilastokeskus.

Youth in India: Situation and Needs 2006-07, published by International Institute of Populations Sciences and Population Council, Mumbai.

Youth in the Labour Market in OECD Countries, OECD Social, Employment and OECD Migration Working Paper, 8.

Youth Indicator, The (1994-2009) Advisory Council for Youth Affairs.

Zeman, K., (2007) A first look at provincial differences in educational pathways from high school to college and university. *Education Matters* 4(2). www.statcan.gc.ca/pub/81-004-x/2007002/9989-eng.htm [Accessed 25 May 2012]

Zhou, M., (1997) Segmented assimilation: issues, controversies, and recent research on the new second generation, *Internal Migration Research*, 31(4): 179-191.

Zubok J.A. and Chuprov V.I., (2009) *Social regulation under conditions of uncertainty. Theoretical and methodological questions in studying youth*, Moscow: Academia.

Zubok J.A., (2005) Risk among youth in modern Russia: problems and trends, in: Helve, H. and Holm, G. (eds.) *Contemporary Youth Research. Local Expressions and Global Connections*, Farnham: Ashgate.

Zubok J.A., (2007) *Risk as a fenomenon in sociology. Experience of study of youth (in Russian)*. Moscow: Mysl.

Zubok J.A., (2009) *Саморегуляция и рационализация в условиях трансформирующегося общества (Self-regulation and rationalization under conditions of transformation)* www.socionavtika.net/Staty/diegesis/zubok.htm

Zubok J.A., Yakovuk T.I. (2008) *Cultural life of young people in the society undergoing transformation (in Russian)*, Brest: Alternativa.

Zubok J.A., Yakovuk T.I., (2007) *Transgression in Sociology of Youth. Encyclopedic Dictionary.* Moscow: Academia.

Lightning Source UK Ltd.
Milton Keynes UK
UKOW030835210413

209536UK00006B/76/P